McGraw-Hill Education

PSAT /NMSQT

FELICIA (FANG TING) WANG
MERCEDEZ L. THOMPSON

Mc Graw Hill Education

New York   Chicago   San Francisco   Athens   London   Madrid
Mexico City   Milan   New Delhi   Singapore   Sydney   Toronto

1 2 3 4 5 6 7 8 9   LHS   23 22 21 20 19 18

ISBN   978-1-260-12206-0
MHID   1-260-12206-9

e-ISBN   978-1-260-12207-7
e-MHID   1-260-12207-7

McGraw-Hill Education products are available at special quantity discounts to use as premiums and sales promotions or for use in corporate training programs. To contact a representative, please visit the Contact Us pages at www.mhprofessional.com.

Contents

PART 7   # PSAT Practice Tests

PART 1

Introduction to the PSAT

General Approach

This book will take a unique approach and guide students through all the necessary steps to excel on the PSAT exam. First, the book will teach essential knowledge covered by the exam, from core grammar concepts to math subjects. Following each theory section, students can practice using the many targeted practice questions on each core subject. In addition, this book will focus on teaching PSAT test-specific knowledge that will help students maximize their scores. Unlike other books, this book will dedicate more pages to teaching students what types of questions will be tested on the PSAT and how to solve these specific types of questions. There will be sections focusing on test-specific knowledge and tip boxes within other sections on how to solve the PSAT's targeted questions. Finally, this book includes multiple practice exams just like the actual PSAT, so students can practice the concepts and strategies they've learned in test-like conditions.

Approach for the Reading Section

The reading section teaches how to attack each type of reading question and gives general tips to help students improve on the section. For example, skimming is not encouraged in this book because many questions in the reading section are detail questions. For students with normal reading speed, there is enough time to read each passage carefully only once. Therefore, skimming a passage and going back to reread for details can be costly to students. Also, although the PSAT exam can seem dull and stressful, taking an interest in the content of the reading will help the students achieve a higher score. Interest in the passage will help students understand the main idea and pay attention to details as there are detail-oriented questions in the reading section.

Approach for the Writing and Language Section

If English isn't your strength, don't worry. The writing and grammar questions are often the most straightforward for students to learn because the same types of questions are asked over and over. First, all essential grammar lessons are taught, followed by sufficient practice questions. Armed with this knowledge, students can then attack all the grammar questions in the writing and language section. Following the grammar section, the book will teach students to tackle the editing questions, which are a new addition to the revised PSAT exam. Most of the editing questions will focus on how to solve questions using knowledge of how sentences interact within the paragraph, and how to use the passage as a whole.

Approach for the Math Section

The math section will start with math lessons to help students learn different math concepts that will appear in the PSAT. Then the math section will focus on exam-targeted knowledge. For example, the math section will have questions in which solving the presented math problem is not the goal; the goal is to answer the question. Therefore, students need to learn how to solve the question backward, starting with the answers. These are often problems where it is much easier to solve the questions by plugging in the answers. There are even some questions that are impossible to solve without plugging in the answers. In this case, students should always start with the middle choices, then move to the first and last answer choices, often depending on if the question is looking for a larger or smaller number.

What You Need to Know About the PSAT

You can think of the PSAT/NMSQT® (or Preliminary Scholastic Aptitude Test/National Merit Scholarship Qualifying Test) as a practice SAT that assesses student progress and determines eligibility for the $180+ million dollars in scholarships that are awarded in the National Merit Scholarship. The PSAT is not about memorizing words and facts but instead tests overall knowledge accumulated in high school and the skills you will need to succeed in college.

- Students are given 2 hours and 45 minutes to complete the PSAT.
- The test has two major components: (1) Evidence-Based Reading and Writing and (2) Math
- Each section is scored 160–760, for a total score of 320–1520.
- There is no penalty for guessing.

Format

1. Evidence-Based Reading and Writing
   a. Reading: 60 minutes, 47 questions
   b. Writing and Language: 35 minutes, 44 questions
2. Math
   a. No Calculator: 25 minutes, 17 questions
   b. Calculator: 45 minutes, 31 questions

Scores

Raw Scores

SECTION	RAW SCORE	EQUATED SCORE
Reading Section and Writing and Language Section	91	160–760
Math No-Calculator Section and Calculator Section	48	160–760
Total		320–1520

Score Reports

The online score report will have a summary of your score on each subject. You will get a percentile rank along with your score to see how you did compared to others. On the online test report, you can filter results and see your performance on different difficulty level questions. The detailed feedback on the online report will help guide you to understand where you need more practice.

There are two percentile ranks. One is the Nationally Representative Sample percentile, which compares your score to other U.S. students in a particular grade. The other is the User Percentile—National, which compares your score to other U.S. College Board test-takers in a particular grade.

Score Calculation

The raw score is the number of questions correct. Then it is converted to scores from 160–760. The total score will fall between 320 and 1520.

Mean Scores and Benchmark

You will see the average score of the U.S. students who take the PSAT. There will also be a benchmark for each section of the PSAT; these scores will tell you about your college readiness. It is good to score above the benchmark. Scores below the benchmark represent areas where you will need more practice.

Practicing a Good Pace

Unlike a lot of the tests you see in class, the PSAT and other standardized tests are not created with the idea that all students will or can finish them. In fact, students who try to complete all parts of the test often find that by overextending themselves, they fail to showcase their best performance. As you prepare and complete practice tests, you need to be thinking about your pace—the timing you should follow to do your best. This book's chapters offer some alternative strategies for students who are trying to find the right pace for them. Very generally, the PSAT does not ask you to speed read in the same ways some other tests might. An average reader will have time to read the passages through once and still complete the test on time. The Reading test is 60 minutes with 5 passages, so a 12 minute/ passage pace is what's necessary to complete the test. The Writing and Language test is 35 minutes with 4 passages, so practice at an 8.5 minutes per passage pace to be able to complete the test. The no-calculator Math test gives you 25 minutes for 17 questions, while the calculator permitted Math test gives you 45 minutes for 31 questions. In the math section, the questions generally get more difficult as you go, and as such you need to pace yourself so that you allow more time for the latter half of the math questions. All math formulas are provided for your reference at the beginning of the test. Remember that the PSAT does NOT penalize you for guessing, so no question should be left blank.

Students will find that their skills are better suited to meet the timing demands of some sections than others. Again, standardized tests like the PSAT are not created with the idea that all students will be able to finish every section in its entirety. For instance, one student may know that he or she can meet the timing demands of the Writing and Language test and the Math test but will have to guess on one passage of the Reading. This book is designed to help you decide on a pace that you are successful at. The best thing you can do for yourself is to come to the PSAT comfortable with the timing and with your own plan for success so you can best execute the pace that works for you.

How Does the PSAT Compare with the SAT?

The PSAT is a lot like the SAT; think of it as a shorter, practice version of the SAT. The big difference is that the PSAT determines eligibility for National Merit®, while the SAT impacts college admissions. However, preparing for the PSAT will absolutely help prepare you for the SAT. The PSAT does not have any essay section (an optional part of the SAT), and the PSAT is only administered once a year—in the fall—while the SAT is offered multiple times throughout the year. When you take the PSAT, consider opting in for the National Merit Scholarship, which primarily uses PSAT scores to distribute millions of dollars in college scholarships. As you can imagine, National Merit is highly competitive.

The National Merit Scholarship Program

The National Merit Scholarship Program was established in 1955 and grants students scholarships and recognition every year. To qualify for the National Merit Scholarship Program, the student must be a U.S. citizen or permanent resident, a high school student, and taking the exam in the specified year. Students enter this competition through taking the PSAT/NMSQT. Each year approximately 50,000 students, out of approximately 1.6 million students, will receive a varying degree of recognition and/or scholarship. The process will take place over a few months.

Commended Student

In September, approximately 50,000 high scorers will be contacted through their schools. They will receive notification that they have been selected as either a Commended Student or Semifinalist. Then approximately 34,000 of the students will receive Letters of Commendation.

Semifinalists

Approximately 16,000 students are notified through their schools that they have been selected as Semifinalists. These students are the highest scoring students in each state and are provided with scholarship application materials.

Finalist

About 15,000 Semifinalists are notified in February that they have been selected as Finalists.

Winners

Around 7,500 Finalists are notified that they are selected to receive a Merit Scholarship® award. This process will take place from March until mid-June. There are three types of awards: National Merit $2,500 Scholarships, Corporate-sponsored Merit Scholarship awards, and College-sponsored Merit Scholarship awards.

How to Register for the PSAT

Students register for the PSAT through their high schools and not through the College Board. It is possible to find more information about the registration process online, but the actual registration will be done through the school. The high school you attend will provide information regarding the registration. If you have not received any information regarding the PSAT registration by the fall of the year that you are taking the exam, ask your guidance counselor about the specific details.

Accommodations for Taking the PSAT

A request is needed to take the PSAT with accommodations. To make the request you need to contact the College Board's Services for Students with Disabilities (SSD).

Some of the common accommodations include:

- **Extended time.** Some of the options for extended time are 50% additional time, 100% additional time, and so on.
- **Computer use for essays.** Computers can be used for essay and short-answer responses, but additional technology cannot be used unless granted with additional requests.
- **Extra and extended breaks.** Often extended breaks will be twice the standard time.
- **Reading and seeing accommodations.** Some of the reading and seeing accommodations include large-print test book, braille test book, braille graphs, MP3 audio test format, reader, magnifier/magnifying machine.
- **Four-function calculators are allowed** .If you believe you qualify for accommodations, discuss this with your guidance counselor as soon as possible. They can help guide you through College Board's request process. It can take weeks to have your request answered, so do this well in advance.

What You Need to Bring to the Test

◆ No. 2 pencils and erasers (no mechanical pencils)
◆ A scientific calculator (find the list of approved calculators at https://college readiness.collegeboard.org/psat-nmsqt-psat-10/taking-the-tests/test-day -checklist/approved-calculators)
◆ Photo ID
◆ A watch (DO NOT bring one that makes noise or has an alarm, DO NOT bring a smartwatch)
◆ Be aware that you CANNOT bring your cell phone, other devices, or your snacks into the testing room

Reading Section

The focus of the reading section is on answering questions based on evidence from a variety of passages. It is important to remember that all answers must be supported by the passage. There may be answer choices that are tempting. However, if the answer choice is not supported by the passage, it is not correct. It is also important to think about what is the main idea that the author expresses.

Time: 60 minutes
Number of Questions: 47 questions

What to expect:

◆ There are only multiple-choice questions in the reading section.
◆ Graphs sometimes accompany the passages.
◆ There are no math questions about the graphs.
◆ There are sometimes paired passages.

Some types of questions include:

◆ Words and vocabulary
◆ Details in the passage
◆ Inference from the information given in the passage
◆ Main idea questions
◆ Hypotheses questions
◆ Analysis of data
◆ Lines and evidence that supports the answer to the previous question

Types of passages include:

◆ U.S. history
◆ Social studies
◆ U.S. or world literature
◆ Economics
◆ Psychology
◆ Science

Writing and Language Section

The Writing and Language test is focused on proofreading and editing skills like fixing mistakes and weaknesses of a passage. The Writing and Language test asks you to look at single sentences, and even single words, as well as to consider the main idea of a passage and how it relates to a graphic. Even with recent revisions that focus more on rhetorical choices, there are still many grammar-focused questions.

Time: 35 minutes
Number of Questions: 44 questions

What to expect:

- There are only multiple-choice questions in the Writing and Language section.
- Graphs sometimes accompany the passages.
- There are no math questions about the graphs.

Some types of questions include:

- Word choice and vocabulary
- Improve the passage/paragraph
- Enhance the sentence
- Correct the grammar of the sentence
- Organize the paragraph/passage

Some grammar structures tested include:

- Punctuation
- Clauses
- Verb tense
- Punctuation
- Parallel construction
- Sentence structure
- Subject-verb agreement
- Comma use

Types of passages include:

- History
- Social studies
- Science
- Humanities
- Careers

Math Section

There are two math sections in the PSAT, a calculator section and a non-calculator section. In both the calculator and non-calculator sections there will be multiple-choice and grid-in questions. It is important to read the instructions for the grid-in questions carefully. Always try to solve the question with the fastest and easiest method regardless of what the conventional method is.

> **No Calculator Section Time:** 25 minutes
> **No Calculator Section Number of Questions:** 17 questions
> **Calculator Section Time:** 45 minutes
> **Calculator Section Number of Questions:** 31 questions

What to expect:

- The test consists of mostly multiple-choice questions.
- There are some grid-in questions where no answer choices are given.
- There are questions where calculators are allowed.
- There are questions where calculators are not allowed.
- Multiple questions are sometimes asked based on the same initial information given.

The types of questions include:
1. Heart of Algebra
2. Problem Solving and Data Analysis
3. Passport to Advanced Math
4. Additional Topics in Math

How to Use This Book

You can use this book to prepare for the PSAT regardless of how long you have before the test. It is designed to give you more than ample practice on the types of questions you will see on test day. Like the SAT, the PSAT comprises a Reading test, a Writing and Language test, and a Math test. And like the SAT, the PSAT is written with college readiness and success in mind, so it is not focused on memorizing facts or formulas, but instead on using your knowledge to think critically and solve complex problems. If you have plenty of time before test day, say a month or more, you should do this book in its entirety. In each section, you will find concept reviews/lessons, useful strategies, and practice problems. You can best prepare for the PSAT by completing a full practice test in a timed environment, so that you know exactly what will be expected of you. If you have some time before test day, say a week or two, you should read the concept reviews/lessons in each of this book's chapters and then take a full-length practice test in a timed environment. This preparation strategy allows you to refresh the necessary concepts and skills you will be tested on and then put them into practice. If you have very little time before test day, say a day or two, you should read the Introduction carefully so you are familiar with the format and with general test-taking strategies, and then try 5 to 10 questions in each section of a practice PSAT.

General Test-Taking Strategies

1. Solve the question with the help of the answer choices. Glance over the answers very briefly, especially for the math section. There are usually questions that are easier to solve with the answer choices. In certain questions, the answer choices can be used as a guide. For example, if there are two answer choices that are extremely similar, chances are they are both incorrect. Also, when there are two answers that are the opposite, at least one must be eliminated.

2. When you do not know the correct answer, use elimination and cross off the wrong answers first. Then, go through each of the answers left and try to solve the question again. If you are still unable to solve the question, you should guess between the best two choices and not leave any of the questions empty. Also, choices that include extremes such as the words NEVER or ALWAYS are usually not the correct answer.

3. When you have no clue how to solve the question, you should guess. Remember there is a 25% chance of getting the correct answer if you are guessing randomly. Also, if you have eliminated the choices that are obviously wrong, your chance of guessing right can be as high as 50%. You can also mark the questions you are unsure of. If you have time left over at the end of the section, you can come back and give these questions another try. If you are running out of time at the end of the section, make sure to put a choice down even if you do not know the correct answer.

4. Read all directions carefully. Students often overlook the directions. If you are not familiar with the exam, read the directions carefully. If you are familiar with the exam, make sure there are no discrepancies between your knowledge and the directions. Don't forget to use what is on the page with the equations in the directions section to help you solve math problems.

5. Read the questions carefully. Look out for words like NOT or EXCEPT. It is easy to overlook the question when you are stressed for time and just go straight for the correct answer.

6. Take timed exams as practice. Practice the exam weeks or months before the exam date. Try to take a full timed practice exam in one sitting. This is a good way to familiarize yourself with the exam before the exam date and learn the format, question types, and timing of the exam.

7. Write on the test as you go. Keep a list of questions that you would like to go back to within the section if time allows. You can also add small relevant notes to the list of questions, but do not spend too much time on the notes. These notes should help you and not take up all your time. When doing the Reading section, you can write as you are reading the passage. Focus on thinking about

the author's purpose and audience as well as the passage's main idea. These notes should also help guide you to find the answer when you do not have the line reference in the question. Focus on thinking about the author's purpose and audience as well as the passage's main idea.

Test Anxiety

Many students experience test anxiety. Test anxiety is a common problem that can have many causes. Usually students care deeply about their scores and worry about their performance, especially on standardized tests that feel very high-stakes. As a result, students can suffer from sleepless nights before their exam and can go blank during the exam. This problem may be exacerbated if the exam is early in the morning, and the student must wake up much earlier than usual on the test date.

How to Reduce the Chances of Having Test Anxiety Before the Exam Date

- Prepare in advance for your exam. Most juniors take the PSAT at their own high school in the fall. However, there are options if you are homeschooled or if your high school doesn't offer the PSAT to take it at nearby schools. Talk to your guidance counselor early and decide when and where you'll test. According to College Board, the PSAT costs about $16 per student, but many schools cover the costs. You may also want to discuss test fees with your guidance counselor in advance.
- Get into the habit of going to sleep early and waking up at the time you need to wake on the day of the exam. For example, if you need to wake up at 6:30 a.m. on the day of the exam, start going to bed early and waking early at 6:30 starting a week before the exam. Also, try to review and study for the exam at the same time of day that you will be taking the test and get into a habit. This will help you feel more comfortable on the exam day.
- Familiarize yourself with the exam before the test date. This may be your first serious standardized test. Use this book as a resource to become familiar with the content and format of the test as well as the timing. By test day, you should feel as if you know exactly what to expect.
- The revised PSAT is a bit longer than its predecessor. You need to get used to studying for a full 2 hours and 45 minutes. However, even students who are used to concentrating for this long may have a difficult time focusing on test day when anxiety is highest. Take advantage of your breaks and refuel with snacks if your school or test center allows it.
- Do not do last-minute studying on the night before or the day of the exam. This usually makes students more nervous and does not help students prepare better for the exam.

* Exercise regularly during the weeks before the exam. Exercising will not only help you focus, but also it will help you sleep better at night.

How to Fight Test Anxiety on the Exam Date

* Make sure to eat a healthy breakfast on the day of the exam. Do not go to the exam hungry.
* If you are stressed for time in the morning, at least bring something to eat on the way.
* Make sure that you leave plenty of time to travel to the test location. If you are not testing at your own school, allow time to acquaint yourself with parking and find the test room. If you are rushing to the exam location, it will add unnecessary stress before the test.
* Try to arrive early and find a good seat. It may be a good idea to sit far from doors, so you will not be distracted by outside noises.
* Bring water and stay hydrated, but do not overdrink. Having to use the bathroom outside of a scheduled break is going to cost you valuable time during the exam, so have a good balance.
* If you blank out during the exam or get too nervous, take 30 seconds to a minute to take deep breaths and even close your eyes and put your head down. This should help relax you and clear your head. Remember you don't have to be perfect to do well on the PSAT. Recollect and reassure yourself that your preparation has more than equipped you for everything you'll see.
* Try not to get distracted by other people. There are often people coughing in the exams or making other noises—focus on your own exam. A good way to stay focused is to mouth the words as you read them. You are not permitted to talk, but mouthing the words will help you hear them inside your head and prevent you from being distracted by your neighbors.
* Practice your timing and make a plan for test day. Try to stick to this plan. Do not rush through the exam, and do not leave too little time toward the end. Moving through the exam at a reasonable pace will help you reduce stress.

PART 2

Diagnostic Test

How to Use the Diagnostic Test

It is important to take a diagnostic test so you can understand your strengths and weaknesses. Take the test in conditions as close to the testing day conditions as possible. This diagnostic test is the same length as a full PSAT/NMSQT, so allow yourself enough time to complete it. When you are done, you can use the resources that follow the exam to score your own test.

Before Taking the Test

Take the diagnostic test under conditions similar to the real test

It is important to take the test in conditions as similar to the real testing conditions as possible. Try to find a solid block of time when you can finish the entire test in one sitting. Time the exam so that you are spending the exact amount of time on each of the sections as instructed. Try not to be disturbed in the middle of the exam.

Do not leave any questions blank

Try to answer all the questions to the best of your knowledge. Use techniques to eliminate answer choices when you are unsure of the answer. Because there are no penalties for guessing, do not leave any of the questions blank. You will have a higher chance of guessing the correct answer than simply leaving it blank. Even if you have no idea what the answer is, choose a letter and move on. It makes sense to always use the same letter for your blind guesses.

Check your answers

You may want to leave a few minutes at the end of each section to go back to questions that you are unsure of and check the answers. Also, double check if you missed any questions or intentionally left any questions blank. If you do not have enough time to solve these questions, at least take a guess.

Do not go back to other sections

It is important not to go back to any other sections in the exam if you have extra time left over from a different section. In the real exam, you are not allowed to go between sections. Therefore, refrain from trying to use the time you have for one section toward a different section.

Be prepared

Make sure you have pencils, a calculator, and access to a clock or timer before you start. You should have practiced with your calculator beforehand and ensured that the batteries were fresh. Make sure you get a good night's sleep and wake up in time to eat a full breakfast. By being prepared and not rushed, you can eliminate any unnecessary stress.

Read the instructions

Take the time to read the instructions carefully. It is important to have good habits for the real exam. Learn the rules of the exam and what resources are provided, including how to enter the answers for the grid-in math questions. Fully utilize the information and resources provided in the instructions to your advantage.

Answer Sheet

Last Name: _____   **First Name:** _____

Date: _____   **Testing Location:** _____

Administering the Test

- Remove this answer sheet from the book and use it to record your answers to this test.
- This test will require 2 hours and 10 minutes to complete. Take this test in one sitting.
- Use a stopwatch to time yourself on each section. The time limit for each section is written clearly at the beginning of each section. The first four sections are 25 minutes long, and the last section is 30 minutes long.
- Each response must completely fill the oval. Erase all stray marks completely, or they may be interpreted as responses.
- You must stop ALL work on a section when time is called.
- If you finish a section before the time has elapsed, check your work on that section. You may NOT move on to the next section until time is called.
- Do not waste time on questions that seem too difficult for you.
- Use the test book for scratchwork, but you will only receive credit for answers that are marked on the answer sheets.

Scoring the Test

- Your scaled score, which will be determined from a conversion table, is based on your raw score for each section.
- You will receive one point toward your raw score for every correct answer.
- You will receive no points toward your raw score for an omitted question.
- For each wrong answer on a multiple-choice question, your raw score will be reduced by 1/4 point. For each wrong answer on a numerical "grid-in" question (Section 4, questions 29–38), your raw score will receive no deduction.

SECTION 1 **Reading Test** 60 MINUTES

Time: 60 minutes

Start: _____

Stop: _____

1. Ⓐ Ⓑ Ⓒ Ⓓ
2. Ⓐ Ⓑ Ⓒ Ⓓ
3. Ⓐ Ⓑ Ⓒ Ⓓ
4. Ⓐ Ⓑ Ⓒ Ⓓ
5. Ⓐ Ⓑ Ⓒ Ⓓ
6. Ⓐ Ⓑ Ⓒ Ⓓ
7. Ⓐ Ⓑ Ⓒ Ⓓ
8. Ⓐ Ⓑ Ⓒ Ⓓ
9. Ⓐ Ⓑ Ⓒ Ⓓ
10. Ⓐ Ⓑ Ⓒ Ⓓ
11. Ⓐ Ⓑ Ⓒ Ⓓ
12. Ⓐ Ⓑ Ⓒ Ⓓ
13. Ⓐ Ⓑ Ⓒ Ⓓ
14. Ⓐ Ⓑ Ⓒ Ⓓ
15. Ⓐ Ⓑ Ⓒ Ⓓ
16. Ⓐ Ⓑ Ⓒ Ⓓ
17. Ⓐ Ⓑ Ⓒ Ⓓ
18. Ⓐ Ⓑ Ⓒ Ⓓ
19. Ⓐ Ⓑ Ⓒ Ⓓ
20. Ⓐ Ⓑ Ⓒ Ⓓ
21. Ⓐ Ⓑ Ⓒ Ⓓ
22. Ⓐ Ⓑ Ⓒ Ⓓ
23. Ⓐ Ⓑ Ⓒ Ⓓ
24. Ⓐ Ⓑ Ⓒ Ⓓ
25. Ⓐ Ⓑ Ⓒ Ⓓ
26. Ⓐ Ⓑ Ⓒ Ⓓ
27. Ⓐ Ⓑ Ⓒ Ⓓ
28. Ⓐ Ⓑ Ⓒ Ⓓ
29. Ⓐ Ⓑ Ⓒ Ⓓ
30. Ⓐ Ⓑ Ⓒ Ⓓ
31. Ⓐ Ⓑ Ⓒ Ⓓ
32. Ⓐ Ⓑ Ⓒ Ⓓ
33. Ⓐ Ⓑ Ⓒ Ⓓ
34. Ⓐ Ⓑ Ⓒ Ⓓ
35. Ⓐ Ⓑ Ⓒ Ⓓ
36. Ⓐ Ⓑ Ⓒ Ⓓ
37. Ⓐ Ⓑ Ⓒ Ⓓ
38. Ⓐ Ⓑ Ⓒ Ⓓ
39. Ⓐ Ⓑ Ⓒ Ⓓ
40. Ⓐ Ⓑ Ⓒ Ⓓ
41. Ⓐ Ⓑ Ⓒ Ⓓ
42. Ⓐ Ⓑ Ⓒ Ⓓ
43. Ⓐ Ⓑ Ⓒ Ⓓ
44. Ⓐ Ⓑ Ⓒ Ⓓ
45. Ⓐ Ⓑ Ⓒ Ⓓ
46. Ⓐ Ⓑ Ⓒ Ⓓ
47. Ⓐ Ⓑ Ⓒ Ⓓ

SECTION 2 **Writing and Language Test** 35 MINUTES

Time: 35 minutes

Start: _____

Stop: _____

1. Ⓐ Ⓑ Ⓒ Ⓓ
2. Ⓐ Ⓑ Ⓒ Ⓓ
3. Ⓐ Ⓑ Ⓒ Ⓓ
4. Ⓐ Ⓑ Ⓒ Ⓓ
5. Ⓐ Ⓑ Ⓒ Ⓓ
6. Ⓐ Ⓑ Ⓒ Ⓓ
7. Ⓐ Ⓑ Ⓒ Ⓓ
8. Ⓐ Ⓑ Ⓒ Ⓓ
9. Ⓐ Ⓑ Ⓒ Ⓓ
10. Ⓐ Ⓑ Ⓒ Ⓓ
11. Ⓐ Ⓑ Ⓒ Ⓓ
12. Ⓐ Ⓑ Ⓒ Ⓓ
13. Ⓐ Ⓑ Ⓒ Ⓓ
14. Ⓐ Ⓑ Ⓒ Ⓓ
15. Ⓐ Ⓑ Ⓒ Ⓓ
16. Ⓐ Ⓑ Ⓒ Ⓓ
17. Ⓐ Ⓑ Ⓒ Ⓓ
18. Ⓐ Ⓑ Ⓒ Ⓓ
19. Ⓐ Ⓑ Ⓒ Ⓓ
20. Ⓐ Ⓑ Ⓒ Ⓓ
21. Ⓐ Ⓑ Ⓒ Ⓓ
22. Ⓐ Ⓑ Ⓒ Ⓓ
23. Ⓐ Ⓑ Ⓒ Ⓓ
24. Ⓐ Ⓑ Ⓒ Ⓓ
25. Ⓐ Ⓑ Ⓒ Ⓓ
26. Ⓐ Ⓑ Ⓒ Ⓓ
27. Ⓐ Ⓑ Ⓒ Ⓓ
28. Ⓐ Ⓑ Ⓒ Ⓓ
29. Ⓐ Ⓑ Ⓒ Ⓓ
30. Ⓐ Ⓑ Ⓒ Ⓓ
31. Ⓐ Ⓑ Ⓒ Ⓓ
32. Ⓐ Ⓑ Ⓒ Ⓓ
33. Ⓐ Ⓑ Ⓒ Ⓓ
34. Ⓐ Ⓑ Ⓒ Ⓓ
35. Ⓐ Ⓑ Ⓒ Ⓓ
36. Ⓐ Ⓑ Ⓒ Ⓓ
37. Ⓐ Ⓑ Ⓒ Ⓓ
38. Ⓐ Ⓑ Ⓒ Ⓓ
39. Ⓐ Ⓑ Ⓒ Ⓓ
40. Ⓐ Ⓑ Ⓒ Ⓓ
41. Ⓐ Ⓑ Ⓒ Ⓓ
42. Ⓐ Ⓑ Ⓒ Ⓓ
43. Ⓐ Ⓑ Ⓒ Ⓓ
44. Ⓐ Ⓑ Ⓒ Ⓓ

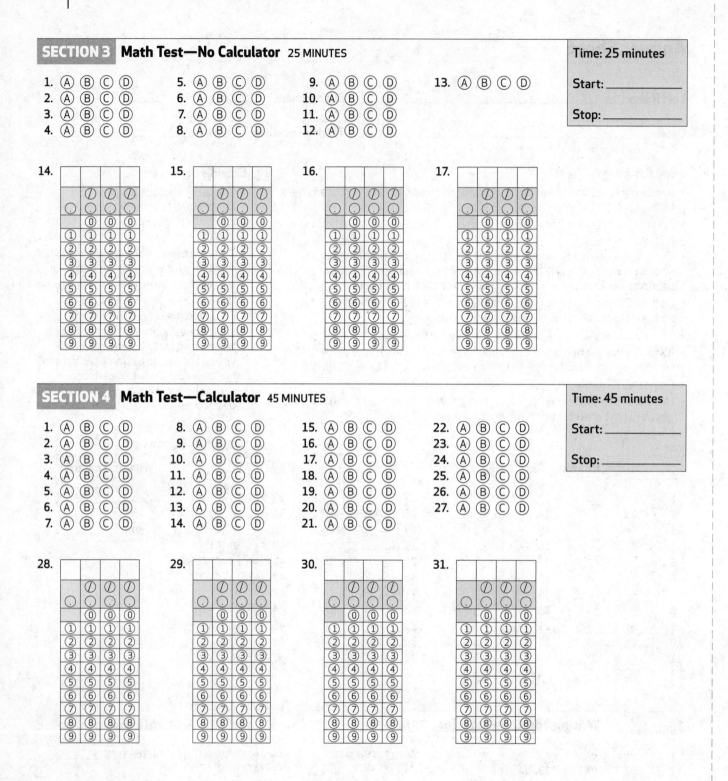

READING TEST
60 MINUTES, 47 QUESTIONS

Turn to Section 1 of your answer sheet to answer the questions in this section.

Directions: Each passage or pair of passages below is followed by a number of questions. After reading each passage or pair, choose the best answer to each question based on what is stated or implied in the passage or passages and in any accompanying graphics (such as a table or graph).

Questions 1–9 are based on the following passage.

The following passage is the beginning of the fourth chapter of Virginia Woolf's Jacob's Room, *first published in 1922. It depicts the beginning of Jacob's voyage to meet Timothy Durant's family.*

What's the use of trying to read Shakespeare, especially in one of those little thin paper editions whose pages get ruffled, or stuck together with sea-water? Although the plays of Shakespeare had
5 frequently been praised, even quoted, and placed higher than the Greek, never since they started had Jacob managed to read one through. Yet what an opportunity!

For the Scilly Isles had been sighted by Timmy
10 Durrant lying like mountain-tops almost a-wash in precisely the right place. His calculations had worked perfectly, and really the sight of him sitting there, with his hand on the tiller, rosy gilled, with a sprout of beard, looking sternly at the stars, then at a
15 compass, spelling out quite correctly his page of the eternal lesson-book, would have moved a woman. Jacob, of course, was not a woman. The sight of Timmy Durrant was no sight for him, nothing to set against the sky and worship; far from it. They
20 had quarreled. Why the right way to open a tin of beef, with Shakespeare on board, under conditions of such splendor, should have turned them to sulky schoolboys, none can tell. Tinned beef is cold eating, though; and salt water spoils biscuits; and

25 the waves tumble and lollop much the same hour after hour—tumble and lollop all across the horizon. Now a spray of seaweed floats past—now a log of wood. Ships have been wrecked here. One or two go past, keeping their own side of the road. Timmy
30 knew where they were bound, what their cargoes were, and, by looking through his glass, could tell the name of the line, and even guess what dividends it paid its shareholders. Yet that was no reason for Jacob to turn sulky.
35 The Scilly Isles had the look of mountain-tops almost a-wash. . . .

Unfortunately, Jacob broke the pin of the Primus stove.

The Scilly Isles might well be obliterated by a
40 roller sweeping straight across.

But one must give young men the credit of admitting that, though breakfast eaten under these circumstances is grim, it is sincere enough. No need to make conversation. They got out their pipes.

45 Timmy wrote up some scientific observations; and—what was the question that broke the silence— the exact time or the day of the month? anyhow, it was spoken without the least awkwardness; in the most matter-of-fact way in the world; and then Jacob
50 began to unbutton his clothes and sat naked, save for his shirt, intending, apparently, to bathe.

The Scilly Isles were turning bluish; and suddenly blue, purple, and green flushed the sea; left it grey;

GO ON TO THE NEXT PAGE ⟹

struck a stripe which vanished; but when Jacob had
55 got his shirt over his head the whole floor of the
waves was blue and white, rippling and crisp, though
now and again a broad purple mark appeared, like a
bruise; or there floated an entire emerald tinged with
yellow. He plunged. He gulped in water, spat it out,
60 struck with his right arm, struck with his left, was
towed by a rope, gasped, splashed, and was hauled
on board.

The seat in the boat was positively hot, and
the sun warmed his back as he sat naked with
65 a towel in his hand, looking at the Scilly Isles
which—confound it! the sail flapped. Shakespeare
was knocked overboard. There you could see him
floating merrily away, with all his pages ruffling
innumerably; and then he went under.

1. Which choice gives the best description of what
   happens in the passage?

   (A) One small boy becomes infatuated with
       Shakespeare but then loses his book.
   (B) Two professional sailors stranded at sea
       finally spot land and celebrate together.
   (C) One young man records a very technical
       scientific experiment.
   (D) Two young men bicker with one another
       while on a sea voyage to the Scilly Isles.

2. How is Timmy described in the passage?

   (A) serious and intriguing
   (B) playful and handsome
   (C) dull and ill-humored
   (D) stern and unsightly

3. As used in line 8, "moved" most nearly means

   (A) relocated
   (B) impressed
   (C) transferred
   (D) disturbed

4. The passage implies that Jacob and Timmy
   argued because

   (A) Jacob didn't appreciate Timmy's
       favorite poet
   (B) lunch was unpleasant and they were
       aggravated with the length of their journey
   (C) Timmy attracted the attention of more girls
       than Jacob did
   (D) Jacob was seasick and wanted to return
       home, but Timmy refused

5. Which choice provides the best evidence for the
   previous question?

   (A) Lines 9–11 ("For the Scilly . . . right place.")
   (B) Lines 11–16 ("His calculations . . . a
       woman.")
   (C) Lines 20–26 ("Why the right . . . the
       horizon.")
   (D) Lines 29–36 ("Timmy knew . . . almost
       a-wash. . .")

6. As used in line 50, "save" most nearly means

   (A) preserve
   (B) except
   (C) rescue
   (D) stockpile

7. Which choice describes a possible relationship
   between Timmy and Jacob?

   (A) Timmy is Jacob's father.
   (B) Timmy and Jacob are strangers meeting for
       the first time.
   (C) Timmy and Jacob are good friends on an
       adventure together.
   (D) Timmy is a famous scientist whom Jacob is
       considering hiring.

8. What does the passage imply about Timmy?

   (A) He is knowledgeable and familiar with this part of the sea.

   (B) He has never navigated a boat before.

   (C) His scientific observations are the results of fifty years of study and observation.

   (D) He works for one of the ships that passes by.

9. What is the most likely significance of the Shakespeare text drowning?

   (A) To foreshadow the death of the great poet

   (B) To emphasize how much Jacob disliked reading Shakespeare and suggest that he threw the book

   (C) To supply a reason for Jacob and Timmy's next argument which will be about the lost book

   (D) To mark the ending of the journey and the closing of a part of Jacob's life

Questions 10–19 are based on the following passage.

This passage was adapted from the profile of Felix Mendelssohn included in Francis Jameson Rowbotham's Story-Lives of Great Musicians.

To those who visited the home of Abraham Mendelssohn, the wealthy Berlin banker, the fact that his son Felix had a remarkable genius for music did not admit of a doubt. The capacity for learning
5 music had begun very early, but his wonderful gift of extemporization, which gave his genius wings as well as voice, had only lately revealed itself at the time at which our story opens. Nevertheless, it had made great strides, and opened up all sorts of possibilities
10 with regard to the future. And withal there was such an unaffected modesty and simplicity about the boy, so complete an absence of anything like a desire to show off his talents, as sufficed to disarm any tendency towards captiousness on the part of his
15 hearers.

Felix's whole wish was to satisfy himself as to his progress in music, and, young as he was, he had the sense and determination to pursue his bent without regard to the plaudits of his father's
20 friends. Abraham Mendelssohn, notwithstanding his business capacities, was himself a great lover of the arts, and especially of music. That his children should exhibit similar tastes to his own was,

therefore, to him a matter of delightful satisfaction,
25 for he shared with his wife Leah a deep interest in all that affected his children's education. He watched Felix with peculiar care, for it seemed to him that he inherited many of the traits as well as the capacity for learning which had distinguished the
30 grandfather and philosopher, Moses Mendelssohn.

Felix undoubtedly possessed the bright dark eyes and the humorous temperament of his grandfather, for he was one of the brightest and merriest of children. The family was not a large one. The three
35 elder children were born in Hamburg, where the family continued to reside until the occupation of the town by the French soldiers in 1811 made life there so miserable for the German inhabitants that as many families as could contrive to do so escaped
40 to other towns of Germany which were free from the presence of the invading army. With his wife and children Abraham fled to Berlin to make his home in the house of the grandmother.

No happier surroundings could have been
45 imagined than those amidst which Felix Mendelssohn's childhood was passed. The residence was in the Neue Promenade, a broad, open street, bounded on one side only by houses, and extending on the other side to the banks of the canal. Here a
50 wide stretch of grass-land, with a plentiful dotting of

GO ON TO THE NEXT PAGE ➡

trees, imparted a pleasant suggestion of the country, whilst the waters of the canal reflected the blueness of the sky, or, when rippled by the breeze, lapped the grassy banks with a murmuring sound that
55 was half sigh, half song. To this spot daily resorted the Mendelssohn children in company with the occupants of other nurseries in the promenade, and here amongst the rest might often have been seen little Felix, his eyes sparkling with merriment, and
60 his black curls tossed by the wind.

Every encouragement was given to the development of Felix's musical talent as soon as his fondness for the art made itself apparent. In company with his sister Fanny he began to receive
65 little lessons on the pianoforte from his mother when he was about four years old. Then came a visit to Paris, when Abraham Mendelssohn, taking the two children with him, placed them under the care of a teacher named Madame Bigot. Their progress
70 was so satisfactory—for the lady was an excellent musician and quick to recognize the abilities of her pupils—that on their return to Berlin it was decided to engage the services of professional musicians to carry on the instruction in the pianoforte, violin,
75 and composition as a regular part of the children's education. There was a continual round of lessons in the Mendelssohn home at this time, for in addition to music the children were taught Greek, Latin, drawing, and other subjects. No amount of lessons,
80 however, could detract from the happiness of a home wherein love was the dominant note, and in which each strove for the good of all; whilst as for Felix himself, no name could have been more symbolical of his true nature than that by which he was called.
85 Nothing served to check the flow of his spirits. Both in work and play he was thoroughly in earnest—indeed, he regarded both in the same enjoyable light.

10. How do the words "remarkable," "genius," and "possibilities" in the first paragraph (lines 1–8) set the tone?

(A) They create a tone of optimism that the author later rejects.

(B) They create a tone of admiration that establishes the author's esteem for the child virtuoso.

(C) They create a critical tone that mocks the early expectations for children musicians.

(D) They create an uncertain tone that will later be dispelled with the child's success.

11. As used in line 16, "satisfy" most nearly means

(A) please

(B) persuade

(C) assure

(D) repay

12. According to the passage, what made Felix even more likable than his talent?

(A) his laugh

(B) his serious stare

(C) his confidence

(D) his modesty

13. Which choice provides the best evidence for the previous question?

(A) Lines 1–8 ("To those who . . . our story opens.")

(B) Lines 10–15 ("And withal . . . his hearers.")

(C) Lines 20–26 ("Abraham Mendelssohn . . . children's education.")

(D) Lines 31–41 ("Felix undoubtedly . . . invading army.")

14. According to the passage, why did Felix in particular catch the attention of his father?

(A) Felix was the only child to take an interest in music.

(B) Felix was the only boy.

(C) Felix was like his grandfather.

(D) Felix was the eldest.

15. Which choice provides the best evidence for the previous question?

(A) Lines 16–20 ("Felix's whole . . . father's friends.")

(B) Lines 20–26 ("Abraham Mendelssohn . . . children's education.")

(C) Lines 26–30 ("He watched . . . Moses Mendelssohn.")

(D) Lines 55–60 ("To this spot . . . by the wind.")

16. As used in line 51, "imparted" most nearly means

(A) spread

(B) blurted

(C) awarded

(D) conveyed

17. What is the purpose of the fourth paragraph (lines 44–60)?

(A) describe the setting of Felix's childhood

(B) compare Felix's childhood to that of his father

(C) differentiate Felix from other children his age

(D) explain where Felix's greatest inspirations began

18. What does the author suggest about Madame Bigot?

(A) She was a very grave woman who believed music was more important than the children's other studies.

(B) She was a brilliant musician, but a mediocre instructor.

(C) She was only in Paris for a brief time, so the students needed another instructor.

(D) She quickly discerned Felix's exceptional talent for music.

19. According to the passage, Felix can be best described as

(A) eager for musical study, but resistant to other topics

(B) somber and talented

(C) naturally happy and diligent

(D) free-spirited and reluctant to study

Questions 20–29 are based on the following passage.

This passage was adapted from an 1893 article by A. Mueller titled "On Snake-Poison: Its Action and its Antidote."

Snakebite and its cure have always been the despair of medical science. On no other subject has our knowledge remained for centuries so unsatisfactory, fragmentary and empirical. The
5 history of the subject, in fact, may be summed up briefly as a series of vain and spasmodic attempts to solve the problem of snakebite-poisoning and wring from nature the coveted antidote.

Various and contradictory theories of the action
10 of snake-poison have been propounded, some absolutely erroneous, others containing a modicum of truth mixed with a large proportion of error, but none but one fulfilling the indispensable condition of accounting for all the phenomena observable
15 during the poisoning process and of reducing the formidable array of conflicting symptoms to order by finding the law that governs them all. We have the advocates of the blood-poison theory ascribing the palpable nerve-symptoms to imaginary blood
20 changes produced by the subtle poison, and alleged to have been discovered by the willing, but frequently deceiving microscope.

Even bacteriology has been laid under service and innocent leucocytes have been converted under the
25 microscope into deadly germs, introduced by the reptile, multiplying with marvelous rapidity in the blood of its victims, appropriating to themselves all the available oxygen and producing carbonic acid, as the saccharomyces does in alcoholic fermentation.
30 Others again, and among them those supposed to be the highest authorities on the subject now living, divide the honors between nerve and blood. Some snakes they allege are nerve-poisoners others as surely poison the blood, but with one solitary
35 exception they assume the terminations of the motor-nerves and not the centers to be affected.

Thus then with regard to theories we have hitherto had "confusion worse confounded," and as with theories so it has been with antidotes. They
40 were proposed in numbers, but only to be given up again, some intended to decompose and destroy the subtle poison in the system, others to counteract its action on the system with that action unknown. It is scarcely too much to assert that there are but few
45 chemicals and drugs in the world of medicine that have not been tried as antidotes in experiments on animals and dozens upon dozens that have been tried in vain on man.

The reasons for this somewhat chaotic state of our
50 science on a subject of so much interest to mankind are various. The countries of Europe, in which scientific research is most keenly pursued, have but few indigenous, and these comparatively harmless snakes. The best scientific talent has, therefore,
55 only exceptionally been brought to bear on the subject. In those countries on the other hand in which venomous snakes abound and opportunities for observing the poison-symptoms on man are more plentiful, the observing element has been
60 comparatively deficient.

A still more potent source of failure must be sought in the faulty methods of research pursued by most investigators. Experiments on animals were far too much resorted to, and their frequently
65 misleading results accepted as final, whilst observations on man did not receive the attention their importance demanded.

One important point has been completely left out of sight and ignored in all this experimenting
70 on animals. It is the fact that the action of snake-poison on the human system and on that of animals, more especially dogs, though very similar, is not absolutely identical, and that for this reason alone results of experiments on the latter cannot be
75 indiscriminately applied to man. But the difference between man and dog becomes more marked yet when strychnine is administered to a dog suffering

GO ON TO THE NEXT PAGE ➡

from snake-poison. It counteracts the latter quite as effectually in a dog as in man, but has to be injected
80 with extreme caution, for whilst in man a slight excess in the quantity required to subdue the snake-virus is not only harmless, but actually necessary, any excess of it in a dog will at once produce violent tetanic convulsions and cause the animal to die even
85 quicker than the snake-poison would have killed it, if allowed to run its course.

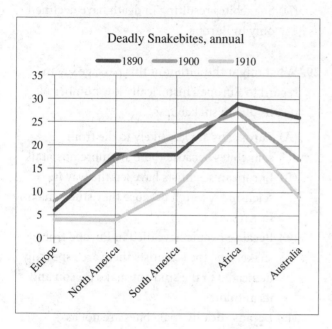

20. Which choice best summarizes the first paragraph (lines 1–8)

   (A) The writer believes he has just found the cure for all snakebites.
   (B) Recently, scientists have given up on studying snakebites because each bite is so different.
   (C) Snakebites presented an especially difficult mystery for scientists for many years.
   (D) Nature has a simple and universal cure for snakebites, but science will never lead us to it.

21. As used in line 2, "despair" most nearly means

   (A) resignation
   (B) hopelessness
   (C) distress
   (D) pessimistic

22. As used in line 6, "vain" most nearly means

   (A) unsuccessful
   (B) conceited
   (C) egocentric
   (D) bootless

23. The passage is written from the perspective of someone who is

   (A) an obvious lover of all animals, but especially reptiles and rare, venomous snakes
   (B) an advocate of animal testing
   (C) confident only in European scientists
   (D) cynical about how scientists have historically approached the question of snakebites

24. What is the main idea of lines 9–22?

   (A) There are few theories about how snake poison works, and more research needs to be done.
   (B) There are many theories about how snake poison works, but none but one is wholly correct.
   (C) Microscopes are not effective tools for studying snake poison.
   (D) Scientists used to believe poison attacks the blood, but now they know it attacks the nerves.

25. According to the author, what is the relationship between theories of snake poison and its antidote?

    (A) Both mysteries have baffled scientists.
    (B) Both mysteries were solved centuries ago.
    (C) Snake poison confounded scientists, but antidotes have been known for years.
    (D) How poison spread was easy to understand, but how to stop it from spreading is undetermined.

26. Which choice provides the best evidence for the previous question?

    (A) Lines 9–17 ("Various and . . . them all.")
    (B) Lines 17–22 ("We have . . . deceiving microscope.")
    (C) Lines 30–36 ("Others again . . . to be affected.")
    (D) Lines 37–43 ("Thus then . . . action unknown.")

27. Based on the passage, all of the following are reasons scientists failed to solve the question of snake venom and its antidote EXCEPT

    (A) flawed methods of research
    (B) snakes are rare and hard to catch
    (C) the world's best scientists weren't focusing their research on this topic
    (D) animal testing doesn't directly apply to humans

28. Which statement about the deadly effects of snakebites is supported by the graph?

    (A) Snakebites resulting in death have remained steady, so we need to increase scientific research.
    (B) Snakebites resulting in death have skyrocketed, so more scientists need to dedicate themselves to studying snakes.
    (C) Snakebites resulting in death have steadily declined.
    (D) Snakebites resulting in death have declined only in Europe.

29. What might the author of this passage say in regard to Europe's historically low number of deaths due to snakebites?

    (A) Europeans are less likely to die from snakebites because there are more hospitals.
    (B) European scientists have led the way in scientific research because they study snakes in Africa.
    (C) Because people have died in Europe from snakebites, the scientists there are especially dedicated to the study of snake poison and its antidotes.
    (D) Because deadly snakebites are not as common in Europe, the world's best scientists haven't spent enough time studying snake poison and its antidotes.

Questions 30–38 are based on the following passage.

The following passage is from a 1980 interview with Adrien Arpel, a best-selling beauty author who grew up in New Jersey and moved to New York's East Side.

As a young girl in Englewood, New Jersey, Adrien Arpel was determined that one day she would transform herself into a beautiful woman. After having her nose bobbed, she began to pester
5 the ladies behind every cosmetic counter she could reach, and by the time she graduated from high school at 17, she knew more than they did. That same year she opened a small cosmetics shop in her hometown with $400 earned from baby-sitting.
10 Today, at 38, she is the president of a $12 million-a-year company selling more than 100 beauty products throughout the U.S. and Europe.

Not content with mere business success, she recently turned her talent to writing her first
15 book, Adrien Arpe's *Three-Week Crash Makeover/ Shapeover Beauty Program* (1977). It was on the *New York Times'* best-seller list for six months, and is still selling briskly in paperback. Miss Arpel received $275,000 from *Pocket Books* for the reprint rights—
20 the most ever for a beauty book.

"I have always been a rebel," she proclaims regally, dressed in a stylish Edwardian outfit with padded shoulders at her midtown office. Quite heavily made up, with hot pink lipstick and a Cleopatra hairdo, she
25 looks considerably younger than her age. For some reason, she declines to say much about her new book, *How to Look 10 Years Younger*, which is scheduled for publication in April. Instead, she stresses the simple, common-sense rules about beauty that have guided
30 her career from the beginning. Probably her two most important innovations are her exclusive use of nature-based, chemical-free products (chosen from leading European health spas) and her policy of try-before-you-buy makeup.

35 Upon being complimented for her attire, Miss Arpel gasps, "Thank you!" with schoolgirlish delight. There is something almost surreal in her creamy white complexion. "I think sunbathing is absolutely deadly, and that there is no reason in the world for
40 a woman to sunbathe," she says. Moments later, she admits that "high heel shoes are not very good for you," but that she wears them anyway, "because they're very fashionable. They are something that really can be a problem—if they're pitched wrong.
45 If you have a good shoe and it's pitched well, you shouldn't have a problem."

Does she think it would be a good idea for women to give up high heels altogether? "No, no. I don't think you'll ever get women to give up fashion. So
50 we can tell what creates problems, what's really hazardous, what's going to be injurious to your health, and what's going to just hurt a little bit."

She never thought of writing a book until about four years ago, says Arpel, because "every second
55 when I was away from my business, I spent with my daughter. Now my daughter's 16 and a half, and has a boyfriend, and goes out, and doesn't want to spend every minute with me. This all started when she was about 13." Adrien and her husband,
60 manufacturer Ronald Newman, moved to the New York metropolitan area right after they were married in 1961, and acquired an Upper East Side apartment last summer.

For her own health and beauty regimen, Adrien
65 begins her typical day with jumping rope. She thinks weight training for women is "terrific," but considers jogging the best all-around exercise. She has a facial twice weekly. "Facials are not luxuries. They are necessities to peel off dead surface skin. . . .
70 Air pollution is the reason. If it wears away stone on buildings, think what it can do to the skin." A facial, she explains, consists of "all different sorts of hand massages to deep-cleanse the skin with coconut-like milk, or some sort of sea kelp cleanser. Then there's
75 a skin vacuum which takes blackheads out—electric brushes with honey and almond scrubs which clean out the pores. And at the end, a mask. Nature-based again—orange jelly, sea mud, or spearmint."

GO ON TO THE NEXT PAGE ⇒

Arpel believes that a woman's makeup should be
80 largely determined by her profession. She reveals
a humorous side when asked whether a woman
stockbroker, for example, should always dress
conservatively. "Well, if she was wearing a see-
through blouse and no bra in her office, I'd certainly
85 think she had poor taste," she laughs.

A nonsmoker who consumes little alcohol, she
confesses to at least one vice: "I drink two cups of
coffee in the morning, sometimes more. Also not
wonderfully good for you—but I never said I was a
90 hundred percent good."

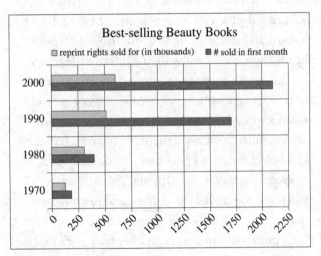

Best-selling Beauty Books

30. The writer most likely began the passage with
the first paragraph to illustrate

(A) the dramatic difference between successful
and unsuccessful people

(B) the amount of money Adrien is likely worth

(C) how a girl's early fascination with
beauty and cosmetics evolved into a
successful career

(D) that you don't have to have a lot of talent and
money to become famous

31. Why might the writer have included the details
about Adrien's $400 startup money in the
paragraph?

(A) To show she had help starting her business

(B) To show how determined she was to start
her own business

(C) To suggest that babysitting experience is
preferred in the cosmetics industry

(D) To suggest that her modest beginning led to
her downfall

32. As used in line 18, "briskly" most nearly means

(A) rapidly

(B) impatiently

(C) energetically

(D) sharply

33. The author suggests that Adrien's biggest
accomplishment thus far is

(A) her nose job

(B) her babysitting career

(C) her promotion to president of her company

(D) the success of her first book

34. Which choice provides the best evidence for the
previous question?

(A) Lines 4–7 ("After having . . . more than
they did.")

(B) Lines 7–9 ("That same year . . . from
baby-sitting.")

(C) Lines 10–12 ("Today, at 38, . . . and Europe.")

(D) Lines 18–20 ("Miss Arpel . . . a beauty
book.")

35. The passage suggests that what differentiates Adrien's beauty products/services from others is

    (A) their unique locations
    (B) her reputation
    (C) her nature-based, chemical-free products and an insistence that you try makeup before you purchase it
    (D) her dedication to her own beauty and her insistence on trying everything herself before supplying it in her stores

36. According to the passage, Adrien would most likely think a woman who is a construction worker should

    (A) wear high heels to emphasize her femininity
    (B) wear modest makeup to complement her features while remaining professional
    (C) have no beauty regimen whatsoever
    (D) change professions immediately because she will be exposed to too much sunlight

37. The writer says Adrien made the most money for reprint rights on a beauty book ever. Does the chart disprove this claim?

    (A) Yes, because the chart shows reprint rights selling for near $600,000.
    (B) Yes, because the chart shows beauty books selling over 2,000 copies in the first month.
    (C) No, because $275,000 had never been made by the year Adrien's book was released.
    (D) No, because Adrien's book sold the most in its first month the year it was released.

38. What does the chart suggest about the beauty industry?

    (A) Its popularity has been growing steadily since the interview discussed in the passage.
    (B) Its popularity was growing during the time of the interview but then plateaued.
    (C) Its popularity declined for two decades but is thriving once again.
    (D) Its popularity flourished for two decades but no longer has a promising future.

Questions 39–47 are based on the following passage.

Passage 1 is taken from a speech given by J. Hamilton Lewis to the U.S. Senate in 1918. Passage 2 is taken from a speech delivered by President Wilson that same year.

PASSAGE 1

No democracy was ever founded in any Government of earth that did not have to fight to continue its existence or maintain its ideals. Hear Goethe proclaim to Prussia, "Those who have liberty
5 must fight to keep it." The test of every free land that tries out its worthiness or unworthiness to exist as a Government of freedom has been its willingness or refusal to fight and die for its faith. No Government that has not exhibited a capacity to sacrifice all it has
10 for the theory for which it was founded, and to prove

its ability to protect and perpetuate the institutions it has created, has ever yet existed for a length of time sufficient to be recorded in history as having fostered liberty or transmitted democracy to men. No
15 Government has yet been accorded by civilization a place among the nations of the earth until it had first demonstrated its worthiness to administer justice by doing justice to itself, and then to prove its power in conflict to overcome its natural enemies, whether
20 from within or without.

Our United States, too, must pass under the rod. America's institutions of freedom, inspiring mankind to her example and awakening oppressed lands to follow her course if they would know
25 liberty, inflamed the souls of the royal rulers of Prussia with fear and fired them to war of

GO ON TO THE NEXT PAGE ⟹

destruction upon all that America stood for and was living for.

PASSAGE 2

Fellow-citizens: This is the anniversary of our
30 acceptance of Germany's challenge to fight for our right to live and be free, and for the sacred rights of freemen everywhere. The nation is awake. There is no need to call to it. We know what the war must cost, our utmost sacrifice, the lives of our fittest men,
35 and, if need be, all that we possess.

The loan we are met to discuss is one of the least parts of what we are called upon to give and to do, though in itself imperative. The people of the whole country are alive to the necessity of it and are
40 ready to lend to the utmost, even where it involves a sharp skimping and daily sacrifice to lend out of meagre earnings. They will look with reprobation and contempt upon those who can and will not, upon those who demand a higher rate of interest,
45 upon those who think of it as a mere commercial transaction. I have not come, therefore, to urge the loan. I have come only to give you, if I can, a more vivid conception of what it is for.

The reasons for this great war, the reason why it
50 had to come, the need to fight it through, and the issues that hang upon its outcome, are more clearly disclosed now than ever before. It is easy to see just what this particular loan means, because the cause we are fighting for stands more sharply revealed
55 than at any previous crisis of the momentous struggle. The man who knows least can now see plainly how the cause of justice stands, and what the imperishable thing he is asked to invest in. Men in America may be more sure than they ever were
60 before that the cause is their own, and that, if it should be lost, their own great nation's place and mission in the world would be lost with it.

39. In Passage 1, Lewis suggests that World War II was

   (A) overrated
   (B) dubious
   (C) irresolute
   (D) inevitable

40. According to Lewis, a nation must do what two things to earn respect and rank?

   (A) be just and defeat enemies
   (B) write a constitution and promote equality
   (C) give all suffrage and go to war
   (D) write out laws and build infrastructure

41. As used in line 25, "inflamed" most nearly means

   (A) swollen
   (B) incensed
   (C) lit up
   (D) provoked

42. The purpose of President Wilson's speech is to

   (A) secure financial support
   (B) rouse the military to action
   (C) persuade other countries to join the war
   (D) gain supporters for the next election

43. As used in line 36, "least" most nearly means

   (A) smallest in amount
   (B) smallest in significance
   (C) barely
   (D) remotely

44. According to President Wilson, this time is different than any other because

   (A) the country is more financially unstable than ever before
   (B) women will fight alongside men
   (C) the reason for the fight is clearer than ever
   (D) he is asking directly

45. Which choice provides the best evidence for the previous question?

   (A) Lines 32–35 ("The nation . . . we possess.")
   (B) Lines 38–42 ("The people . . . meagre earnings.")
   (C) Lines 42–48 ("They will . . . what it is for.")
   (D) Lines 49–56 ("The reasons . . . momentous struggle.")

46. Which choice shows the relationship between the two passages?

   (A) Passage 2 challenges the argument put forth in Passage 1.
   (B) Passage 2 uses reasoning similarly to Passage 1 to advocate for a cause.
   (C) Passage 2 is in complete disagreement with Passage 1.
   (D) Passage 2 exemplifies an attitude discredited by Passage 1.

47. The main purpose of both passages is to

   (A) intimidate enemies into surrender
   (B) weaken support for an avoidable conflict
   (C) garner support for a necessary conflict
   (D) discuss the relationship between people and their government

STOP

If you finish before time is called, you may check your work on this section only.

Do not turn to any other section.

WRITING AND LANGUAGE TEST

35 Minutes, 44 Questions

Directions: Answer the following questions on Section 2 of your answer sheet. Each passage is accompanied by questions that ask you to revise or edit the passage to improve its flow, organization, clarity, and sentence mechanics. For most questions, you will be directed to an underlined portion of the passage to either choose "NO CHANGE" or select the appropriate revision. For other questions, you'll be asked to think about the passage as a whole. Some passages may also include a graphic to consider as you edit.

Questions 1–11 are based on the following passage.

Paid Family Leave in the U.S.

For many Americans, paid family leave **1** is simply not a reality. Those people who need it the most are, in fact, the least likely to reap its benefits. For new parents, paid family leave seems not only reasonable but necessary. A **2** moving percentage— the Department of Labor reports less than 15%—of non-government employers work for companies that offer paid leave, and very few employers **3** extended these benefits to men as well as women or equally consider circumstances such as adoption and fostering. The lack of paid family leave doesn't necessarily mean that new parents cannot receive time off work, but instead that this time may be very limited and generate more trouble than it alleviates.

1. (A) NO CHANGE
   (B) proves to be rather farfetched overall.
   (C) doesn't exist annually.
   (D) saves them from financial ruin.

2. (A) NO CHANGE
   (B) touching
   (C) dismaying
   (D) melancholy

3. (A) NO CHANGE
   (B) extend
   (C) extending
   (D) has extended

[1] The Family and Medical Leave Act of 1993 mandates employers to provide employees with job-protected **4** leave, for qualified medical and family reasons, but many employees don't qualify for FMLA and even those that do go unpaid. [2] New parents rely on FMLA for time off work after the birth or adoption of **5** a child, but eligibility varies state to state. [3] New parents may be ineligible if they have not been employed by their current employer for more than 12 months or have not worked full time during that year. [4] Let us not forget that even those fortunate enough to qualify for up to 12 weeks off work can rarely afford to go that long without pay, especially when in the midst of expanding their family. [5] **6** Furthermore, even if the employee meets the federal requirements, the employer may not be eligible if it doesn't meet the criteria for the number of employees within a certain distance from the workplace.

7 As one might expect, the unfair policies tend to misuse already vulnerable populations, coming down hardest on low-income and households of color. Government and corporate employers are much more likely to offer paid benefits in addition to the FMLA standards, while retail companies like Walmart and Starbucks that pay the majority of their employees low wages are less likely to offer these benefits, and when they do, often restrict them to the top-level employees. **8** In fact, the vast majority of new parents take ten or less days off when a child is born, adopted, or fostered into their family.

4. (A) NO CHANGE
   (B) leave
   (C) leave;
   (D) leave:

5. (A) NO CHANGE
   (B) a child, so
   (C) a child yet
   (D) a child; moreover,

6. To make this paragraph flow most logically, sentence 5 should be placed:

   (A) where it is now
   (B) before sentence 2
   (C) after sentence 1
   (D) after sentence 3

7. (A) NO CHANGE
   (B) Fortunately,
   (C) Occasionally,
   (D) Sometimes,

8. At this point, the writer is considering adding the following sentence.

   > Large populations of new parents—those who are paid the least and are without access to adequate resources and benefits—suffer the most.

   Should the writer make this addition?

   (A) Yes, because it explains the FMLA standards.
   (B) Yes, because it connects the previous sentence to the following sentence.
   (C) No, because it contradicts the main idea.
   (D) No, because it adds irrelevant details.

At the **9** founding of the campaign to win paid family leave for everyone in the United States (led by Paid Leave for the United States or PL+US) **10** lies a startling fact: only 2 countries in the world are without a national maternity leave policy—the United States and Papua New Guinea. **11** The time for indifference has long ago passed.

9. (A) NO CHANGE
   (B) inauguration
   (C) middle
   (D) core

10. (A) NO CHANGE
    (B) lay
    (C) lie
    (D) lays

11. The writer wants a concluding sentence that serves as a call to action. Which choice is most appropriate?

    (A) NO CHANGE
    (B) If that doesn't surprise you, I don't know what will.
    (C) Americans are hopeful that these issues will work themselves out.
    (D) Paid family leave, as it exists currently, is reserved for the elite.

Questions 12–22 are based on the following passage.

The following passage is adapted from a 1917 Spalding sports guide titled Girls and Athletics.

Basketball needs no introduction. **12** Its' probably the most popular game played by girls. Through the work of the Executive Committee on Basketball Rules, headed by Mrs. Senda Berenson Abbott, chairman, the playing rules and the conditions under which the game may best be played have been **13** thoroughly studied and set forth in the Spalding Official Basketball Guide for Women, No. 7A.

[1] Basketball undoubtedly fills this need. [2] The game may be played either outdoors or indoors, depending upon conditions. [3] The writer is a firm believer in outdoor exercise wherever and whenever possible, **14** and there is a decided need for a wholesome, interesting game for indoors during the long winter months. **15**

12. (A) NO CHANGE
    (B) Its
    (C) It's
    (D) Basketballs

13. (A) NO CHANGE
    (B) significantly
    (C) warily
    (D) carelessly

14. (A) NO CHANGE
    (B) but
    (C) thus
    (D) moreover

15. For this paragraph to be most logical, sentence 1 should be placed
    (A) where it is now
    (B) after sentence 2
    (C) after sentence 3
    (D) It should be omitted.

GO ON TO THE NEXT PAGE ⟼

The game 16 was played by two teams consisting of five players each. The three general positions call for three different kinds of skill. The forwards should possess a good eye, should have the knack of handling the ball well and should have agility and speed. The center should have height, ability to get possession of the ball and the knack of feeding well, that is, passing the ball to her forwards. 17 The guard's, as their name implies: must 18 defeat the opposing forwards from shooting, so must be quick, active and able to jump well.

The game begins with each team in position. The referee puts the ball in play by tossing it up 19 between the centers, who jump and bat it (they must not catch it). Once in play, the ball must be passed from one player to another—not handled, nor rolled, nor kicked. Nor may any player carry it, but she may bounce it. The play continues until a score is made, or a player fouls, or the ball goes out of bounds. A score is made when a player shoots the ball into the basket from the court. A foul is made when a player of one side transgresses a rule of the game. 20 When a player fouls, a free-throw from a mark fifteen feet from and directly in front of the basket is allowed to the player who was fouled. 21 When the ball passes through the basket, rim and net, one point is added to the score of the team. When the ball goes over the boundary lines, the game is stopped and the ball is given to the opponent of the girl who touched it last. She then passes the ball to one of her teammates, thus starting play again.

The winning of the game is determined by the scoring of the most points (both field goals and free throws) in a given time—usually fifteen-minute halves with a ten-minute intermission. Baskets are exchanged at the end of the first half. 22

16. (A) NO CHANGE
    (B) are played by
    (C) plays by
    (D) is played by

17. (A) NO CHANGE
    (B) The guards as their name implies,
    (C) The guards—as they're name implies—
    (D) The guards, as their name implies,

18. (A) NO CHANGE
    (B) circumspect
    (C) cease
    (D) prevent

19. (A) NO CHANGE
    (B) to
    (C) amidst
    (D) among

20. The writer is considering deleting the underlined sentence. Should the writer make this deletion?
    (A) Yes, because it does not transition into the next sentence.
    (B) Yes, because it fails to support the main idea of the passage.
    (C) No, because it expands upon the previous sentence.
    (D) No, because it provides a counterargument.

21. Which choice makes the most sense within the context of the paragraph?
    (A) NO CHANGE
    (B) The guard is probably the most coveted position in basketball.
    (C) If a player moves with the ball without bouncing it, traveling is called.
    (D) The basket is mounted to a backboard and is exactly 10 feet high.

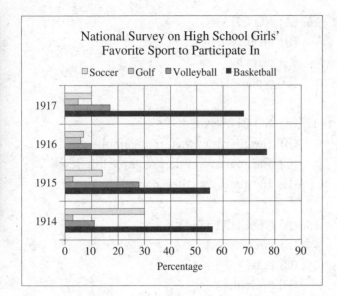

National Survey on High School Girls' Favorite Sport to Participate In

22. At this point, the writer wants to conclude with specific information about the popularity of basketball among girls. Which choice effectively completes the passage with accurate information based on the graph?

(A) In 1917 alone, well over 70% of surveyed high school girls voted basketball as their favorite sport to participate in.

(B) Perhaps basketball needs no introduction because it has consistently been the favorite sport for the majority of girls to participate in.

(C) Girls are active in a variety of sports including soccer, golf, volleyball, and basketball—proving once and for all that girls can do whatever boys can do.

(D) Last year, only 10% of girls preferred volleyball to basketball.

Questions 23–33 are based on the following passage.

A Woman of Many Faces

In reading Shakespeare's *Antony and Cleopatra*, I found Cleopatra as captivating as Antony did. She is advised to "cross him in nothing," to which she scoffs and decides instead that if she finds him sad, she will act contented, but if she finds him happy, she will perform as if she is "sudden sick." The reader recognizes Cleopatra's 23 agency, and independence in her refusal to obediently and passively comply. 24 In performing to contradict the mood of her lover, the reader witnesses her immature stubbornness. Regardless of whether Cleopatra is read as agreeably or obnoxiously defiant, I couldn't help but admire her vivacity. 25 Hitherto, she is manipulative and deceitful, but she is also assertive, resolute, and ambitious. In showing the extremes of human nature, Shakespeare once again creates a character which emboldens and amplifies those parts of us which we love and those others which we despise.

23. (A) NO CHANGE
    (B) agency, and independence,
    (C) agency—and independence—
    (D) agency and independence

24. (A) NO CHANGE
    (B) The reader witnesses Cleopatra's immature stubbornness in her impulse to contradict the mood of her lover.
    (C) The reader is immature and stubborn when Cleopatra contradicts her lover.
    (D) Cleopatra performs by contradicting the mood of her lover and the reader realizes how immature and stubborn she really is.

25. (A) NO CHANGE
    (B) Fortunately,
    (C) Thus,
    (D) Certainly,

I found a similarly complex character in Plutarch's *Antony and Cleopatra*. Cleopatra is first described as "layed under a pavilion of cloth of gold of tissue, appareled and attired like the goddess Venus." Yet, while Cleopatra is unquestionably beautiful, it is not her beauty which captures and bewitches Antonius, but instead her grace and compelling conversation. I noticed often that she distinguished herself not by her appearance, but by her kindness, insight, and lively spirit. In her, Antony **26** find a beautiful and intelligent woman who can do it all. **27** She exceeds not only other women but Antony himself in her luxury, decadence, tastes, intelligence, and sport.

28 Cleopatra, the last active ruler of Ptolemaic Egypt, has a special place in popular myth. Readers meet her as that which has transformed the brave military leader "[i]nto a strumpet's fool." She is blamed for her lover's neglected responsibilities and overindulgence—**29** an enchanting witch who makes Antony the "noble ruin of her magic." Importantly, when Cleopatra **30** flies from battle not once but twice, she leaves Antony vulnerable to Caesar.

26. (A) NO CHANGE
   (B) finds
   (C) found
   (D) has found

27. Which choice most clearly shows that Cleopatra is exceptional?
   (A) NO CHANGE
   (B) She captures Antony mainly with her charm and beauty.
   (C) Cleopatra's appeal lies in her unapologetic mediocrity.
   (D) Despite the many choices he has for potential lovers, Antony is spellbound by Cleopatra's pedestrian ways and falls deeply in love with her.

28. Which choice most appropriately introduces the paragraph?
   (A) NO CHANGE
   (B) Shakespeare's Cleopatra far surpasses Plutarch's Cleopatra.
   (C) Shakespeare's Cleopatra is framed from the onset through Antony's recklessness.
   (D) It goes unsaid that readers will find Cleopatra distasteful.

29. (A) NO CHANGE
   (B) a chanting witch
   (C) an evil girl
   (D) a really bad person

30. (A) NO CHANGE
   (B) flees
   (C) flew
   (D) flown

While she isn't **31** unlikable she is excessive in everything she does. **32** It might be easy to write her off as childish, dramatic, and demanding, but Shakespeare creates a much more complex character in Cleopatra. She is at once noble and frivolous, generous and cruel, **33** disloyal and treacherous.

31. (A) NO CHANGE
    (B) unlikable, she
    (C) unlikable; she
    (D) unlikable, but she

32. (A) NO CHANGE
    (B) The reader writes Cleopatra
    (C) Don't you dare think of her
    (D) One could easily assume, if not careful, that Cleopatra should ultimately be read

33. (A) NO CHANGE
    (B) untrustworthy
    (C) backstabbing
    (D) loyal

Diagnostic Test

Questions 34–44 are based on the following passage.

A Carbon Crisis

Recent measurements of atmospheric carbon dioxide concentrations approach numbers as high as **34** 410 parts per million—a fifty percent increase from pre-Industrial Revolution levels, according to Scripps Institution. In 1958, climatologists at Mauna Loa Observatory measured carbon dioxide levels in the Earth's atmosphere **35** at approximately 310 ppm. Since then, emission levels have soared and carbon dioxide concentrations **36** increase at record rates. Essentially, carbon dioxide and other greenhouse gases trap heat in the Earth's atmosphere, and as the oceans absorb that heat, sea levels rise. **37** In order to cool, oceans radiate that heat back out, and we see a steady incline in global temperatures. Perhaps the most urgent problem we face is that greenhouse gases don't just go away, but instead remain trapped in the atmosphere decades and even centuries later. **38**

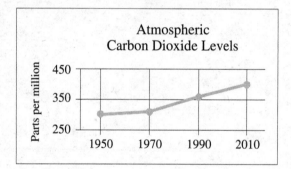

34. (A) NO CHANGE
(B) 410 parts per million.
(C) 410 parts per million;
(D) 410 parts per million

35. Which choice offers an accurate interpretation of the data in the chart?

(A) NO CHANGE
(B) at approximately 390 ppm.
(C) at approximately 410 ppm.
(D) at approximately 550 ppm.

36. (A) NO CHANGE
(B) has increased
(C) are increasing
(D) have increased

37. (A) NO CHANGE
(B) To cool,
(C) To reduce their heat,
(D) In order to regain their former temperatures,

38. According to the chart, when were the carbon dioxide levels closest to the safe zone?

(A) 1950
(B) 1960
(C) 1980
(D) 2010

[1] With scientists designating the carbon dioxide safe zone at 350 ppm, the question remains not only of how to **39** increase the flux of emissions but also of how to remove the already trapped greenhouse gases. [2] Recently, 175 countries opted to sign the Paris Agreement, initiating a global movement to reduce emissions and hold temperatures steady. [3] To address the former, we are working on small and large scales to reduce pollution and explore green energy options. [4] **40** Yet, scientists are adamant that this is not enough. [5] To merely slow down the increase or maintain current rates puts us on a fast trajectory to carbon dioxide levels of 450 ppm and higher, numbers Earth hasn't reached in 50 million years and estimated sea levels that threaten to swallow coastal cities. **41**

39. (A) NO CHANGE
    (B) reduce
    (C) omit
    (D) eliminate

40. Which choice best transitions to the following sentence?

    (A) NO CHANGE
    (B) This is a great start to a long journey.
    (C) A team of scientists at NASA urge everyone to do their part, from recycling to carpooling.
    (D) However, it is too late to prevent destruction.

41. To make this passage most logical, sentence 3 should be placed:

    (A) Where it is now
    (B) Before sentence 1
    (C) Before sentence 2
    (D) After sentence 5

So, if stopping our wasteful and reckless habits right now still cannot prevent large scale climate change and unprecedented sea levels, what can we do? **42** Is all hope lost? Scientists at Columbia and Harvard don't think so; although, they do caution that disaster and destruction are headed our way if we don't make big changes fast. **43** Scientists across the globe are gathering to have conversations about what to do next. Extracting billions of tons of carbon dioxide from the atmosphere, however, is hardly economical. Recent estimates by scientist James Hansen put the cost somewhere over $100 billion a year for several decades. Other researchers advocate for a large-scale investment in tree planting and soil fertilization, options that will help to naturally absorb carbon and offset global warming. The urgency of the situation and the dire consequences of further inaction **44** demands that we devote time and resources to all of these measures: reduce current emissions, remove trapped greenhouse gases, and maximize plant life.

42. The writer is considering deleting the underlined sentence. Should the writer make this deletion?

(A) Yes, because it distracts the reader.

(B) Yes, because it poses a rhetorical question.

(C) No, because it raises a question that is answered by the following sentence.

(D) No, because it draws attention to the serious nature of the main topic.

43. Which choice provides a possible solution to the main question posed and flows logically with the rest of the paragraph?

(A) NO CHANGE

(B) Carbon dioxide levels, at their current levels, threaten our very way of life.

(C) The way to solve the problem is to stop being so wasteful immediately.

(D) To reach safe levels once again, we literally need to remove greenhouse gases from the atmosphere.

44. (A) NO CHANGE

(B) will demand

(C) has demanded

(D) demand

STOP

If you finish before time is called, you may check your work on this section only.

Do not turn to any other section.

MATH TEST – NO CALCULATOR

25 MINUTES, 17 QUESTIONS

To answer questions in this section turn to Section 3 of your answer sheet.

Directions: Choose the best answer choice for questions 1–13 and fill in the answer sheet accordingly. Solve questions 14–17 and fill in the answer sheet accordingly. Before moving on to question 14, refer to the directions on how to fill in the answers on the answer sheet. Use of available space on the test booklet is allowed.

Notes

1. **No calculator use** is permitted.
2. Unless indicated, variables and expressions represent real numbers.
3. Figures are drawn to scale.
4. Figures lie in a plane.
5. The domain of a function f is the set of all real numbers x where $f(x)$ is a real number.

Reference

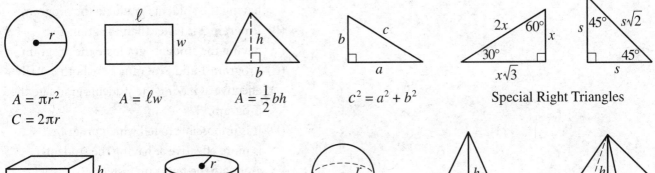

$A = \pi r^2$
$C = 2\pi r$

$A = \ell w$

$A = \dfrac{1}{2}bh$

$c^2 = a^2 + b^2$

Special Right Triangles

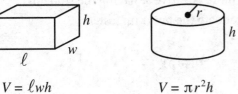 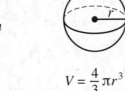 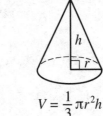 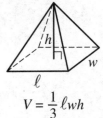

$V = \ell wh$

$V = \pi r^2 h$

$V = \dfrac{4}{3}\pi r^3$

$V = \dfrac{1}{3}\pi r^2 h$

$V = \dfrac{1}{3}\ell wh$

There is a total of 360 degrees in the arc of a circle.

There is a total of 2π radians in the arc of a circle.

There is a total of 180 degrees in the internal angles of a triangle.

GO ON TO THE NEXT PAGE

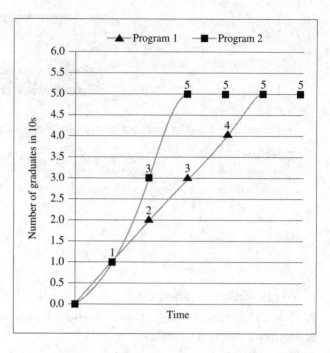

1. The figure above shows the graph of $f(x)$. Which of the following is $f(0)$ equal to?

(A) 5

(B) 0

(C) −3.5

(D) −2

2. A school is putting two classes of the same level of ESL, each of 50 students, into two different programs, Program 1 and Program 2. Based on the above graph, which of the following statements below is true?

(A) Program 1 is faster than Program 2 at having the students graduate the program.

(B) Program 2 is faster than Program 1 at having the students graduate the program.

(C) Program 1 and Program 2 are both equally effective at having the students graduate the program.

(D) It is impossible to tell which program is more effective at having the students graduate the program faster.

3. If $\dfrac{3x}{5y} = 5x^2$, then $xy = ?$

(A) 3

(B) $\dfrac{3}{5}$

(C) $\dfrac{3}{25}$

(D) $-\dfrac{5}{3}$

4. If $n^{3/4} = 8$, what is n?

(A) 6

(B) 8

(C) 10.66

(D) 16

5. A student is watching a live sports game, taking place in London, on TV in New York. It is 3:55 a.m. in New York, and the game will take another 2 hours and 16 minutes to finish. London is 5 hours ahead of New York. What time is it going to be in London when the game finishes?

(A) 5:55 a.m.

(B) 6:11 a.m.

(C) 8:55 a.m.

(D) 11:11 a.m.

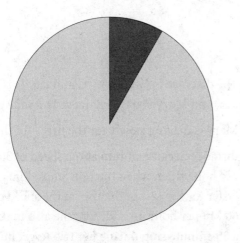

6. A circle with a radius of 12 is cut into slices through the center. One piece has an angle of 30°. What is the area of this piece?

(A) 12π

(B) 30π

(C) 46π

(D) 144π

x	0	3	–21	–33
y	0	1	–7	?

7. What is the missing y coordinate of this straight line?

(A) –11

(B) –33

(C) –21

(D) –7

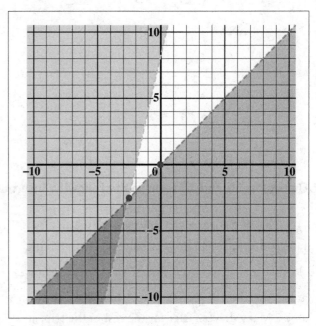

8. $y > 4x + 8$

$y < x$

Which of the following is a solution to the two inequalities shown above?

(A) (0, 5)

(B) (–5, –7)

(C) (–5, 0)

(D) (5, 7)

9. If $f(x) = \dfrac{-1}{x}$ and $g(x) = \dfrac{1}{3x}$, what is the value of $f(g(5))$?

(A) –5

(B) –15

(C) $\dfrac{1}{5}$

(D) $\dfrac{1}{15}$

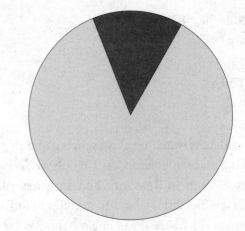

10. A circle has a diameter of 12, and the angle of the shaded region is 30°. What is the perimeter of the shaded region?

(A) $12 + 11\pi$

(B) 30π

(C) $12 + 1\pi$

(D) 33π

Questions 11 and 12 refer to the following information.

Jane and Mary are driving from city A to city B. Jane is driving at 45 km per hour. Mary is driving slowly because of rain for the first $\dfrac{1}{3}$ of the distance at the speed of 30 km per hour. Then when the rain stops, Mary drives faster for the rest of the trip, at the speed of 60 km per hour.

11. If the distance between city A and city B is 450 km and they both start the trip at 10 a.m., what is the difference in their arrival time?

(A) 0 hour

(B) 1 hour

(C) 3 hour and 35 minutes

(D) 5 hours

12. The distance between city C and city D is 540 km, and Mary starts driving at 11 a.m. Again, Mary is driving slowly for the first $\dfrac{1}{3}$ of the distance because of rain at the speed of 30 km per hour. Then when the rain stops, Mary drives faster for the rest of the trip, at the speed of 60 km per hour. In addition, she also makes a 35-minute stop during her trip to get lunch. When will Mary get to city D?

(A) 4:45 p.m.

(B) 7:25 p.m.

(C) 11:35 p.m.

(D) 12 a.m.

13. Which of the following quadratic equations has no solution?

(A) $3(x + 1)(x - 1) = 0$

(B) $2x(x + 11)(x + 8) = 0$

(C) $3 + (x + 3)^2 = 0$

(D) $(x + 1)(x + 2) = 1$

GO ON TO THE NEXT PAGE ⟹

Directions: Solve questions 14–17 and fill in the answer sheet accordingly. Refer to the following directions on how to fill in the answers on the answer sheet.

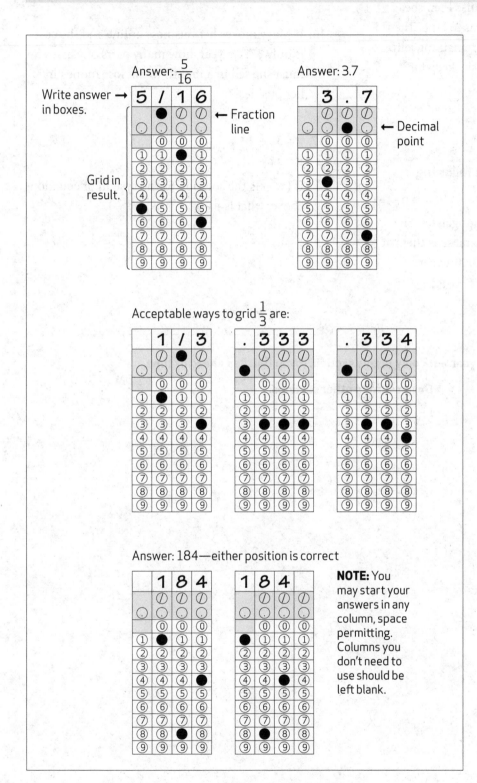

Answer: $\frac{5}{16}$

Write answer → in boxes.

← Fraction line

Grid in result.

Answer: 3.7

← Decimal point

Acceptable ways to grid $\frac{1}{3}$ are:

Answer: 184—either position is correct

NOTE: You may start your answers in any column, space permitting. Columns you don't need to use should be left blank.

1. Only the filled-in circles are graded. The directions suggest writing the answer in the box at the top, but it is not scored.

2. Fill in only one circle in any column.

3. There are no negative answers.

4. Only fill in one correct answer, even if there are more than one.

5. **Mixed numbers** like $2\frac{1}{2}$ should be filled in as 2.5 or 5/2.

6. **Decimal answers:** If you obtain a decimal answer with more digits, it should be filled in to fill the entire grid.

GO ON TO THE NEXT PAGE ⟹

14. Mandy is giving her friends some jelly beans. She starts with 50 jelly beans and gives her friend Beth 10% of her jelly beans. Then she gives 20% of the rest of the beans to Jane. Then she is keeping one-third of the remaining jelly beans herself. How many does she keep for herself?

Questions 15 and 16 refer to the following information.

Mary is starting a business selling sunglasses. She imports the sunglasses at $5 a pair and sells them at $15 a pair. She rents a store for $60,000 a year.

15. How many pairs of glasses must she sell in a month to not lose money in her business?

16. If Mary moves her business online and the cost is only $720 a year, how many pairs of glasses must she sell in a month to not lose money in her business?

17. $y = 3x + 2$
$y = 5x - 10$

If (x, y) is the solution to the system of equations above, what is $y - x$?

You can check your work only in this section, if you finished ahead of time.

Do not turn to other sections.

MATH TEST—CALCULATOR

45 MINUTES, 31 QUESTIONS

To answer questions in this section turn to Section 4 of your answer sheet.

Directions: Choose the best answer choice for questions 1–27 and fill in the answer sheet accordingly. Solve questions 28–31 and fill in the answer sheet accordingly. Before moving on to question 28, refer to the directions on how to fill in the answers on the answer sheet. Use of available space on the test booklet is allowed.

Notes

1. **Calculator use** is permitted.
2. Unless indicated, variables and expressions represent real numbers.
3. Figures are drawn to scale.
4. Figures lie in a plane.
5. The domain of a function f is the set of all real numbers x where $f(x)$ is a real number.

Reference

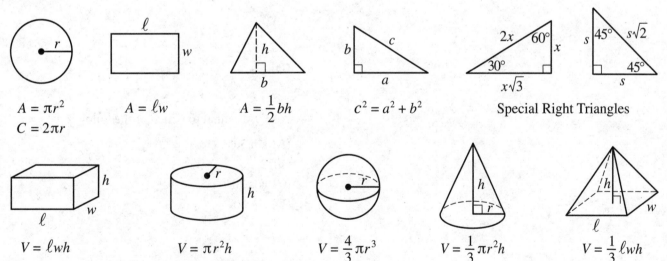

$A = \pi r^2$
$C = 2\pi r$

$A = \ell w$

$A = \frac{1}{2}bh$

$c^2 = a^2 + b^2$

Special Right Triangles

$V = \ell wh$

$V = \pi r^2 h$

$V = \frac{4}{3}\pi r^3$

$V = \frac{1}{3}\pi r^2 h$

$V = \frac{1}{3}\ell wh$

There is a total of 360 degrees in the arc of a circle.

There is a total of 2π radians in the arc of a circle.

There is a total of 180 degrees in the internal angles of a triangle.

GO ON TO THE NEXT PAGE ⫸

1. What number is halfway between $\frac{64}{13}$ and $-\frac{24}{14}$?

   (A) $-\frac{40}{27}$

   (B) $1\frac{110}{182}$

   (C) $\frac{84}{27}$

   (D) 40

2. A student bought 4 packs of gum at $1.39 per pack, and a tax of 7.8% is added. How much did the student pay in total?

   (A) $1.33
   (B) $4.33
   (C) $5.99
   (D) $5.56

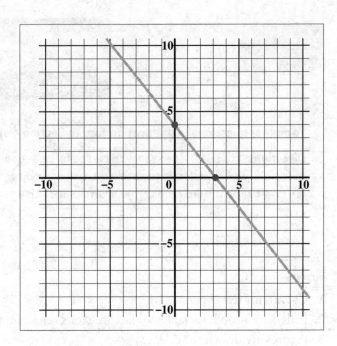

3. What is the slope of the graph above?

   (A) $-\frac{5}{4}$

   (B) $\frac{4}{5}$

   (C) $\frac{5}{4}$

   (D) $-\frac{4}{5}$

4. cos 60° is equal to which of the following?

   (A) sin 30°
   (B) 2
   (C) cos 30°
   (D) sin 60°

TYPE OF DOUGHNUT	NUMBER OF DOUGHNUTS
Jelly	25
Chocolate	54
Maple	13
Cream	12

5. The chart above shows the types of doughnuts in a box. If a doughnut is picked out at random, which type will have the likelihood of $\frac{1}{8}$ of being selected?

   (A) Jelly
   (B) Chocolate
   (C) Maple
   (D) Cream

6. $y = \frac{1}{4}x - 3$

What is the value of y when $2x = \frac{1}{4}$?

   (A) $-\frac{95}{32}$

   (B) $\frac{1}{32}$

   (C) -3
   (D) -2

7. $3x^3 - 12x = ?$

   (A) $3x(x - 2)^2$
   (B) $3x(x + 2)(x - 2)$
   (C) $(x + 2)(x - 2)$
   (D) $3(x + 2)^2$

8. A student has a summer job doing gardening work. He is paid \$28 for every tree that he has to trim in a yard and \$8 for every hour of grass cutting. How much did he make for a work day where he cut grass for 8 hours and trimmed 3 trees?

   (A) \$64
   (B) \$84
   (C) \$92
   (D) \$148

GO ON TO THE NEXT PAGE ⟹

Questions 9 and 10 are based on the following information.

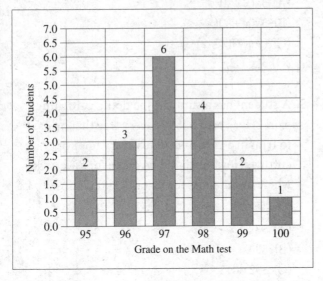

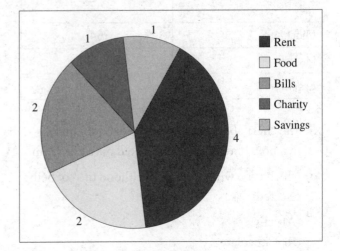

9. The school keeps track of the Math team's midterm math scores. In this set of data, which of the following number is the biggest?

   (A) median
   (B) mean
   (C) mode
   (D) range

10. The teacher of the Math team would like to know how many points were lost on average by each team member. Which of the following is the most relevant for her?

   (A) median
   (B) mean
   (C) mode
   (D) range

11. Andy divides his salary into 10 portions when he receives it. He spends 4 portions on rent, 2 portions on food, 2 portions on bills, 1 portion on charity, and 1 portion on savings. If he receives $5,450 of salary per month, how many dollars does he spend on rent and food in a year?

   (A) $2,180
   (B) $3,270
   (C) $39,240
   (D) $32,700

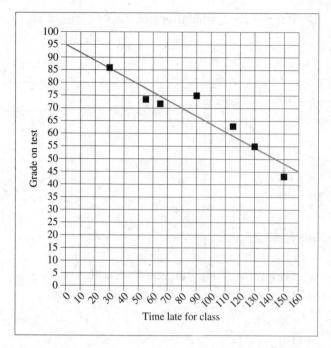

Grade on test / Time late for class

12. A school is conducting a study regarding the amount of cumulative time a student is late in the semester and its relationship with the grade on the student's test. Which of the following statements is true regarding the graph above?

(A) The slope represents the increase in the grade on the students' tests as students have a longer cumulative late time.

(B) The slope represents the decrease in the grade on the students' tests as students have a longer cumulative late time.

(C) The slope represents the increase in the amount of cumulative late time as a student receives a higher score on the test.

(D) The slope represents the decrease in the amount of cumulative late time as a student receives a lower score on the test.

13. If the percent increase from 30 to x is the same as the percent increase from 72 to 108, what is x?

(A) 60

(B) 45

(C) 66

(D) 102

14. Ken walked from his home to the office in 50 minutes. The distance between his office and home is 3.5 km. On the way back from the office to his home, he took the car for half of the distance. The speed of the car is three times the speed of his walking. He then walked the rest of the way home. How many minutes did it take for him to get home?

(A) 8 minutes

(B) 23 minutes

(C) 25 minutes

(D) 33 minutes

15. $4x - 3xy + 4z - 3yz = ?$

(A) $(3x - 1)(4y + 1)$

(B) $(x + z)(4 - 3y)$

(C) $(3xy - z)(4x + 1)$

(D) $(4x - 3)(x - yz)$

16. $\dfrac{5(q-3)+2}{3} = q - 2(q+1)$

    What is the value of q in the equation above?

    (A) 12
    (B) 11
    (C) $\dfrac{19}{8}$
    (D) 3

17. The size of a bacteria culture decreased by 25% during an experiment. What is the ratio of the new size of the culture to the decrease in the size?

    (A) 3 to 4
    (B) 4 to 3
    (C) 1 to 3
    (D) 3 to 1

18. If $6x^2 + x = 2$, what is one of the solutions of x?

    (A) $-\dfrac{1}{3}$

    (B) $-\dfrac{1}{6}$

    (C) $\dfrac{1}{6}$

    (D) $\dfrac{1}{2}$

19. $\dfrac{x^2 + 7x + 12}{x+3} > -10$

    Given that x does not equal -3, which of the following is the same as the inequality above?

    (A) $x > 2$
    (B) $-x < 14$
    (C) $x > -3$
    (D) $x > 3$

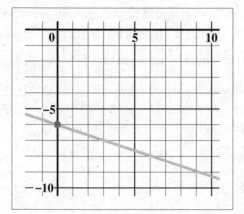

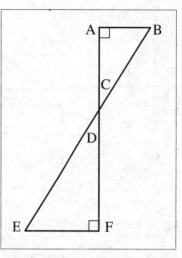

20. In the graph above, where does the line intersect the *x* axis?

(A) –18

(B) –12

(C) $-\dfrac{32}{3}$

(D) $-\dfrac{23}{4}$

21. Ting has two cylindrical mugs. The first mug has a base that has a radius of 7 cm, and the second mug has a base that has a radius 8.5 cm. The first mug with a base radius of 7 cm is filled with coffee up to 8.5 cm, and the second is empty. If Ting pours all of the coffee from the first mug into the empty mug, the second mug now has coffee filled up to where?

(A) 4.33π

(B) 5.76π

(C) 8.5π

(D) 15.5π

22. In the figure above, if line AC is 4, line AF is 16, line DE is 15, and angle B is 53.13°, what is the sum of line AB + line EF?

(A) 4

(B) 9

(C) 12

(D) 15

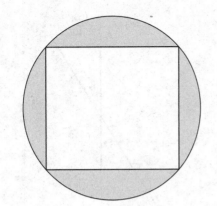

23. In the figure above, a square is inscribed inside a circle. If the radius is $\dfrac{\sqrt{2}}{2}$, what is the area of the shaded region?

   (A) 4π

   (B) $\dfrac{1}{2}\pi - 1$

   (C) $\dfrac{\sqrt{2}}{2}\pi - 2$

   (D) $\sqrt{2}\pi$

24. David and Avi are working together to fill an order. David can fill the order in 12 hours. It takes David and Avi 6 hours to fill the order if they work together. How long would it take for Avi to fill the order by himself? Round to the nearest minute.

   (A) 6 hours
   (B) 12 hours
   (C) 9 hours
   (D) 6 hours and 12 minutes

25. Sam is using a grid to make a map of her town, and she drew a line to represent the highway, represented by the equation $y = \dfrac{1}{5}x - 4$. Each unit on the grid is 1 km long. If she drew two points on the graph $(5, n)$ and $(m, 2)$, how far are these points from each other in km?

   (A) $\sqrt{226}$

   (B) 32

   (C) $\sqrt{650}$

   (D) $\dfrac{1}{5}$

26. $\dfrac{5(q-3)+2}{3} = q - 2(q + 1)$

   What is the value of q in the equation above?

   (A) 12

   (B) $\dfrac{7}{8}$

   (C) $\dfrac{19}{8}$

   (D) 3

27. A store sold two types of miniature sculptures, brass and ceramic. The brass sculpture cost $15 more. If the store made $14,625 from selling 125 brass sculptures and 130 ceramic sculptures per month, on average, how much did the store make selling the ceramic sculpture per year?

   (A) $50
   (B) $600
   (C) $6,500
   (D) $78,000

Directions: Solve questions 28–31 and fill in the answer sheet accordingly. Refer to the following directions on how to fill in the answers on the answer sheet.

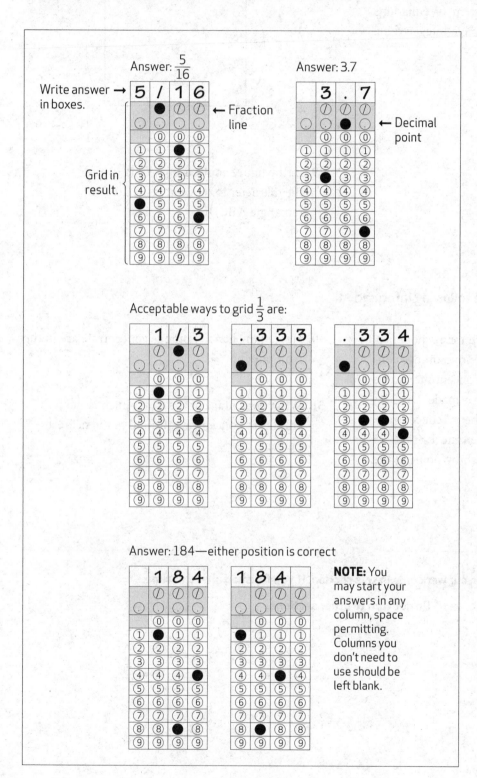

Answer: $\frac{5}{16}$

Write answer in boxes.

← Fraction line

Grid in result.

Answer: 3.7

← Decimal point

Acceptable ways to grid $\frac{1}{3}$ are:

Answer: 184—either position is correct

GO ON TO THE NEXT PAGE ⟹

NOTE: You may start your answers in any column, space permitting. Columns you don't need to use should be left blank.

1. Only the filled-in circles are graded. The directions suggest writing the answer in the box at the top, but it is not scored.

2. Fill in only one circle in any column.

3. There are no negative answers.

4. Only fill in one correct answer, even if there are more than one.

5. **Mixed numbers** like $2\frac{1}{2}$ should be filled in as 2.5 or 5/2.

6. **Decimal answers:** If you obtain a decimal answer with more digits, it should be filled in to fill the entire grid.

Diagnostic Test

28. $y > -2x + 4$

$y < 3x - 1$

(x, y) is a solution to the system of equations above. What is the largest possible integer value of y, if x is 5?

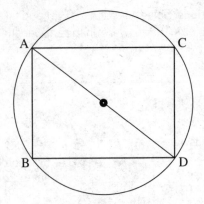

29. In the figure above if line AB is 10 and the diameter is 26, what is the area of rectangle ABCD?

Questions 30 and 31 refer to the following information.

A teacher is making fruit punch for a school trip. She made 1 liter of orange juice from orange concentrate; there is 10% orange concentrate in this 1 liter of orange juice. She also made 2.5 liters of cranberry juice from cranberry concentrate; there is 15% cranberry concentrate in this 2.5 liters. She made the fruit punch by pouring the two juices together.

30. How many liters of orange concentrate are in the fruit punch?

31. What percentage of the fruit punch is the cranberry concentrate? Round to the nearest percent.

 STOP

You can check your work only in this section, if you finished ahead of time.

Do not turn to other sections.

Diagnostic Test Answer Key

Reading Test

1. **(D)** Remember this is about the passage as a whole, so don't get caught up in the details. In the passage, Jacob and Timmy are at sea headed toward Scilly Isles and, despite the adventure, they are finding reasons to argue.

2. **(A)** Timmy "would have moved a woman" because he is handsome and stern and knowledgeable. He is always very serious, taking calculations and checking his compass. Eliminate (B) because he is not playful. Eliminate (C) because he's not dull. And eliminate (D) because he's not unsightly.

3. **(B)** Put this in your own words. Timmy looks very appealing and intriguing; he would have impressed a woman.

4. **(B)** Look for evidence. The first reason given for their argument is "the right way to open a tin of beef." The passage explains that while they should have been having fun, the beef was cold and the biscuits spoiled and the journey long and "much the same hour after hour." There is no evidence for the other choices.

5. **(C)** These lines address the bad food and the monotony of the journey, which are the reasons for the quarrel.

6. **(B)** Here, he sat naked "save" for his shirt, meaning everything was off except his shirt.

7. **(C)** Look for evidence. Eliminate (A) right away. The two seem to know each other, and there's no evidence that they are just now meeting, so get rid of (B) too. And while Timmy is performing scientific calculations, there's no evidence that he's a famous scientist or that Jacob is looking to hire him.

8. **(A)** Not only does Timmy calculate right where the isles will be, he is also familiar with the boats passing them and the cargo they carry.

9. **(D)** This is a tough question. Try to eliminate the answers that are definitely incorrect. Eliminate (A) because Shakespeare has been long dead. Eliminate (C) because we have absolutely no evidence that there is another argument. The passage does imply that Jacob is not a fan of Shakespeare, but it does not suggest he threw the book—it's obvious that the book went overboard by accident when the sail flapped. So, (D) is the correct answer. This makes sense considering the journey is coming to an end, and a new adventure will be starting soon.

10. **(B)** Eliminate (C) and (D) because the tone, or attitude, of the writer is far from critical or uncertain. The author is obviously very fond of Felix. Eliminate (A) because at no point does the author reject optimism and turn to negativity.

11. **(A)** Here, Felix works hard at his music in order to "satisfy," or please himself. It's all about the enjoyment he gets from playing.

12. **(D)** Felix's talent is obvious; but, early in the passage, the author states that his talent is made better by the fact that he never tries to show off. So look for humility or modesty, as in (D).

13. **(B)** These lines give the evidence for the previous question. They state that his "unaffected modesty and simplicity" deterred his audiences from noticing any faults in him.

14. **(C)** Felix's father favored Felix and Fanny because of their devotion to music. According to the passage, Abraham paid particular attention to Felix because he had inherited the traits that made his grandfather great.

15. **(C)** These are the specific lines that state why Abraham "watched Felix with particular care." Felix inherited the traits that had distinguished his grandfather, Moses Mendelssohn.

16. **(D)** Read the sentence with all the choices. The grass and trees "imparted" a suggestion of the country. So, they conveyed or emanated that country feeling.

17. **(A)** This is a purpose question. Ask what the fourth paragraph does, not what it says. Quite simply, this paragraph describes where Felix grew up. It does not make any comparisons as in (B) and (C). Nor does it directly link Felix's upbringing to any of his later work.

18. **(D)** Madame Bigot is the instructor in Paris who noticed both children's talent and arranged for them to receive musical lessons as part of their regular education. Thus, (D) is the correct answer. There is no evidence of her disposition, and while she wanted music to be just as important as other aspects of the children's education, she never says it's more important. Eliminate (B) because she was a great instructor. And there's no evidence for (C); the children leave Paris, not Madame Bigot.

19. **(C)** First, you know that Felix worked hard at his music just because he enjoyed it. Next, you know that he was "the brightest and merriest of children." Finally, you know that nothing could get his spirits down—he was earnest in work and play. There is no evidence that he was resistant to topics other than music. Somber is the opposite of his disposition. And he was not reluctant to study.

20. **(C)** This is a summary question. What happens in the first paragraph? The author introduces the topic—snakebite and its cure—and says that for centuries our scientific knowledge on this topic was unsatisfactory. This paragraph doesn't introduce a cure, as in (A). It doesn't say scientists have given up, as in (B). And it doesn't say science will never find the cure, just that it had a really difficult time with it in the past.

21. **(C)** Here, snakebite and its cure have caused despair or distress since the science, for so long, didn't deliver any answers.

22. **(A)** Read the sentence with each choice. In this first paragraph, the author is talking about all the fruitless or unsuccessful attempts to solve the question of snakebite and its cure.

23. **(D)** The author doesn't mention which animals he favors, as in (A). He doesn't believe animal testing can give us the answer, as in (B). And while he does think some of the best science comes out of Europe, it's much too extreme to say he isn't confident in any other scientists, as in (C). (D) is correct because the author is obviously frustrated with the scientific process used to solve the problem of snakebite and its cure.

24. **(B)** This is a main idea question, so don't get lost in the details. Topic sentences can help you with these types of questions. In the second paragraph, the author begins describing the "various and contradictory theories" of snake venom. He says there's only one that is universal, but he doesn't dive into the correct theory, instead he begins explaining why all the others are incorrect. Eliminate (A) because there are not "few" theories. Eliminate (C) and (D) because they are details of the passage, not the main idea of this paragraph.

25. (A) The author begins talking about the relationship between theories and antidotes in the fourth paragraph, describing them as "confusion worse confounded." The point here is that scientists had an equally difficult time figuring out snake-poison antidotes as they did understanding the poison itself. So look for the answer that says they were both scientific mysteries.

26. (D) These lines specifically relate theories to antidotes and describe how antidotes were proposed over and over unsuccessfully.

27. (B) For EXCEPT questions, eliminate all answers that are true. The author mentions (A) at the start of paragraph 7. Right above that, in paragraph 6, he mentions (C). And (D) is discussed thoroughly in the final paragraph.

28. (C) The graph is a bit confusing, so take a moment to study it. It's obvious that overall the snakebites resulting in death have generally decreased, so eliminate (A) and (B). Since this isn't just true for Europe, eliminate (D).

29. (D) This question is tough. First, consider what the author says about Europe. He says that scientific research is keenly pursued in Europe, but that snakebites are not a popular topic of study because Europe has few snakes and they are comparatively harmless. So, if he looked at the graph and saw Europe didn't have a lot of deaths by snakebite, he would not be surprised. He would explain that this low number of deaths is why Europe hasn't dedicated a lot of time and energy to studying snakebites.

30. (C) Ask yourself what the first paragraph does. It very quickly tells the reader about Adrien Arpel's early fascination with beauty and how that made her into the person she is now, "president of a $12 million-a-year company." The writer introduces her through her past and tracks her past into her present. (C) is the only answer that captures that. The writer doesn't discuss unsuccessful people. And while the value of her company is mentioned, her monetary value is not. The writer also doesn't suggest that Adrien doesn't have a lot of talent.

31. (B) Another question asking about rhetorical choices. Here, the writer was showing how Adrien used the little bit of money she did have to follow her dreams. (A) is not mentioned. There is no evidence for (C). And she hasn't had a "downfall" but instead is living out her dream.

32. (A) In this context, the writer is talking about her book selling briskly, or quickly. (A) is the only word that conveys the idea that her book sales are still going well. It isn't appropriate to say a book is selling "impatiently," "energetically," or "sharply."

33. (D) First, eliminate (A) and (B)—these are minor details that are mentioned but in no way praised by the author. You may struggle between (C) and (D) but ask yourself which choice the writer specifically comments on. In the second paragraph, the writer introduces the book and then goes on to talk about its accomplishments—being on the best-seller list for six months and earning the most money ever for the reprint rights of a beauty book. Her book's success is clearly what distinguishes her to the author.

34. **(D)** In these lines, the author compares Adrien's success to that of others. Her book has distinguished itself from others by continuing to be a bestseller and by earning the most for reprint in its genre. While Adrien is impressive in many ways, it's her book that has truly put her at the forefront of her career.

35. **(C)** This question asks specifically about the beauty products. According to the passage, her "innovations" are "her exclusive use of nature-based, chemical-free products" and "her policy of try-before-you-buy makeup." This is stated almost exactly in option (C).

36. **(B)** Toward the end of the passage, the writer addresses Adrien's advice to other women—"a woman's makeup should be largely determined by her profession." Hence, if a woman were a construction worker, Adrien would think that her workplace and duties should determine her beauty choices. So, (B) makes sense here. (A) isn't practical for the profession. There's no evidence for (C); in fact, Adrien is surely the type to think every woman should have some type of routine—she calls regular facials a necessity, after all. And (D) is slightly absurd since there's no evidence in the passage that Adrien wants all women in "feminine" careers away from the damaging effects of weather.

37. **(C)** This is a difficult question. First, check what the writer says about reprint rights. The book Adrien published in 1977 earned the most money ever for a beauty book's reprint rights. So, check the chart to see if there's anything to suggest that before 1977 a beauty book earned more than $275,000. The increments are 50 (thousand), so it isn't until 1980 that reprint rights surpass this amount. So no, the chart doesn't disprove what the writer said. Since we are discussing reprint rights, not book sales, eliminate (D).

38. **(A)** Each year, book sales grow and reprint rights are bought for increasing prices. Hence, all the evidence in the chart suggests that the popularity of the beauty industry has been and is continuing to increase.

39. **(D)** In Passage 1, Lewis insists that every democracy will have to fight for its liberties, so America's test is both expected and necessary. "Inevitable" is closest to necessary. (A) conveys the opposite. (B) means doubtful. (C) means uncertain.

40. **(A)** This is at the end of the first paragraph. A civilization can only earn a place or rank if it does justice to itself and defeats its enemies.

41. **(D)** Read this sentence with all the choices. Here, America's freedoms inflamed Prussia's rulers with fear and caused them to go to war, so it provoked them. (B) is an appealing choice, but it actually means "enraged."

42. **(A)** Right at the beginning of paragraph 2, President Wilson states why he is speaking, a meeting to discuss a loan.

43. **(B)** This sentence compares itself to the previous one, the "utmost sacrifice" of the lives of American men. The loan, then, is the "least" of what the country has to give. So eliminate (C) and (D). Now, does the author mean it is least in amount or in significance? The money is not as important as the lives that will be given, so (B) is the correct choice.

44. **(C)** In the second passage it becomes clear that "now" is different from "before" because the need to fight is "more clearly disclosed." Thus (C) is the correct answer. It's the only one with actual evidence in the passage. While the other choices may or may not be true, they are not supported by the passage itself.

45. (D) These are the lines where President Wilson states directly why he needs the loan now. He says that the reasons the country is at war and what's at stake is more clear than ever before, giving direct evidence for the previous question.

46. (B) This is a tough question. What do the passages have in common? They are both about the necessity of war and sacrifice for freedom. Yet, Passage 2 goes further and uses this argument to ask for money. Thus (B) is the correct answer choice. They are not in conflict or disagreement, so you can eliminate the other choices.

47. (C) This question is also asking you to make connections between the passages. They both are advocating for war, calling it an inevitable sacrifice for democratic ideals. The passages are not targeted at enemies, as in (A). Both are attempting to bolster support, so eliminate (B). And while (D) might be implied by the passages, it is not the purpose.

Writing and Language Test

1. (A) This is correct as is. Eliminate (B) because it is too wordy. Eliminate (C) because it is too extreme to say paid family leave "doesn't exist." Eliminate (D) because there is no evidence to support it; in fact, if you read on, (D) is incorrect since most Americans don't receive paid family leave, and even those that do often suffer financial consequences.

2. (C) Choice (C) expresses the fact that the statistics are alarming, even distressing, and so is the correct answer. (B) can be eliminated because it suggests that the statistics are heartwarming rather than appalling. (D) can be tricky because the statistics can make one feel melancholy or sad, but it isn't appropriate to say the percentage is mournful.

3. (B) Make sure your tense is consistent. The verb "work" in this sentence is in present tense, which should help you choose (B). (C) is present participle and is usually accompanied by a helping verb and used for continuous action, for instance "are extending." (D) is present perfect tense; it is used to show something that has started in the past but continues now.

4. (B) Choose (B) because this sentence does not need to be broken up here in the middle of a long phrase. It is not the end of an independent clause and the beginning of another as in (C); it is not the end of an independent clause that is followed by a list or clarification as in (D).

5. (A) This is correct as is. Here, the comma conjunction separates two independent clauses, and we need "but" to show contrast between the two ideas. (B) has the comma but shows cause and effect rather than contrast. (C) conveys the contrast with "yet," which works just like "but"; however, it is missing the comma. Substitute "moreover" in choice (D) with "additionally," and you'll quickly see that it is incorrect.

6. **(D)** For these types of questions, look for hints in the sentence. Sentence 5 begins with "Furthermore," meaning that it is giving additional information to something already said. Here, the sentence is giving more reasons why employees may not qualify for FMLA. Sentence 3 is also doing this, while sentence 4 moves on to explaining the limitations of FMLA even when employees do qualify. So, sentence 5 should be between these two ideas. If you have trouble with this, notice that you can eliminate (B) and (C) because they are the same answer, then read the sentence where it is now and after sentence 3.

7. **(A)** This is correct as is. Eliminate (B) because misusing vulnerable populations is not a fortunate or good thing. Eliminate (C) and (D) because they are synonyms; if they can't both be correct, they must be incorrect.

8. **(B)** Ask yourself what's happening before and after. The sentence before is explaining how the most vulnerable and low-paid employees are the most exploited. The sentence after states the consequences of the current system: new parents don't get to take ample time off to be with their children. We need to connect these ideas, so (B) is the correct choice. It doesn't explain the standards as in (A), contradict the point of the paragraph as in (C), or supply irrelevant information as in (D).

9. **(D)** The fact is at the center, or core, of the campaign as in Choice (D). (B) suggests the fact is only at the beginning of the movement, while (C) refers to another definition of center used for location or betweenness.

10. **(A)** Memorize this. You use "lay" (present) and "laid" (past) when you mean "to place," so that doesn't fit here. You use "lie" (present) and "lay" (past) when you mean "to recline" like you are going to sleep. You also use lie for examples like this or phrases like "the answer lies in the question."

11. **(A)** This is correct as is. Ask yourself what the question asks. The sentence has to both conclude and serve as a call to action. (A) is the only choice that calls the reader to action as it says indifference or inaction is no longer appropriate.

12. **(C)** Eliminate (A) because "Its'" doesn't exist. Eliminate (B) because it shows possession. Eliminate (D) because it would need an apostrophe to mean "basketball is"—right now it is just the plural form of "basketball." (C) means "It is" and so is the correct choice here.

13. **(A)** Here, you need to decide which word is most precise for the intended meaning. The conditions have been studied carefully and thoroughly. (B) means importantly. (C) means carefully but as in suspiciously, and so it doesn't fit the context. (D) is an antonym of the intended meaning.

14. **(B)** This sentence creates a contrast. The writer prefers outdoor exercise but approves of indoor exercise during winter months. The only conjunction that accomplishes contrast is choice (B).

15. **(C)** For questions like these, look for clues. Sentence 1 says basketball fills a need, so it needs to be after a sentence that establishes the need. Thus, it should come after sentence 3 when the need for an indoor sport during winter is introduced.

16. **(D)** Check the subject-verb agreement and the tense. The subject is "the game," so eliminate (B). The rest of the sentence is in present tense, so eliminate (A). Read the sentence with (C), and you'll quickly see that it doesn't work. (D) is the correct choice.

17. **(D)** First, notice that this question is testing three things: the punctuation surrounding the phrase, the correct form of "guards," and the correct form of "their/they're." The rule is that extra phrases (the sentence can be read without them and still makes perfect sense) should be surrounded by commas. In certain instances, when the phrases are large or distracting, they are surrounded by dashes. Eliminate (A) because "guards" is plural, not possessive. Eliminate (B) because it doesn't surround the phrase with commas. Eliminate (C) because they're (they are) isn't appropriate here.

18. **(D)** This is a word choice question. Try to substitute a word before looking at the choices—an obvious word is "stop." The guards must stop the opposing forwards from shooting. Choice (D) is the only choice that works here. It is not appropriate to say you must "defeat" or "cease" someone from shooting. And (B) is an adjective meaning to be cautious.

19. **(A)** This is correct as is. Since there are two centers, "between" is correct, not "among." (B) and (C) aren't effective because they don't convey the idea that the ball is being thrown up between the two so that they can jump for it.

20. **(C)** For these types of questions, ask yourself what the sentence is doing currently. This sentence is explaining what happens when a player fouls. The sentence before defines a foul. Hence, this sentence is expanding on the sentence before it and giving the reader relevant detail. Eliminate (D) because it is not providing a counterargument.

21. **(A)** This is a difficult question. You have to understand the organization of this paragraph. This sentence is right in middle of the explanation of fouls and free-throws. Only (A) continues this topic and makes sense here. Choices (B), (C), and (D) change the topic abruptly even if they are still relevant to the game of basketball more generally.

22. **(B)** This is also a difficult question. It asks for a concluding sentence that makes sense within the context of the passage and which coincides with the data in the graph. First, eliminate anything that doesn't fit well with the topic and flow of the passage. (C) and (D) bring in other sports, which would be very abrupt to a passage solely about basketball. Eliminate (A) because it doesn't interpret the graph accurately—the percentage of girls voting for basketball in 1917 is about 67%. Choice (B) remains consistent with the context of the passage, and since over 50% of girls voted for basketball each year, it accurately interprets the graph.

23. **(D)** It is not necessary to break up these two items, so choice (D) is correct. The other choices create unnecessary pauses and break up the flow of the sentence.

24. **(B)** Choice (B) is in active voice and is concise, making it correct. (A) incorrectly suggests that the reader is contradicting the mood of her lover rather than Cleopatra. (C) is illogical. (D) is too wordy.

25. **(D)** The "but" in this sentence tells you that the writer is making a contrast, so (D) makes the most sense. (A) means "up until this point;" (B) is illogical since those qualities are not "fortunate"; and (C) suggests a cause and effect relationship with the previous sentence.

26. **(B)** This question tests subject-verb agreement and consistent tense. "Antony" is the subject, so eliminate (A). The rest of the sentence is in present tense, so eliminate (C) and (D).

27. **(A)** Read the question carefully. You are looking for the choice that best expresses the extraordinary nature of Cleopatra. Choices (C) and (D) claim that Cleopatra is ordinary, and so should be eliminated. (B) relies on her physical appearance and personality, and doesn't differentiate her nearly as much as choice (A).

28. **(C)** Another one you'll want to read carefully. The rest of the paragraph is about Cleopatra's relationship with Antony and how they are viewed or understood as a result of that relationship. So, you are looking for a choice that mentions both of them and remarks on how they shape your understanding of each other, making (C) correct. (A), (B), and (D) don't include both characters or hint at the ways Cleopatra is blamed for Antony's faults.

29. **(A)** This is correct as is. For word choice questions like this, read the sentence with each choice. (B) changes the meaning of the sentence. (C) and (D) are equally vague.

30. **(B)** Check tense and subject-verb agreement. (A) is illogical; Cleopatra cannot fly. (C) and (D) are in incorrect tenses.

31. **(B)** Here, we have a dependent clause, or fragment, followed by an independent clause, or complete sentence. The rule is to separate them with a comma, making (B) correct. (A) has no punctuation and, therefore, creates an unclear run-on. Eliminate (C) because semicolons are used just like periods, to separate two independent clauses. In (D), the "but" conflicts with the "While" in the sentence and makes the sentence incomprehensible.

32. **(A)** Try process of elimination. The reader doesn't write Cleopatra at all, so eliminate (B). (C) changes the tone of the passage and doesn't flow with the second half of the sentence. (D) is much too wordy. Note that the writer uses first person and inserts his or her opinion often, so (A) matches the casual tone of the passage.

33. **(D)** This sentence expresses Cleopatra's complexity with pairs of contrasting words, so you are looking for the opposite of "treacherous." (A), (B), and (C) are all synonyms, and so can be eliminated.

34. **(A)** This is correct as is. Eliminate (B) and (C) because they do the same thing, and since they cannot both be correct, neither can be. Now, eliminate (D) because you do need a break here. Think of the dash as a hard pause, like a comma on steroids; the dash is very versatile.

35. **(A)** Look at the chart given for the approximate carbon dioxide level in 1958; it should be very close to 300 ppm. (B), (C), and (D) are all too high according to the chart.

36. **(D)** Keep tense consistent. Earlier in the sentence, the writer used "have soared," so it makes sense to continue using past participle. Also, eliminate (B) because the subject, "carbon dioxide concentrations," is plural, and the verb must agree.

37. **(B)** Remember to be concise; the shortest answer with all the necessary information wins. Choices (A), (B), and (D) all convey the same meaning, but take many more words to do so.

38. **(C)** The reading states that the safe zone is 350 ppm, so look at the chart for the year when levels were at that rate. The line crosses the 350 ppm mark right before 1990, so (C) is the only logical answer.

39. **(B)** The point of this passage is that emission levels are very high and need to go down, so you can eliminate (A). "Omit" means to remove or delete. "Eliminate" has a similar meaning: to get rid of or exclude from consideration. They are both too extreme to make sense here.

40. **(A)** For these, check what's going on around the sentence. Immediately before this sentence, the writer lists efforts to reduce current emissions. The sentence that follows suggests that those efforts alone cannot avert disaster. (A) suggests that more urgent action is needed and flows logically. (B) and (C) are too nonchalant, indicating that these minor efforts are paying off. (D) is too extremely negative since the passage as a whole discusses what can still be done to control the situation.

41. **(C)** These are always tough, but look for clues. Sentence 3 begins with "To address the former," and so should follow a sentence that lists two issues or questions. The first sentence lists two questions, so this sentence should come directly after it. If you read it there, it also flows more logically with the following sentence because the Paris Agreement serves as an example of a large-scale effort. Another approach you might use is to eliminate (B) and (D) because this sentence doesn't work here as a topic or wrap-up sentence.

42. **(C)** The next sentence directly responds to this question, so deleting it would interrupt the logical flow. While the nature of the topic is grave as in (D), the removal of this sentence would not detract from that in any meaningful way.

43. **(D)** Read the question carefully. You are looking for two things: a possible solution and logical flow. The main question is in the topic sentence: "what can we do?" (A) and (B) don't offer solutions, so eliminate them. Immediately after this sentence is a discussion of how to extract carbon dioxide from the atmosphere, so (D) is correct.

44. **(D)** Find the subject. This sentence has a compound subject: "urgency of the situation" and "dire consequences of further inaction." Instead of reading this every time, substitute it with "two things" or "they" and read it with each choice. Eliminate (A) and (C) because they do not agree with a plural subject. The rest of the sentence is in present tense, so go with (D).

Math Test—No Calculator

1. **(D)** This is a simple question about functions. Find the point on the function where $x = 0$. When $x = 0$, $y = -2$.

2. **(B)** This is a data analysis question. The graph shows that the students graduate the program faster when they are in Program 2. Therefore, the answer is B.

3. **(C)** This is a simple algebra question. First divide both sides of the equation to get $\frac{3}{5y} = 5x$. Then rearrange the equation to find what xy is equal to: $5xy = \frac{3}{5}$; $xy = \frac{3}{25}$.

4. **(D)** This is a question about exponents. $n^{3/4} = 8$. First cube root both sides of the equation. $\sqrt[3]{n^{\frac{3}{4}}} = \sqrt[3]{8}$. Then the equation becomes $n^{1/4} = 2$. Then raise both sides of the equation to the power of 4 and get: $(n^{1/4})^4 = (2)^4$. Then the answer will be 16 because $n = 16$.

5. **(D)** This is a word problem. First, find out what time it is in New York when game ends 3:55 a.m. + 2 hour and 16 minutes = 6:11 a.m. Then because London is 5 hours ahead add 5 hours to get to the London time: 6:11 a.m. + 5 hours = 11:11 a.m.

6. **(A)** This is a simple question about a circle. First, find the area of the circle: $A = \pi r^2 = \pi 12^2 = 144\pi$. Then, find out what fraction of the circle is 30°: $30°/360° = \frac{1}{12}$. Then, multiply the area of the circle with the fraction: $\frac{1}{12} \times 144\pi = 12\pi$.

7. **(A)** This is a linear equation question. First, find the slope of the equation by taking two points on the line, $\frac{1-0}{3-0} = \frac{1}{3}$. Then plug the slope into the line equation of $y = mx + b$ to get $y = \frac{1}{3}x + b$. Then plug in a point to get the constant b, $0 = \frac{1}{3}(0) + b$; $b = 0$. The equation of this line is $y = \frac{1}{3}x$. Plug in the x value to get the missing y value, $y = \frac{1}{3}(-33)$; $y = -11$.

8. **(B)** This is a system of inequality question. Look though the answer choices to find the set of coordinates that falls in the region where there is shaded area from both inequalities. The answer is (−5, −7).

9. **(B)** This is a simple function question. First plug 5 into $g(x)$, $g(5) = \frac{1}{3(5)} = \frac{1}{15}$. Then solve for $f(g(5))$, $f(g(5)) = \frac{-1}{\frac{1}{15}} = -15$.

10. **(C)** This is a medium circle question. First, find the radius, $12 \div 2 = 6$. Then find the circumference of the circle, $2\pi 6 = 12\pi$. Find the ratio of the shaded region to the circle $30° \div 360° = \frac{1}{12}$. Then find the arch of the shaded area, $12\pi \times \frac{1}{12} = \pi$. Then add the sides to find the circumference, $1\pi + 6 + 6 = 12 + 1\pi$.

11. **(A)** This is a multistep word problem. Because both Jane and Mary are leaving city A at the same time, the information about both leaving at 10 a.m. can be ignored. Jane is driving at 45 km/hr, so it takes 10 hours for her to get to city B (450 km ÷ 45 km per hr = 10 hr). Then find the time it takes for Mary. First, find the time it takes for the first $\frac{1}{3}$ of the distance. This first $\frac{1}{3}$ of the distance is: 450 km $\times \frac{1}{3} = 150$ km. It took her 5 hours for the first $\frac{1}{3}$ of the distance (150 km ÷ 30 km per hr = 5 hr). Then, find the time it takes for the rest of the distance. This rest of the distance is $\frac{2}{3}$ of the distance, which is: 450 km $\times \frac{2}{3} = 300$ km. It took her 5 hours for the rest of the distance (300 km ÷ 60 km per hr = 5 hr). It takes Mary 10 hours to get there (5 hr + 5 hr = 10 hr). The difference between their arrival is 10 hr − 10 hr = 0 hours.

12. **(C)** This is a multistep word problem. To find the time it takes for Mary, first find the time it takes for the first $\frac{1}{3}$ of the distance. This first $\frac{1}{3}$ of the distance is: 540 km $\times \frac{1}{3} = 180$ km. It took her 6 hours for the first $\frac{1}{3}$ of the distance (180 km ÷ 30 km per hr = 6 hr). Then, find the time it takes for the rest of the distance. This rest of the distance is $\frac{2}{3}$ of the distance, which is: 540 km $\times \frac{2}{3} = 360$ km. It took her 6 hours for the rest of the distance (360 km ÷ 60 km per hr = 6 hr). It takes Mary 12 hours of total driving time (6 hr + 6 hr = 12 hr). Then adding the 35-minute stop in the middle of her trip, it takes her 12 hours and 35 minutes to get to city D. The arrival time will be 11:35 p.m. (11 a.m. + 12 hr and 35 min = 11:35 p.m.).

13. **(C)** This is a difficult algebra question. In this question, it is easy to see that choices A and B are solvable. The only ones that are not solvable could be C and D. Here try to solve both problems to see which one is solvable and which is not. If you try problem D, you will see that it is solvable with the quadratic formula. Then try to see if choice C is solvable. The problem needs to be first FOILed, then rearranged: $3 + x^2 + 6x + 9 = 0$; $x^2 + 6x + 12 = 0$. Then apply the quadratic equation: $x = \dfrac{-b \pm \sqrt{b^2 - 4ac}}{2a}$.

$x = \dfrac{-(6) \pm \sqrt{(6)^2 - 4(1)(12)}}{2(1)}$; $x = \dfrac{-(6) \pm \sqrt{36 - 48}}{2(1)}$.

Here you will see that the inside of the square root becomes a negative number $x = \dfrac{-(6) \pm \sqrt{-12}}{2(1)}$ and therefore choice C cannot be solved.

14. **12** This is a word problem about percents. First, find out how much she has left after giving to Beth, $50 \times 90\% = 45$. Then find out how much is left after she gives to Jane, $45 \times 80\% = 36$. Then divide by 3 to get the answer, $36 \div 3 = 12$.

15. **500** This is a multistep word problem. First, set up an equation with the cost on one side and the revenue on the other side, using p to represent the pairs of sunglasses, ($60,000 ÷ 12) + $5p = $15p. Now solve for p, $5,000 + $5p = $15p; $5,000 = $10p; p = 500. She must sell 500 pairs of glasses in a month to not lose money in her business.

16. **6** This is a multistep word problem. First, set up an equation with the cost on one side and the revenue on the other side, using p to represent the pairs of sunglasses, ($720 ÷ 12) + $5p = $15p. Now solve for p, $60 + $5p = $15p; $60 = $10p; p = 6. She must sell 6 pairs of glasses in a month to not lose money in her business.

17. **14** This is a system of equations question. First, solve the equation to get the x and y values. Set the two equations equal to each other, $3x + 2 = 5x - 10$. Then solve for x, $12 = 2x$; $x = 6$. Then plug in x to find the value of y, $y = 3(6) + 2$, $y = 20$. The value of $y - x$ is $20 - 6 = 14$.

Math Test—Calculator

1. **(B)** This is a simple fraction question. Add the two fractions: $\dfrac{64}{13} + (-\dfrac{24}{14}) = \dfrac{(64)(14)}{(13)(14)} - \dfrac{(24)(13)}{(14)(13)}$

$= \dfrac{896}{182} - \dfrac{312}{182} = \dfrac{584}{182}$. Then divide by 2 to get the answer for this question: $\dfrac{584}{182} \div 2 = \dfrac{292}{182} = 1\dfrac{110}{182}$.

2. **(C)** This is a simple word problem. First find the cost of the 4 packs of gum, $1.39 \times 4 = $5.56. Then add 7.8% tax on it by multiplying $5.56 by 1.078. The answer is $5.99.

3. **(A)** This is a simple graphing question. To find the slope find the rise and run, rise is –5, and run is 4. Therefore the slope is $-\dfrac{5}{4}$.

4. **(A)** This is a simple trigonometry question. The easiest way to solve this question is to plug each term into the calculator and see which equals cos 60°. cos 60° = sin 30°.

5. **(C)** This is a simple problem about probability. First, add the number of doughnuts together, $25 + 54 + 13 + 12 = 104$. Then find $\dfrac{1}{8}$ of 104, $104 \times \dfrac{1}{8} = 13$. The answer is Maple.

6. **(A)** This is an algebra question. First, find the value of x, $x = \frac{1}{8}$. Then plug x into the equation to solve for y, $y = \frac{1}{4}(\frac{1}{8}) - 3$; $y = \frac{1}{32} - 3$; $y = -\frac{95}{32}$

7. **(B)** This is a simple algebra question. This is a difference of square question. First factor the $3x$ out of the equation. $3x(x^2 - 4)$. Then factor the equation. $3x(x + 2)(x - 2)$.

8. **(D)** This is a simple word problem. First, find out the amount the student earned for the 3 trees that he trimmed: $\$28 \times 3 = \$84$. Then find out the amount he earned for the 8 hours of grass cutting he did: $\$8 \times 8 = \$64$. Finally, add the two together. $\$84 + \$64 = \$148$.

9. **(B)** This is a simple data analysis question. Find the median, the number in the middle, which is 97. Find the mean, the average, $[2(95) + 3(96) + 6(97) + 4(98) + 2(99) + 1(100)] \div (2 + 3 + 6 + 4 + 2 + 1) = (190 + 288 + 582 + 392 + 198 + 100) \div 18 = 1{,}750 \div 18 = 97.22$. Find the mode, the number that appears the most often, which is 97. Find the range, the difference between the biggest and smallest number, which is 5. Here the biggest number is the mean.

10. **(B)** This is a simple data analysis question. If she would like to know how many points were lost on average by each team member, she would first need to know the average or mean of this set of data.

11. **(C)** This is a data analysis question. First, find how many portions he spent on rent and food, 2 + 4 = 6. Then, find out how much each portion is worth, $\$5{,}450 \div 10 = \$545$. Then, find how much he spends on rent and food per month, $\$545 \times 6 = \$3{,}270$. Then find how much he spends on food and rent per year, $\$3{,}270 \times 12 = \$39{,}240$.

12. **(B)** This is a data analysis question. The graph shows that as the amount of cumulative time a student is late increases, he or she will have a lower score on the test. The x value is the amount of time, and the y value is the score on the test. Therefore the answer is (B).

13. **(B)** This is a medium difficulty percent question. First, find the percent increase from 72 to 108, $108 \div 72 \times 100\% - 100\% = 50\%$. Then increase 30 by 50%, $30 + 30 \times 50\% = 45$.

14. **(D)** This is a multistep word problem about speed. First, find out his speed of walking, 3.5 km ÷ 50 minutes = 0.07 km/min. Then find out the car speed, 0.07 km/min × 3 = 0. 21 km/min. Then find out the time it took to walk, 3.5 ÷ 2 ÷ 0. 07 km/min = 25 minutes. Then find the time it took in the car, 3.5 ÷ 2 ÷ 0. 21 = 8 minutes. Add the number of minutes together to get the answer, 25 min + 8 min = 33 min.

15. **(B)** This is a medium algebra question. Factor out the x in the first part of the equation and z in the second part of the equation, $x(4 - 3y) + z(4 - 3y)$. Then factor out the $(4 - 3y)$, $(x + z)(4 - 3y)$.

16. **(C)** This is a difficult algebra question. First, simplify $\frac{5(q-3)+2}{3} = q - 2(q+1)$; $\frac{5q-13}{3} = -q + 2$. Then, multiply both sides by a common denominator, $3 \times \frac{5q-13}{3} = = 3 \times (-q + 2)$; $5q - 13 = 6 - 3q = $. Then solve for n, $8q = 19$; $n = \frac{19}{8}$.

17. **(D)** This is a medium difficulty question about percent and ratios. Use an arbitrary number like 100 to start the calculation. If 100 is decreased by 25% then the new size is 75. Therefore the ratio is 75 to 25, 3 to 1.

18. **(D)** This is an algebra question of medium difficulty. The first step is to rearrange the question and to set the equation equal to 0, $6x^2 + x - 2 = 0$. Then factor this equation, $(2x - 1)(3x + 2) = 0$. Then solve for $x = \frac{1}{2}$, $x = -\frac{2}{3}$.

19. (B) This is medium difficulty inequality. First recognize that the top of the fraction can be factored, $\dfrac{(x+4)(x+3)}{x+3} > -10$. Then eliminate $x + 3$ to get $x + 4 > -10$ and simplify to get $x > -14$. Because $x > -14$ is not one of the choices, manipulate the inequality to get, $-x < 14$.

20. (A) This is a graphing question. Use the equation of the straight line, $y = mx + b$, to find the equation for the line in the graph. First, find the slope by looking at the rise over run. The rise here is 1 and run is –3. The slope is $-\dfrac{1}{3}$. Then look at the y intercept to find b, which is –6. The equation for the line is $y = -\dfrac{1}{3}x - 6$. Then to find where the line intersects the x axis, plug in $y = 0$, $0 = -\dfrac{1}{3}x - 6$. Solve to find the x value, $0 = -x - 18$; $18 = -x$; $x = -18$. The answer is –18.

21. (B) This is a difficult word problem. First, find the volume of the water in the first mug by using the formula for the volume of a cylinder, $\pi(7)^2 \times 8.5 = 416.5\pi$. Then find the height of the water by using the formula for the volume again, $416.5\pi \div \pi(8.5)^2 = 5.76\pi$.

22. (C) This is a difficult geometry question. First find the ratio between AC and DF, 16 – 4 = 12, 1:3. Then because DE is 15 and DF is 12, triangles ABC and DEF are both special triangles of 3:4:5. Then use the ratio to find that AB is 3. Multiply 3 by 3 to get 9 for line EF. The sum of line AB + line EF is 3 + 9 = 12. This question can also be solved by using angle B to calculate AB then EF.

23. (B) This is a difficult geometry question. First find the area of the circle, $(\dfrac{\sqrt{2}}{2})^2 \pi = \dfrac{1}{2}\pi$. Then because radius is $\dfrac{\sqrt{2}}{2}$ the diameter is $\sqrt{2}$. Recognize that the square is made with two special triangles of 1:1:$\sqrt{2}$. Then because the sides of the square are 1 and 1, the area of the square is $1 \times 1 = 1$. Then find the area of the shaded region $\dfrac{1}{2}\pi - 1$. This question can also be solved by using the angle to find the sides of the square.

24. (B) This is a speed problem. First find the amount of the order that David can fill in one hour: 1 order ÷ 12 hours = $\dfrac{1}{12}$ order/hour. Then find the amount of order that David and Avi can fill in one hour, 1 order ÷ 6 hours = $\dfrac{1}{6}$ order/hour. Then subtract the amount that David can fill in an hour from the amount that they can fill together in an hour: $\dfrac{1}{6} - \dfrac{1}{12} = \dfrac{1}{12}$ order/hour. Then find how long it takes for Avi to fill the order by himself, 1 order ÷ $\dfrac{1}{12}$ order/hour = 12 hours.

25. (C) This is a linear equation and Pythagorean question. First, plug the number into the equation to solve for n, $n = \dfrac{1}{5}(5) - 4$; $n = -3$. Second, plug the number into the equation to solve for m, $2 = \dfrac{1}{5}m - 4$; $6 = \dfrac{1}{5}m$; $m = 30$. Find the distance between the y coordinates, 2 – (–3) = 5. Find the distance between the x coordinates, 30 – 5 = 25. Then use $a^2 + b^2 = c^2$ to solve for the distance between the two points, $25^2 + 5^2 = 650$, $c = \sqrt{650}$ km.

26. **(B)** This is a difficult algebra question. First, simplify $\frac{5(q-3)+2}{3} = q - 2(q+1)$; $\frac{5q-13}{3} = -q - 2$. Then, multiply both sides by a common denominator, $3 \times \frac{5q-13}{3} = 3 \times (-q - 2)$; $5q - 13 = -3q - 6$. Then solve for q, $8q = 7$; $q = \frac{7}{8}$.

27. **(D)** This is a difficult multistep word problem. First, set up the equations needed to solve the problem and use b for brass and c for ceramic, $b - c = \$15$, $125b + 130c = \$14,625$. Manipulate the first equation to get $b = c + \$15$. Then plug the modified equation into the second equation to get $125(c + \$15) + 130c = \$14,625$. Solve for c, $125c + \$1,875 + 130c = \$14,625$; $255c = \$14,625 - \$1,875$; $255c = \$12,750$; $c = \$50$. Then find out how much the store makes selling the ceramic sculpture per year, $\$50 \times 130$ per month $\times 12$ months/year $= \$78,000$.

28. **13** This is a system of equations question. Plug in the value of x into both equations to get the y value. Plug into the first equation, $y > -2(5) + 4$; $y > -6$. Plug into the second equation, $y < 3(5) - 1$; $y < 14$. The y value will be between -6 and 14, $-6 < y < 14$. The biggest integer value of y would be 13.

29. **240** This is a medium difficulty geometry question. To find the area of ABCB, first find the length of BD. Recognize that triangle ABD is a special triangle of 5 to 12 to 13. Use this ratio to find that BD is 24. Then find the area of rectangle ABCD is $10 \times 24 = 240$.

30. **0.1 or 1/10** This is a simple word problem. To find the amount of orange concentrate just multiply 1 liter by 10% to get 0.1 liter.

31. **11** This is a multistep word problem. First find the amount of cranberry concentrate by multiplying 2.5 liters by 15% to get 0.375 liter. Then find the total amount of punch by adding 1 liter and 2.5 liter to get 3.5 liters. Then find what percentage of the fruit punch is the cranberry concentrate, 0.375 liters ÷ 3.5 liters × 100% = 11%.

Scoring Your Diagnostic Test

Now that you have completed your PSAT diagnostic test, use the answer key, the conversion tables, and the following instructions to score your test.

Section and Total Scores

You will have raw scores from each of the sections, including the Reading and Writing sections and the Math sections. Your raw score is the number of questions you have answered correctly in each of the sections. You will be able to calculate your total score by converting your raw scores into the scaled scores and then adding your scaled scores into a total score.

What You Need to Score the Exam

- You will need the answer key. Compare your answers to the answer key and mark your answers.
- Get your raw score for each of the sections by adding up the number of questions you answered correctly in each section.
- Use your raw score for each of the sections and the conversion tables to calculate your score for the diagnostic test.

Calculate Your Practice Test Scores

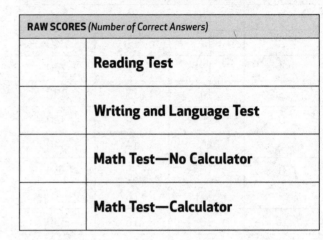

RAW SCORES *(Number of Correct Answers)*	
	Reading Test
	Writing and Language Test
	Math Test—No Calculator
	Math Test—Calculator

Scaled Scores

RAW SCORE (# of correct answers)	READING TEST SCORE	WRITING AND LANGUAGE TEST SCORE	MATH SECTION SCORE
0	8	8	160
1	9	9	1990
2	10	10	210
3	11	11	240
4	12	12	270
5	14	13	290
6	15	14	320
7	16	14	340
8	16	15	360
9	17	15	370
10	18	16	390
11	18	16	400
12	19	17	420
13	19	18	430
14	20	18	440
15	20	19	460
16	21	20	470
17	21	20	480
18	22	21	490
19	22	21	500
20	23	22	510
21	23	23	520
22	24	24	530
23	24	24	540
24	25	25	550

RAW SCORE (# of correct answers)	READING TEST SCORE	WRITING AND LANGUAGE TEST SCORE	MATH SECTION SCORE
25	26	25	560
26	26	26	570
27	27	27	580
28	27	27	580
29	28	28	590
30	28	28	600
31	29	29	610
32	29	29	620
33	30	30	630
34	30	30	640
35	31	31	650
36	31	32	670
37	32	32	680
38	32	33	690
39	33	34	710
40	34	35	720
41	34	36	730
42	35	37	730
43	36	37	740
44	37	38	740
45	37		750
46	38		750
47	38		760
48			760

Total Scaled Score

To calculate your scaled scores, fill in the following chart.

Reading Test   Raw Score (0–47) _____ ➔ Scaled Score (8–38) _____

Writing Test   Raw Score (0–44) _____ ➔ Scaled Score (8–38) + _____

Total Scaled Score (16–76) = _____

× 10

Evidence Based Reading and Writing Test Score (160–760) _____

Math Test
(No Calculator)   Raw Score (0–17) _____

Math Test
(Calculator)   Raw Score (0–31) + _____

Total Raw Score (0–48) = _____ ➔ **Total Scaled Score** (160–760) + _____

PSAT/NMSQT TestScore (320–1520) = _____

PART 3

Reading Test

CHAPTER 1

Introduction to Reading

The PSAT Reading portion assesses if you are ready to read and interpret the kinds of texts you're likely to encounter in college and career. Recall that the Reading test is the first section of the Evidence-Based Reading and Writing portion of the PSAT. The word "evidence" cannot be stressed enough here. You read every day. You've been reading and being asked what you read since your earliest days in school. That being said, you already have the tools you need to succeed on the PSAT Reading portion. *What you're not used to is the way the PSAT will ask you to read*—that's what this chapter is designed to help you with. In school, it is common to read long texts over several class periods and then have a closed-book test. Even in English class, you might read a novel over a few weeks, and take quizzes and then a final exam on the novel. The teacher might ask you big ideas about plot development and character relationships, but might also ask you to recall details about events, characters, imagery, and so on. Thus, generally speaking, you are used to the type of reading where you have unlimited time to read and carefully take notes because you'll have to memorize those details for a later quiz or test. However, this method of reading won't get you very far on the PSAT. Instead, you are taking *an open-book test* in which *you need to read fast* to finish. The test questions are literally designed to make you *go back and check for evidence*, so it is silly to read slowly and closely to try to memorize the small things. You'll have to go back anyway! And you'll run out of time if you approach the test this way. The Reading test will ask you to read passages quickly for the main idea, recalling where things are talked about so you can find them later. The good news is you have the tools to succeed—you've been reading a long time now. But you need to practice this approach to reading because it is very different from what you're used to.

Format

The reading test is a full hour-long test with five passages, with 9 or 10 questions each. Most of the passages you'll read are nonfiction, but there will be one literary passage. Regardless of what you enjoy reading, this format is good news for you. In general, nonfiction passages are a bit easier to predict than fiction passages—there's an introduction to a topic, then evidence to support that topic, maybe a mention of a counterargument or opposing side, then a conclusion to wrap up the topic and any arguments or claims. You are probably familiar with this format from reading but also from your own writing—you may have been trained early on in composing the 5-paragraph essay. Because of that loose format, you can train yourself how to read for the PSAT. All the questions are multiple choice and in random order of difficulty. Besides the literary passage, you'll see two history/social studies passages and two science passages. One of those history/social studies passages will be a U.S. founding document or what the PSAT calls a "Great Global Conversation," so you might see a passage from the Constitution or a presidential speech, for example. It's worth mentioning that one of the five passages will be a paired set, two smaller passages that relate to one another in some way. What the PSAT is trying to test with the paired set is whether you can recognize relationships between different passages. This chapter offers you practice so that you can master the paired set. And you'll find more examples of these in the practice tests at the end of the book. The Reading test also has a few graphics or charts. These questions are low difficulty and meant to ensure that you can recognize patterns and make inferences based on quantitative information. If you review this chapter thoroughly and take a practice exam, you can feel confident about everything you'll encounter on test day.

At a Glance

- 60 minutes long
- 47 questions total
- 5 Passages (4 single and 1 paired set): 1 U.S. and World Literature, 2 History/Social Studies, 2 Science
- 9–10 questions per passage; random order of difficulty
- 12 minutes per passage pace to finish on time

Breaking It Down

Let's review the common types of questions you'll be asked on the PSAT Reading section. Obviously, you'll be asked about what the authors say directly. But you'll also be asked about what's implied—you'll have to read between the lines, so to speak, as to what the passage *suggests*. You'll be asked main idea questions. You're used to these: summarizing what you read. You'll be asked purpose questions—not what parts of a passage say, but *what they do*. And you'll be asked structure questions, about how the passage is organized and how the evidence is presented.

TIP

80% of the reading passages are nonfiction, which is good news for you (despite what you like to read) because nonfiction tends to have a more predictable format than fiction.

For the paired passage, you'll be asked synthesis questions. In these, you have to draw connections between the pair: how are they alike, how are they not, how one author might respond to the other author, and so on. Since the PSAT was recently revised, there has been an emphasis on what the PSAT calls *Command of Evidence* and *Words in Context*. These reading skills are discussed in detail below.

The PSAT asks you to identify and evaluate evidence. You need to be able to identify how authors support the statements they make. And you'll be challenged to find evidence in a passage to support your answers to previous questions. These types of questions are aptly called *Command of Evidence* questions. So, what's important for you to take away is that you won't just have to read closely and determine what's said, you'll have to be able to identify textual evidence for your answers. The PSAT will have several questions asking you to identify which lines best support your answer to the previous question.

You'll also come across *Words in Context* questions—these are sort of like vocabulary questions. However, they aren't the type of vocabulary questions that ask you about really difficult or specialized words that few people recognize and even fewer actually use in conversation. Instead, these questions test words that we use regularly and that will continue to come up in our academic and professional lives. Often, these are words we are familiar with, but that can be used in a variety of contexts. What the PSAT asks you to do is use the context surrounding the word to decipher its intended meaning and usage. The PSAT might point out a word that has three or four meanings, and it'll be up to you, using the context of the passage, to decide which meaning is appropriate to the usage.

The PSAT is no longer asking you about words you've never heard of. Instead, it's asking you about words you hear all the time, but that can be used in many different ways. Replace the word in question with a simple synonym before looking at the answer choices—this strategy will help you decide which usage the author intended.

LET'S PRACTICE

Below is an excerpt from John F. Kennedy's Inaugural Address on January 20, 1961.

We observe today not a victory of party, but a celebration of freedom—symbolizing an end, as well as a beginning—signifying renewal, as well as change. For I have sworn before you and Almighty God the same solemn oath our forebears prescribed nearly a century and three quarters ago.

5   The world is very different now. For man holds in his mortal hands the power to abolish all forms of human poverty and all forms of human life. And yet the same revolutionary beliefs for which our forebears fought are still at issue around the globe—the belief that the rights of man come not from the generosity of the state, but from the hand of God.

TIP

The vocabulary on the PSAT has changed dramatically since the last revision. Whereas it used to be important to memorize and practice uncommon words that showed up on the PSAT, it's now much more important for you to use the context surrounding words to decipher the intended meaning.

10   We dare not forget today that we are the heirs of that first revolution. Let the word go forth from this time and place, to friend and foe alike, that the torch has been passed to a new generation of Americans—born in this century, tempered by war, disciplined by a hard and bitter peace, proud of our ancient heritage—and unwilling to witness or permit the slow undoing of those human rights to
15 which this Nation has always been committed, and to which we are committed today at home and around the world.

    Let every nation know, whether it wishes us well or ill, that we shall pay any price, bear any burden, meet any hardship, support any friend, oppose any foe, in order to assure the survival and the success of liberty.
20   This much we pledge—and more.

1. As used in line 4, "prescribed" most nearly means

(A) wrote a prescription for
(B) advised
(C) forbid
(D) established

2. What does the passage suggest was different at the time the presidential oath was first devised?

(A) Humans had more power than now to give and destroy life.
(B) Humans didn't have as much power to give and destroy life.
(C) There had never been a war.
(D) Democracy wasn't yet part of the nation's values.

3. Which choice provides the best evidence for the previous question?

(A) Lines 3–4 ("For I have . . . quarters ago.")
(B) Lines 5–6 ("The world . . . human life.")
(C) Lines 6–9 ("And yet . . . hand of God.")
(D) Lines 10–12 ("Let the word . . . of Americans")

4. JFK's tone can best be described as

(A) earnest and resolute
(B) scholarly and dispassionate
(C) lighthearted and humorous
(D) literary and knowledgeable

5. As used in line 13, "bitter" most nearly means

(A) unsweetened
(B) sour
(C) painful
(D) glacial

PRACTICE QUESTION ANSWERS

1. **The best choice here is (D).** A great approach to these types of questions is to cover the answers and go back to the passage, placing a synonym where the word currently is. You might say the oath our forebears "made" or "created." Now, uncover the answers and look for a word that means that.

2. **The best choice here is (B).** You may want to put this question in your own words since it's worded oddly. Just simplify it: what was it like when the oath was created? Now, look for evidence. The author talks about the oath being prescribed and then tells how times are different now. Now, we can abolish both poverty and human life. He's referring to advances that have given us more power to both help people and hurt people. Look for an answer that aligns with this idea.

3. **The best choice here is (B).** These evidence questions can be tricky, but they don't have to be. You already did the work in the previous question. Where did you look for your answer? You found it in the lines beginning the second paragraph where the author tells how the world is different now.

4. **The best choice here is (A).** First off, come up with a general answer on your own. What is JFK's attitude? You might say he's very serious and passionate. He's talking about a new generation of Americans taking over that are very serious about democracy and fighting for liberty. It's obviously something he cares a lot about. So, eliminate any answers that don't align with that. Get rid of (B) because "dispassionate" is the opposite of his tone. (C) is all wrong because he's taking these things very seriously, not making jokes. And while he might be knowledgeable, his attitude is not "literary," nor is he merely informing. That leaves you with the correct answer.

5. **The best choice here is (C).** Go back to the sentence and read it with the context. JFK is talking about the current generation running the United States, stating that they are willing to fight for human rights because they have experienced a lot and are unwilling to compromise when it comes to basic rights. They have known war, which led to a hard and "bitter" peace. So, peace can come at a hard, painful, and disagreeable cost. Eliminate (A) and (B) because they both pertain to the usage of the word when it refers to flavor. Eliminate (D) because it refers to "bitter" weather conditions when it's cold and icy.

CHAPTER 2

8 Strategies for Success on the Reading Section

Now you have an idea of the format and content of the Reading test. The recent revisions to the PSAT were all about making the test more applicable to your college and career success. Hence, the Reading test measures how well you understand what you read and how to locate evidence quickly. As discussed earlier, it is not important to read very carefully because the passage is right there for you to return to. In fact, the questions are designed to make you go back and find support. You will be tested on your ability to identify evidence, choose the correct words, and interpret and analyze passages that differ in style and topic. You will not need to recall memorized information but will need to apply years of reading skills. Here are some quick pointers on how to approach the Reading test.

Strategy 1: Slow Down at the Beginning and End

Remember that the vast majority of what you're reading will be nonfiction, and nonfiction generally follows a pattern. A topic is introduced, there are a few supporting paragraphs, a counterargument might be addressed, and then a conclusion wraps up the idea . This is the standard five-paragraph essay structure that you were probably taught when you were first learning to read and write. Your job is not to read closely and memorize details, but instead to read quickly and get the main ideas down plus know where to locate the small stuff. *Don't read closer, read smarter.* Take your time on the first paragraph so you know what the passage is talking about. Speed up in the middle—you'll have to come back for these details anyway. And then slow down again at the close of the passage, paying special care to how the passage ends and how the author wraps up any conclusions, arguments, or claims.

Just because you're an exceptional reader doesn't mean you'll test well on the PSAT Reading. Often, great readers test poorly on standardized reading tests because they are used to reading closely and understanding everything they read. That's not a good approach on the PSAT. It simply takes too long, and frankly, some of the material is much too dry. This is not leisure reading. You are here to test well and demonstrate that you have what it takes to excel in your college and professional life. Do not read slowly and closely to get every detail. Instead, read slowly on the first and last paragraphs, and waterfall the rest (look below for more information on waterfall reading).

Strategy 2: Waterfall Reading

Do you read every word on Facebook? Every caption on Instagram? Every article on msn.com? Chances are, you do not. Today, we are used to feeds overflowing with information. As information becomes more and more accessible, we adapt and learn to take in only the important stuff. There just isn't enough time to read it all. Instead, headlines or captions or compelling pictures tell us when to stop, and otherwise, we keep scrolling. This skill, which comes as naturally to you as lifting your fork to your mouth, is very applicable to the PSAT. You have it in your toolbox already, so use it on the PSAT Reading. Instead of reading word by word, the type of close reading that might be championed in your classroom, read *line by line* like you do on your social media feeds—waterfall reading.

You might be thinking, *so I should scan the passages*. No. Scanning is a technique employed to make for faster reading, but it involves looking only for a specific piece of information and leaving out everything else. This doesn't work on the PSAT Reading because you don't know what specifics you need to be looking for. You might scan for a keyword in your history book or scan for a piece of dialogue you roughly remember in a novel, but you cannot scan when you are completely unfamiliar with what you're reading and have no clue what you're looking for. Okay, so now you're thinking, *so I should skim the passages*. Closer, but not exactly. Skimming is an excellent tool to speed up your reading and get only the main points of what's being said. In fact, in college, you'll use skimming a lot. However, skimming usually entails a superficial glance at the reading—you might omit whole lines or even whole paragraphs. In skimming a text, you still have to decide what material is important enough to read and what should be completely left out. So no, you aren't skimming either. You are waterfalling everything but those first and last paragraphs (which you should read more closely). You aren't leaving anything out, but you are reading quickly to only get the main points. Your eyes, instead of going left to right getting every word, will be going

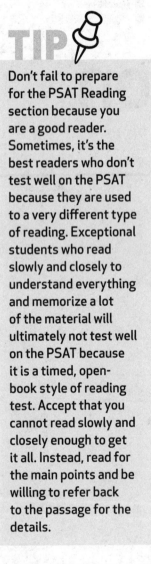

TIP

Don't fail to prepare for the PSAT Reading section because you are a good reader. Sometimes, it's the best readers who don't test well on the PSAT because they are used to a very different type of reading. Exceptional students who read slowly and closely to understand everything and memorize a lot of the material will ultimately not test well on the PSAT because it is a timed, open-book style of reading test. Accept that you cannot read slowly and closely enough to get it all. Instead, read for the main points and be willing to refer back to the passage for the details.

top to bottom, digesting whole lines and keeping you moving. It's just like going through a Facebook news feed. Remember, you have to come back later for the details anyway, so you don't need to know them now, you just need to know where to locate them.

While you are training yourself to read like this, it's a good idea to measure how fast you are reading and if you're getting what you need to get from the passage. Ideally, you want to spend about 5 minutes reading each passage (you have 12 minutes to read and complete all the questions for each passage). If you're a bit over 5 minutes, don't worry—you can definitely still finish the test. To assess whether you are getting what you need to get from the passage, challenge yourself to summarize the main idea and the purpose in one sentence. For example: *the passage is a fictional passage describing a scene between two characters who were once romantically involved and are meeting again after many years.* If you can provide a one-sentence summary, you understand enough about the passage to attack the questions. When you use the technique of waterfall reading, you will not be skipping or leaving out any of the passage, but you'll be reading line by, taking in only the main points.

Strategy 3: Passage Map

As mentioned above, you need to know where to locate details. Even the fastest readers, the best and brightest, will have to refer back to the passages when taking the PSAT Reading. Recall in the practice exercise above how you were asked not only to answer specifics about what the writer or speaker said, but you were also asked to look at word choice in a specific line or locate lines with textual evidence for the previous question. That being said, you will be going back to the reading regardless of your reading skill level. As you can imagine, it will be very time-consuming if you have to scan the entire passage each time you go back (yes, now you'll be scanning because you are looking to locate specific information). What makes a lot more sense is knowing approximately where in the passage things are located. For instance, you might think, *ooh, that was talked about in the third paragraph*, and then you're only scanning a few lines.

A helpful strategy is passage mapping. *When you are first working your way through a passage—slowing down on the first and last paragraphs and waterfalling everything in between—you should be trying to make a blueprint or a map of the passage in your mind.* Something like this: first it introduces the struggle for women's suffrage, then it talks about three leaders of the movement, then it discusses two influential opponents of the movement, then it finishes up with the granting of the vote and its implications for future civil rights movements. This type of mapping allows you to return to the passage quickly and effectively to locate information. Some students find that it helps them to jot three to five words down next to each paragraph as they read so that they know exactly where to return to later. Certainly, it slows them down a bit while they are reading, but the time

TIP

Practice passage mapping to become a better reader (and to get a better score on the PSAT). Make an outline of articles you read. Grab the *New Yorker* or the *Economist* and read an article. On a separate sheet of paper, number each paragraph of the article and try to describe what that paragraph does in just a few words. This type of reading will certainly make you a better reader. It will also help you prepare for the PSAT, SAT, ACT, and other tests.

they make up for later is well worth it. Try this method while you are practicing. Even if you decide not to jot down words next to each paragraph on the actual PSAT, the practice itself will get you used to mentally mapping the passage as you read. Think of it as creating an outline of what you read—a skill you've most likely employed in school before.

Strategy 4: Write as You Go

You know you have to be able to locate information quickly. And you know that there's no point in trying to memorize all the details when you read the passage. Life would be much easier then if, while you were reading, you could predict exactly the parts of the passage you were going to be tested on. Well, you can't do that. But you can notice patterns and anticipate the types of things that will be asked. In nonfiction (which makes up most of the PSAT reading), certain things tend to be important over and over. First, you need to know who is arguing what—the position or the thesis is the main argument or claim being made. Then, you need to know numbers, dates, and other stats. Think about it. If the passage is about a fossil discovery, it's probably important that you know who discovered it and when the person discovered it. Thus, if you know there's a good chance these facts will be tested, and you know it's pointless to try to read slowly enough to memorize them all, then it makes sense to flag these things so you can find them right away.

You do not have time to take notes while you test. Even jotting down a few words as in the strategy above might not be realistic for you if your timing is near 12 minutes per passage. But what you can do is underline, circle, and star those parts of the passage that are likely to be tested. As you read, *underline any arguments, claims, or thesis statements; circle any names, dates, or important numbers; and star any counterarguments or opposing sides.* You may want to read the questions before reading the passage so you know exactly which lines or items to flag. For instance, if you know question 3 asks about the exact date the fossil was discovered, you'll know to circle that when you're reading through. Then when you get to the questions, you know exactly where to look.

Strategy 5: Read the Specific Lines First

Consider these two ways to approach a question.

Student 1 reads the question, looks at option A, thinks, "Ooh, I remember that somewhere, let me look for it," goes back to the passage and locates it. Looks at option B, thinks, "Hmm, I don't remember that, but it has words that match the passage exactly, so let me check," goes back to the passage and locates it. Looks at option C, "That sounds a lot like the previous option, let me check," goes back to the passage and locates it. Looks at option D, "That sounds even better than B and

C, let me look again," goes back to the passage for the fourth time. Now, student 1 eliminates B and C, and chooses between A and D based on her fourth or fifth return to the passage.

Student 2 reads the question and immediately goes back to the passage to the specific lines applicable to the question. Student 2 finds where the question is discussed and makes his own answer based on the evidence in the passage. Then student 2 returns to the question, quickly eliminates B and C because they sound nothing like the answer he came up with, then chooses A because it sounds most like the answer he came up with.

Which approach do you think is most effective? Hopefully, you see that student 2 employs the better approach here. That student goes back to the passage only once, or twice at the most, whereas student 1 goes back four or five times to verify each answer option. Student 1 will likely run out of time if she uses this approach on all or even most of the questions. Even if student 1 doesn't run out of time, she'll likely confuse herself because many of the choices will have words and ideas that match part of the passage. If you are relying on matching each answer choice to the passage, most of the answer choices will tempt you, and you'll ultimately take too much time. It's very easy to get confused if you're considering three or four choices at once. However, if you approach the test like student 2, you are less likely to get caught up matching information and confusing yourself. Consider the question fully and refer back to the specific lines in the passage before considering the answer choices to maximize your time on the PSAT Reading.

Whereas this book encourages you to use the answer choices to work backward on the Math test, you do NOT want to rely on the answer choices to direct you on the Reading test. Go back to the passage and come up with your own answer, then compare it with the choices given. The PSAT is not just some test. It isn't put together overnight or even over a month. The writers of the test make sure that more than one answer is appealing. After all, they are testing how well you locate and interpret evidence. Consider the question and come up with an answer instead of weighing each choice given. It will save you time and limit your anxiety.

TIP

Considering each answer option separately takes a lot of time and will end up confusing you.

Strategy 6: Try to Answer the Question First

Strategy 6 is very closely related to strategy 5, but it's so important that it's worth it to make it separate and reiterate it. You should go back to the passage and answer the question before considering each answer choice closely. Your answer doesn't have to be specific, but it can be a general guide for what you are looking for. This protects you from getting caught up in the "choose the best answer" mentality. How often have you been told by your teachers to choose the best answer? That doesn't work so well on the PSAT. College Board is not going to sit down and say, *Hmm the correct answer was C, but Johnny put B. We can tell what he was thinking though and why he thought that option might be the best, so we will give him some credit.* There is one correct answer for each question on the PSAT Reading.

You are not looking for the best answer; you are looking for the correct answer. The way to get the correct answer is not to get bogged down in comparing the answer options. Whereas on the Math portion of the PSAT, it makes a lot of sense to look right at the answers and even use them to work backward, this approach will only confound you on the PSAT Reading. A much better approach is to go back to the specific lines in the passage first and come up with your own answer. Then you can get rid of anything that doesn't align with what you came up with.

Consider question 2 from the example exercise in Chapter 1:

What does the passage suggest was different at the time the presidential oath was first devised?

To attack this question, read it closely and put it in your own words to make sure you understand what's being asked. *What does the author/speaker say has changed?* Now, go back to the passage, and using the evidence given, answer the question. The evidence given in the passage is as follows: "The world is very different now. For man holds in his mortal hands the power to abolish all forms of human poverty and all forms of human life." So, your answer might be something like, *when the presidential oath was first devised men didn't have as much power.* Now, you are not comparing the four answer choices and picking the best. You are seeing which one aligns with your answer and eliminating all that don't. *Answer the question first,* then consider the options given.

Strategy 7: Use Process of Elimination

Sometimes you'll follow the preceding strategies, do everything right, and still be left with two very appealing answers. What do you do now? *You look for the word that makes one of those choices incorrect and you eliminate it.*

This might seem counterintuitive. You might naturally want to go back to your old way of doing things and try to decide which of the two is the best. But this chapter has already explained why that mentality isn't very effective. Instead, understand that there is only one completely correct answer, only one that will be scored as correct. That means somewhere hiding in one of those two answer choices is a word or phrase that makes it incorrect. Finding that word or phrase is the key to choosing the correct answer. *It's easier to eliminate the incorrect answers than to go back and forth trying to determine which answer is correct.*

Strategy 8: On the Paired Set, Split up the Questions

The paired set passage intimidates a lot of students. It not only includes the regular questions you are used to, but it also has synthesis-type questions that ask you to make connections and identify relationships between two passages. *Synthesis* might be an intimidating word for you, but really it just means connecting ideas, bringing them together in a meaningful way. A useful way to think about synthesis is as a dinner conversation. Imagine you know the authors of both passages and, after reading their selections, you invite them both over to your house for dinner. Now, here they are sitting at the same table—what would they agree on, disagree on? How would they respond to one another? This is what synthesis is all about—putting texts in conversation with one another.

A useful strategy for the paired set passage is to read passage 1 and answer the questions referring to that passage, then read passage 2 and answer the questions referring to that passage, and then tackle the questions that pertain to both passages. When you finish the questions for passage 2, take a moment to ask yourself what the relationship is between the two passages. Are they in agreement? Opposition? How might the authors feel about one another? What is it they have in common? Thinking about how the passages relate to one another will get you in the right mindset to tackle the synthesis questions.

Trying to read both passages and ask these questions of yourself first might be overwhelming. So, break it down. The questions are generally in order, so it's easy for you to employ this strategy. Read passage 1 and answer only those questions about passage 1. Read passage 2 and answer only those questions about passage 2. Then consider the relationship between the two passages and tackle the questions asking about both passages. Doing it this way makes it more manageable and can alleviate any anxiety around the synthesis questions.

LET'S PRACTICE

Questions 1–9 are based on the following passage.

The following passage is the beginning of Edith Wharton's novel Ethan Frome *(1911).*

I had the story, bit by bit, from various people, and, as generally happens in such cases, each time it was a different story.

If you know Starkfield, Massachusetts, you know the post-office. If you know the post-office you must have seen Ethan Frome drive up to it, drop the reins on
5 his hollow-backed bay and drag himself across the brick pavement to the white colonnade; and you must have asked who he was.

It was there that, several years ago, I saw him for the first time; and the sight pulled me up sharp. Even then he was the most striking figure in Starkfield, though he was but the ruin of a man. It was not so much his great height that

10   marked him, for the "natives" were easily singled out by their lank longitude from the stockier foreign breed: it was the careless powerful look he had, in spite of a lameness checking each step like the jerk of a chain. There was something bleak and unapproachable in his face, and he was so stiffened and grizzled that I took him for an old man and was surprised to hear that he was not more than fifty-

15   two. I had this from Harmon Gow, who had driven the stage from Bettsbridge to Starkfield in pre-trolley days and knew the chronicle of all the families on his line.

"He's looked that way ever since he had his smash-up; and that's twenty-four years ago come next February," Harmon threw out between reminiscent pauses.

20   The "smash-up" it was—I gathered from the same informant—which, besides drawing the red gash across Ethan Frome's forehead, had so shortened and warped his right side that it cost him a visible effort to take the few steps from his buggy to the post-office window. He used to drive in from his farm every day at about noon, and as that was my own hour for fetching my mail I often

25   passed him in the porch or stood beside him while we waited on the motions of the distributing hand behind the grating. I noticed that, though he came so punctually, he seldom received anything but a copy of the Bettsbridge Eagle, which he put without a glance into his sagging pocket. At intervals, however, the post-master would hand him an envelope addressed to Mrs. Zenobia—or

30   Mrs. Zeena—Frome, and usually bearing conspicuously in the upper left-hand corner the address of some manufacturer of patent medicine and the name of his specific. These documents my neighbor would also pocket without a glance, as if too much used to them to wonder at their number and variety, and would then turn away with a silent nod to the post-master.

35   Everyone in Starkfield knew him and gave him a greeting tempered to his own grave mien; but his taciturnity was respected and it was only on rare occasions that one of the older men of the place detained him for a word. When this happened he would listen quietly, his blue eyes on the speaker's face, and answer in so low a tone that his words never reached me; then he would climb stiffly

40   into his buggy, gather up the reins in his left hand and drive slowly away in the direction of his farm.

"It was a pretty bad smash-up?" I questioned Harmon, looking after Frome's retreating figure, and thinking how gallantly his lean brown head, with its shock of light hair, must have sat on his strong shoulders before they were bent out

45   of shape.

"Wust kind," my informant assented. "More'n enough to kill most men. But the Fromes are tough. Ethan'll likely touch a hundred."

"Good God!" I exclaimed. At the moment Ethan Frome, after climbing to his seat, had leaned over to assure himself of the security of a wooden box—also with

50   a druggist's label on it—which he had placed in the back of the buggy, and I saw

his face as it probably looked when he thought himself alone. "That man touch a hundred? He looks as if he was dead and in hell now!"

Harmon drew a slab of tobacco from his pocket, cut off a wedge and pressed it into the leather pouch of his cheek. "Guess he's been in Starkfield too many 55 winters. Most of the smart ones get away."

1. Which choice best describes what happens in the passage?

   (A) One character argues with another character who has been in a grave accident.
   (B) One character becomes interested in the story of a local man after seeing him at the post office.
   (C) One character shows another character around a new town and introduces him to the townspeople.
   (D) Two characters exchange stories about the people of Starkfield and are grateful that they escaped the small town.

2. Which choice best describes how the passage develops?

   (A) a careful analysis of a medical accident and its effects
   (B) a cheerful recounting of a local story passed down several generations
   (C) a detailed description of one event followed by an internal monologue
   (D) a meditation of one man's memories followed by a dialogue with another man

3. As used in line 8, "striking" most nearly means

   (A) breathtaking
   (B) inconspicuous
   (C) dramatic
   (D) noticeable

4. According to the narrator, the obvious difference between the native townspeople and those who have moved here from other places is

   (A) their physical build and height
   (B) their accent
   (C) their habits at the post office
   (D) their dress

5. Which choice provides the best evidence for the previous question?

   (A) Lines 3–6 ("If you know . . . who he was.")
   (B) Lines 7–9 ("It was there . . . ruin of a man.")
   (C) Lines 9–11 ("It was not . . . foreign breed.")
   (D) Lines 12–15 ("There was something . . . than fifty-two.")

6. The relationship between the narrator and Harmon Gow is best described as

   (A) amiable and familiar
   (B) objective and distanced
   (C) friendly but alien
   (D) uninvolved but ritualistic

7. According to the narrator, Ethan's disposition is best described as

   (A) somber and commanding
   (B) boisterous and firm
   (C) approachable and sociable
   (D) serious and affectionate

8. From the passage, we can assume the "smash-up" refers to what?

   (A) a recent accident that Ethan is trying to recover from
   (B) a very big fight that killed Ethan and left several of his family members in bad shape
   (C) a serious accident that happened many years ago and left Ethan disabled
   (D) a disease that is slowly killing Ethan

9. The narrator and Harmon Gow disagree on

   (A) how serious Ethan's accident was
   (B) how long Ethan will live
   (C) how tall Ethan is
   (D) how sick Ethan's mother is

PRACTICE QUESTION ANSWERS

1. **(B)** This question asks about the passage as a whole, so try to outline or summarize what happens. The narrator tells the reader about when he first saw Ethan at the post office and then talks with an old railroad man about Ethan's history. So, (B) is the correct choice. There is no argument as in (A). We have no clue how long the narrator has been in this town, but he's definitely not just now being shown around it as in (C). And you can eliminate (D) because they are not exchanging stories, but rather the narrator is getting a story from Harmon, and they have not escaped the town because they live there themselves.

2. **(D)** This is another question about the passage as a whole. First, the narrator recalls a memory, then he reflects on the conclusions he drew from seeing Ethan. Next, the narrator gets information about Ethan from Harmon and they discuss Ethan's family and how long he might live. So, (D) is the best choice here.

3. **(D)** Try to put each word in the sentence. Here, the narrator is saying that Ethan is the most noticeable—he attracts a lot of attention.

4. **(A)** The narrator says that natives are lanky while foreigners are stocky, so (A) is the correct choice. There is no discussion of accents, habits, or dress.

5. **(C)** It is in these lines that the narrator distinguishes natives from foreigners. Ethan's height gives him away as a local even if it is his powerful look that sets him apart. Thus the "lank longitude" of the natives contrasts with the "stockier foreign breed."

6. **(A)** For this question, consider the interactions between the narrator and Harmon. The narrator gets all of his information about Ethan's past and his family from Harmon. They talk easily and openly as if they are very friendly. Eliminate (B) because they are not distanced but instead very open. Eliminate (C) because while they are friendly, they are not "alien" or unfamiliar. Eliminate (D) because the conversation seems engaging rather than uninvolved, and it's definitely not ceremonial and formal.

7. **(A)** Ask yourself what you know about Ethan from the passage. He is tall and strong and rather imposing. He doesn't talk much, and his silent demeanor is respected by the community. Thus (A) is the correct choice. "Boisterous," "approachable," and "affectionate" are not words that describe Ethan as the narrator knows him to be.

8. **(C)** The "smash-up" is referenced throughout the passage. Harmon says it happened twenty-four years ago. The narrator lists the results of it as a gash across the forehead plus an injury to Ethan's right side that warped him and made even taking a few steps a chore. Later, Harmon confirms that it was the type of accident that would kill most men. Thus, (C) is the correct choice.

9. **(B)** At the end of the passage, Harmon predicts that Ethan will live to be a hundred, while the narrator rejects that prophecy saying Ethan looks dead already. The two have very different opinions regarding Ethan's life expectancy.

Questions 1–10 are based on the following two passages.

Passage 1 is from a chapter titled "Establishing the Revolution" in Ida Husted Harper's 1899 autobiography of Susan B. Anthony. Passage 2 is from a chapter titled "Woman in Newspapers" in History of Woman Suffrage, *which was edited by Susan B. Anthony herself.*

PASSAGE 1

The first entry in the diary of 1868, January 1, reads: "All the old friends, with scarce an exception, are sure we are wrong. Only time can tell, but I believe we are right and hence bound to succeed." Immediately after the meeting at Steinway Hall, Mr. Train had brought with him to call on Miss Anthony, David
5 M. Melliss, financial editor of the *New York World*, and they entered into an agreement by which the two men were to supply the funds for publishing a paper until it was on a paying basis. It was to be conducted by Miss Anthony and Mrs. Stanton in the interests of women, and Mr. Train and Mr. Melliss were to use such space as they desired for expressing their financial and other opinions.

10 Ten thousand copies were printed and, under the congressional frank of Representative James Brooks, of New York, were sent to all parts of the country. The advent of this element in the newspaper world created a sensation such as scarcely ever has been equaled by any publication. *The New York Sunday Times* said:

15 THE LADIES MILITANT.—It is out at last. If the women as a body have not succeeded in getting up a revolution, Susan B. Anthony, as their representative, has. Her Revolution was issued last Thursday as a sort of New Year's gift to what she considered a yearning public, and it is said to be "charged to the muzzle with literary nitroglycerine." If Mrs. Stanton would attend a little more to her domestic
20 duties and a little less to those of the great public, perhaps she would exalt her sex quite as much as she does by Quixotically fighting windmills in their gratuitous behalf, and she might possibly set a notable example of domestic felicity. No married woman can convert herself into a feminine Knight of the Rueful Visage and ride about the country attempting to redress imaginary wrongs without
25 leaving her own household in a neglected condition that must be an eloquent witness against her. As for the spinsters, we have always said that every woman has a natural and inalienable right to a good husband and a pretty baby. When, by proper "agitation," she has secured this right, she best honors herself and her sex by leaving public affairs behind her, and endeavoring to show how happy she
30 can make the little world of which she has just become the brilliant center.

PASSAGE 2

Many foreign papers devoted to woman's interests have been established within the last few years. The *Women's Suffrage Journal*, in England, Lydia E. Becker, of Manchester, editor and proprietor; the *Englishwoman's Journal*, in

London, edited by Caroline Ashurst Biggs; *Woman and Work* and the *Victoria*
35 *Magazine*, by Emily Faithful, are among the number. Miss Faithful's magazine
having attained a circulation of fifty thousand. *L'Ésperance*, of Geneva, an
Englishwoman its editor, was an early advocate of woman's cause. *La Donna*,
at Venice, edited by Signora Gualberti Aläide Beccari; *La Cornelia*, at Florence,
Signora Amelia Cunino Foliero de Luna, editor, prove Italian advancement.
40 Germany, Spain, and the Netherlands must not be omitted from the list of those
countries which have published Woman's Rights papers. In Lima, Peru, we find a
paper edited and controlled entirely by women; its name, *Alborada*. The Orient,
likewise, shows progress. At Bukarest, in Romaine, a paper, the *Dekebalos*,
upholding the elevation of woman, was started in 1874. *The Bengalee Magazine*,
45 devoted to the interests of Indian ladies, its editorials all from woman's pen,
shows Asiatic advance.

   In the United States the list of women's fashion papers, with their women
editors and correspondents, is numerous and important. For fourteen years
Harper's Bazaar has been ably edited by Mary L. Booth; other papers of similar
50 character are both owned and edited by women. So important a place do women
writers hold, *Harper's Monthly* asserts, that the exceptionally large prices are paid
to women contributors. The spiciest critics, reporters, and correspondents today, are women—Grace Greenwood, Louise Chandler Moulton, Mary Clemmer.
Laura C. Holloway is upon the editorial staff of the Brooklyn Eagle. The *New*
55 *York Times* boasts a woman cattle reporter, one of the best judges of stock in
the country. In some papers, over their own names, women edit columns on
special subjects, and fill important positions on journals owned and edited
by men. Elizabeth Boynton Harbert edits "The Woman's Kingdom" in the
Inter-Ocean, one of the leading dailies of Chicago. Mary Forney Weigley edits
60 a social department in her father's—John W. Forney—paper, the *Progress*, in
Philadelphia. The political columns of many papers are prepared by women, men
often receiving the credit. Among the best editorials in the *New York Tribune*,
from Margaret Fuller to Lucia Gilbert Calhoun, have been from the pens
of women.

65   If the proverb that "the pen is mightier than the sword" be true, woman's
skill and force in using this mightier weapon must soon change the destinies of
the world.

1. Passage 1 indicates which of the following about Mr. Train and Mr. Melliss?

   (A) They supported women's roles in newspapers.
   (B) They did not support women's roles in newspapers.
   (C) They were economists who needed Anthony's expertise.
   (D) They were hopeful Anthony would make them very rich men.

2. As used in line 6, "supply" most nearly means

   (A) hoard
   (B) provision
   (C) provide
   (D) fulfill

3. According to Passage 1, the first issue of Anthony and Stanton's paper

   (A) caused a public outcry
   (B) received very little attention
   (C) almost put the *New York Sunday Times* out of business
   (D) focused on the role of women in families

4. Which choice provides the best evidence for the answer to the previous question?

   (A) Lines 7–9 ("It was to . . . other opinions.")
   (B) Lines 12–13 ("The advent of . . . any publication.")
   (C) Lines 19–22 ("If Mrs. Stanton . . . gratuitous behalf.")
   (D) Lines 22–26 ("No married . . . witness against her.")

5. What is the purpose of the first paragraph of Passage 2 (lines 31–46)?

   (A) To compare European and Asian women.
   (B) To name the most famous newspapers in the world.
   (C) To draw a contrast between international women and American women.
   (D) To establish the international presence of women in newspapers.

6. As used in line 44, "elevation" most nearly means

   (A) height
   (B) mountain
   (C) eminence
   (D) advancement

7. The author of Passage 2 believes

   (A) Women should have their own newspapers separate from men.
   (B) Women are integral to newspapers and are paid well to contribute.
   (C) Women will someday be very important to newspapers.
   (D) Women should leave politics to men but write about everything else.

8. The last lines of Passage 2 (65–67) have which effect?

   (A) They allude to women's shrinking role in media.
   (B) They employ humor to evoke an inflated sentiment.
   (C) They use a common saying to make an important prediction.
   (D) They criticize men for their continued role in war and violence.

9. Which choice best describes the relationship between Passage 1 and Passage 2?

   (A) Passage 2 relays the firsthand experiences of a woman briefly mentioned in Passage 1.
   (B) Passage 2 gives the standpoint of the person discussed by the author of Passage 1.
   (C) Passage 2 takes a specific position on a topic that is objectively evaluated in Passage 1.
   (D) Passage 2 predicts the reactions of the findings discussed in Passage 1.

10. The authors of the two passages would most likely agree that

   (A) Media must contain voices that represent all the public in order to be whole and authentic.
   (B) International papers are far more advanced than those in the United States.
   (C) It's more important for women to be involved in economics and finance than in fashion.
   (D) Women are better writers than men.

PRACTICE QUESTION ANSWERS

1. **(A)** Go back to the lines that first introduce Mr. Train and Mr. Melliss. According to the passage, the two men supply funds for a paper run by Stanton and Anthony. That being said, it is logical that they support women's roles in newspapers. Eliminate (B) because they are investing in women to run a newspaper. Eliminate (C) because there is no evidence that they are economists. Eliminate (D) because there is no evidence the paper will make money, and in fact, at the time, it was probably highly unlikely that a paper run by women would be extremely profitable.

2. **(C)** Cover those answers and go back to the line. Substitute "supply" with your own word. You might say the men were to "give" the funds. Look for a word that sounds like "give."

3. **(A)** Go back to the passage first and look for evidence. We know a lot of copies of the newspaper went out and "caused a sensation." And we also know a very reputable paper responded to the newspaper by saying women should stay at home and raise babies, leaving public affairs behind. Eliminate (B) because the paper got a lot of attention. Eliminate (C) because there's no evidence for this answer. Eliminate (D) because this is the topic that the *New York Sunday Times* focused on, not Anthony and Stanton's paper.

4. **(B)** It is in these lines that the author states that the women's paper created a sensation like no other publication had ever caused. Hence, it is here that we get evidence for the public response to the paper. Everyone was talking about it; everyone was shocked; many were disturbed.

5. **(D)** This is a purpose question. Ask yourself what the first paragraph does. It shows how international papers dedicated to women's interests are prevalent and growing. It gives examples from all over the globe. Find an answer like that.

6. **(D)** Again, make sure you go back and substitute your own word in. A paper upholds the elevation of women, so it shows their progress or advancement. (A) and (B) are fairly easy to eliminate here. But many students might choose (C) just because they are unfamiliar with the word and it sounds smart. Don't make the mistake of choosing a word just because it's unknown. "Eminence" means fame or superiority and so is too extreme here.

7. **(B)** Eliminate (A) because the argument is not that women need to stay separate from men, but instead that they need to be involved and represented. Eliminate (C) because women are already very important to newspapers— this is pretty much the whole point of the passage. And eliminate (D) because the author is supportive of women writing about politics. Since Passage 2 is about how essential women are to papers and it gives evidence of the "large prices" given to women contributors, (B) is the correct choice.

8. **(C)** What do the last lines do? They use a well-known proverb to suggest that women's power in writing will continue to advance them and change the world.

9. **(B)** This is a synthesis question. Ask yourself the relationship between the passages. The first one is an autobiography of Susan B. Anthony talking about the splash her newspaper made. The second is a chapter edited by Susan B. Anthony that talks about the widening role of women in newspapers. So, the second passage is Anthony's opinion or stance, and the first passage is an objective look into Anthony's life. Eliminate (A) because Anthony is the topic of Passage 1 (much more than briefly mentioned), and she's not recounting her experiences in Passage 2. Eliminate (C) because the two passages are not evaluating a topic and taking a side. Eliminate (D) because there were no findings in Passage 1 to predict a response to.

10. **(A)** If you had dinner at your house with Harper and Anthony, how would it play out? First, Harper would be very interested in Anthony (after all, she wrote an autobiography about her) and adamant about all the things Anthony did to improve the lives of women. Harper doesn't mention international papers, and we can't assume anything about her opinion of them. Besides, Anthony doesn't believe they are more advanced than those in the United States, but that they are both important. Anthony doesn't devalue fashion, but instead thinks women should contribute to everything from fashion to politics. And (D) is too extreme—the authors are interested in women's writing, but not in proving that it's superior to men's writing.

CHAPTER 3

Attacking Informational Graphics Questions

One important change to the PSAT is the inclusion of informational graphics. This isn't something to be worried about, but it is something to expect and be prepared for. Most of the time, within the Evidence-Based Reading and Writing section, you'll find a chart or table or other graphic and will be asked whether that graphic clearly and accurately reflects the passage. You may be asked to edit the passage to ensure that it reflects the graph. Either way, you won't need any prior knowledge— everything you need is right in front of you. And these aren't extremely complex graphs. Instead, they are designed to assess how well you can interpret data and compare that to information in the accompanying passage.

Informational Graphics at a Glance

- Informational graphics will come up in every single PSAT.
- Informational graphics *do not* make up a large portion of the PSAT. There are only one or two graphics in the Reading section and one or two in the Writing and Language section.
- You'll be asked to find patterns and interpret data in basic graphs, charts, and tables, etc.
- You'll be asked to revise texts to be consistent with the data presented in those graphs, charts, and tables, etc.

While it doesn't make sense to spend all your time preparing for the PSAT practicing the types of questions you'll encounter with informational graphics (because of the small percentage of the test they make up), it does make a lot of sense to be familiar with them and comfortable reading and interpreting diverse graphics.

LET'S PRACTICE

Graphs

In the following example, Mrs. Smith had her eleventh grade class plant the same number of sunflowers, green beans, and potatoes in a small garden beside the Biology classroom for four consecutive years. Look at the graph below and answer the accompanying questions.

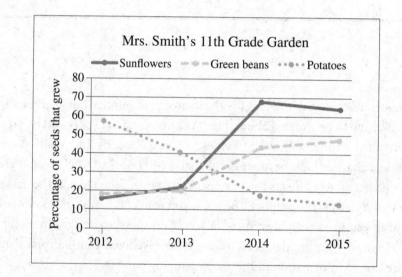

1. According to the graph, the percentage of sunflowers that grew in 2014 was

   (A) less than the percentage that grew in 2012
   (B) consistent with the percentage that grew in 2012
   (C) more than triple the percentage that grew in 2012
   (D) exactly half the percentage that grew in 2012

2. According to the graph, green beans

   (A) grew best in 2013
   (B) had a lack of sunlight in 2014
   (C) grow mutually with potatoes
   (D) grew better each year

3. The growth rate of sunflowers and green beans was roughly equal in which of the following years

   (A) 2012 and 2013
   (B) only 2012
   (C) 2013 and 2014
   (D) only 2015

4. According to the graph, the percentage of potatoes grown in 2014 was

   (A) almost half that of sunflowers
   (B) almost half that of green beans
   (C) double that of sunflowers
   (D) double that of green beans

5. Based on the information in the graph, it can be assumed that

   (A) sunflowers and potatoes are mutual species
   (B) sunflowers and potatoes are competing species
   (C) there was more sunlight in 2015 than 2014
   (D) students forgot to water the plants in 2013

PRACTICE QUESTION ANSWERS

1. **(C)** For this question, you are comparing the percentage of sunflowers that grew in 2014 to the percentage of sunflowers that grew in 2012. In 2014, nearly 70% of the planted sunflowers were successful. In 2012, about 17% were successful. Therefore, the only answer that makes sense here is (C).

2. **(D)** Look at the pattern of green bean growth. Since the first planting, green beans have increased each year. Eliminate (A) because the highest rate of growth was 2015. Eliminate (B) because there is no evidence for this answer. Eliminate (C) because as green bean growth has increased, potato growth has decreased—so this is not a mutual or common relationship.

3. **(A)** Look for where the two lines meet or overlap. In the first two planting years, sunflowers and green beans were almost exactly equal, so (A) is the best answer. Eliminate (C) and (D) quickly because the spread is much greater in those later years. Then realize that (B) leaves out information.

4. **(B)** First, check the percentage of potatoes in 2014—maybe 18% or so. Then, work your way down the answer choices. Sunflower growth was nearly 70%—much more than double—so eliminate (A). Green bean growth was about 43% give or take, so 18% is nearing half of that. You can then quickly eliminate (C) and (D) because potato growth is less than sunflower and green bean growth. Choice (B) is the only one left standing.

5. (B) This question might be the toughest because you aren't just reading the graph, but making an inference based on your interpretation. Eliminate (A) because there is an inverse relationship between sunflowers and potatoes—as one goes up, the other goes down. Eliminate (C) and (D) because there is no evidence to support these answers. Sunflower growth went down a bit in 2015, while green bean growth still increased. And there are many factors that can influence plant growth. We know nothing about how the students tended to the plants, so (D) isn't applicable. Besides, two of three plants grew better in 2013 than the previous year, so there's nothing to support the idea of neglect. (B) is the correct answer because of the obviously inverse relationship between sunflowers and potatoes. The two appear to compete with one another and not grow well together.

Tables

In the following example, the relationship between the wolf and deer populations was examined in a small regional park.

Annual Count of Wolves and Deer in Flagstone Park

YEAR	WOLF COUNT	DEER COUNT
1997	0	157
1998	6	155
1999	8	121
2000	16	88
2001	29	65
2002	32	66
2003	32	60

1. According to the table, the deer population at Flagstone Park increased in which of the following years?

(A) 1998 and 1999
(B) 2002
(C) 2003
(D) 2004 and 2005

2. According to the table, the wolf population in 1999

   (A) decreased by half the following year
   (B) doubled that of 1998
   (C) doubled the following year
   (D) fell slightly due to a harsh winter

3. Which claim is supported by the data given in the table?

   (A) Deer numbers declined every year since the introduction of wolves to Flagstone Park.
   (B) Deer numbers declined the first year wolves came to Flagstone Park, but then stabilized.
   (C) Deer numbers showed an overall decline as the wolf population in Flagstone Park grew.
   (D) Deer numbers do not appear to have a relationship with wolf numbers.

4. According to the table, the deer population dropped most dramatically in which of the following years?

   (A) 1998
   (B) 1999
   (C) 2002
   (D) 2003

5. Which claim is supported by the data given in the table?

   (A) The deer population was native to Flagstone Park, while the wolves were later introduced.
   (B) The wolf population was native to Flagstone Park, while the deer were later introduced.
   (C) Both species were always present in Flagstone Park.
   (D) Both species came to Flagstone Park between 1997 and 1999.

PRACTICE QUESTION ANSWERS

1. **(B)** Of the data shown, the deer population only showed an increase one year, 2002. Every other year showed a decline in deer.

2. **(C)** The wolf population was 8 in 1999. It was 6 the year before and 16 the following year. (C) is the correct choice here. It increased the following year, so eliminate (A). Eight is not twice the amount of 6, so eliminate (B). And the population didn't fall, nor do we have any evidence of a harsh winter, so eliminate (D).

3. **(C)** Questions like these can be a bit tough. Go through each choice carefully. We know there was one year that the recorded number of deer increased, so (A) is not correct. There were dramatic decreases in the deer population after the first year the wolves came, so eliminate (B) as well. You can eliminate (D) because it's obvious that the wolf population is growing while the deer population topples—there is an obvious relationship here. Generally speaking, as wolves increase, deer decrease.

4. **(B)** You don't have to do the math here. Just look at the numbers and get an estimate to answer the question. The greatest drops in the number of deer at Flagstone Park occurred during 1999 and 2000. Only 1999 is listed as an answer, so that's the correct choice.

5. **(A)** Here, you are considering which population was original to the park and which came later. According to the table, wolves were not present at all in 1997, but the deer population flourished. So, given the evidence, you can assume that deer were native to the park while wolves came later. (A) is the only choice that backs up this inference. Of course, deer didn't come after as in (B). We know wolves weren't always present as in (C). And (D) isn't correct because deer were already doing very well in the region by the given years.

Charts

In the following example, Jermaine has tracked the macronutrient information of his regular diet for four weeks as instructed by his athletic trainer. His trainer advised him that to meet his muscle building goals, at least 35% of his diet should come from protein. After averaging his daily protein, carbohydrate, and fat intake, he came up with the following graph.

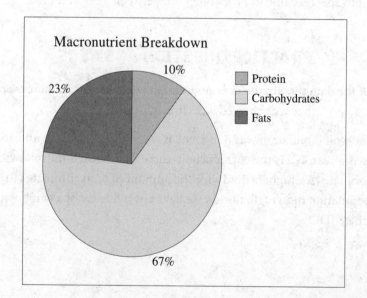

1. Based on the information given, Jermaine needs to

   (A) increase his carbohydrate intake
   (B) increase his fat intake
   (C) increase his protein intake
   (D) maintain his current diet

2. If the National Dietary Association recommends that Americans take in 50–60% carbohydrates per day, Jermaine consumes

   (A) more carbohydrates than recommended
   (B) less carbohydrates than recommended
   (C) the recommended carbohydrate intake
   (D) not enough information given

3. If the National Dietary Association recommends that Americans take in 20–30% fats per day, Jermaine consumes

   (A) more fats than recommended
   (B) less fats than recommended
   (C) the recommended fat intake
   (D) not enough information given

4. Based on the information given, Jermaine will most likely

   (A) replace some of his daily protein with fats
   (B) replace some of his daily protein with carbohydrates
   (C) replace some of his daily fats with protein
   (D) replace some of his daily carbohydrates with protein

5. Which claim is supported by the data given in the chart?

   (A) Jermaine's fat intake is half his carbohydrate intake.
   (B) Jermaine's carbohydrate intake is about double his protein intake.
   (C) The majority of Jermaine's diet is made up of proteins and fats.
   (D) Jermaine's combined protein and fat intake is about half of his carbohydrate intake.

PRACTICE QUESTION ANSWERS

1. **(C)** Use only the information you are given. To meet his goals, Jermaine must consume 35% of his calories in protein. His current number is significantly less. Thus, he needs to increase his protein intake as in (C).

2. **(A)** Currently, Jermaine consumes 67% carbohydrates per day on average. This is higher than the recommended percentage. Thus, he consumes more carbohydrates than recommended as in (A).

3. **(C)** Look at Jermaine's average fat intake—23%. This is right in the recommended percentage, making (C) the correct choice.

4. **(D)** This one is tough because you not only have to interpret the graph but analyze it with the information given to make an inference. Ask yourself what you know. Jermaine needs more protein to hit his goal. He currently consumes too much carbohydrates and just the right amount of fats. So, it makes the most sense that he would replace some of his current carbohydrates with protein. Eliminate (A) and (B) first because he does not want his protein intake to decrease. Then eliminate (C) because his fats are in the proper range as they are.

5. **(D)** This is another tough one. Work your way through each answer choice: 23 is not half of 67, so get rid of (A); 67 is far more than double 10, so get rid of (B). When you add 23 and 10, you get 33—33 is not the "majority" because it does not make up more than 50% of his diet, so get rid of (C); 33 is about half of 67, so (D) is the correct answer here.

PART 4

Writing and Language Test

CHAPTER 4

Introduction to the Writing and Language Section

The Writing and Language test is poorly named—you won't be writing so much as editing. What does it mean to edit? Simply put, you will read the content, correct errors, and make rhetorical choices. Making rhetorical choices is a fancy way of saying you will have to "think like a writer," and we will go into this more a little later. The Writing and Language Test will ask you to make choices about which word fits the context of the sentence best, or which order the sentences should be in, or which details should be included and which should be omitted. You won't have to write, as in come up with your own content. And reading comprehension was tested in the previous section. Instead, *you have to read like a writer*: find mistakes, fix them, and think about whether the writing is as clear and organized as it can be. *You are more than qualified to do this.* You do this every time you proofread something before turning it in. How many papers have you turned in by now? How many writing assignments have you revised and turned in again? The fact is you've been doing this for years. Plus, unlike the Reading and Math sections, the Writing and Language Test tests the same concepts over and over, so just by practicing some key grammar and language skills, you can know what to expect and how to excel on this section of the PSAT.

TIP

Unlike in the Reading section, you should read word by word in the Writing section.

It's tough to train yourself to read one way on one part of the test and another way on the other. So, try underlining the words as you read. It will help you slow down and train your eyes to read like an editor. A successful editor not only has a clear understanding of convention but also an eye for detail.

Format

The Writing and Language Test is the second section of the PSAT, after the Reading. Recall that together the Reading Test and the Writing and Language Test make up the Evidence-Based Reading and Writing portion of the PSAT. The second portion of the test is, of course, the Math component. The Writing and Language Test is 35 minutes and 44 questions. Of those 44 questions, 24 will be "Expression of Ideas" questions and 20 will be "Standard English Conventions" questions (both types of questions are discussed below). All questions are multiple choice and based on four passages. The passage topics are generally split up into four themes or subjects: one careers passage, one history/social studies passage, one humanities passage, and one science passage. You will *not* need any prior background knowledge of the passage content—in other words, you do not have to know the material discussed in the passages whatsoever. You are just editing that material. Each passage has 11 test questions. You should work at an 8.5 minutes per passage pace to finish on time. This is the same pace as the Revised SAT and is very doable. You have the time to read every word, so do it. This doesn't mean the timing is easy and you shouldn't practice that pace—it just means it is manageable, and with a bit of practice, you'll know exactly how you should pace yourself on test day. It is worth noting that you will see a few graphics on the PSAT Writing and Language Test. These are very low difficulty—they are there to test if you can interpret graphs and charts. While these questions are not too difficult and make up a very small portion of the test, they can take you by surprise if you are not expecting them. The practice questions that follow and especially the full-length practice tests in this book will more than prepare you for everything you'll see on the PSAT.

At a Glance

- 35 minutes long
- 44 questions total; 24 Expression of Ideas and 20 Standard English Conventions
- 4 Passages: 1 career, 1 history/social studies, 1 humanities, 1 science
- 11 questions per passage; random order of difficulty
- 8.5 minutes per passage pace to finish on time

Breaking It Down

The PSAT describes Expression of Ideas questions as those that deal with development, organization, and effective language use. But what does that really mean? And how can you prepare for these types of questions? Expression of Ideas questions focus on the rhetorical context. *Rhetorical context* just means the choices a writer has to make while writing, the circumstances around that writing. You know you are in the right mindset if you are thinking about *purpose, audience, and focus. Purpose is the why.* Why is this passage being written? You might want to say this passage was written so students can be tested on the PSAT, but that mindset won't help you test well. Instead, consider whether the writer wrote this passage to inform you about a topic, argue an issue, persuade you to agree with him or her, tell you a story, and so on. *Audience is the for whom.* Again, you might want to say that obviously this passage was written for me, the student taking the test. But instead, try to get specific. The writer might be targeting a person who disagrees with him or her, a person interested in the topic, a person who has no clue about the topic, and so on. Thinking about who the passage was intended for can help you make tough decisions about tone, organization, and which details need to be included. *Focus is the what.* Of course, it refers to the topic of the passage, but it also includes the organization, transitions, and evidence or details the writer uses to convey a message or prove a thesis or claim. The focus is informed by the *why* and the *for whom*. What the writer chooses to include and how he or she organizes it depends on the purpose for the writing and the audience the writer has in mind. All of this makes up the rhetorical context—*rhetoric* meaning the use of language to effectively inform, persuade, entertain, and so on, and *context* meaning the circumstances in which the writer communicates. So what do these types of questions look like on the PSAT?

Expression of Ideas questions might ask you to add evidence or support, remove sentences or details that aren't important or are distracting, reorganize or reorder the sentences so they make sense together, choose which word expresses an idea best, combine or revise sentences, eliminate repetition, and so on. Let's look at a few examples:

LET'S PRACTICE

The following passage is accompanied by questions that ask you to revise or edit the passage to improve its flow, organization, and clarity. For most questions, you will be directed to an underlined portion of the passage to either choose "NO CHANGE" or to select the appropriate revision. For other questions, you'll be asked to think about the passage as a whole.

The Electric Takeover

[1] The big news in the automobile industry is Elon Musk and his affordable, yet **1** fancy electric car. **2** [2] For a decade, Tesla has been a manufacturer of high-end electric cars to its few, elite consumers. **3** [3] Now, the company's mission has changed; large-scale production is in full bloom. [4] But not without complications. [5] While stock market value has soared, an indication of investors' confidence in Musk's prospects, producing a half-million vehicles for interested buyers **4** who have already put down deposits is no small task. **5**

1. (A) NO CHANGE
   (B) luxurious
   (C) really nice
   (D) grand

2. The writer is considering adding the following sentence:

   Tesla's cars surpass the competition because they combine extravagance and affordability.

   Should the writer make this addition?

   (A) Yes, because it provides new detail.
   (B) Yes, because it transitions to the next sentence.
   (C) No, because it distracts the reader.
   (D) No, because it is repetitive.

3. What's the best way to combine the following two sentences?

   (A) Now, the company's mission has changed, but not without complications.
   (B) Large-scale production is in full bloom since the news that the company's mission has changed, moreover, not without complications.
   (C) Now, the company's mission has changed and large-scale production is in full bloom, but not without complications.
   (D) It is not without complications that the company changed its mission and began producing on a large scale.

4. Which detail is most relevant and logical?

   (A) NO CHANGE
   (B) who don't have the money to spare
   (C) who have prominent reputations throughout the industry
   (D) who are increasingly interested

5. To make this paragraph most clear, sentence 5 should be

   (A) where it is now.
   (B) before sentence 1
   (C) after sentence 1
   (D) before sentence 3

PRACTICE QUESTION ANSWERS

1. **(B)** The correct answer choice is (B), luxurious. This is a word choice question, so you are asked to decide which word most clearly communicates the meaning. Here, the writer is trying to convey that the Tesla cars are upscale, or luxurious. Eliminate (C) because it is too informal and vague. And while (A) and (D) can be synonymous, "fancy" means elaborately decorated and "grand" means imposing. Neither word choice conveys what the writer is going for—elegant and upscale.

2. **(D)** Read the sentence before and the sentence after. Directly before this the writer tells us that the car is affordable and luxurious, so to say it again would be repetitive. Even if the sentence is correct and sounds nice, you have to make the choice as a writer whether it is logical and necessary. Since the information isn't new, eliminate (A). Since we don't need it to move logically into the next sentence, eliminate (B). And because it doesn't change topics or distract from the main idea, eliminate (C).

3. **(C)** Currently, the paragraph has a run-on. You are trying to decide how to combine these sentences logically and correctly. (A) loses information. (B) is wordy and changes the meaning, suggesting that it was complicating to change the company's mission. (D) is appealing, but ultimately does the same thing as choice (B). Even though it sounds good, it suggests that the complications were in changing the mission. (C) is the correct choice. If you read the next sentence, it becomes clear that after the mission changed and large-scale production began, the complications arose to meet the demand for the cars.

4. **(A)** Here, you have to make a choice about which detail should be included. You must ask yourself which choice is relevant and logical within the context of the paragraph. First, eliminate (D) because it is repetitive. Then, eliminate (C) because someone's reputation doesn't influence how difficult it is to produce more cars. Likewise, there's no evidence for (B). (A) is the correct choice. It is an important detail that the interested buyers have already put a deposit down because that means there's more stress to hurry up and produce the cars.

5. **(A)** The best way to approach the questions asking about sentence order is to read the paragraph as it is and see if anything seems out of place. The first sentence introduces the issue. The second tells us about Tesla's mission in the past. The third and fourth sentences are now combined to tell us about Tesla's new mission. The fifth sentence describes the complication—producing half a million cars. Everything makes logical sense how it is, so (A) is the correct choice. You can also try to move the sentence to all the suggested choices and see if it sounds better there. You'll find in this example that it does not.

The PSAT describes the rest of the questions you'll encounter as those that ask you to apply your knowledge of the conventions of standard English. But is there really a standard? How do you know the difference between preferences and actual rules? Standard English Conventions questions focus on what you might collectively call grammar and mechanics—these questions test sentence structure, usage, punctuation, subject-verb agreement, commonly confused words, and so on. The good news is these concepts can be learned and/or reviewed pretty easily. The bad news is a lot of students go through school without ever really being taught and tested on grammar and mechanics. Sure, they hear about the teachers' pet peeves and adapt stylistically, but they never learn and practice the conventions. These questions might ask you to correct incomplete sentences and run-ons; decide where commas, colons, semicolons, and dashes should and shouldn't be; address lack of agreement between subjects and verbs; correctly punctuate essential and nonessential elements; make sentences parallel; and so on. Don't worry if you aren't sure how to go about these conventions. As mentioned previously, these concepts are tested again and again on the PSAT, so the practice in this book will absolutely prepare you for everything you'll see on test day. The best part? The PSAT doesn't test whether you know *why* something is correct, so this book does not focus on memorizing grammatical terms. It doesn't matter nearly as much that you know the difference between a subordinate and insubordinate clause, but instead that can identify a fragment and correct it so that it is a complete thought. Let's look at a few examples:

LET'S PRACTICE

The following passage is accompanied by questions that ask you to revise or edit the passage to improve its sentence mechanics. For most questions, you will be directed to an underlined portion of the passage to either choose "NO CHANGE" or to select the appropriate revision.

The 36th President of the United States

President Lyndon B. Johnson is ranked favorably by **1** historians, who praise him for policies, that improved civil rights, gun control, poverty rates, and social **2** security: but he was greatly criticized during his presidency for his handling of the Vietnam War. Johnson, who was born on a farm in Stonewall, Texas, taught high school and **3** worked as a Congressional aide before winning election to the House of Representatives. Later, he won election to the Senate. In 1960, he failed to gain nomination for the presidential election, but **4** John F. Kennedy offered and he accepted the offer to run as his vice president. President Kennedy was sworn into office in 1961. When tragedy struck on November 22, 1963, it was Johnson who succeeded Kennedy **5** for president.

1. (A) NO CHANGE
   (B) historians who praise him for policies,
   (C) historians—who praise him for policies—
   (D) historians who praise him for policies

2. (A) NO CHANGE
   (B) security, but
   (C) security; and
   (D) security nonetheless

3. (A) NO CHANGE
   (B) works
   (C) has worked
   (D) working

4. **(A)** NO CHANGE
   (B) accepted John F. Kennedy's offer to run as his vice president
   (C) John F. Kennedy had offered him a position as vice president thus he
       gladly accepted
   (D) accepted an offer to be vice president which was given to him by
       John F. Kennedy

5. (A) NO CHANGE
   (B) like
   (C) in
   (D) as

PRACTICE QUESTION ANSWERS

1. **(D)** If we need the phrase, no commas. If we don't need it, surround it by
   commas. Read the sentence without the phrase and it becomes clear that we
   need it, so (D) is the correct choice. Eliminate (A) for that same reason—
   we cannot take out the phrase and still have a complete, logical sentence.
   Eliminate (B) because it adds an unnecessary break that disrupts the flow
   of the sentence. Eliminate (C) because the dashes work as hard commas,
   meaning they do the same thing but put more emphasis on the pause. Dashes
   are usually used like this to separate out a long phrase that is nonessential but
   gives relevant details or information.

2. **(B)** Here, we have two independent clauses that connect logically, so we need to combine them with a comma and conjunction. Semicolons are used just like periods. Colons are used after complete thoughts before a list or clarification. And (D) can be eliminated because it forms a run-on. You can also look at the conjunctions, or connecting words, to eliminate some choices here. (C) doesn't show contrast. And (D) is like "in spite of," so it isn't appropriate.

3. **(A)** This is correct as is. We want to maintain the tense for consistency and parallelism. Since "taught" is past tense, you are looking for the past tense of "work."

4. **(B)** Choice (B) is the only choice that is concise, or brief and to the point. The others are all wordy and hard to read. In general, you want to look for choices that are clear, specific, and concise. Trust your instinct. When something sounds lengthy and wordy, chances are it is. Never choose an answer just because its wordiness makes it sound smart—the PSAT is looking for the answer that is direct and to the point.

5. **(D)** Read the sentence with each choice. Here, "as" is a preposition meaning "in the role of," and so it is the correct choice. Again, trust your instinct. The others don't sound correct because they aren't correct.

Okay, so now you've seen what both types of questions look like—Expression of Ideas and Standard English Conventions. As mentioned earlier, you can prepare for the Writing and Language portion of the PSAT by learning some concepts that are tested over and over. Hence, Chapter 5 contains instructional exercises or mini-lessons that will prepare you for test day. As you learn, review, and practice these mini-lessons, you will notice patterns and understand what the PSAT expects you to know. This gives you a great advantage over students who come to the test unclear on what the Writing and Language portion tests.

Writing and Language Review

You now know how the Writing and Language portion of the PSAT is formatted. You know what types of questions it asks. You know you must *edit* to *correct errors* and *make rhetorical choices*. You've seen examples of test questions. But how do you prepare? Grammar, mechanics, and usage are often skimmed over in school. Your junior high teachers introduced you to the basics and then assured you that your high school teachers would make you experts. Your high school teachers reminded you of the basics but were convinced that your junior high teachers were the ones who should have spent a lot of time here. The point is, a lot of students graduate without an extensive education in the conventions that the Writing and Language section tests. Even the students exposed to all these concepts have often learned them sporadically and inconsistently. Then, there's the fact that a "standard" way of writing and speaking is hardly realistic. We all speak a bit differently. And even the best writers employ different techniques and styles. Don't let this overwhelm you. The previous introduction to this section of the PSAT stated that the Writing and Language test, unlike other tests within the PSAT, is a bit more predictable (and therefore manageable) because it tests the same concepts over and over. Hence, if you use the following mini-lessons to familiarize yourself with the concepts that will be tested, you are on your way to success.

There are several ways to approach the mini-lessons. If you have ample time to prepare, and especially if your goal is to score high and/or earn National Merit, you will want to review each concept closely, not only practicing the concepts but reading the explanations for each answer. *Reading answer explanations is critical—it teaches you how the PSAT thinks!* If you are just reviewing your life's worth of English grammar quickly the week before the test, then read the introduction to each lesson and try three to five practice questions from each section. Again, check your answers and read the answer explanations so you notice patterns and refrain from making the same mistakes over and over. Or, maybe the test is later this week and you just want to brush up on the stuff you haven't seen in years. If that's the case, circle a few lessons you want to review in particular, and complete the practice questions for those lessons paying close attention to the answer explanations. Don't overlook the explanations!

Sentence Basics

A sentence expresses a complete thought and is made up of a subject and a predicate. The subject is the person, place, or thing performing the action within the sentence. The predicate is the action within the sentence—it contains the verb plus modifying words, phrases, and/or clauses. Together, a subject and a predicate make up a complete idea, or a sentence. In this book, you will also hear simple sentences referred to as independent clauses. An independent clause is a group of words within a sentence that can stand alone because it contains both a subject and a verb.

> **Sentence:** a group of words containing a subject and a verb that expresses a complete thought

EXAMPLES: The dog lies on the carpet.

Jimmy and Samantha, old friends from their college days, met again in the terminal and spent the afternoon catching up with each other.

Stop.

Is that you?

These examples are all complete sentences because they express a complete thought and have both subject (or implied subject as in the third example) and verb.

When a group of words lacks a subject or a verb, or doesn't express a complete thought, it is a fragment. Since we use fragments in spoken conversation all the time, they can be difficult to identify. To help you identify fragments, the exercises below will teach you to find the subject and verb of a sentence and then to decide whether a complete thought is expressed. In this book, you will also hear fragments referred to as dependent clauses. A dependent clause is a group of words within a sentence that contains a subject and verb but does not express a complete thought, so it cannot be a complete sentence.

Fragment: a group of words lacking one or more of the three things that constitute a complete sentence—a fragment may be missing a subject or a verb or may fail to express a complete thought

EXAMPLES: Is swimming in the pond.

Sarah, the president of Student Council and the teacher's pet.

While I walked down the block in the pouring rain.

The three dogs, who had lived for years in the abandoned house on the corner of Wilson Street and Riverdale Drive and who had always eaten their share from the neighborhood trash cans.

These examples are all fragments because they express an incomplete thought. They are corrected below:

Jerome is swimming in the pond.

Sarah, the president of Student Council and the teacher's pet, earned high honors this year.

While I walked down the block in the pouring rain, I wondered why I hadn't brought my umbrella.

The three dogs, who had lived for years in the abandoned house on the corner of Wilson Street and Riverdale Drive and who had always eaten their share from the neighborhood trash cans, seemed happy with their arrangement.

> **TIP**
>
> Fragments aren't always short. Don't make your decision based on the length of sentences. There are fragments several lines long and complete sentences that are just one or two words.

A run-on sentence occurs when two or more independent clauses have been combined without proper punctuation. The most common form of a run-on sentence is a comma splice, when two independent clauses are connected by only a comma—to properly combine two independent clauses with a comma, we also need a conjunction (the most common conjunctions are represented by the acronym FANBOYS: *for, and, nor, but, or, yet, so*). To recognize run-ons, ask yourself whether we could put a period somewhere in the sentence and make two complete sentences.

Run-on Sentence: a group of words consisting of two or more independent clauses that are not punctuated properly

EXAMPLES: The cat napped, she was always sleepy.

Are you going to clean up is it always a mess in here?

Stop correcting everything I say, it is really annoying.

The books sat on the table and they looked as if they were all a hundred years old.

These examples are all run-on sentences because they express more than one complete thought and do not include proper punctuation or transition. They are corrected below:

The cat napped because she was always sleepy.

Are you going to clean up? Is it always a mess in here?

Stop correcting everything I say; it is really annoying.

The books sat on the table, and they looked as if they were all a hundred years old.

TIP

There are several ways to correct run-ons: a period, a comma plus conjunction, a semicolon, and a dash.

Run-on: Chocolate is my favorite I eat it every day.

Possible corrections:

Chocolate is my favorite. I eat it every day.

Chocolate is my favorite, so I eat it every day.

Chocolate is my favorite; I eat it every day.

Chocolate is my favorite—I eat it every day.

LET'S PRACTICE

For the exercises below, try to first locate the verb. Then locate the subject by asking who or what is performing the verb. Lastly, decide if the sentence contains a complete thought. For each question, say whether it is a sentence, fragment, or run-on.

1. Anthony swims.

2. Anthony went swimming and hiking on Tuesday.

3. While Anthony went swimming and hiking on Tuesday.

4. If I'd known that Anthony went swimming and hiking on Tuesday.

5. Go swimming!

6. Anthony went swimming and Anthony went hiking.

7. Anthony and I went swimming and hiking on Tuesday.

8. A boy I know swims his name is Anthony.

9. Because I am interested in both swimming and hiking.

10. He's interested too.

PRACTICE QUESTION ANSWERS

1. Sentence   The verb is *swims*. The subject is *Anthony*. Together, they form a complete thought. Just because a sentence is short doesn't mean it is a fragment. This is grammatically correct as it is.

2. Sentence   Here, we have a gerund (it isn't important you know this term, but you do need to recognize the verb). With a gerund, we use a verb plus the *-ing* form of an action verb. So, the verb is compound, *went swimming* and *went hiking*. The subject is *Anthony*. We have a complete thought, so this is a complete sentence.

3. Fragment   This is a dependent clause or a fragment because of the word "while." Despite it being longer than the previous sentence, it doesn't express a complete thought. To fix it, you could omit the word "while," or you could finish the thought: "While Anthony went swimming and hiking on Tuesday, I finished my homework."

4. Fragment   This has the same issue as the previous sentence. It doesn't express a complete thought because of the word "if." To fix it, you could say, "If I'd known that Anthony went swimming and hiking on Tuesday, I would have joined him."

5. Sentence   Any request or command has the understood subject *you*. So, despite not being able to locate a subject, this sentence is correct because it is implied that the subject is *you*. It means the same as, "Hey you, go swimming!" You'll see this with other commands. Believe it or not, "Stop!" is a complete sentence since the verb is *stop*, the subject is the implied *you*, and it expresses a complete thought.

6. **Run-on** This example has two independent clauses. So, we need to separate them with either a period, a semicolon, or a comma plus a conjunction. To fix it, you could say, "Anthony went swimming. Anthony went hiking." An even better way to fix it is to say, "Anthony went swimming, and he also went hiking." Perhaps the best way to fix it is to remove the unnecessary second subject and just say, "Anthony went swimming and hiking."

7. **Sentence** The verb is *went swimming* and *hiking*. The compound subject is *Anthony and I*. The sentence expresses a complete thought. Bingo! This is grammatically correct.

8. **Run-on** Here, we have two independent clauses without correct punctuation. Make this two complete sentences by adding a period: "A boy I know swims. His name is Anthony."

9. **Fragment** This example is missing a complete thought. You can fix it by completing the thought as in, "Because I am interested in both swimming and hiking, I was upset that Anthony didn't invite me to join him." Or you can fix it by omitting the word "because," as in, "I am interested in both swimming and hiking."

10. **Sentence** This one might seem tricky, but it is correct as it is. Remember that "He's" is a contraction for "he is." So, the verb is *is*, and the subject is *he*. The sentence expresses a complete thought.

The Weird Stuff

Everyone knows the English language is full of weird stuff. It's confusing and irregular. This section is designed to help you identify some of the weird stuff with sentence basics so that you can avoid common pitfalls or misunderstandings.

The Most Common Verbs: "To Be" Verbs

When we talk about verbs, we often talk about action words. However, the most common verbs don't sound like an action at all—they are indicative of *being*. These "to be" verbs are the most common verbs you'll see; they are tested often on tests like the PSAT, SAT, and ACT; they are irregular and tough. However, if you know them and know how to identify them, you can make your life much easier and your PSAT score much higher. And later, in college and in your professional life, you'll learn to replace these verbs with stronger verbs—you may be learning to do this already.

Am/are/is/was/were/(have, has, had) been/being

In the following examples, the verbs are underlined for your reference.

EXAMPLES: I <u>am</u> exhausted.

My brother <u>is</u> messy.

Thanksgiving dinner <u>was</u> excellent.

Airplane seats <u>are</u> tiny and cramped.

The research findings <u>were</u> significant to the scientists but boring to the public.

You <u>are</u> being too thorough.

It <u>has been</u> ages since I watched the original *Star Wars* movie.

After she wrote me, I <u>was</u> grateful.

Gerunds and Infinitives

As mentioned before, it is not important that you know grammatical terms for the PSAT. For instance, the test will not ask you to define *gerund* or *infinitive*. Yet, you do need to understand these concepts to master the art of identifying subjects and verbs so that you can decide whether a sentence is complete or not. Gerunds and infinitives are not the verbs of the sentence, even though they might look like it. A gerund is a noun made from a verb. In these instances, the verb of the sentence will be followed by the *-ing* form of another verb.

In the following examples, the verb of the sentence is underlined, and *the gerund is italicized*.

EXAMPLES: Brigitte <u>stopped</u> *smoking*.

She <u>is</u> *studying* in her bedroom.

We <u>started</u> *working* together on the project.

I <u>am</u> *jogging* to the store.

He <u>has been</u> *coming* over every evening.

Another weird thing you'll see in sentences is the infinitive. It's the verb plus "to." Again, the infinitive is not the verb. So, you should be able to identify an infinitive and realize that it doesn't mean a sentence is complete. It can absolutely be part of a complete sentence, but don't mistake it for the verb of the sentence.

In the following examples, the verb of the sentence is underlined, and *the infinitive is italicized*.

EXAMPLES: *To sleep* <u>is</u> the only thing I want.

She <u>refused</u> *to look* at the puppy.

<u>Bring</u> a book *to read* in case there is a long wait.

Kodi <u>agreed</u> *to come*.

Mary <u>seems</u> *to be* disappointed with her score.

Understood Subjects

Sentences that express a request or command might have an implied subject. In these instances, even if you cannot locate a verb in the sentence, the sentence may be complete. Put simply, if the request or command has an implied subject *you*, the sentence is complete.

In the following examples, the verb of the sentence is underlined, and the subject is implied. All examples are complete sentences.

EXAMPLES: Stop!

Walk slowly.

Please bring me your homework.

Go to bed.

Read the instructions carefully.

Semicolons, Colons, Dashes

Punctuation is one of those things that will come up again and again on the PSAT. The bad news is you'll be tested on punctuation that you most likely don't use often, like semicolons, colons, and dashes. The good news is a quick review of each and how you'll likely encounter them on test day will set you up for success.

Semicolons

1. Use the semicolon like a period to join two related independent clauses.

EXAMPLE: Vernon wasn't feeling well; he asked Katie to check his temperature.

2. Use the semicolon like a period to join two independent clauses when the second begins with a transition word (*however, therefore, meanwhile, in fact, for instance, even so,* etc.).

EXAMPLE: Stacy cleaned the bedrooms on Tuesday; therefore, she was upset when the children made them messy on Wednesday.

3. Use the semicolon like a comma to separate items in a list that contains commas.

EXAMPLE: Morgan visited the office February 2, 2018; August 12, 2018; and January 25, 2019.

Colons

1. Use the colon after a complete thought before a clarification.

EXAMPLE: I was surprised at what I found under my sister's bed: my favorite pair of shoes.

2. Use the colon after a complete thought before a list.

> **EXAMPLE:** During the summer months, I spend every weekend doing my favorite three hobbies: swimming, hiking, and fishing.

Dashes

Dashes are weird. They are weird because they are uncommon and very versatile. They can do pretty much anything, which makes them very useful and very frustrating. Don't worry, though. The PSAT basically wants you to know that they are versatile, that they can be used in many different ways.

1. Use the dash like a comma for a hard pause or to separate nonessential information.

> **EXAMPLE:** All three dogs—a black Great Dane, a fawn pit bull, and a red mastiff—walked perfectly on their leashes.

2. Use the dash like a period or a semicolon to denote a change in thought or voice or an interruption.

> **EXAMPLES:** I wanted to eat at the sports bar—Joe preferred the Italian spot on the corner.
>
> Chelsea asked me to the dance—I had already said yes to Laura—on Thursday evening after dinner.

3. Use the dash like a colon to denote a clarification or list.

> **EXAMPLE:** She left everything at my house—her shoes, makeup, and car keys.

TIP

Stay consistent when separating out nonessential information. Commas and dashes can both be used, but they shouldn't be mix and matched.

Correct: Kodi, the prettiest girl in the eleventh grade, asked me to the dance, and I said yes.

Correct: Kodi—the prettiest girl in the eleventh grade—asked me to the dance, and I said yes.

Incorrect: Kodi, the prettiest girl in the eleventh grade—asked me to the dance, and I said yes.

LET'S PRACTICE

For the exercises below, first decide if each is correct or incorrect. For those that are incorrect, correct them using semicolons, colons, or dashes.

1. Put your shoes where they go I don't want to have to do it later.

2. Although you are late for class, I will let you take the exam.

3. I smelled something burning the candle.

4. Clay took three things a shotgun, a tent, and a bag of supplies on his hunting trip.

5. My stomach was full I couldn't take another bite of the macaroni and cheese.

6. Tracy is so loud—I can hear her down the hall.

7. This semester I am visiting St. Louis, Missouri Tampa, Florida and Raleigh, North Carolina.

8. I saw Chloe she was wearing those brown boots you bought her just yesterday when I went to the mall.

9. While you are out, grab a few groceries bread, coffee, and milk.

10. Many freshmen and sophomores are beginning to take the PSAT more seriously in fact, several of my students have formed weekly study groups.

PRACTICE QUESTION ANSWERS

1. **Incorrect**   Put your shoes where they go; I don't want to have to do it later. Since there are two complete thoughts (independent clauses), they need to be separated with a semicolon. A period or a dash would also work here.

2. **Correct.**

3. **Incorrect**   I smelled something burning: the candle. Since there is a complete thought followed by a clarification, the best way to fix this sentence is with the colon. The dash would also work here.

4. **Incorrect**   Clay took three things—a shotgun, a tent, and a bag of supplies— on his hunting trip. Here, you have nonessential information that requires commas already, so it is best to separate this with dashes.

5. **Incorrect**   My stomach was full; I couldn't take another bite of the macaroni and cheese. Since there are two complete thoughts (independent clauses), they need to be separated with a semicolon. A period or dash would also work here.

6. **Correct.**

7. **Incorrect**   This semester I am visiting St. Louis, Missouri; Tampa, Florida; and Raleigh, North Carolina. Since there is a list that already requires commas, separate these items with semicolons. Note that you do not need a colon before the list because it does not follow a complete sentence.

8. **Incorrect**   I saw Chloe—she was wearing those brown boots you bought her—just yesterday when I went to the mall. Since there is an interruption right in the middle of this sentence, separate it with dashes.

9. **Incorrect**   While you are out, grab a few groceries: bread, coffee, and milk. Since there is a list following a complete thought, use the colon. A dash would also work here.

10. **Incorrect**   Many freshmen and sophomores are beginning to take the PSAT more seriously; in fact, several of my students have formed weekly study groups. Since there are two independent clauses separated by a transition word, use the semicolon.

Commas

Commas might be the most frustrating and difficult concept tested on the PSAT Writing and Language Test. Furthermore, commas are tested *a lot*. If you are a big reader, you probably already know that writers use commas in different ways and often stylistically, meaning they use commas to complement their style and voice, not necessarily in line with convention. However, the PSAT will test commas as convention dictates. Students can see a drop in their scores if they haven't prepared for correct comma usage. Think about it this way: if the test asks the same type of question 10 times, you are probably going to answer it the same way those 10 times. So, if you're answering it correctly, good for you—10 easy points. But, if you're answering it incorrectly, ouch! The only way to be prepared for all the ways you might encounter commas is to practice. If you've seen it before and know *how the PSAT tests it*, you are much more likely to do well.

When to Use Commas

1. Use a comma after a dependent clause before an independent clause.

> **EXAMPLE:** If you practice this section of the book, you will get a better score.

2. Use a comma plus conjunction to join two independent clauses (remember the most common conjunctions are denoted by the acronym FANBOYS: *for, and, nor, but, or, yet, so*).

> **EXAMPLE:** You can choose not to practice, but you will regret it.

3. Use commas to surround nonessential information and appositives.

> **EXAMPLE:** Carol, the president of Yearbook Club, never responds to her e-mails.

4. Use commas to separate items in a list.

> **EXAMPLE:** Can I get my pizza with banana peppers, sausage, and pineapple?

5. Use a comma for a natural pause.

> **EXAMPLE:** Well, I suppose you can come inside.

LET'S PRACTICE

For the exercises below, first decide if each is correct or incorrect. For those that are incorrect, correct them by adding commas where necessary.

1. The boy lives next door.

2. The boy in the red truck lives next door.

3. The boy in the red truck who lives next door waved at me.

4. If the boy in the red truck waves it's because he lives next door to me.

5. The boy in the red truck lives next door and he just waved at me.

6. Chloe is the best hairstylist around.

7. Chloe whose salon is on Main Street is the best hairstylist around.

8. Chloe the best hairstylist around is famous for color cuts retouches and updos.

9. When I want my hair done I go to Chloe.

10. I call Chloe when I want my hair done.

11. I know you want it done today but Chloe books appointments three weeks out.

12. My boss is easy to work for.

13. My boss William Smith is easy to work for.

14. No he doesn't micromanage.

15. After all he knows I work hard while I'm on the clock.

16. If you work hard he will acknowledge it and trust you to get the job done.

17. William Smith is easy to work for because he is honest concise and prepared.

18. Because my boss is honest concise and prepared he is easy to work for.

19. Dogs not cats are my favorite domestic animals.

20. Cats however are easier to care for.

PRACTICE QUESTION ANSWERS

1. **Correct.**

2. **Correct.**

3. **Incorrect**   The boy in the red truck, who lives next door, waved at me. This falls under rule 3. Since the subject is specific, anything more becomes nonessential information and can be surrounded by commas.

4. **Incorrect**   If the boy in the red truck waves, it's because he lives next door to me. This falls under rule 1. Put a comma here after the dependent clause but before the independent clause. You know the independent clause because it's the complete sentence—it could stand alone without the first part.

5. **Incorrect**   The boy in the red truck lives next door, and he just waved at me. This falls under rule 2. "The boy in the red truck lives next door" is an independent clause. "He just waved at me" is also an independent clause. Here, we use the comma plus "and" to combine them into one sentence. Without the comma, this is a run-on.

6. **Correct.**

7. **Incorrect**   Chloe, whose salon is on Main Street, is the best hairstylist around. This falls under rule 3. Since the subject is given by name, it is specific enough on its own; any further information becomes nonessential and is surrounded by commas.

8. **Incorrect**   Chloe, the best hairstylist around, is famous for color, cuts, retouches, and updos. This falls under rules 3 and 4. The extra information is surrounded by commas, and the items in a list are separated by commas.

9. **Incorrect**   When I want my hair done, I go to Chloe. This falls under rule 1. Again, the independent clause "I go to Chloe" is a complete sentence, while the dependent clause "When I want my hair done" cannot stand on its own.

10. **Correct.**

11. **Incorrect**   I know you want it done today, but Chloe books appointments three weeks out. This falls under rule 2. Here, the two independent clauses are combined with a comma plus conjunction.

12. **Correct.**

13. **Incorrect**   My boss, William Smith, is easy to work for. "My boss" refers to one person and is specific, so the name is nonessential here. According to rule 3, nonessential information needs to be surrounded by commas.

14. **Incorrect**   No, he doesn't micromanage. This falls under rule 5.

15. **Incorrect**   After all, he knows I work hard while I'm on the clock. This also falls under rule 5.

16. **Incorrect**   If you work hard, he will acknowledge it and trust you to get the job done. According to rule 1, you place a comma after a dependent clause before an independent clause.

17. **Incorrect**   William Smith is easy to work for because he is honest, concise, and prepared. This falls under rule 4.

18. **Incorrect**   Because my boss is honest, concise, and prepared, he is easy to work for. This falls under rules 1 and 4. First, there needs to be a comma after "prepared" to separate the dependent clause from the proceeding independent clause. Next, place commas between the items in a list.

19. **Incorrect**   Dogs, not cats, are my favorite domestic animals. This falls under rule 3. A quick way to check this is to see if the sentence would still be complete and make sense if you removed the information within the commas.

20. **Incorrect**   Cats, however, are easier to care for. This also falls under rule 3 and for the same reason.

The Weird Stuff

Essential Versus Nonessential Information

Essential words, phrases, and clauses are those that are *essential* to the sentence—they are necessary. Since we need them, these essential elements are *not* surrounded by commas.

Nonessential words, phrases, and clauses are those that are *not essential* to the sentence—they are unnecessary. Since we could remove them without hurting the sentence, these nonessential elements are surrounded by commas.

But, how do you decide if something is essential or nonessential? Let's start with some examples of essential and nonessential words. Then we will look at some more complex examples with phrases and clauses.

> Tommy's hypothesis, however, was inaccurate.

Here, "however" is nonessential because it can be removed from the sentence without changing its meaning. It is unnecessary.

> The chemistry prodigy Tommy made an inaccurate hypothesis.

Here, "Tommy" is essential because it specifies which chemistry prodigy. If we remove it, we lose information.

> Tommy, eager to please, made a rash hypothesis that turned out to be inaccurate.

Here, "eager to please" is nonessential, giving us more information but not necessary information. We can remove it, and we still have a complete sentence with a specific noun.

> The person verifying Tommy's hypothesis noticed the mistake right away.

Here, "verifying Tommy's hypothesis" is essential because it tells us which person. If we removed it, we would have a very ambiguous noun; we wouldn't know enough about our subject for the sentence to make sense.

> Tommy, who is nineteen years old, has a lot to learn.

Here, "who is nineteen years old" is nonessential. Without it, we still know exactly who we are talking about. It gives important information, surely, but the information is additional or nonessential.

> The famous scientist who mentored Tommy is proud of how far he's come.

Here, "who mentored Tommy" is essential because without it we do not know which famous scientist. Again, the subject is too broad without this information, so it's necessary.

TIP

Need it = No commas

Can do without it = Commas

A good way of thinking about essential and nonessential information is in terms of vague versus specific subjects. If the noun the phrase or clause is describing is vague, more information is needed (no commas). But if the noun the phrase or clause is describing is specific, no further information is needed (commas). Notice above that every time the subject was "Tommy," any further information was nonessential. Since we had a specific noun—a name—we had enough information to know exactly who our subject was. Hence, any other descriptive phrases were separated by commas. But, when the subject was vague as in "the person" or "the famous scientist," we needed more information to know which person or which scientist. Since we needed more information, the descriptive phrases were not separated by commas. See the correct sentences below:

> The birds sat on the bench.

> The birds with the yellow feathers sat on the bench.

> The birds with the yellow feathers, eating seeds, sat on the bench.

> Paulie, my favorite bird with yellow feathers, loves to sit on the bench and eat his seeds.

Oxford Commas

The Oxford comma is the final comma in a list of things—it's the one before the "and" or "or."

> Please bring me a cup of soup, a slice of bread, and two spoons.

In this example, the Oxford comma is the comma between "bread" and "and." It is stylistic, meaning whether you use it or not is up to you. Since there is no standard convention regarding the Oxford comma, the PSAT will generally not test it. For you, that means if it's there, great. If it's not, great. That won't be the issue either way.

Subject-Verb Agreement

Subject-verb agreement is another commonly tested concept on the Writing and Language Test. By now, this probably comes naturally to you—singular subjects need singular verbs, and plural subjects need plural verbs. However, the PSAT will make this basic principle more complicated by separating the subject and the verb with modifiers and using indefinite pronouns and collective nouns.

> **EXAMPLES:** **Singular subject:** <u>Mary</u> *eats* cake.
>
> **Plural subject:** The <u>students</u> *eat* cakes.

It may look simple to match singular subjects with singular verbs and plural subjects with plural verbs. However, the PSAT can make this simple question more difficult by separating the subject and the verb.

> **EXAMPLE:** The <u>book</u>, written by Jane Austen in 1811, *is* a story about Elizabeth Bennet.

Here the subject and verb are separated by the phrase *written by Jane Austen in 1811*. This separation makes subject-verb agreement questions more difficult.

> The <u>*book*</u> *is* a story about Elizabeth Bennet.

Here, when the phrase between the subject and verb is taken out, it is much easier to see that the subject is *book* and the verb is *is*. When you encounter this, try to locate the subject and the verb and read them as if nothing is between them—it will make it much clearer.

TIP

The subject-verb agreement is much easier to work with when the phrase between the subject and the verb is crossed out.

LET'S PRACTICE

For the following exercises, decide whether the sentence is correct or incorrect. If it's incorrect, change the nouns, pronouns, and verbs as necessary.

1. The teacher who taught my sister's seventh grade class are instructing my class today.

2. The dog looking through the windows upstairs smile at me all the time.

3. Everyone in the room is happy to see you.

4. The group of poets read twice a week at open mic.

5. Each of the boys have his own pair of green socks.

6. A pair of my pants are still on the floor.

7. My mom, who is constantly asking me about my future but refuses to ever talk about her own issues, bother me about getting married.

8. Neither my mother nor my father have been over to see my new apartment.

9. The news is bad.

10. Anyone who eats like she does are going to stay lean.

11. Women who love a good romantic comedy is going to enjoy this.

12. Inside the house, children walks slowly and talks quietly.

13. My earnings have gone up significantly over the years.

14. Either the rice or the bread are fine with me.

15. My dog, which likes to sleep with all four blankets, snores loudly.

PRACTICE QUESTION ANSWERS

1. **Incorrect**   The teacher who taught my sister's seventh grade class *is* instructing my class today.

2. **Incorrect**   The dog looking through the windows upstairs *smiles* at me all the time.

3. **Correct.**

4. **Incorrect**   The group of poets *reads* twice a week at open mic.

5. **Incorrect**   Each of the boys *has* his own pair of green socks.

6. **Incorrect**   A pair of my pants *is* still on the floor.

7. **Incorrect**   My mom, who is constantly asking me about my future but refuses to ever talk about her own issues, *bothers* me about getting married.

8. **Incorrect**   Neither my mother nor my father *has* been over to see my new apartment.

9. **Correct.**

10. **Incorrect**   Anyone who eats like she does *is* going to stay lean.

11. **Incorrect**   Women who love a good romantic comedy *are* going to enjoy this.

12. **Incorrect**   Inside the house, children *walk* slowly and *talk* quietly.

13. **Correct.**

14. **Incorrect**   Either the rice or the bread *is* fine with me.

15. **Correct.**

Remember that a good way to attack subject-verb agreement issues is to locate the subject and the verb and read them next to one another. For instance, in number 7 above, the correct answer becomes clear if I read the sentence, "My mom bothers me about getting married." By reading the sentence without the extra modifiers and phrases, you can more easily spot the discrepancy.

Verb Tenses

Verbs provide key information about timing. The verbs in the sentences give information on whether the action takes place in the past, present, or future. Sometimes these verbs can give more information and express the time frames of the actions.

Simple Tenses

Past: Nancy *studied* for the PSAT.
Present: Nancy *studies* for the PSAT.
Future: Nancy *will study* for the PSAT.

Past Perfect Tense

Past perfect tense is used to describe actions that took place before a different past event. Think of it as talking in past tense about something that happened before that. The past perfect tense is used to describe noncontinuous actions.

EXAMPLE: Nancy *had studied* for the PSAT before she ate dinner.

Here Nancy *had studied* for the PSAT before she performed a different past action, which is *ate dinner*.

Present Perfect Tense

Present perfect tense is used to describe actions that started in the past and continue into the present, or to describe repeated actions in an unspecified period between the past and now.

EXAMPLE: Nancy *has worked* for the hospital for a decade.

Here, the *has worked* means that Nancy started working for the hospital in the past and that this action continues into the present.

I *have studied* for the PSAT several times but never taken it.

Here, studying is a repeated action that takes place in an unspecified time between the past and now.

Future Perfect Tense

Future perfect tense is used to describe actions that finish in the future before another future event.

EXAMPLE: Nancy *will have studied* enough by the time she takes the PSAT.

Here *will have studied* means that the action will finish before she takes the exam.

Verbs That Change Forms to Show Time

PRESENT	PAST	PAST PARTICIPLE (USE WITH *HAS, HAVE, HAD,* ETC.)
awake	awaked, awoke	awaked, awoken
begin	began	begun
bind	bound	bound
break	broke	broken
bring	brought	brought
build	built	built
burst	burst	burst
buy	bought	bought
catch	caught	caught
choose	chose	chosen
come	came	come
do	did	done
draw	drew	drawn
drink	drank	drunk
drive	drove	driven
eat	ate	eaten
fall	fell	fallen
feed	fed	fed
feel	felt	felt
fight	fought	fought
find	found	found
fly	flew	flown
forbid	forbade	forbidden
forget	forgot	forgot, forgotten
forgive	forgave	forgiven
freeze	froze	frozen
get	got	got, gotten
give	gave	given
grow	grew	grown
have, has	had	had
hold	held	held

(continued)

Verbs That Change Forms to Show Time, *continued*

PRESENT	PAST	PAST PARTICIPLE (USE WITH *HAS, HAVE, HAD,* ETC.)
know	knew	known
lead	led	led
leave	left	left
lend	lent	lent
lose	lost	lost
make	made	made
meet	met	met
pay	paid	paid
put	put	put
raise	raised	raised
read	read	read
ride	rode	ridden
rise	rose	risen
run	ran	run
see	saw	seen
sell	sold	sold
send	sent	sent
set	set	set
shake	shook	shaken
shoot	shot	shot
shrink	shrank, shrunk	shrunk, shrunken
sing	sang	sung
sit	sat	sat
sleep	slept	slept
slide	slid	slid
speak	spoke	spoken
steal	stole	stolen
stick	stuck	stuck
sweat	sweat, sweated	sweated
swim	swam	swum
take	took	taken

Verbs That Change Forms to Show Time, *continued*

PRESENT	PAST	PAST PARTICIPLE (USE WITH *HAS, HAVE, HAD, ETC.*)
teach	taught	taught
tell	told	told
think	thought	thought
throw	threw	thrown
wake	waked, woke	waked, woken
wear	worn	worn
win	won	won
work	worked, wrought	worked, wrought
write	wrote	written

Apostrophes

Apostrophes are used to (1) combine two words in a contraction, and (2) show ownership. Apostrophes are never used just to make nouns plural. Contractions are very common, and most students are used to them by time they take the PSAT. "Will not" becomes "won't," and "I am" becomes "I'm," and so on. However, possession can be quite difficult.

Possession

1. When you want to show possession with a singular subject, use apostrophe plus *s*.
2. When you want to show possession with a plural subject, use *s* plus apostrophe.
3. Do not use apostrophes just to make nouns plural.
4. Do not use apostrophes to show ownership with pronouns.

LET'S PRACTICE

For the following examples, decide if the sentence is correct or incorrect. If incorrect, correct the apostrophe usage to fix the sentence.

1. Sams toys are scattered all over the room.

2. Be careful not to step on the dog's toys.

3. The dog's keep running in and out of the room with their toys.

4. One lady's dog is at the water bowl.

5. It's bowl is full of slobber.

6. Two dog's leashes were left hanging in the front room.

7. Where did your's go?

8. Every time the kid's pick up the toys, they just end up right back on the floor.

9. Ann and Terry's dog barks the loudest by far.

10. Anthony's and Millie's dogs are clearly the fastest two of the party.

PRACTICE QUESTION ANSWERS

1. **Incorrect**   Sam's toys are scattered all over the room.

2. **Correct.**

3. **Incorrect**   The dogs keep running in and out of the room with their toys.

4. **Correct.**

5. **Incorrect**   Its bowl is full of slobber.

6. **Incorrect**   Two dogs' leashes were left hanging in the front room.

7. **Incorrect**   Where did yours go?

8. **Incorrect**   Every time the kids pick up the toys, they just end up right back on the floor.

9. **Correct**   (Since the dog collectively belongs to Ann and Terry, only one apostrophe is necessary.)

10. **Correct**   (Since there are two separate dogs belonging to two separate people, both names need apostrophes.)

The Weird Stuff

Some irregular nouns become plural by changing their spelling. So these words are plural but don't end in *s*. The most common on the PSAT are words like *women*, *men*, and *children*, which do not have an *s* in their plural form. For these, use the apostrophe plus *s* (the women's rights rally, the children's coats, etc.).

Commonly Misused Words

It is most appropriate after the previous mini-lesson to address four sets of words that are commonly misused and thus commonly tested by the PSAT. Possessive pronouns can be very tricky. Memorize the following four sets of words—they will come up, and they can be easy points if you complete this mini-lesson.

Word Set 1: There/Their/They're

There: refers to a place or acts as a pronoun introducing a noun or clause.

EXAMPLES: Hey you, stop right there.

There is my hat!

No way I'm going in there.

Their: shows possession

EXAMPLES: The children left their books on the table.

Is it their house?

Their differences are most pronounced in their behaviors.

They're: a contraction for "they are"

EXAMPLES: They're always testing tough grammar concepts on the PSAT.

I cannot believe they're not here.

They're older than I realized.

Word Set 2: Its/It's

Its: shows possession

EXAMPLES: I can see its colors from here.

The university is having the most profitable year in its history.

My rabbit hardly eats its food.

It's: a contraction for "it is" or "it has"

EXAMPLES: It's beginning to look a lot like the holidays.

It's been below freezing all week.

After you've seen the movie, you understand why it's considered the best.

Word Set 3: Your/You're

Your: shows possession

EXAMPLES: Your cereal is getting soggy.

If you take off those glasses, I can see your eyes.

Mother never had any patience for your sarcasm.

You're: a contraction for "you are"

EXAMPLES: You know that you're my favorite.

You're constantly getting into trouble these days.

You've been at the bottom before, so you know you're lucky to be at the top now.

Word Set 4: Whose/Who's

Whose: shows possession

EXAMPLES: Whose jacket are you wearing?

I've met the man whose wallet was stolen.

The news of the layoff wasn't well received by the managers whose employees were going to lose work.

Who's: a contraction for "who is" or "who has"

EXAMPLES: I'm the one who's most affected by her decision.

Who's going to wash the dishes tonight?

I met the gentleman who's moving in next door.

LET'S PRACTICE

For the following exercises, choose the correct usage of the commonly misused words.

1. (Whose/Who's) turn is it to watch the baby?

2. (There/Their/They're) constantly leaving without saying goodbye.

3. I've been over (there/their/they're) before, but never in (there/their/they're) bedroom.

Writing and Language Review | **151**

4. (Its/It's) (there/their/they're) turn to buy lunch, but (there/their/they're) canceling last minute.

5. (Whose/Who's) performing tonight?

6. Cheryl, (whose/who's) desk is messy, was the one complaining about (your/you're) lack of organization.

7. (Your/You're) over (there/their/they're), and I'm stuck here.

8. Have you seen (its/it's) wheels yet?

9. (Your/You're) probably wondering why (its/it's) so dark outside.

10. (There/Their/They're) very concerned about where (your/you're) brother is.

PRACTICE QUESTION ANSWERS

1. **Whose** turn is it to watch the baby?

2. **They're** constantly leaving without saying goodbye.

3. I've been over **there** before, but never in **their** bedroom.

4. **It's their** turn to buy lunch, but **they're** canceling last minute.

5. **Who's** performing tonight?

6. Cheryl, **whose** desk is messy, was the one complaining about **your** lack of organization.

7. **You're** over **there**, and I'm stuck here.

8. Have you seen **its** wheels yet?

9. **You're** probably wondering why **it's** so dark outside.

10. **They're** very concerned about where **your** brother is.

Parallelism

Parallelism isn't one of those things tested over and over directly on the PSAT. But it is one of those things that comes up, and it can really help you decide between two answers that both sound right. Parallelism is about how you say things—how they flow. It means that the components of a sentence are similar in construction or sound. Not only is parallel structure a standard expected of you, but it's also what makes your writing sound good.

Consider the difference between the two following sentences:

> Brittany is a talented athlete and an excellent student.

Brittany is a talented athlete, and excels at school.
You should notice that the first sentence flows better. That's because it's parallel.
Look at another example:

> On vacation, I went swimming, hiking, and boating.

On vacation, I went swimming, hiked, and on a boat.
Again, you should notice that the first sentence is better than the second sentence because it maintains parallel structure.
Let's look at one more example:

> My mother insists that my brother will find his way because he enjoys talking to people, helping others, and being friendly.

My mother insists that my brother will find his way because he enjoys talking to people, helped others, and his demeanor is so friendly.
So, what it really comes down to is not mixing and matching. You want sentences to use the same pattern and correspond so that they are parallel and read well.

LET'S PRACTICE

In the following exercises, decide if the sentence is parallel or not. If it's not, fix it.

1. In the dictionary, you'll find definitions, how to pronounce, and origins for each word.

2. I expect that you'll be there on time and ready to play.

3. If you want to exercise more, try jogging, biking, and to lift weights.

4. Dedication and to be disciplined are what create results.

5. Win or losing, hold your head high.

6. Your attitude has ruined your relationship, your career, and it has made you unhealthy.

7. Betty wrote down her resolutions: a new house and driving a new car.

8. You can reach me by telephone, e-mail, or Facebook.

9. Melissa liked Italian food, while to Meghan it was Greek that was preferable.

10. For breakfast, I made pancakes, bacon, and fried an egg.

PRACTICE TEST ANSWERS

1. Incorrect In the dictionary, you'll find definitions, pronunciations, and origins for each word.

2. Correct.

3. Incorrect If you want to exercise more, try jogging, biking, and lifting weights.

4. Incorrect Dedication and discipline are what create results.

5. Incorrect Win or lose, hold your head high.

6. Incorrect Your attitude has ruined your relationship, your career, and your health.

7. Incorrect Betty wrote down her resolutions: a new house and a new car.

8. Correct.

9. Incorrect Melissa liked Italian food, while Meghan preferred Greek food.

10. Incorrect For breakfast, I made pancakes, bacon, and an egg.

Modifiers

Modifier placement is the next concept we need to address. It can seem trivial at first, but it's integral to good writing. A reader can easily get confused if modifiers are misplaced. First, you need to know that a modifier is just a word, phrase, or clause that adds description to the sentence. Ideally, this modifier should be close to whatever it's describing. If it's not, the meaning of the sentence can get lost.

Consider this example:

> Looking out the window, Rachel saw a bird with a dark blue head and red wings.

> Looking out the window, a bird with a dark blue head and red wings caught Rachel's eye.

What's the difference between the sentences above? In the first sentence, the subject is right after the modifier that describes it—Rachel is the one looking out the window. This is what the writer means; it's correct. However, in the second sentence, "a bird" comes directly after the modifier, so if we read this sentence literally, it's the bird looking out the window. That's not what the writer meant.

Let's look at another:

> Mary ate the sandwich, soggy from sitting in the fridge all day.

> Mary, soggy from sitting in the fridge all day, ate the sandwich.

I think you're getting the point here. The first sentence is correct because it's the sandwich that is soggy, not Mary. The modifier needs to be with whatever it's describing.

LET'S PRACTICE

Decide if the modifiers are placed correctly or incorrectly in the following exercises.

1. The dog fetched its Frisbee, running back and forth.

2. The dog, running back and forth, fetched its Frisbee.

3. The dog fetched, running back and forth, its Frisbee.

4. Smiling at me, my sister waved from the backseat.

5. My sister, smiling at me, waved from the backseat.

6. My sister waved from the backseat, smiling at me.

7. Blowing in the wind, we watched the trees as the storm approached.

8. As the storm approached, we watched the trees blowing in the wind.

9. I told Katie not to wear the yellow dress, which was stained with barbecue sauce.

10. Stained with barbecue sauce, I told Katie not to wear the yellow dress.

PRACTICE QUESTION ANSWERS

1. **Incorrect**   Here, the sentence literally means that the Frisbee is running back and forth.

2. **Correct.**

3. **Incorrect**   Again, "running back and forth" needs to be located next to the thing it's describing: the dog.

4. **Correct.**

5. **Correct.**

6. **Incorrect**   Here, the backseat is what's smiling. That modifier needs to be relocated next to the thing it's describing as in the two previous examples.

7. **Incorrect**   Here, "we" are blowing in the wind. What the writer means is that the trees were blowing in the wind, so that modifier needs to be right beside what it's describing.

8. **Correct.**

9. **Correct.**

10. **Incorrect**   If we read this sentence literally, it means that "I" was stained with barbecue sauce, which is not the intended meaning.

The takeaway here is that the literal meaning should match the intended meaning. Think about where descriptions are placed and get them as close to whatever they're describing as possible. A lot of questions on the Writing and Language portion of the PSAT will test conciseness and flow—you will be charged with the task of making sure sentences are not wordy or repetitive and that they are parallel with accurate modifier placement. For you, that means choosing the sentence that is direct and to the point, but it also means applying this mini-lesson and the previous mini-lesson to choose the best sentence structure. Flow matters.

Active Versus Passive

The rule is: use active voice whenever you can. In active voice, the noun performing the action comes first and then the action of the sentence. In passive voice, the action comes first, so the action is done *by* or *for* or *to* whoever of whatever is performing the action. To identify whether the sentence is active or passive, first ask yourself what action is being done in the sentence. Then, ask yourself who or what is performing that action. If the actor comes first, it's active. If the action comes first, it's passive. Look for the word *by*, which can be a good indicator that the sentence is passive. This does not mean that the passive voice should never be used—there are good reasons to sometimes use the passive voice (check out the "Weird Stuff" section below). However, for the purposes of the PSAT, if you are given a choice, go with active voice. It tends to be more clear and direct.

TIP

If the PSAT is asking you, choose the active voice.

Passive voice is much less common and only used in special circumstances.

EXAMPLES: Mario hit the ball. (*active*)

The ball was hit by Mario. (*passive*)

I enjoyed the book. (*active*)

The book was enjoyed by me. (*passive*)

Researchers proved that people using the app are less likely to be overweight. (*active*)

It was proven by researchers that people using the app are less likely to be overweight. (*passive*)

LET'S PRACTICE

In the following exercises, decide if the sentence is active or passive—ask yourself is there an actor performing an action (active) or is an action being done by an actor (passive). If it's passive, change it appropriately to make it active.

1. The kitchen was cleaned by Jackson.

2. The package was delivered to my door by the postman.

3. Snowballs, coming from all different directions, were dodged by the laughing children.

4. Sarah, the club administrator, is writing the memo now.

5. The project had been completed on time.

6. Black coffee was being poured for all the meeting's attendees.

7. The man struggling to get out of his cuffs had been arrested by the police officer.

8. The dog ran back and forth between Lucy and Mark.

9. You must explain your decision to me.

10. My presentation was approved by my boss.

PRACTICE QUESTION ANSWERS

1. **Passive**   Jackson cleaned the kitchen.

2. **Passive**   The postman delivered the package to my door.

3. **Passive**   The laughing children dodged the snowballs coming from all different directions.

4. **Active.**

5. **Passive**   They had completed the project on time. (Note how the passive voice might actually be preferred here because of the ambiguous actor and the emphasis on the project itself.)

6. **Passive**   I poured black coffee for all the meeting's attendees. (Again, note how without a clear subject, the passive voice might have been intended by the writer.)

7. **Passive**   The police officer had arrested the man who was now struggling to get out of his cuffs. (Who actually did the action of arresting? It was the police officer.)

8. **Active.**

9. **Active.**

10. **Passive**   My boss approved my presentation.

The Weird Stuff

Some sentences are passive for good reason. Usually, if the writer wants to emphasize the action, it's a good idea to employ the passive voice. Consider the following examples where a writer might choose to use the passive voice because the emphasis is on the action much more than on the actor performing that action.

> The love letter was passed down the line of students. (*passive*)
>
> The line of students passed down the love letter. (*active*)
>
> The safety policy was not followed correctly. (*passive*)
>
> Someone did not follow the safety policy correctly. (*active*)
>
> Thousands of people were diagnosed with the disease. (*passive*)
>
> Doctors diagnosed thousands of people with the disease. (*active*)
>
> The plan was finally approved by Congress. (*passive*)
>
> Congress finally approved the plan. (*active*)

It's worth noting that the passive voice is not always bad. In some instances, it's desirable. In these examples, the emphasis is on the action because it's more important than the actor(s). However, when the PSAT gives you the choice, choose the active voice. Remember the PSAT is trying to eliminate wordiness and vagueness.

Transitions

Transitions and sequence questions come up a lot on the PSAT. Transitions are words that show relationships between ideas. The PSAT will ask you to connect different parts of a sentence or paragraph or passage. It will also ask you to consider if sentences are in the correct order based on how the transitions work and how the sentences flow together. This is definitely one of the tougher concepts on the PSAT Writing and Language test.

Let's start at a sentence level. To transition within sentences, we use connecting words like *and, but, or, yet, rather, while, also, because, in fact, moreover, likewise, otherwise, however, nonetheless,* and so on. If we want to connect things because they are similar, we use words like "and" and "also." If we want to connect things because they show contradiction, we use words like "but" and "or." If we want to connect things to show cause and effect, we use words like "because" and "therefore." Your job will be to understand the relationship being shown and select the transition word that makes that relationship most clear.

LET'S PRACTICE

For the exercises below, decide if the underlined transition word fits the intended meaning of the sentence. If not, change it appropriately. Note that there are many ways to fix the incorrect sentences; the solutions below are just one way of many.

1. Chelsea is pregnant, <u>and</u> she eats much more than normal.

2. I should be able to go home at five, <u>hence</u> my boss keeps me late on Wednesdays.

3. We stayed inside <u>and</u> it was raining all day.

4. <u>Because</u> he studied so hard this year, he passed all his exams.

5. Candace excelled in biology, <u>thus</u> so did her sister.

6. <u>Because</u> the freezing temperatures, they went for a walk.

7. Juan played baseball well, <u>plus</u> he particularly excelled on the wrestling mat.

8. <u>As a result of</u> Brad's negligence, his bedroom became unbearable.

9. Tammy asked for Tuesday off well in advance; <u>therefore,</u> her request was granted.

10. My mom knew about it, <u>or</u> your dad figured it out eventually.

PRACTICE QUESTION ANSWERS

1. **Incorrect** Chelsea is pregnant, so she eats much more than normal.

2. **Incorrect** I should be able to go home at five, but my boss keeps me late on Wednesdays.

3. **Incorrect** We stayed inside because it was raining all day.

4. **Correct.**

5. **Incorrect** Candace excelled in biology, and so did her sister.

6. **Incorrect** Despite the freezing temperatures, they went for a walk.

7. **Incorrect**   Juan played baseball well, but he particularly excelled on the wrestling mat.

8. **Correct.**

9. **Correct.**

10. **Incorrect**   My mom knew about it, and your dad figured it out eventually.

The PSAT won't always ask about transition words within a sentence but might instead ask about the order of sentences and how transitions can be used to organize sentences logically. In these questions, you'll be asked to order the sentences of a paragraph so that they are logical and meaningful. It's important then that you read like a writer. Don't trust what's on the page already, but instead ask yourself if the sentences connect logically.

LET'S PRACTICE

Put the following sentences into the correct order.

[1] But standardized testing allows little room for creativity and doesn't account for the many ways students can think critically.

[2] Let's not forget to consider other factors like race, gender, and class that are proven again and again to influence test scores.

[3] The most controversial issue with standardized testing, of course, is whether it really measures a student's ability to critically think and problem solve.

[4] On one hand, students with higher critical thinking skills continually test better than their peers.

[5] While it appears that standardized testing is a far from perfect way to assess academic potential, there seem to be no immediate alternatives taking its place.

[6] For instance, there are very intelligent students who test poorly simply because they exhibit their skills and talents in a different medium like art or music.

PRACTICE QUESTION ANSWER

The correct order is 3–4–1–6–2–5. Let's talk about how you'd know this. First, look for an introduction sentence, something that tells you what the paragraph might be about. That's sentence 3. "On one hand" sets up one side of the issue, so sentence 4 logically comes next. Read the remaining sentences; you either want an *and* statement (something that supports this or adds to this idea) or a *but* statement (something that contradicts it and shows a counterargument). You find the latter in sentence 1—it shows the opposing side. Sentence 6 comes next because it gives evidence for the opposing side—the "For instance" should clue you in. You only have two sentences left. Read them both and you'll see that 5 should be the concluding sentence, the last sentence, because it sums up the paragraph. So, the order is 2 then 5.

CHAPTER 6

8 Strategies for Success on the Writing and Language Section

The introduction to the Writing and Language section in Chapter 4 mentions a scary term: *rhetorical context*. But you now know that's a fancy way of saying you have to make choices about writing. The context around any writing revolves around purpose, audience, and focus. (1) What is the point of the passage? What does it do? Why might the writer have written it? (2) Who is the intended audience? How can it maintain a consistent tone and voice? What sort of evidence is appropriate for this type of reader? (3) What is the focus or main idea of the passage? What is it trying to say, argue, discuss? What sort of evidence supports this focus in a meaningful way?

Strategy 1: Read like a Writer

Since the Writing and Language test is first and foremost an editing test, you'll be charged with the task of *reading like a writer*—slowing down and not just reading for the content, but instead considering how that content was written and why it was written that way.

You're used to reading for the *what*. If you're reading a book in your room and your sister walks in, she might ask you, "What's your book about?" If you're reading a selection out of one of your textbooks, you might be expected to summarize it and pick out key terms. Even if you're reading a short story in English class, your teacher might test you on main ideas and themes. You are very used to being asked about the *what*. What you might not be as comfortable with is the *why* and *how*? Why might a writer add or delete this sentence? Why might a writer use this word or choose another? If a writer wants to convey this idea, how should he or she go about it? How should a writer transition from one idea to the next? How should the writer connect ideas in a sentence? You get the idea. How you read is different on the Writing and Language test, but it is designed to get you ready for the questions and assignments that will come up in college classrooms.

Perhaps the most challenging aspect of this change is that you cannot trust what you read. You've been programmed since your first days at school to trust what you read. When you read your textbooks, you rarely stop and question if the information is correct or if it's written correctly—you take it for granted that it is. When you read a novel, you may never wonder, *Hmmm, are those sentences in the correct order?* or *Is that the best way to transition between these ideas?* But that's exactly what you are charged with doing on the PSAT. You cannot trust how a passage is written. You cannot trust what you read. Instead you must read it with a critical eye and be ready to change words, reorder phrases and sentences, correct punctuation and usage, and so on.

This is particularly important for the logical sequence questions like the one in Chapter 5 where you have to decide the order of all sentences in a paragraph. For these, don't trust the sequence the sentences are currently in. Be suspicious and read like a writer, looking for transition words that clue you in as to the appropriate order like "first," "for example," "next," "thus," "as a result," and so on.

Strategy 2: Play like You Practice

We have all heard the saying that we must practice how we play. On the PSAT, you must play like you practice. So many students prepare for tests and practice strategies for success, but then, for whatever reason, when they sit down at the test, all of their preparation goes out the window. This book is your best resource. Get to know the format of the test, make a game plan based on your skill set, and stick with that on test day. Having a plan and knowing how you will approach the test will mitigate anxiety on test day and help you to perform your very best.

Memorize this about the Writing and Language test:

- 4 passages
- 44 questions
- 35 minutes
- 8.5 minutes per passage

If you're noticing that math is a bit off, you're right. The timing is nearly 9 minutes per passage, but with the bubbling in of answers and turning of pages and the guy in the third row coughing, you'll lose a second here and there. It's better that you finish with a few seconds to go than not finish. That being said, you don't want to finish with a full two minutes left. Having too much time left is not always a good thing. You'll be tempted to go back and second-guess yourself and change answers that maybe shouldn't be changed. So, you need to use this book to practice, and then you need to test just like you've been practicing.

Begin by trying out the 8.5 minute/passage pace. Set a timer as you complete the passage at the end of this chapter. If you're close to that 8.5 minute mark (say you finish in 8 minutes or 9 minutes), no worries, you can make small adjustments as you practice on the full-length practice tests. But if you're not close to that mark, you need to make bigger adjustments. Here are some tips:

1. **If you're moving too fast** (finishing each passage in less than 7 minutes): Underline as you read. You can write all over the PSAT, so take advantage of it. By running your pencil under the words you are reading, you'll be forced to slow down and read each word.
2. **If you're moving too slow** (finishing each passage in 10 minutes or more): Pick a letter (A, B, C, or D) and use that same letter on all the questions that are designed to take a longer time, like those asking you to put the sentences in the correct order. Don't even waste time considering these questions—as soon as you come across them, fill in your letter, and keep moving. Remember, your chances are better if you always use the same letter.

Strategy 3: Get It Right the First Time

On tests like the PSAT, it's generally not a good idea to speed through the test in hopes of having time to go back and double-check your answers. We all work at a different pace, but most students find that they have ample time to finish this section of the test. That being said, you should read everything. There may be sentences or whole paragraphs without a question, but you can count on them being important to the questions that require context like the transition and organization questions. It is much more effective on these types of tests to take your time and work through the test once. Reading and considering a question one time slowly is still faster and more effective than rushing through it three or four times. This isn't to say you can't flag a difficult question and come back to it if you have time. It's just not a good strategy to rush through and rely on double-checking. You want to answer the questions when the passage is fresh in your mind.

This can be particularly difficult if you have test anxiety. You may feel rushed and antsy. Or maybe you are worried you won't have time to check your answers. But the fact is, doing the questions one time thoroughly is much more effective than rushing through them and coming back to check your work. Remember the PSAT is not only asking you to make sentence-level changes like punctuation and subject-verb agreement, but it's also asking you to make paragraph and passage-level changes like transitioning between ideas and reordering sentences. These questions will be much harder if you've been rushing through and don't have an idea of the passage as a whole.

Read the entire passage. Practice doing each question once slowly. Take your time, trust your gut, and make a decision. Then move on. And remember, if you are finishing very early, you can underline as you read to slow yourself down.

Strategy 4: Use Process of Elimination

You've certainly heard of process of elimination. The idea is that even if you don't know the correct answer right away, you can eliminate those answers you know are definitely not correct. This same concept can be applied to the PSAT, and it can be taken a step further. Get rid of the answers you know are incorrect. On the Writing and Language test, you can often identify incorrect answers because they are very similar to other choices.

Process of elimination allows you to get rid of any obviously wrong answers and any answers that do the same thing:

The bird, green and blue in color, was singing, it was a song from my childhood.

(A) NO CHANGE
(B) The green bird, which also had blue in its feathers, was singing a song I recognized from my childhood.
(C) The blue bird, which also had green in its feathers, was singing a song from my childhood that I recognized.
(D) The green and blue bird was singing a song from my childhood.

Using process of elimination, eliminate the answers that are obviously wrong and that make the same mistakes, like being too wordy. Using just this strategy, you can select (D) as the correct answer.

Consider the following exercises:

The bird sat on the window ledge, its wings fluttering.

(A) NO CHANGE
(B) ledge.
(C) ledge;
(D) ledge:

Here, the answer must be A. First, eliminate B and C because semicolons and periods do the exact same thing. Then, you're deciding between the comma and colon. Since this doesn't open to a clarification or a list, the colon isn't appropriate. That leaves you with A.

Will earned first place at the <u>tournament, though</u> he was invited back for the championships the following weekend.

(A) NO CHANGE
(B) tournament, and
(C) tournament, but
(D) tournament, yet

Here, B has to be the correct answer. A, C, and D all transition with a word that shows contrast. Since they all three do the same thing, eliminate them. It makes your job a lot easier when you can get rid of two or three of the answer choices right away.

Strategy 5: Don't Get Caught Up in Preferences

The PSAT tests conventions, not pet peeves or styles. By reviewing the concepts in this chapter, you've already prepared yourself for the rules you'll be tested on. What you don't want to do is get caught up in stylistic issues. Students often say they knew the correct answer was correct, but they didn't choose it because it used first person ("I") or because the sentence began with "and" or "because." There is no rule against using informal language. There is no rule against beginning a sentence with "and" or "because," permitting that it's still a complete and logical sentence. The truth is, in an effort to stop young writers from being too personal and informal on academic assignments, teachers banned first person. And in an effort to discourage fragments, teachers told students never to begin sentences with a conjunction. But, these are not rules of standard English. They are merely well-intentioned preferences that have stuck way too long.

In Chapter 5, the Oxford comma was also discussed. The Oxford comma is the comma before the "and" in a list of items. Some people prefer not to use this, saying it's unnecessary. Others swear by it, saying sentences can get very confusing without it. Once again, this is a style issue. It will not be tested by the PSAT.

Can you think of any others? Is there something one of your past teachers told you never to do simply because it drove him or her insane? (I had an English teacher who hated first person. I had another who told us never to use dashes.) Remember that the PSAT is testing whether you know the rules, so don't waste time and energy getting hung up on styles.

Strategy 6: "It Sounds Right" Is Good Enough

Even after you review all the mini-lessons in Chapter 5 and master the grammar concepts, you won't be asked to recall the rules or to explain your choices. When you fix a comma, you won't be asked how you made that decision. You won't be asked to define or explain prepositional phrases or misplaced modifiers.

You might recognize that active voice sounds more precise and concise, but you might not remember that active voice is when the actor comes before the action in a sentence. You might not even remember that it's called active voice. That's okay! Put simply, if you know it's right, that's good enough. You don't necessarily have to know *why* it's right. You won't be tested on terminology at all.

You use language constantly. Just by speaking and reading, you become familiar with a lot of these concepts and you can *hear* what's correct. Many times, you'll encounter a question and choose the answer based on the fact that it's the one that *sounds right*. Good for you. That's a legitimate enough reason. Certainly, there are exceptions. In daily speech, we say things incorrectly all the time. We use *who* when we mean *whom*. We almost always converse in run-on sentences. We employ slang and double negatives. But generally speaking, we can tell a lot about what's correct by how it sounds. Trust yourself. Mouth the words and hear them. If they sound weird, chances are something is wrong. And when all else fails, choose the answer that sounds correct.

Strategy 7: "It Sounds Smart" Is Not Good Enough

A huge mistake that students make on standardized testing is choosing an answer because it sounds smart. Don't do that. Never opt for a choice because it uses unnecessarily big words and goes on and on. In fact, these wordy, embellished sentences are not what the test is looking for at all. Instead, the PSAT is looking for the concise answer. The definition of *concise*, according to the Oxford Living Dictionaries online, is "giving a lot of information clearly and in a few words; brief but comprehensive." So, the PSAT is looking for the answer choice with the necessary information but in a manner that is short and to the point.

This doesn't mean that the shortest answer is always correct. However, it does mean that answer choices that are lengthy, wordy, and overly complex can be eliminated. Think of it this way: say yes to detail, no to repetition. If extra words are being used to describe something more specifically and fully, it's probably safe to say they should stay. But if extra words are fluff—they're just there to sound fancy and repeat things already said—get rid of them.

Strategy 8: Never Leave a Question Blank

There is no guessing penalty on the PSAT. That's worth saying twice. *There is no guessing penalty.* What that means for you is that you should never, ever leave a question blank. Have a letter ready for your guesses, and always use the same letter. If you truly have no clue about a question, don't waste your time on it. Fill in your letter and keep chugging along. A mistake many students make is wasting time on a difficult question that they are probably going to end up getting incorrect anyway. As a result of getting hung up for say two or three minutes on one question, they have to hurry through the last five questions of the test. So they missed the difficult question that they spent so much time on, but then they also missed three easier questions that they would have gotten correct had they had appropriate time to address them. You see where this is going—four missed questions instead of just the one.

Smart test-takers know that getting an excellent score doesn't mean you get every question right. Instead, it means that you come to the test with a plan and make sound decisions. You never leave a question blank. And when one tricky question is holding you back from getting to several other more manageable questions, you guess and move on. Students who score the highest on these tests are not necessarily smarter than their peers. Rather, these students have prepared, and they know how the test works. They don't sacrifice a group of questions just to get one particularly aggravating question right.

Guessing can be painful for many students, especially gifted students who are used to exceptional grades and high test results. You can avoid the panic that comes with this by already including guessing in your game plan. Pick your letter now. It doesn't matter which letter. Take one of the full-length practice tests and score yourself. Based on that score, decide how many guesses you'll allot yourself. For instance, a student who scores 38/44 and finishes with a minute to go might decide he or she has three free guesses. A student who scores 28/44 and finishes 30 seconds after the time might decide he or she has 10 free guesses. Regardless of what you decide, work these guesses into your plan so that there's no anxiety around them. You already know you'll be guessing on a few questions, and you already know which letter you'll be guessing. It's part of your plan for test day.

LET'S PRACTICE

Directions: Each passage is accompanied by questions that ask you to revise or edit the passage to improve its flow, organization, clarity, and sentence mechanics. For most questions, you will be directed to an underlined portion of the passage to either choose "NO CHANGE" or to select the appropriate revision. For other questions, you'll be asked to think about the passage as a whole. Some passages may also include a graphic to consider as you edit.

Questions 1–11 are based on the following passage.

The following passage is adapted from an 1890 travel guide by E. L. Lomax, titled Oregon, Washington and Alaska: Sights and Scenes for the Tourist.

Portland is a very beautiful city of 60,000 inhabitants, and situated on the Willamette river twelve miles from its junction with the Columbia. It is perhaps true of many of the growing cities of the West, that they **1** cannot possibly offer no matter what the same social advantages as the older cities of the East. But this is principally the case as to what may be called boom cities, **2** where the larger part of the population is of that floating class which follows in the line of temporary growth for the purposes of speculation, and in no sense applies to those centers of trade whose prosperity is based **3** in the solid foundation of legitimate business.

1. (A) NO CHANGE
   (B) simply cannot offer despite their best efforts
   (C) do not provide as desired
   (D) do not offer

2. (A) NO CHANGE
   (B) who
   (C) which
   (D) whereas

3. (A) NO CHANGE
   (B) on
   (C) about
   (D) within

As the metropolis of a vast section of country, having broad agricultural valleys filled with improved farms, surrounded by mountains rich in mineral wealth, and boundless forests of as fine timber as the world produces, the cause of Portland's growth and prosperity **4** are the trade which it has as the center of collection and distribution of this great wealth of natural resources, and it has attracted, not the boomer and **5** speculator, who find their profits in the wild excitement of the boom, but the merchant, manufacturer, and investor, who seek the surer if slower channels of legitimate business and investment.

These have come from the **6** East; most of them within the last few years. They came as seeking a better and wider field to engage in the same occupations they had followed in their Eastern homes, and bringing with them all the love of polite life which they had acquired there, have established here a new society, **7** that promises to be worth the current sacrifice down the road when it eventually prospers. Here are as fine churches, as complete a system of schools, as fine residences, **8** as great a love of music and art, as can be found at any city of the East of equal size.

4. (A) NO CHANGE
   (B) is
   (C) was
   (D) were

5. (A) NO CHANGE
   (B) speculator—whom find they're profits in the wild excitement of the boom—
   (C) speculator, who find there profits in the wild excitement of the boom—
   (D) speculator: who find their profits in the wild excitement of the boom,

6. (A) NO CHANGE
   (B) East
   (C) East,
   (D) East:

7. Which choice best concludes the sentence and conveys the idea that the overall quality of life in Portland is comparable to that of eastern cities?

   (A) NO CHANGE
   (B) with more affordable real estate than New York offers.
   (C) equaling in all respects that which they left behind.
   (D) inferior but propitious.

8. (A) NO CHANGE
   (B) upon a passion
   (C) and a love
   (D) with a love

9 Thus, Portland may justly claim to be the peer of any city of its size in the United States in all that pertains to social life, in the attractions of beauty of location and surroundings, it stands without 10 its peer. The work of art is but the copy of nature. What the residents of other cities see but in the copy, or must travel half the world over to see in the original, the resident of Portland has at his very door. In short, within a few hours' walk of the heart of this busy city are beauties surpassing the White Mountains or Adirondacks, and the grandeur of the Alps lies within the limits of a day's picnicking.

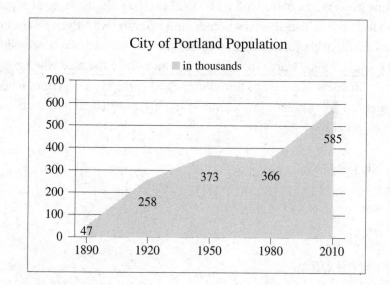

9. (A) NO CHANGE
   (B) But, while Portland
   (C) Consequently, Portland
   (D) As a result, Portland

10. (A) NO CHANGE
    (B) it's
    (C) its'
    (D) their

11. Does the information in the graph align with the information given in the passage?

   (A) Yes, because the growing population in the 1990s proves that Portland is prosperous.

   (B) Yes, because more easterners came to Portland once they read the travel guide.

   (C) No, because the population given in the graph is less than the population reported by the writer.

   (D) No, because the population given in the graph is more than the population reported by the writer.

12. Based on the information given in the passage, what might be a contributing reason for Portland's population growth?

   (A) its social advantages that far outweigh those of eastern cities

   (B) its abundance of silver for mining

   (C) its proximity to Seattle

   (D) its great wealth of natural resources

PRACTICE QUESTION ANSWERS

1. **(D)** Remember to look for the concise answer. (A), (B), and (C) are all too wordy. Choice (D) effectively gets the point across and manages to stay brief and to the point.

2. **(A)** Decide what the modifier is describing. It's describing "boom cities," a location. For people, use "who" and "whom." For things, use "that" and "which." For places, use "where" and "in which."

3. **(B)** Here, mouth it out and hear which choice sounds best. Prosperity is based *on* the solid foundation. You can also think about this literally—you rest *on* a foundation. Another approach is to eliminate (A) and (D) because they are doing the same thing and then decide between (B) and (C).

4. **(B)** This is a subject-verb agreement question. Locate your subject: "the cause." Now, read it with nothing in between: "the cause is the trade." You know to stay in present tense because the sentence starts with "As the metropolis," and so you want to maintain that.

5. **(A)** This question has a lot going on, but use it to your advantage. First, eliminate (B) and (C) because they don't have the correct usage of "their." Then, eliminate (D) because of the colon. Remember that for additional information, we either surround it by commas or, if we need a hard pause because it's an interruption, dashes. Either way, the punctuation needs to stay consistent.

6. **(C)** First eliminate (A) and (D). The semicolon doesn't work because the second portion is not a complete sentence. The colon doesn't work because it isn't appropriate, because we aren't clarifying or beginning a list. Now, you're deciding between (B) and (C). When you read it, you realize that we need a pause there, so a comma is appropriate.

7. **(C)** This is a difficult question. Read it carefully. We are looking for the choice that says Portland is generally comparable or equal to eastern cities when it comes to quality of life. Eliminate (A) and (D) because they are both saying the same thing, that Portland is not comparable now but will be in the future. Now, (B) focuses on real estate rather than overall quality of life, so get rid of it too.

8. **(A)** Remember to keep the sentence parallel. The current sentence structure lists each item, beginning with "as," so you want to maintain that pattern.

9. **(B)** Here, you are looking for an appropriate transition. The easiest way to approach this question is to eliminate (A), (C), and (D) because they are all doing the same thing—establishing a cause and effect relationship. Those transition words are synonymous. Another way to approach this question is to read the sentence carefully and see that the writer is making a contrast. Portland is a peer in size, but a superior in beauty. "But" is the only contrast word.

10. **(A)** The intended meaning here is possessive. Remember that "its" shows possession, and "it's" is a contraction for "it is." That being said, this is correct as it is.

11. **(C)** The graph records Portland's population. The passage doesn't predict anything for the 1990s, so eliminate (A). There's no evidence to show that the travel guide itself inspired any great migration, so (B) is out too. In the first lines of the passage, the author gives the population as 60,000. We know from the introduction to the passage that it was written in 1890. According to the graph, the population of Portland in 1890 was about 47,000. Therefore, (C) is the correct answer.

12. **(D)** The passage focuses heavily on Portland's natural resources and beauty. It doesn't mention silver specifically, nor does it mention Seattle. And if you check the passage, (A) is not supported. The author believes that Portland can match the social advantages of the East but does not suggest it can surpass those. Instead, Portland surpasses the East in natural resources and beauty.

PART 5

Math

CHAPTER 7

Introduction to the Math Section

There are two math sections in the PSAT. The No Calculator section comes first; it is 25 minutes long and there are 17 questions in this section. This section has 13 multiple-choice questions and 4 grid-in questions. Then there is the Calculator section; it is 45 minutes long and there are 31 questions in this section. This section has 28 multiple-choice questions and 4 grid-in questions.

SECTION	TIME	MULTIPLE CHOICE	GRID-IN	TOTAL
No Calculator	25 Minutes	13	4	17
Calculator	45 Minutes	28	4	31

Calculator Section

It is important to use your calculator in the calculator section of the Math test. Correctly using the calculator will save you valuable time. However, even in the calculator section, there are many questions where use of the calculator is not essential. Use your judgment as you do questions in this section; decide if it is faster to do the question using a calculator or if it is faster to do the question without the calculator. Do not over-rely on the calculator.

No Calculator Section

The No Calculator section is the shorter of the two sections, but it is also important to do well in this section. This section will test you on math concepts from the simple to the complicated. You will have to rely on hand calculations, but most questions will not test you on very complicated calculations. It is important to review your basic math skills, but know that most of the questions in this section will test your math knowledge on various concepts.

Multiple-Choice Questions

The multiple choice questions are straightforward. Use the multiple choices to your advantage. If you cannot find the correct answer, take a guess. There is no penalty for guessing. Use elimination to rule out answers that are not possible or plausible. This will increase the likelihood that you will guess correctly. Be aware of the trick answer choices as well; there are often answer choices that are included to mislead you. For example, there are some answer choices that are answers to only part of the question or answers that look similar to the correct answer. After you finish the question, make sure your answer choice answers the entire question and not only part of the question.

Grid-in Questions

The grid-in questions only represent a small part of the math section. These questions can seem more difficult because there are no answer choices as guidance. However, these questions may not be more difficult than the multiple-choice questions. It is critical to mark the answer sheet correctly. Please review the directions before moving forward on this section.

Follow these guidelines when filling in the answers:

- Mark only one circle in each column.
- Only the filled-in answer will be graded. Any additional work written elsewhere will not be graded.
- There may be different possible answers to questions in this section, but only fill in one answer.
- You can choose which column you would like to start filling in your answer.
- The answers should be within four decimal places.
- The answers should be positive numbers. There are no negative answers in this section.
- The answers can be fractions or decimals.
- Fractions should be simplified.
- Only improper fractions can be used and not mixed numbers.

The figure shows a sample of the grid-in instructions.

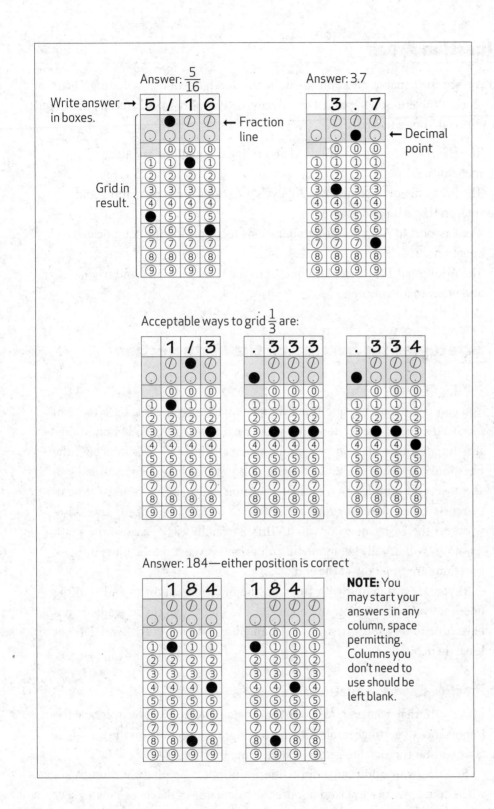

Answer: $\frac{5}{16}$

Write answer → in boxes.

← Fraction line

Grid in result.

Answer: 3.7

← Decimal point

Acceptable ways to grid $\frac{1}{3}$ are:

Answer: 184—either position is correct

NOTE: You may start your answers in any column, space permitting. Columns you don't need to use should be left blank.

1. Only the filled-in circles are graded. The directions suggest writing the answer in the box at the top, but it is not scored.

2. Fill in only one circle in any column.

3. There are no negative answers.

4. Only fill in one correct answer, even if there are more than one.

5. **Mixed numbers** like $2\frac{1}{2}$ should be filled in as 2.5 or 5/2.

6. **Decimal answers:** If you obtain a decimal answer with more digits, it should be filled in to fill the entire grid.

Question Areas

There are four major question areas in the math sections, including Heart of Algebra, Problem Solving and Data Analysis, Passport to Advanced Math, and Additional Topics in Math.

- The Heart of Algebra questions focus on linear equations and linear inequalities.
- The Problem Solving and Data Analysis questions focus on reading and interpreting data and graphs.
- The Passport to Advanced Math questions focus on solving complicated equations.
- The Additional Topics in Math questions focus on geometry and trigonometry and other math concepts.

Strategies for Success on the Math Section

Skip Questions

You can try to skip the questions you are stuck on and come back to them toward the end of the section, after you have finished all the other questions. It is important to stay on pace and answer all the questions. Since all the questions are worth the same amount of points, it is not a good strategy to spend several minutes on a difficult question and not give yourself time to complete other questions that may prove to be less difficult for you. Also, work on the easier questions first. This is usually easy because the math questions will usually get more difficult progressively, and the more difficult questions are generally at the end.

If you are struggling with time, do the questions in order and skip the ones that you are stuck on and come back to them later. If you really do not have time to do these questions, take an educated guess at the end. Do not leave them blank.

Practice Basic Calculations

Make sure that you practice your basic calculations. Do not overlook the importance of getting simple calculations right. Doing well on the no calculator section is crucial to getting a high score on your PSAT.

Practice your addition, subtraction, multiplication, and division. Also, when doing practice tests, do not use the calculator in the no calculator section. The calculations in the no calculator section are usually easy, but be careful not to make simple mistakes.

Use the Calculator Correctly

It is important to use the calculator correctly in the calculator section. Do not over-rely on using the calculator; some questions require almost no calculation. Try to think about how to solve the questions first before jumping to calculations. Write down the information each question gives you and make sure you understand what the questions is asking you for. Taking the time to understand the question before relying on your calculator will save you time in the long run.

Do try to use the calculator for the calculations because it will be more time efficient. Using the calculator even for simple questions may save you from making simple calculation mistakes as well.

The Aim Is to Get the Correct Answer

The aim is to get the correct answer. Therefore, solve the question using the easiest and most time-efficient way possible. Because you will not be graded on the work you have done on the questions and no partial grade will be given for work shown, you should focus on getting the answer correct using the easiest method.

This means that sometimes you will need to solve the questions backward by plugging in each of the answers to the question. You may even start by plugging in the most likely answer, based on your judgment, to try to solve the question backward.

Understand Your Mistakes

Use the practice questions to understand your mistakes. Every time you get a question wrong, it is an opportunity for you to learn what you did wrong and improve your skills. Focus your efforts on reviewing the questions that you did not answer correctly and make sure you understand them after looking through the answer explanation.

Make sure you mark the questions you have skipped or guessed on. Even if you have guessed these questions correctly, you probably do not understand how and why. Treat these questions like the ones you did not get correct.

Study Your Weak Areas

Use the questions you did not answer correctly as a guide to help you understand your areas of weakness. Go to these areas and focus your effort on learning and improving your weakness.

If you are confident about a section in the math section, you may focus more of your studying on sections that you are less competent in.

Do Not Jump to Calculations

Read the question carefully, and do not jump to calculations. Think about what is the easiest way to solve the question. Think before you calculate everything whether all the calculations are needed. There are questions in which you are asked to give an answer that is traditionally only a middle step in that type of question. There are also questions where calculations are not needed. Do not assume you know what the question is about before reading the whole question. Decide what the question is asking before you do the math.

CHAPTER 8

Heart of Algebra

The Heart of Algebra questions focus on key algebra concepts and especially on linear equations and inequalities.

Linear Equations with One Variable

Linear equations are the basics of the Heart of Algebra. It will require multiple steps to solve this type of question. First simplify the equation, then solve for the variable.

Example

$y = -3x - 6$

At which value of x does the line crosses the x-axis?

(A) -2
(B) -3
(C) -6
(D) 6

Solution

STEP 1
First, recognize that when the line crosses the x-axis, $y = 0$.

STEP 2
Set $y = 0$.

$-3x - 6 = 0$

STEP 3
Add 6 to both sides to move the number to the other side of the equation.

$-3x = 6$

STEP 4

Divide both sides by -3 to solve for the x value.

$$\frac{-3x}{-3} = \frac{6}{-3}$$

$$x = -2$$

STEP 5

Select the correct answer; the answer is A.

A System of Two Linear Equations with Two Variables

A system of two linear equations can be more difficult than linear equations with one variable. Solving a system of two linear equations requires multiple steps. First simplify the equations. Then use both equations to solve for the first variable, and use the first variable to solve for the second variable.

Example

$$y = 4x + 6$$

$$y = 3x + 8$$

If (x, y) is the solution to the system of equations, above what does $y - x$ equal?

(A) 2
(B) 10
(C) 12
(D) 14

Solution

STEP 1

Recognize that this is a system of equations question. You must solve the equation to get the x and y values.

STEP 2

Set the two equations equal to each other.

$$4x + 6 = 3x + 8$$

STEP 3

Solve for x.

$$4x + 6 - 6 = 3x + 8 - 6$$

$$4x = 3x + 2$$

$$4x - 3x = 3x - 3x + 2$$

$$x = 2$$

STEP 4

Plug in x to one of the equations to find the value of y.

$$y = 4x + 6$$

$$y = 4(2) + 6$$

$$y = 14$$

STEP 5

Find the answer of $y - x$

$$14 - 2 = 12$$

STEP 6

Select the correct answer; the answer is C.

A System of Two Linear Inequalities with Two Variables

A system of two linear inequalities is similar to a system of two linear equations but can be more difficult. The inequalities are multistep problems. First simplify the inequality. Then use both inequalities to solve for the first variable, and use the first variable to solve for the second variable. Sometimes it is easier to solve these questions using trial and error.

Example

Which point satisfies both $4y - x > 4$ and $y > -\dfrac{3x}{4} + 4$?

(A) (4, 3)

(B) (2, –5)

(C) (0, 0)

(D) (–1, –5)

Solution

STEP 1

First, recognize that it is easiest to solve this question using trial and error. Try each of the answer choices.

STEP 2

To see which pair satisfies both equations, plug each of the points into both equations and find the point that satisfies both equations.

STEP 3

Plug in answer choice A. Plug (4, 3) into the first equation.

$$4(3) - (4) > 4$$

and get $8 > 4$

This means that the point satisfies the first equation

STEP 4

Plug in answer choice A. Plug (4, 3) into the second equation.

$$3 > -\frac{3 \times 4}{4} + 4$$
$$3 > -3 + 4$$

$$3 > 1$$

This means that the point also satisfies the second equation.

STEP 5

At this point, the correct answer is A, and there is no need to test the other answer choices. Select the correct answer.

Please note that another way of solving this question is to graph out the two equations and see which points satisfy both equations.

Linear Functions and Graphical Representations

It is important to understand the relationship between linear functions and their graphical representations. Use the line equation $y = mx + b$ to help you graph the lines.

$y = mx + b$

m is the slope of the line

b is the y intercept

Example

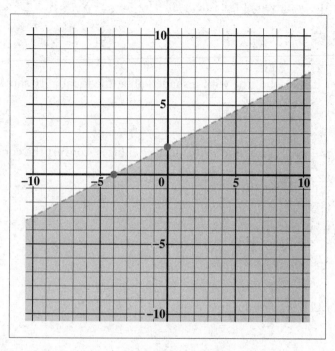

The inequality shown in the above graph is which of the following?

(A) $x + 4 \geq 2y$

(B) $y \leq -\dfrac{1}{2}x + 2$

(C) $y \geq -\dfrac{1}{2}x + 4$

(D) $y \leq -\dfrac{1}{2}x - 2$

Solution

STEP 1

Recognize that this is a graphing question. Use the equation of the straight line, $y = mx + b$, to find the equation for the line in the graph.

STEP 2

Find the slope by looking at the rise over run. The rise here is 1 and run is 2. The slope is $\dfrac{1}{2}$.

STEP 3

Look at the y intercept to find b, which is 2.

STEP 4

Put together the equation of the line.

$$y = \frac{1}{2}x + 2$$

STEP 5

Then because it is a solid line with a shaded area, the inequality shown is $y \leq \frac{1}{2}x + 2$.

STEP 6

Because is $y \leq \frac{1}{2}x + 2$ is not one of the answer choices, convert the equation to get $x + 4 \geq 2y$.

$$y \times 2 \leq (\frac{1}{2}x + 2) \times 2$$

$$2y \leq x + 4$$

$$x + 4 \geq 2y$$

STEP 7

Select the correct answer; the answer is A.

LET'S PRACTICE

1. What is the x intercept of $y = -\frac{2x}{3} + 6$?

   (A) 9

   (B) $-\frac{2}{3}$

   (C) −18

   (D) 18

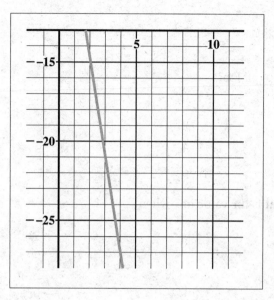

2. What is the *x* intercept of the line shown in the graph above?

   (A) –6
   (B) 3
   (C) –3
   (D) $-\dfrac{1}{2}$

   $y = 3x - 10$

   $y = 5$

3. At which coordinate do the two lines intersect?

   (A) (3, 5)
   (B) (15, 5)
   (C) (5, 5)
   (D) (5, 15)

4. Which point satisfies both $x > 3$ and $-x + 2y < 6$?

   (A) (–2, 5)
   (B) (4, 0)
   (C) (0, 0)
   (D) (3, 6)

$$7x - 1 = 10y$$
$$x - 1 = y$$

5. What is $x + y$ equal to?

    (A) 1
    (B) 4
    (C) 5
    (D) 10

6. If $y = \dfrac{21}{11}$, what is the value of x when $\dfrac{x}{7} = \dfrac{3}{y}$?

    (A) 11

    (B) $\dfrac{11}{7}$

    (C) $\dfrac{11}{63}$

    (D) $\dfrac{77}{21}$

7. What is the slope of the line $2y - x = 6$?

    (A) $\dfrac{1}{2}$

    (B) 2

    (C) $-\dfrac{1}{2}$

    (D) -2

8. What is the y intercept of line $4y = 8 - x$?

    (A) -4
    (B) 2
    (C) 4
    (D) 8

9. If $y = 3$, what is x when $\dfrac{x}{y} = \dfrac{3}{4}$?

   (A) 4

   (B) –4

   (C) $\dfrac{4}{9}$

   (D) $2\dfrac{1}{4}$

$$2y = 7x$$
$$y - 2x = 3$$

10. What is $y - x$ equal to?

   (A) –9

   (B) 5

   (C) 6

   (D) 9

PRACTICE QUESTION ANSWERS

1. **(A)** This is a simple graphing question. The x intercept is when $y = 0$, so plug 0 into the equation for y. $0 = -\dfrac{2x}{3} + 6$. Take away 6 on both sides, $-6 = -\dfrac{2x}{3}$. Then multiply both sides by 3, $18 = 2x$. Then divide both sides by 2, $9 = x$ Then the x intercept is 9.

2. **(D)** This is a linear algebra question. First find the equation of this line by using the line equation of $y = mx + b$. Find m, the slope: the line is negative because it is dropping as it goes from left to right. The line drops 6 units for every one unit to the right, so the slope is –6. Then because the y intercept is not shown, pick a point to plug into the new equation, which is now $y = -6x + b$. (2, –15) is an easy point to work with. Plug in this point to get $-15 = -6(2) + b$. Then, $b = -3$ and the equation of the line is $y = -6x - 3$. Because the x intercept is when $y = 0$, plug in $y = 0$. $0 = -6x - 3$; $x = -\dfrac{1}{2}$ and the x intercept is $-\dfrac{1}{2}$.

3. **(C)** This is a system of equations problem. First, substitute $y = 5$ into the first equation ($5 = 3x - 10$). Then take away –10 from both sides ($15 = 3x$). Then solve for x ($x = 5$). The x coordinate will be 5. Because the $y = 5$, the y coordinate does not need to be solved and will be 5. The coordinates of the intersection are (5, 5). The correct answer is then C.

4. **(B)** This is a simple inequality question. To see which points satisfies both equations, plug each of the points into both equations and find the point that satisfies both equations. For example, plug $(4, 0)$ into the first equation: $4 > 3$. This means that the point satisfies the first equation. Next plug $(4, 0)$ into the second equation: $-4 + 2(0) < 6$, and get $-4 < 6$. This means that the point also satisfies the second equation. Another way of solving this question is to graph out the two equations and see which points satisfy both equations.

5. **(C)** This is a system of equations problem. First, multiply the second equation by 10 to get $10x - 10 = 10y$. Then take away the first equation from the second one to get $3x - 9 = 0$; $3x = 9$; $x = 3$. Then plug x into the second equation to get y; $3 - 1 = y$; $y = 2$. Then, find what $x + y$ is equal to: $3 + 2 = 5$.

6. **(A)** This is a fraction question. First, plug in the value of y into the equation to get $\dfrac{x}{7} = 3 \div \dfrac{21}{11}$. Then, simplify to get $\dfrac{x}{7} = 3 \times \dfrac{11}{21}$. Simply again to get $\dfrac{x}{7} = \dfrac{11}{7}$. The answer is $x = 11$.

7. **(A)** This is a simple linear algebra question. Rearrange the question according to the equation of the line, $y = mx + b$, to get the answer. First, add x to both sides to get $2y = x + 6$. Then divide both sides by 2 to get $y = \dfrac{1}{2}x + 6$. The slope of this line is $\dfrac{1}{2}$.

8. **(B)** This is a simple linear algebra question. Because the y intercept is when $x = 0$, plug in $x = 0$. $4y = 8 - 0$; $4y = 8$; $y = 2$. The y intercept of the line is 2.

9. **(D)** This is a simple algebra question. Plug in $y = 3$ to the equation to get $\dfrac{x}{3} = \dfrac{3}{4}$. Then multiply both sides by 12 to get $4x = 9$. Then divide both sides by 4 to get $x = 2\dfrac{1}{4}$.

10. **(B)** This is a system of equations problem. First, multiply the second equation by 2 to get $2y - 4x = 6$. Then rearrange this equation to get $2y = 4x + 6$. Then set this equation as equal to the first equation to get $7x = 4x + 6$. Then add $4x$ to both sides to get $3x = 6$ and $x = 2$. Then plug x into the first equation to get y; $2y = 7(2)$; $2y = 14$; $y = 7$. Then, find what $y - x$ is equal to: $7 - 2 = 5$.

CHAPTER 9

Problem Solving and Data Analysis

The Problem Solving and Data Analysis section focuses on solving problems in which data and different levels of analysis are required.

Ratios

You will use ratios to solve multistep problems. These questions generally range from medium difficult to difficult and can involve multiple sets of ratios.

Example

Questions 1 and 2 are based on the following information:

A gum ball machine contains three flavors of gum: strawberry, blueberry, and cherry, at a ratio of 7:3:5.

1. If there are 21 strawberry-flavored gum balls, how many gum balls are there in total?

   (A) 15
   (B) 45
   (C) 56
   (D) 84

2. If there are 36 blueberry-flavored gum balls, how many more strawberry-flavored gum balls are in the machine than the cherry flavor gum balls?

(A) 24
(B) 36
(C) 56
(D) 64

Solution

Question 1

STEP 1

This is a ratio question, so first set up the ratio.

STEP 2

If there are 21 strawberry-flavored gum balls, then the ratio of the gum balls would be 21:9:15.

$$3 \times 7 = 21$$

The other two will be $3 \times 3 = 9$ and $3 \times 5 = 15$

STEP 3

Therefore, the total will be 45.

$$21 + 9 + 15 = 45$$

STEP 4

Select the correct answer; the answer is B.

Question 2

STEP 1

This is a ratio question, so first set up the ratio.

STEP 2

If there are 36 blueberry- flavored gum balls, then the ratio of the gum balls would be 84:36:60.

$$12 \times 3 = 36$$

The other two will be $7 \times 12 = 84$ and $5 \times 12 = 60$

STEP 3

Therefore, the difference will be 24.

$$84 - 60 = 24$$

STEP 4

Select the correct answer; the answer is A.

Rates

Rate questions can be tricky for students. It is key to remember that rate questions are similar to speed questions, and time × rate = amount.

Example

> Felicia and Shimi are working together to pack toys. Felicia can pack 8 bags of toys in one hour. Shimi can pack 6 bags of toys in one hour. How long would it take for Shimi and Felicia to pack 10 bags of toys if they work together? Round to the nearest minute.
>
> (A) 1 hour 5 minutes
> (B) 43 minutes
> (C) 1 hour 13 minutes
> (D) 2 hours

Solution

STEP 1

This is a multistep word problem. Find the number of bags of toys the two can pack in one hour if they work together

> 8 + 6 = 14 bags per one hour

STEP 2

Then find how long it would take to pack 10 bags of toys if they work together:

> 10 bag ÷ 14 bags per hour = 0.71 hours

STEP 3

Because the answer needs to be in minutes, convert the answer from hours to minutes.

> 0.71 hours × 60 minutes per hour = 43 min

STEP 4

Select the correct answer; the answer is B.

Scatterplot and Relationship Between Variables

Interpret the scatterplot and the line of best fit to judge the relationship between variables.

Example

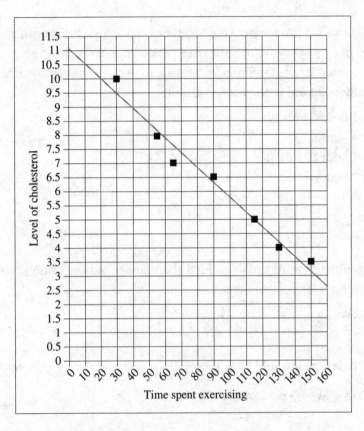

A researcher is conducting a study regarding the number of minutes a person spends exercising in a day and its relationship with the person's cholesterol level. Which of the following statements is true regarding the graph above?

(A) The slope represents the increase in the person's cholesterol level as the number of minutes a person spends exercising in a day increases.

(B) The slope represents the decrease in the person's cholesterol level as the number of minutes a person spends exercising in a day increases.

(C) The slope represents the increase in the number of minutes a person spends exercising in a day as a person has a higher cholesterol level.

(D) The slope represents the decrease in the number of minutes a person spends exercising in a day as a person has a lower cholesterol level.

Solution

STEP 1

This is a data analysis question. First find the relationship between the variables. The graph shows that as the number of minutes a person spends exercising in a day increases, he or she will have a lower cholesterol level.

STEP 2

Find what each variable represents.

The x value is the amount of time and y value is the cholesterol level. Based on this information, the slope represents the decrease in the person's cholesterol level as the number of minutes a person spends exercising in a day increases.

STEP 3

Select the correct answer; the answer is B.

Median, Mode, Mean and Range

It is important to know how to calculate the median, mode, and range of a data set and to use these to solve questions.

* Median: The number that is in the middle of the data set and separates the higher numbers in the set from the lower numbers in the set.
* Mode: The number that appears the most often in the set of data.
* Mean: The average of the data set.
* Range: The difference between the biggest number and the smallest number in the data set.

Example

Questions 1 and 2 refer to the following information:

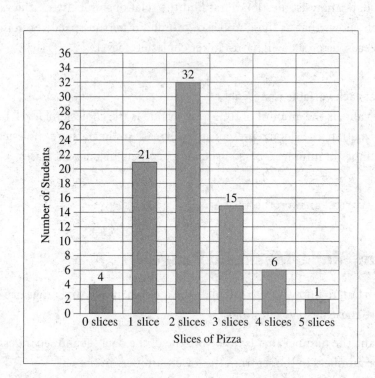

The debate club of a school is having a pizza party at the beginning of the year. The secretary of the club is keeping track of how many slices of pizza each person has to be able to estimate how many pizzas he has to order for the next event. The graph shows how many students have 0 slices, 1 slice, 2 slices, 3 slices, 4 slices, and 5 slices. For example, there are 4 students who did not have any pizza.

1. The secretary is trying to decide how many slices of pizza to order for each student. Which of the following information should he base his decision on?

   (A) Median
   (B) Mean
   (C) Mode
   (D) Range

2. What is the difference between the mode and the median of this set of data?

   (A) 1
   (B) 11
   (C) 17
   (D) 0

Solution

Question 1

STEP 1

This is a question about the median, mean, mode, and range, so look at the given information to see which would be important for answering this question.

STEP 2

In this question if the secretary needs to find out how many slices of pizza to order for each student, he needs the average or the mean of the set of data.

STEP 3

Select the correct answer; the answer is B.

Question 2

STEP 1

This is a question about the median, mean, mode, and range, so look at the given information to see which would be important for answering this question. In this case the mode and median are both important.

STEP 2

First find the mode, the number that appears the most often, which is 2.

There are 12 students who took 2 slices of pizza.

STEP 3

Then find the median, the number in the middle, which is also 2.

To find the median. Find the total number of students there are, $4 + 21 + 32 + 15 + 6 + 1 = 79$. Then find the middle number of 79, which is $\frac{(79-1)}{2} + 1 = 39$. Then find where the 39th number falls. Because 39 is bigger than the total number of students taking 0 and 1 slice, $4 + 21 = 25$, and smaller than the total number of students taking 0, 1, and 2 slices, $4 + 21 + 32 = 57$, The median of this data set is 2.

STEP 4

Find the difference between 2 and 2.

$2 - 2 = 0$

STEP 5

Select the correct answer; the answer is D.

LET'S PRACTICE

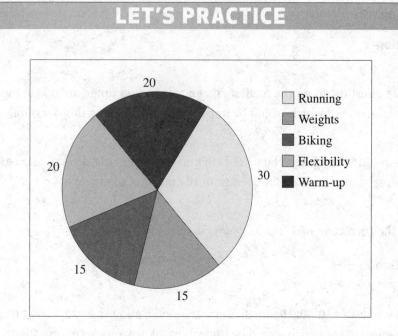

1. A student trains for 100 minutes each day to get ready for the school's running contest. He spends 30 minutes on running, 20 minutes on warm-ups, 20 minutes on flexibility, 15 minutes on biking, and 15 minutes on weights. In total, how many more hours does he spend on running than on weights?

   (A) 0.25
   (B) 1.5
   (C) 15
   (D) 20

Questions 2 and 3 refer to the following information.

Cecil and Nigel are driving from city A to city B. Cecil is driving at 50 km per hour. Nigel is driving slowly for the first $\frac{1}{3}$ of the distance at the speed of 40 km per hour. Then he drives faster for the rest of the trip at the speed of 80 km per hour.

2. Cecil starts driving at 8:30 a.m. and needs to be at city B for a meeting. If the distance between city A and city B is 250 km and Cecil needs to arrive at 3 p.m., how early or late will Cecil be?

   (A) 3.5 hours early
   (B) 1.5 hours early
   (C) on time
   (D) 1 hour late

3. The distance between city A and city B is 300 km. Nigel starts driving at 9:45 a.m. When will Nigel get to city B?

(A) 2:45 p.m.

(B) 4:25 p.m.

(C) 6:35 p.m.

(D) 7 p.m.

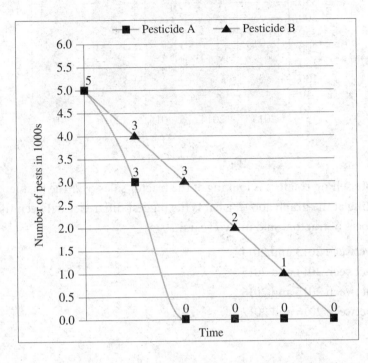

4. A farmer is testing two types of pesticides on her land, Pesticide A and Pesticide B. Which of the following statements is true about the two types of pesticides illustrated in the graph above?

(A) Pesticide A is faster than Pesticide B at killing pests.

(B) Pesticide B is faster than Pesticide A at killing pests.

(C) Pesticide A and Pesticide B are both equally effective at killing pests.

(D) It is impossible to tell which pesticide is more effective at killing pests.

5. After starting a new health regulation at a school, the number of unhealthy snacks sold at school was reduced by 20% during the first year and an additional 25% during the second year. If there are now only 12 kinds of unhealthy snacks sold at school, how many kinds were sold before the start of the health regulation?

(A) 18

(B) 20

(C) 21.81

(D) 26.67

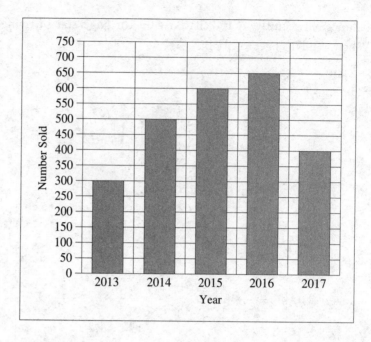

6. A store selling tractors is looking at the tractor sales over the past few years. Looking at the graph above, what is the biggest difference between the numbers of tractors sold in two years?

(A) between 2013 and 2014
(B) between 2014 and 2015
(C) between 2015 and 2016
(D) between 2016 and 2017

Questions 7 and 8 are based on the following information.

The school is starting a new program for its grade 9 students. Students are allowed to choose only one out of the following three classes: Arts, Home Economics, and Ceramics. The ratio of students who choose Arts class to Home Economics to Ceramics class is 2:3:5.

7. What is the percentage of students who choose Arts class?

(A) 20%
(B) 22%
(C) 40%
(D) 80%

8. If there are 24 students who chose Home Economics class, how many students are there in grade 9?

    (A) 48
    (B) 60
    (C) 72
    (D) 80

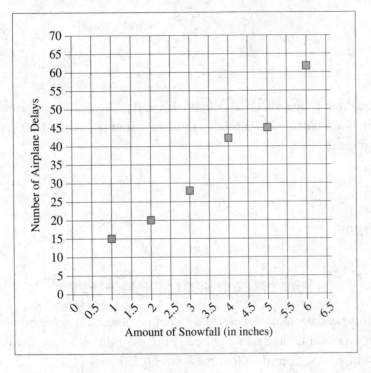

9. The international airport of a state collected data regarding airplane delays and the weather conditions. According to the graph above, what is the relationship between the amount of snowfall and the number of airplane delays at the airport?

    (A) low negative correlation between the amount of snowfall and the number of airplane delays at the airport
    (B) positive correlation between the amount of snowfall and the number of airplane delays at the airport
    (C) high negative correlation between the amount of snowfall and the number of airplane delays at the airport
    (D) no correlation between the amount of snowfall and the number of airplane delays at the airport

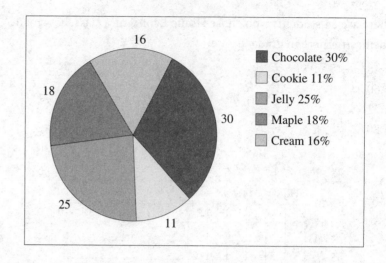

10. A doughnut shop sells 4,500 doughnuts per day. According to the above chart, how many more Maple doughnuts are sold per week than Cookie doughnuts?

(A) 315

(B) 351

(C) 450

(D) 2,205

PRACTICE QUESTION ANSWERS

1. **(A)** This is a data analysis question. First, find how many more minutes he spent on running than on weights, 30 min – 15 min = 15 min. Then convert that into hours: 15 min ÷ 60 min/1 hour = 0.25 hours.

2. **(B)** This is a multistep word problem. First find out how long it will take for Cecil to drive. Cecil is driving at 50 km/hr, so it takes 5 hours for him to get to city B (250 km/50 km per hr = 5 hr). Then find out when Cecil will arrive: 8:30 a.m. + 5 hours = 1:30 p.m. Cecil will arrive 1.5 hours early for the 3 p.m. meeting (3 p.m. – 1:30 p.m. = 1 hour 30 minutes/1.5 hours).

3. **(A)** This is a multistep word problem. To find the time it takes for Nigel, first find the time it takes for the first $\frac{1}{3}$ of the distance. This first $\frac{1}{3}$ of the distance is 300 km $\times \frac{1}{3}$ = 100 km. It took him 2.5 hours for the first $\frac{1}{3}$ of the distance (100 km / 40 km per hr = 2.5 hr). Then, find the time it takes for the rest of the distance. This rest of the distance is $\frac{2}{3}$ of the distance, which is: 300 km $\times \frac{2}{3}$ = 200 km. It took him 2.5 hours for the rest of the distance (200 km / 80 km per hr = 2.5 hr). It takes Nigel 5 hours of total driving time (2.5 hr + 2.5 hr = 5 hr). The arrival time will be 2:45 p.m. (9:45 a.m. + 5 hr = 2:45 p.m.).

4. **(A)** This is a data analysis question. The graph shows that the pests decline in numbers faster when using Pesticide A. Therefore, the answer is (A).

5. **(B)** This is a medium difficulty percent question. Although it might seem that this question is easier to solve backward, it is probably easier to start with 100% and reduce. Start with 100%, reduce by 20% to get to 80%, then reduce by another 25% to get to 60% of the original amount. Then, because 12 kinds of snacks left is 60% of the original number of snacks, set an equation to solve for the original 100%, $\dfrac{x}{100\%} = \dfrac{12}{60\%}$. Multiple both sides of the equation by 100% to get $x = \dfrac{12\,(100\%)}{60\%}$, $x = 20$. There were originally 20 unhealthy snacks sold in the school.

6. **(D)** This is a simple data analytics question. The answer to this question is (D) because the biggest difference between any two years is between 2016 and 2017 where the drop in sales is 250 (650 – 400 = 250).

7. **(A)** This is a simple ratio to percent question. First find the ratio of the students who took Arts class to the total number of students, which is 2:10 (2 + 3 + 5 = 10). Then set up an equation to solve for the percentage, $\dfrac{x}{100\%} = \dfrac{2}{10}$. Then solve the equation to get the percentage $x = \dfrac{2\,(100\%)}{10}$, $x = 20\%$.

8. **(D)** This is a medium difficulty level ratio question. First find the ratio of the students who took Home Economics class to the total number of students, which is 3:10 (2 + 3 + 5 = 10). Then set up an equation to solve for the total number of students, $\dfrac{x}{24} = \dfrac{10}{3}$. Then solve the equation to get the total number of students in grade 9, $x = \dfrac{10\,(24)}{3}$, $x = 80$.

9. **(B)** This is a simple question about data analytics. Because as the amount of snowfall increases the number of airplane delays at the airport also increases, there is a positive correlation between the amount of snowfall and the number of airplane delays at the airport. Therefore, the correct answer is (B).

10. **(D)** This is a medium difficulty question about data analytics and ratios. First, find the number of Maple doughnuts sold per day, 18% × 4,500 = 810. Then find the number of Cookie doughnuts sold per day, 11% × 4,500 = 495. Then find the difference between the number of Maple doughnuts sold and the number of Cookie doughnuts sold, 810 – 495 = 315. Then find the how many more Maple doughnuts are sold per week than Cookie doughnuts, 315 × 7 = 2,205.

CHAPTER 10

Passport to Advanced Math

The Passport to Advanced Math section focuses on topics and skills needed for studying advanced math.

Quadratic Equation

It is important to know how to solve quadratic equations. It is crucial to know how to FOIL and factor quadratic equations and how to use the quadratic equation.

Example

$16 - 9x^2 = ?$

(A) $(16)(9x^2)$
(B) $(4 + 3x)(4 - 3x)$
(C) $(x - 2)(x - 8)$
(D) $(4 + 3x)(4 + 3x)$

STEP 1

This is a simple algebra question. It is a difference of squares.

STEP 2

Factor the equation.

$(4 + 3x)(4 - 3x)$

STEP 3

Choose the correct answer, which is choice B.

Quadratic Formula

It is important to know how to use the quadratic formula to solve questions.

Quadratic formula: $x = \dfrac{-b \pm \sqrt{b^2 - 4ac}}{2a}$

Example

Which of these quadratic equations has no solution?

(A) $(x + 6)^2 = 1$
(B) $2(x + 12)(x - 11) = 0$
(C) $(x - 10)(x - 3) = 0$
(D) $(x - 7)(x - 8) = -3$

Solution

STEP 1

This is a difficult algebra question. First try to eliminate choices that are not correct. In this question, it is easy to see that choices B and C are solvable. Therefore eliminate choices B and C.

STEP 2

The only ones that are not solvable could be A and D. Here try to solve both problems to see which one is solvable and which is not.

STEP 3

If you try problem A, you will see that it is solvable with the quadratic formula.

STEP 4

Then try to see if choice D is solvable.

STEP 5

The problem needs to be first FOILed, then rearranged:

$(x - 7)(x - 8) = -3$

$x^2 - 15x + 56 = -3$

$x^2 - 15x + 56 + 3 = 0$

$x^2 - 15x + 59 = 0$

STEP 6

Then use the quadratic equation:

$x = \dfrac{-b \pm \sqrt{b^2 - 4ac}}{2a}$

$x = \dfrac{-(15) \pm \sqrt{(15)^2 - 4(1)(59)}}{2(1)}$

$$x = \frac{-(15) \pm \sqrt{225 - 236}}{2(1)}$$

STEP 7

Here you will see that the inside of the square root becomes a negative number.

$$x = \frac{-(15) \pm \sqrt{-11}}{2(1)}$$

Therefore choice D cannot be solved.

STEP 8

Select the correct answer, which is choice D.

Exponents

Exponent questions can be tricky and will sometimes require some trial and error to solve.

Example

If $x^{-\frac{4}{3}} = 16$, what is x?

(A) $-\frac{64}{3}$

(B) $\frac{1}{8}$

(C) 2

(D) $\frac{64}{3}$

Solution

STEP 1

This is a question about exponents. You will need to rearrange the equation to solve the problem.

STEP 2

First rearrange the equation $x^{-\frac{4}{3}} = 16$ to get:

$$\sqrt[4]{x^{-\frac{4}{3}}} = \sqrt[4]{16}$$

STEP 3

Then rearrange the equation $\sqrt[4]{x^{-\frac{4}{3}}} = \sqrt[4]{16}$ again to get:

$$x^{-\frac{1}{3}} = 2$$

STEP 4

Then raise both sides of the equation $x^{-\frac{1}{3}} = 2$ to the power of 3 and get:

$$\left(x^{-\frac{1}{3}}\right)^3 = (2)^3$$

STEP 5

Next the equation $\left(x^{-\frac{1}{3}}\right)^3 = (2)^3$ becomes $x^{-1} = 8$ and $x = \dfrac{1}{8}$.

STEP 6

Then the answer will be $\dfrac{1}{8}$ and choice B is the correct answer.

Polynomials and Fractions

There will sometimes be questions in which the polynomial will come in the form of a fraction. These questions may look difficult, but the bottom of the fraction can often be eliminated.

Example

$$\frac{3x^3 + 9x^2 - 4x + 12}{x + 3} = ?$$

(A) $3x^2 - 4$

(B) $x + 4$

(C) $x - 4$

(D) $x + 3$

Solution

STEP 1

This is an algebra question. This question looks difficult but is actually very simple. First factor out $x + 3$ from the equation on the top and get:

$$\frac{3x^2(x+3) - 4(x+3)}{x+3}$$

STEP 2

Then rearrange the equation to get:

$$\frac{\left(3x^2 - 4\right)\left(x + 3\right)}{x + 3}$$

STEP 3

Then eliminate $x + 3$ to get:

$$3x^2 - 4$$

STEP 4

Select the correct answer, which is choice A.

Nonlinear Equations

It is important to know how to solve nonlinear equations like parabolas.

Example

The axis of symmetry of the parabola with the equation $(x + 3)^2 - y = 0$
is $x = ?$

(A) 3
(B) 2
(C) –3
(D) –2

Solution

STEP 1

This is a simple parabola question. Use the equation of a parabola to solve this question:

$$y = (x - a)^2 + b$$

where (a, b) is the vertex

and a is also the axis of symmetry

STEP 2

Rearrange the equation.

$$(x + 3)^2 - y = 0$$

$$y = (x + 3)^2$$

$$y = (x - (-3))^2$$

The axis of symmetry is $x = -3$.

STEP 3

Select the correct answer, which is choice C.

1. If $n^{-\frac{1}{3}} = 15$, what is n?

(A) $-\dfrac{1}{5}$

(B) $\dfrac{1}{3,375}$

(C) $\dfrac{33}{75}$

(D) 5

2. If $f(x) = 27$ and $g(x) = |-x^2 - 2x| - 354$, what is $g(f(x))$?

(A) –729

(B) 156

(C) 321

(D) 429

3. $x^{\frac{2}{6}} = ?$

(A) $\sqrt[3]{x}$

(B) $\dfrac{x}{3}$

(C) $\sqrt{x}$

(D) $\dfrac{3}{6x}$

4. If $f(x) = x^2 + x - 10$, $g(x) = ((-x)^3)^2$, and $x = 10$, what is $g(f(x))$?

(A) 100,000

(B) 100,000,000

(C) 1,000,000,000,000

(D) 10,000,000,000,000

5. If $g(x) = x + 3$ and $f(x) = \dfrac{1}{2x}$, what is the value of $g\big(f(6)\big)$?

(A) $\dfrac{37}{12}$

(B) $-\dfrac{36}{12}$

(C) 36

(D) 9

6. If $f(x) = -x$ and $g(x) = |x^3 - x| + x^2$, and $x = 6$, what is $g\big(f(x)\big)$?

(A) −174

(B) 36

(C) 216

(D) 246

7. $\dfrac{x^2 + 3x - 10}{x - 2} < -8$

Given that x does not equal 2, which of the following is the same as the inequality above?

(A) $-x > 13$

(B) $x < -3$

(C) $x > -3$

(D) $x < -10$

8. If $8x^2 - 2x = 3$, which is a possible solution for x?

(A) $-\dfrac{1}{2}$

(B) $-\dfrac{3}{4}$

(C) $\dfrac{4}{3}$

(D) 2

9. If $f(x) = 13$ and $g(x) = 17 + x^2 - 2x$, what is $g\big(f(x)\big)$?

(A) 13

(B) 26

(C) 78

(D) 160

10. Which of the following is the same as $x^3 + 3x^2 - 4x - 12$?

    (A) $(x - 3)(x^2 + 4)$

    (B) $(x^2 + 3)(x - 4)$

    (C) $(x + 3)(x + 2)(x - 2)$

    (D) $x(x + 3)(x - 4)$

PRACTICE QUESTION ANSWERS

1. **(B)** This is a question about exponents. $\frac{1}{n^{\frac{1}{3}}} = 15$. First raise both sides of the equation to the power of 3 and get: $\left(n^{-\frac{1}{3}}\right)^3 = (15)^3$. Then the equation becomes $n^{-1} = 3{,}375$. Then the answer will be $\frac{1}{3{,}375}$ because $n = \frac{1}{3{,}375}$.

2. **(D)** This is a medium algebra question. If $f(x) = 27$, 27 can be plugged into $g(f(x))$. $g(f(x)) = g(27) = |-(27)^2 - 2(27)| - 354 = |-729 - 54| - 354 = 783 - 354 = 429$

3. **(A)** This is a question about exponents. $x^{\frac{2}{6}} = \sqrt[3]{x}$. First, simplify $x^{\frac{2}{6}} = x^{\frac{1}{3}}$. Then, $x^{\frac{1}{3}} = \sqrt[3]{x}$.

4. **(C)** This is a difficult algebra question. If $f(x) = x^2 + x - 10$, and $x = 10$, then $f(x) = (10)^2 + 10 - 10$. Here $f(x) = 100 + 10 - 10 = 100$. Then 100 can be plugged into $g(f(x))$. $g(f(x)) = ((-100)^3)^2 = (-1{,}000{,}000)^2 = 1{,}000{,}000{,}000{,}000$.

5. **(A)** This is a simple function question. First plug 6 into $f(x)$, $f(6) = \frac{1}{2(6)} = \frac{1}{12}$. Then solve for $g(f(6))$, $g(f(6)) = \frac{1}{12} + 3 = \frac{1}{12} + \frac{36}{12} = \frac{37}{12}$.

6. **(D)** This is a difficult algebra question. If $f(x) = -x$, and $x = 6$, then $f(x) = -6$. Then -6 can be plugged into $g(f(x))$. $g(f(x)) = g(-6) = |(-6)^3 - (-6)| + (-6)^2 = |-216 - (-6)| + 36 = |-216 + 6| + 36 = |-210| + 36 = 246$.

7. **(A)** This is medium difficulty inequality. First recognize that the top of the fraction can be factored, $\frac{(x+5)(x-2)}{x-2} < -8$. Then eliminate $x - 2$ to get $x + 5 < -8$ and simplify to get $x < -13$. Because $x < -13$ is not one of the choices, manipulate the inequality to get $-x > 13$.

8. **(A)** This is a difficult quadratic equation to solve. First, rearrange the equation by taking away 3 on both sides to get $8x^2 - 2x - 3 = 0$. Then factor this equation to get $(2x + 1)(4x - 3) = 0$. Then solve for the first bracket to get $2x + 1 = 0$; $2x = -1$; $x = -\dfrac{1}{2}$. Then solve for the second bracket to get $4x - 3 = 0$; $4x = 3$; $x = \dfrac{3}{4}$.

9. **(D)** This is an algebra question. In this question, if $f(x)$ is 13, then we can put 13 into the equation of $g(x)$ to solve for $g(f(x))$. $g(f(x)) = g(13) = 17 + (13)^2 - 2(13) = 17 + 169 - 26 = 160$.

10. **(C)** This is a difficult quadratic equation to solve. It is probably easier to solve this question backward working from the answers. It is easy to FOIL all the answer choices to see which one is correct. Choice C is correct when FOILed, $(x + 3)(x + 2)(x - 2) = (x + 3)(x^2 - 4) = x^2(x + 3) - 4(x + 3) = x^3 + 3x^2 - 4x - 12$.

CHAPTER 11

Other Essential Math Topics

The Additional Topics in Math section will include geometry and trigonometry and other concepts in math. Questions in this section can be tricky because it can be harder to predict which questions are going to be on the exam. It is worth mentioning that these advanced topics don't make up the majority of the test. Therefore, if you haven't taken Pre-Calculus, don't spend too much time worrying about foreign mathematical concepts. You can learn and review the basic concepts right here. However, please note that these topics do not make up the majority of the test.

Trigonometric Concepts

Use the properties of right triangles and special triangles to solve problems, including the proportions of the side length, proportions of the angles, and so on.

Example

In a certain triangle two sides are 8 and 17. What cannot be the side length of the third side?

(A) 1
(B) 8
(C) 15
(D) 26

Solution

STEP 1

This is a simple geometry question. This question tests the properties of triangles. Understand that the length of the third side of the triangle cannot be equal to or smaller than the other two sides added together.

STEP 2

The two given sides added together equal 25.

$$8 + 17 = 25$$

Therefore, the third side cannot be 26, and the answer is 26.

STEP 3

Select the correct answer, which is choice D.

Circles

Solve for areas, circumference, arc length, and so on using the properties of a circle and the equation of a circle.

Example

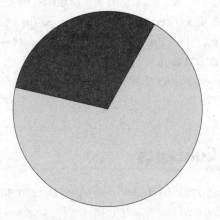

A circle has a diameter of 20, and the angle of the shaded region is 108°. What is the perimeter of the shaded region?

(A) $20 + 6\pi$
(B) 20
(C) 20π
(D) $20\pi + 10$

Solution

STEP 1

This is a circle question. First, find the radius using the diameter,

$$20 \div 2 = 10$$

STEP 2

Then find the circumference of the circle by using the formula of the circumference (circumference = $2\pi r$).

$2\pi10 = 20\pi$

STEP 3

Find the ratio of the shaded region of the circle to the entire region of the circle by using the respective angles:

$108° \div 360° = 0.3$

STEP 4

Then find the arc of the shaded area by using the circumference and the ratio,

$20\pi \times 0.3 = 6\pi.$

STEP 5

Then add the sides to find the perimeter,

$6\pi + 10 + 10 = 20 + 6\pi$

STEP 6

Select the correct answer, which is choice A.

Angles

Use triangles and complementary triangles to solve questions.

Example

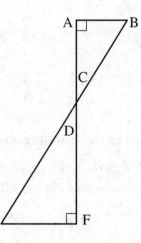

In the figure above, if angle D is 22°, what is angle B?

(A) 56°

(B) 22°

(C) 68°

(D) 88°

Solution

STEP 1

This is a simple angles question. First find angle C.

STEP 2

Angle C is equal to angle D, therefore angle C = 22°.

STEP 3

Then find angle B by using the property of the triangle and the 90 degree angle,

$$180° - 90° - 22° = 68°$$

STEP 4

Select the correct answer, which is choice C.

LET'S PRACTICE

1. sin 30° is equal to which of the following?

   (A) sin 60°

   (B) 2

   (C) cos 30°

   (D) cos 60°

2. If an analog clock is showing 4 o'clock, what is the interior angle that is shown between the two hands?

   (A) 33°

   (B) 40°

   (C) 77°

   (D) 120°

Questions 3 and 4 are based on the following information

Sally has a square tank with the base dimensions of 1 meter by 1 meter filled with water to 0.8 meters tall, and she pours that water into a new tank with a circle base that is now filled to $\dfrac{2}{10\pi}$ meters tall.

3. What is the radius of the base of the tank with the circle base?

   (A) 0.16 meters

   (B) 0.2 meters

   (C) 2 meters

   (D) 4 meters

4. What is the height of the water if the water from the square base tank is poured into a difference tank with a circle base and this tank base has a radius of 1?

   (A) 2 meters

   (B) 0.2 meters

   (C) 0.8 meters

   (D) $\dfrac{8}{10\pi}$ meters

5. There is a ladder leaning against a wall. If the distance between the base of the ladder and the base of the wall is 4 feet and the distance between the top of the ladder and the ground is 8 feet, how tall is the ladder?

   (A) 5 feet

   (B) $4\sqrt{5}$ feet

   (C) 8 feet

   (D) 80 feet

PRACTICE QUESTION ANSWERS

1. **(D)** This is a simple trigonometry question. The easiest way to solve this question is to plug each term into the calculator and see which equals sin 30°. sin 30°= cos 60°.

2. **(D)** This is a simple question about the internal angle of a circle. First, the clock is divided into 12 segments corresponding with the hours. Then because at 4 o'clock the minute hand is at 12 and the hour hand is at 4, the internal angle between the two hands is 4 out of the 12 segments. Next set up an equation to solve for the interior angle that is shown between the two hands and use 360° because that is the internal angle within the circle, $\dfrac{x}{360°} = \dfrac{4}{12}$. Multiple both sides of the equation by 360° to get the answer, $x = \dfrac{4(360°)}{12}$; $x = 120°$.

3. **(C)** This is a difficult question about volume. First find the volume of water in the square tank: 1 meter × 1 meter × 0.8 meter = 0.8 cubic meters. Because the height × base = volume, volume ÷ height = base. The base is 0.8 cubic meters ÷ $\dfrac{2}{10\pi}$ meters = 4π square meters. Then solve for the radius using the formula of the circle, area of circle = πr^2. 4π square meters = πr^2. The radius is equal to 2 meters.

4. **(D)** This is a difficult question about volume. First find the volume of water in the square tank, 1 meter × 1 meter × 0.8 meter = 0.8 cubic meters. Because the height × base = volume, volume ÷ base = height. Solve for the base by using the formula of the circle, area of circle = πr^2. The area of the base is equal to π. Then solve for the new height, 0.8 cubic meters ÷ π square meters = $\dfrac{8}{10\pi}$ meters.

5. **(B)** This is a simple trigonometry question. Use the Pythagorean theorem to solve this question, $a^2 + b^2 = c^2$. Solve for how tall the ladder is, $(4 \text{ feet})^2 + (8 \text{ feet})^2 = c^2$; 16 feet square + 64 feet square = c^2; $c^2 = 80$ feet square; $c = \sqrt{80}$ feet; $c = 4\sqrt{5}$ feet.

PART 6

The National Merit Scholarship Qualifying Test

CHAPTER 12

Introduction to the National Merit Scholarship Qualifying Test

The National Merit Scholarship Corporation recognizes and rewards academically talented students. Its main scholarship program is based principally on performance on the PSAT. In fact, another name for the PSAT is the National Merit Scholarship Qualifying Test. What this comes down to is big money for college for those students who score the highest on the PSAT. To participate in the National Merit Scholarship Program, all you have to do is take the PSAT by the time you're a junior in high school, be a current high school student planning to enter college after high school graduation, and be a U.S. citizen or permanent resident. You will bubble in those requirements on the PSAT answer sheet in order to qualify.

Only the top scorers are recognized by the NMSC. If you are a strong student and looking to earn National Merit, this section is designed especially for you. The idea is simple: practice the most advanced stuff you'll see on test day, so you can perform your very best. This section might not be for everyone—and you definitely shouldn't beat yourself up if you find the material in this section to be very challenging. It's the hardest stuff you'll see, so expect to miss a bit more than you do normally. Approach this section knowing that it's generally more difficult than the actual PSAT and that by practicing the really difficult stuff, you'll be in a better position to qualify for National Merit. Be encouraged! Just like a freshman basketball player might practice with the varsity team in order to improve his or her game, you are practicing advanced questions so that the actual PSAT is easier. Additionally, this section will help you big time when it comes to the SAT.

What's This NMSQT All About?

So, you know a bit about National Merit, but to really understand the Scholarship Program and all the potential resources available, we need to dive deeper. High school students who take the PSAT are screened at a national level with the intent of spotlighting particularly bright students and increasing support for outstanding scholastic talent. Of the 1.6 million students who participate each year, about 50,000 qualify for some sort of recognition. Of those 50,000, the majority receive letters of commendation. While these letters don't come with scholarships themselves, they look great on college applications and often qualify students for other private scholarships. About 16,000 students—the top scorers from each state—become National Merit Semifinalists. All semifinalists are notified and given an application to qualify as finalists. In the end, nearly 15,000 of those 1.6 million become finalists. Finalists may be recipients of a variety of scholarships, up to and including full, renewable scholarships for up to four years of undergraduate study. Furthermore, a lot of schools use National Merit status to award further academic scholarships. These numbers aren't meant to scare you. But it does mean that only the top 5% of test takers are recognized, and those students are rewarded well for their hard work. There are a lot of opportunities for students who receive National Merit, so don't take it lightly.

Revisiting the Test

If you are aiming for National Merit, this section is your best tool. First, review the PSAT format, consider the strategies for exceptional students, and practice the advanced PSAT questions. You may want to complete a full practice test, tackle this section, and then complete a second practice test to evaluate your progress and make note of any areas of weakness that need further preparation.

PSAT Format

- ◆ 2 hours and 45 minutes
  - 2 Sections:
  - Evidence-Based Reading and Writing
    - Reading: a reading comprehension test; 60 minutes, 47 questions, 5 passages
    - Writing and Language: an editing and grammar/mechanics test; 35 minutes, 44 questions, 4 passages
  - Math
    - No Calculator: 25 minutes, 17 questions
    - Calculator: 45 minutes, 31 questions

How to Study for the NMSQT

In general, this book is designed to be versatile and flexible—useful for the student who has six months to prepare as well as the student who has six days to prepare. However, if you are aiming for National Merit, chances are you plan on doing a bit more test preparation than the average PSAT taker. That being said, this section is designed to be done in its entirety. Regardless of how comfortable you feel with the Reading, Writing, and Math material in the rest of this book, you should complete the exercises in this section if National Merit is a goal of yours.

Since the competition is so stiff for National Merit, you need to spend ample time preparing. Your study plan might look something like the following. This plan could take place over two weeks, or you could stretch it out over several months. Just make sure you're revisiting this book at least every week. It's not a good strategy to prepare six months out, forget all about the test, and then glance at the book the night before test day.

- First, complete the Diagnostic test if you haven't yet done so. Score yourself and make note of the types of questions that were incorrect. For instance, you might notice you continuously missed comma questions in the Writing and Language. Or, you might notice most of the math questions you had incorrect were intermediate algebra questions.
- Then, review those concepts specifically until you feel comfortable with them. The quick reviews included in this book can help you refresh concepts you haven't seen in a while.
- Read the strategies and tips in each chapter and become extremely familiar with the timing of the PSAT. Remember, on timed tests it doesn't matter how well you know the material if you don't pace yourself to finish on time.
- Take a second practice exam now that you have reviewed the challenging concepts and familiarized yourself with the timing. Make sure you recreate test-like conditions. Take the whole test in one sitting and time each section. Don't leave any questions blank. Score yourself and note any progress you've seen since the diagnostic test.
- Now it's time to complete this section. You are familiar with the test by this point and ready to see the really challenging stuff. By reviewing the most difficult concepts, you can be sure that nothing will take you by surprise on test day. It's like preparing to run a 5k by practicing running four miles a day. Four miles is longer and more challenging than a 5k, so if you get used to doing it, the 5k will seem easy in comparison.
- Take a final practice exam in a test-like environment. Score yourself and make note of your progress since the Diagnostic test. You should see changes in your scores and confidence levels. For those questions you're continuing to get incorrect, make use of answer explanations to really learn from your mistakes. Remember that you need to test in the top 5% of test takers to earn National Merit recognition—so practice, practice, practice!

CHAPTER 13

Strategies for Success When Aiming for National Merit

Don't Rely on Double-Checking

Gifted students are often perfectionists with the habit of double- and triple-checking their work. But, on timed, standardized tests like the PSAT, working through problems very quickly and then coming back to double-check your answers isn't the best strategy. After all, you are on a time limit. Instead, work carefully through each problem once and only come back to revisit the few that you were unsure of if you have the time. Doing each question once thoroughly is a much better strategy than doing each question twice hastily.

Use Process of Elimination

Students are used to "choosing the best answer." Often, teachers say something like *both of those are close, but choose the best one.* That approach will leave you confused and behind on time on the PSAT. There is only one correct answer for each question on the PSAT. If process of elimination has you down to two answers, look for a word or phrase that corrupts one answer. In other words, change your thinking from finding the correct answer to *eliminating the incorrect answer*. It takes only one word to make a choice the wrong answer. Finding which answer is incorrect is often easier and faster than finding which one is correct.

Don't Check the Clock Too Often

Exceptional students aiming for National Merit will likely be the most prepared on test day. They will have practiced timing and know how to pace themselves to finish the PSAT. They will have completed practice tests and know about how long it should take them to read a passage or answer a series of math questions. While all of that preparation is obviously an advantage, hyperawareness of time can be a weakness if it results in students checking their stopwatch every minute or two. Don't make the mistake of constantly having your eyes on the time—it will slow you down and create higher anxiety. Instead, have a plan for checking the time, maybe after every passage on the Reading or every 10 questions on the Math. It might make sense to mark what time it should be at the halfway point of each section and check the clock then. Do what works for you, but practice it just how you will do it on the test and minimize anxiety by not checking the clock too often.

You Don't Have to Be Perfect

Even to earn National Merit, you don't have to be perfect. Do not get caught up in the idea that you have to get every single question correct. One, that's frightening and leads to test anxiety. Two, it could cause you to give up when you're still very much in the race. Three, it's not true. On tests like the PSAT, scores are calculated based on averages so that every test is fair and equivalent. Even a perfect or nearly perfect score doesn't indicate a faultless test. You don't need to get a perfect score—you just need to be in the top 5% of all scores. So, focus on what you can control. You don't need to get every question right—but you do need to answer every question. You are not penalized for guessing, so don't leave anything blank. Know going in that you can miss a handful of questions and still score very well, even well enough to earn National Merit.

Know Your Guess Letter

It's a good idea to have a go-to letter for questions you have no idea how to answer or for ones that are taking much too long to answer. There is no letter more commonly used than any other, so don't spend your time worrying about that. Instead, pick a letter and stick with that letter. And in instances where you have no idea what the correct answer is, don't waste time going over the question again and again. Each question is worth the same, so if you don't get to three or four questions because of one, it's a great misuse of time. The better strategy is to choose A, B, C, or D before the test, know your letter, and when you encounter a question you have no idea how to answer, select that letter and move on. Do not leave anything blank. Do not waste too much time on one question. If you have time, you can always come back to these questions later and reevaluate. If you don't have time, no worries—you've already bubbled in an answer.

Paraphrase Confusing Questions

"Paraphrase" is one of those overused words that is still underrated. Yes, underrated. Because putting things in your own words always helps, *always*. If you can simplify what's being asked and put it in your own words, you have a much better understanding of what you're reading. And, if you slow it down and read the question once thoroughly, it's still faster than reading it three or four times fast. Slow down, underline or circle words as you go, and then put the question in your own words so you know exactly what's being asked of you. Many students test poorly not because they don't have knowledge of the material, but because they don't understand what they are being asked. Slow it down and then break it down. Challenge yourself while you are practicing to simplify questions without repeating parts of the question itself. For instance, if a question asks you the purpose of the second paragraph as it relates to the passage in its entirety, you might paraphrase it into something like: "What is the second paragraph doing?" Train yourself to read questions one time carefully and to simplify them as much as possible.

Write on the Test

Don't be afraid to write on the test. Even underlining as you read has been proven to improve test scores. While you don't get any credit for showing your work, and taking lengthy notes that use up your precious time isn't advisable, underlining and circling or even jotting a few words can be extremely helpful. This strategy is really what you make it. Some students jot down a word or two next to each paragraph as they read the passages in the Reading section. This passage-mapping allows them to locate information quickly when asked about it. Some students find it helpful to trace their pencil under the words as they read on the Writing and Language—it's an editing test, so you have to train yourself to read slower than you normally do. Other students underline and circle words as they read difficult questions, forcing themselves to slow down and read a question carefully one time instead of having to read it four or five times. Sometimes it makes sense to write all over the graphs and charts, circling relevant numbers or dates or drawing lines to establish patterns. On the Math section, it's very helpful to write down what the problem supplies and what it is specifically asking for. A lot of the math problems are visual: you have to see them and move around the pieces to understand what's expected of you. Regardless of how you choose to implement this strategy, realize its utility and don't hesitate to mark up your test and/or scratch paper.

On the Math Portion, Use the Answers to Guide You. On the Reading Portion, Don't Look at the Answers Right Away.

This can be confusing—sometimes you should read the answer choices right away, other times you should avoid looking at them until you have your own answer already in mind. But when is each strategy appropriate? It's actually less complicated than it seems. On the Reading test, refer to the passage first. The Reading passages are written so that you must go back to the passage and look for evidence. Even the closest readers will have to return to the passage. Think of it as an open-book reading test—the information is all there for you, but you are in charge of finding it in a timely manner. For those who try to avoid returning to the passage, the choices are written so that all of them, or most of them, have words and details that match some part of the passage. What this means for you is that the choices might seem very close to one another, you might remember reading each of them at some point, and two or even three answers might seem correct. Thus, you only confuse yourself by looking at the answers right away.

On the Math test, however, it makes a lot of sense to look at the answer choices. The most obvious reason to do this is because oftentimes those choices will give you a much better idea of what you're supposed to do. The choices guide your problem solving. But there are other reasons to employ this strategy as well. By looking at the answers, you can accurately gauge where in the problem solving you should stop. Especially on a timed test, you don't want to go three steps past what you needed—don't oversolve. Additionally, a lot of times you can use the answer choices to eliminate choices right away, making your job easier and allowing you to finish the problem faster. Get rid of the choices that don't make sense and move quicker so that you have more time for the tough questions. Lastly, for some Math problems, the best approach might be to plug in a number and try it out. For these, start in the middle, maybe B or C, see what you get, and then work up or down as needed. Again, those answer choices act as a tool, helping you reach the correct answer quicker. On the Math section, it makes a lot of sense to look at the choices and use them as a guide.

Know When to Walk Away

Most likely, the audience of this chapter is a certain type of student—a student who excels academically and has high expectations. Unfortunately, a lot of very gifted students don't test well on standardized tests for a number of reasons. These students are often used to really understanding the material they are being tested on. They want to "get it." They strive for perfection. They get easily frustrated when they don't understand something or when they don't know what's being asked of them or when they sort of remember something and could probably get the correct answer eventually, but it's been a long time since they've seen the material. Exceptional students have a hard time, in other words, walking away. They don't know how to just let it go and guess.

Understandably, you want to get the problem correct. Understandably, you want to understand what's being asked of you. But, the PSAT isn't testing one chapter, one book, or even one year of scholarly material. It might test something you learned three years ago. It might test something you won't cover until next semester. The point is you can't know everything. And even the students who have covered all the material on the PSAT will happen across a question where they aren't sure exactly what's being asked of them or a question that they could solve, but it'd take them too long. All of this comes down to this: know when to walk away. Each question on the PSAT is worth the same number of points. If you refuse to leave one question and don't get to four others as a result, you've made a terrible mistake—one that might cost you the score you want. Don't make the mistake of being a perfectionist—keep the big picture in mind. If you have spent too long on a question, or have no clue what to do with it, guess and keep moving.

Read Challenging Works

For most students, this strategy isn't applicable, and that's because most students start preparing for the PSAT a week or two before test day. Even the better-than-average students who pick up a test prep book two months before test day will likely try out one practice test and then forget about the test until test week. For the students aiming for National Merit, though, preparing for the PSAT should be a rather big deal, something to be taken seriously and done months in advance with some sort of consistency. And for those students, the best thing to do is to read, widely and extensively. Reading challenging writing makes you better, period. It not only expands your knowledge and vocabulary, but it also improves focus and concentration, leading to higher analytical skills and memory capacity. The brain is like a muscle—exercise it!

Reading regularly, no matter what you read, will help you become a better test taker. You become a better critical thinker, a better problem solver, a better questioner, and a better debater. (And as an added benefit, reading also decreases stress and therefore leads to a healthier, longer life, even delaying dementia or Alzheimer's in the long term.) However, it's not true that all things you read are created equal. Reading deeply or reading challenging work is far more beneficial than scanning headlines or glancing through Facebook. Pick up a novel. Google a high school or college reading list and start working your way through the works. Grab *The New Yorker* or *National Geographic*. The effects of this strategy transcend the PSAT—you'll be a better test taker certainly, but you'll also be better poised for college and career.

CHAPTER 14

75 Vocabulary Words to Know for the NMSQT

Vocabulary used to be a big deal on the PSAT and SAT, *a really big deal*. Students could expect to see a bunch of words they'd never used and even some words they'd never seen. So, it made a lot of sense to buy 500 vocabulary flashcards and memorize them over a few months. Since the revisions to the PSAT, the narrative has spread that vocabulary is no longer important for your success. And while it is certainly true that vocabulary looks a lot different on the new test, it's not true that you won't encounter tough words or that you cannot benefit from knowing the difficult words that come up again and again. In fact, if you are aiming for National Merit, you should absolutely spend some time becoming familiar with the more obscure terms known to appear on the test. Following is a list of 75 words that come up over and over. Even if these words are not asked about directly, you can bet that a working knowledge of them will allow you a greater understanding of what you read and lead to a better overall performance.

Abeyance	a state of temporary suspension; postponement
Abdicate	renounce; resign; relinquish
Aesthetic	concerned with beauty; artistic; tasteful
Ambiguous	unclear; open to interpretation; having a double meaning
Ambivalent	having mixed feelings; uncertain; indecisive
Amicable	friendly; likable
Anachronistic	outdated; belonging to an earlier period; antiquated
Apathetic	uninterested; unconcerned; indifferent
Autonomous	self-governing; independent
Benevolent	kind; caring; benign
Benign	kind; friendly; benevolent
Blithe	indifferent; unconcerned; careless
Callow	inexperienced; immature; naive
Capricious	unpredictable; volatile
Contentious	controversial; heated
Cumbersome	awkward; unmanageable; difficult to carry
Digress	to deviate or go off subject
Divergent	differing; varying; unalike
Dogmatic	opinionated; unyielding; offering opinions and principles as truths
Eminent	respected and famous
Empathy	the ability to understand the feelings of others
Ephemeral	fleeting; brief
Esoteric	specialized; obscure; intended for a small audience
Evanescent	quickly disappearing; temporary; ephemeral
Frugal	cheap; thrifty; economical
Garrulous	talkative; verbose; chatty
Haughty	arrogant; snobbish; conceited
Hedonistic	pleasure-seeking; self-indulgent
Ignominious	deserving shame; embarrassing; humiliating
Impecunious	poor; indigent; destitute
Impetuous	impulsive; rash; careless
Impudent	disrespectful; impertinent; insolent
Indifferent	unconcerned; uninterested; nonchalant
Intrepid	fearless; adventurous; daring
Intrinsic	inherent; essential; inborn
Magnanimous	generous; forgiving; charitable
Malinger	to fake an illness
Mercurial	unpredictable; volatile; capricious

Obdurate	stubborn; obstinate; unyielding
Obfuscate	to make unclear; to confuse or overcomplicate
Opulent	rich and luxurious; wealthy
Ostentatious	showy; flashy; extravagant
Pervasive	widespread; prevalent
Placate	make calm; pacify
Precocious	talented; advanced for one's age
Pretentious	attempting to impress; artificial; pompous
Prodigy	an exceptional person; genius
Prosaic	ordinary; commonplace; lacking beauty
Prudent	wise; sensible; showing care for the future
Reclusive	avoiding the company of others; solitary; secluded
Resilient	able to spring back; hardy; tough
Sagacious	wise; knowledgeable
Sanctify	approve; bless; endorse
Sanctimonious	self-righteous; superior; preachy
Sanguine	optimistic; positive
Sentiment	a view or attitude; general feeling
Sullen	gloomy; bad-tempered
Superfluous	unnecessary; excessive
Surreptitious	secretive; concealed
Tactful	diplomatic; considerate
Tandem	alongside; together
Tangential	going off in another direction; irregular
Tenacious	firm; persistent; determined; unwavering
Tenuous	slight; flimsy; questionable
Transcend	to go beyond the limit; surpass
Transient	short-lived; impermanent; ephemeral
Trivial	of little value; unimportant; superficial
Undulate	move in waves; ripple; rise and fall
Usurp	take by force; seize; overthrow
Vehement	passionate; intense; enthusiastic
Verbose	wordy; talkative; garrulous
Vindicate	clear of blame; acquit
Vindictive	having a desire for revenge; bitter
Wanton	immoral; indecent; wicked
Whimsical	unconventional; eccentric; quirky

CHAPTER 15

Advanced Practice for the NMSQT

In this chapter you'll find extra opportunities to test your abilities on the Reading, Writing and Language, and Math sections of the exam. The following practice questions are examples of the level of difficulty you will want to familiarize yourself with as you pursue success on the NMSQT . Remember, the following exercises are for students with a goal of earning National Merit. They are advanced and represent the most difficult stuff you will see on test day. They should not be used to gauge your readiness for the PSAT in general, but instead your readiness for the toughest questions on the PSAT.

ADVANCED READING PASSAGE

Questions 1–10 are based on the following passage.

The following passage is an excerpt from "Of the Origin and Use of Money," the fourth chapter of An Inquiry into the Nature and Causes of the Wealth of Nations *by Adam Smith (1776).*

When the division of labor has been once thoroughly established, it is but a very small part of a man's wants which the produce of his own labor can supply. He supplies the far greater part of them by exchanging that surplus part of the produce of his own labor, which is over and above his own consumption, for such
5　parts of the produce of other men's labor as he has occasion for. Every man thus lives by exchanging, or becomes, in some measure, a merchant, and the society itself grows to be what is properly a commercial society.

But when the division of labor first began to take place, this power of exchanging must frequently have been very much clogged and embarrassed in its
10 operations. One man, we shall suppose, has more of a certain commodity than he himself has occasion for, while another has less. The former, consequently, would be glad to dispose of, and the latter to purchase, a part of this superfluity. But if this latter should chance to have nothing that the former stands in need of, no exchange can be made between them. The butcher has more meat in his shop
15 than he himself can consume, and the brewer and the baker would each of them be willing to purchase a part of it. But they have nothing to offer in exchange, except the different productions of their respective trades, and the butcher is already provided with all the bread and beer which he has immediate occasion for. No exchange can, in this case, be made between them. He cannot be their
20 merchant, nor they his customers; and they are all of them thus mutually less serviceable to one another. In order to avoid the inconveniency of such situations, every prudent man in every period of society, after the first establishment of the division of labor, must naturally have endeavored to manage his affairs in such a manner, as to have at all times by him, besides the peculiar produce of his own
25 industry, a certain quantity of one commodity or other, such as he imagined few people would be likely to refuse in exchange for the produce of their industry. Many different commodities, it is probable, were successively both thought of and employed for this purpose.

In all countries, however, men seem at last to have been determined by
30 irresistible reasons to give the preference, for this employment, to metals above every other commodity. Metals can not only be kept with as little loss as any other commodity, scarce anything being less perishable than they are, but they can likewise, without any loss, be divided into any number of parts, as by fusion those parts can easily be re-united again; a quality which no other equally
35 durable commodities possess, and which, more than any other quality, renders them fit to be the instruments of commerce and circulation.

1. According to Smith, a commercial society arises from

   (A) the surplus part of one's labor
   (B) lack of consumption
   (C) the necessity of exchange
   (D) the expansion of commodities

2. As used in line 9, "clogged" most nearly means

   (A) hindered
   (B) plugged
   (C) blocked
   (D) sabotaged

3. The author claims that exchange was difficult early on because of

(A) the limited diversity of commodities
(B) cattle numbers were historically low
(C) butchers had access to more than enough bread
(D) the difficulty crossing national borders

4. Which choice provides the best evidence for the previous question?

(A) Lines 5–7 ("Every man . . . commercial society.")
(B) Lines 8–10 ("But when . . . in its operations.")
(C) Lines 11–12 ("The former . . . this superfluity.")
(D) Lines 13–14 ("But if this . . . between them.")

5. As used in line 22, "prudent" most nearly means

(A) reckless
(B) sensible
(C) beneficial
(D) wealthy

6. In lines 21–26 ("In order to . . . their industry."), Smith contends that

(A) it was smart to store one commodity, so you never ran out of it
(B) it made sense to specialize in a common trade
(C) intelligent merchants bought a variety of goods so that they never wanted for anything
(D) wise tradesmen sought and kept valuable commodities that nearly everyone desired

7. Smith claims that which of the following resulted from a desire to expand one's trading options?

(A) communism
(B) innovation
(C) the industrial revolution
(D) inflation

8. Which choice provides the best evidence for the previous question?

(A) Lines 27–28 ("Many different . . . for this purpose.")
(B) Lines 29–31 ("In all countries . . . other commodity.")
(C) Lines 31–33 ("Metals can not . . . number of parts,")
(D) Lines 33–36 ("as by fusion . . . commercial and circulation.")

9. The third paragraph (lines 29–36) primarily

   (A) explains how to disassemble basic metals
   (B) establishes metals as the first true form of currency
   (C) argues for industrial expansion in steel
   (D) demonstrates the transition from an agricultural to an industrial market

10. According to the author, why were metals "above every other commodity"?

    (A) they were durable and hardy
    (B) they were difficult to steal
    (C) they can be divided into parts
    (D) everyone needs metal more than other commodities

PRACTICE QUESTION ANSWERS

1. **(C)** This is a big picture question; it's asking about a main idea the author comes to. You can find this in the first paragraph. Smith says a society grows into a commercial society when men survive via exchange.

2. **(A)** Before looking at the answer choices, see if you can replace the word in question. To summarize the lines, exchange is messy at first—it was difficult without a variety of goods to trade. Continue to read and you'll find an example where exchange becomes hindered or obstructed when one party wants to trade for a good but doesn't have anything that the other needs.

3. **(A)** Paraphrase the question: why was exchange messy at first? The author gives an example to illustrate his claim, saying one person might have extra of something that a second person wants to purchase. Yet, if the second person doesn't have anything the first person needs, there can be no trade. Thus, exchange is difficult if commodities are limited and there isn't a currency that everyone desires.

4. **(D)** These are the lines that identify the obstruction, the messiness of exchange before money. Exchange cannot be made if both parties don't possess something the other wants.

5. **(B)** As always with vocabulary questions, it's a good idea to try to substitute a word in before looking at the answer choices. Here, every "smart" or "wise" man kept something he knew everybody wanted so that he could always trade for his own needs. The only word that fits is "sensible," meaning "logical."

6. **(D)** This question is asking you to summarize the argument made in these lines. Smith says that upon realizing how important exchange was, logical men must have tried to have a supply of things that other people wanted so that they could trade as they pleased. Eliminate (B) and (C) because those don't align with this particular claim. (A) is appealing, but the idea is not to store any commodity so you have a lot of it, but to store a desirable commodity so you can trade at will.

7. **(B)** Because people wanted to be able to exchange at will for those things they wanted most, they began thinking of and producing new goods. If you have something nobody else has, you can count on people wanting it and being willing to trade other commodities for it. Hence, new products and services were developed to give someone the edge in trading. Introducing new ideas and products is innovation.

8. **(A)** You are looking for evidence to the previous question. In other words, you are looking for the lines that state new products were invented so that people could expand their trading options. In these lines specifically "[m]any different commodities" were "thought of and employed."

9. **(B)** What is the third paragraph doing? It transitions into talking about metals as the preferential commodity for a number of reasons. Look for the answer that says something about metals being the best tool of commerce.

10. **(C)** Recall that metals are discussed in the last paragraph. The author gives several reasons why metals are superior to other commodities. Most important, metals have one quality "more than any other quality" which "renders them fit to be the instruments of commerce and circulation." Which quality is that? They can be divided into parts and reunited again.

ADVANCED WRITING AND LANGUAGE PASSAGE

Questions 1–11 are based on the following passage.

The following passage is taken from the introduction to a language education book called The Art of Writing and Speaking the English Language, *1903.*

If there is a subject of universal interest and **1** utility it is the art of writing and speaking one's own language **2** effectively. It is the basis of culture, as we all know; but it is infinitely more than that: it is the basis of business. No salesman can sell anything unless he can explain the merits of his goods in effective English, or can write an advertisement equally effective, or present his ideas, and the facts, in a letter. Indeed, the way we talk, and write letters, largely determines our success in life.

Now it is well for us to face at once the counter-statement that the most ignorant and uncultivated men often succeed best in business, and that misspelled, ungrammatical advertisements have brought in millions of dollars. It is an acknowledged fact that our business circulars and letters are far inferior in correctness to those of **3** Great Britain yet, they are more effective in getting business. **4**

1. (A) NO CHANGE
   (B) utility;
   (C) utility:
   (D) utility,

2. (A) NO CHANGE
   (B) affectively
   (C) adequately
   (D) exactly

3. (A) NO CHANGE
   (B) Great Britain; yet,
   (C) Great Britain, yet
   (D) Great Britain: yet

4. At this point, the writer is considering adding the following sentence

> Great Britain willingly acknowledges that the U.S. produces better businessmen, but maintains that its artists far exceed ours in talent.

Should the writer make this addition here?

(A) Yes, because it adds significant supporting details.
(B) Yes, because it justifies a questionable claim.
(C) No, because it distracts the reader with irrelevant material.
(D) No, because it merely repeats the information from the previous sentence.

Let us examine the facts in the case more closely. First of all, language is no more than a **5** medium; its like air to the creatures of the land or water to fishes. If it is perfectly clear and pure, we do not notice it any more than we notice pure air when the sun is shining in a clear sky, or the taste of pure cool water when we **6** drank a glass on a hot day. Unless the sun is shining, there is no brightness; unless the water is cool, there is no refreshment. So it is with language. Language is merely a medium for **7** thinking, emotions, the intelligence of a finely wrought brain, and a good mind will make far more out of a bad medium than a poor mind will make out of the best. A great violinist will draw such music from the cheapest violin that the world is astonished. **8** However, is that any reason why the great violinist should choose to play **9** for free?

5. (A) NO CHANGE
   (B) medium: its
   (C) medium; it's
   (D) medium, it's

6. (A) NO CHANGE
   (B) drinks
   (C) drunk
   (D) drink

7. (A) NO CHANGE
   (B) thinking, feeling the intelligence of a finely wrought brain,
   (C) thinking, having emotions, and a brain of which is intelligent and finely wrought,
   (D) thoughts, emotions, the intelligence of a finely wrought brain,

8. (A) NO CHANGE
   (B) Thus,
   (C) Consequently,
   (D) Moreover,

9. Which choice results in the most logical sentence in the context of this paragraph?

(A) NO CHANGE

(B) on a poor violin?

(C) on a wooden stage?

(D) on Broadway for free?

   While language as the medium of thought may be compared to air as the medium of the sun's influence, in other respects it is like the skin of the body; a scurvy skin shows bad blood within, and a scurvy language shows **10** inaccurate thought and a mind ridden with confusion. And as a disease once fixed on the skin reacts and poisons the blood in turn as it has first been poisoned by the blood, so careless use of language if **11** acquitted reacts on the mind to make it permanently and increasingly careless, illogical, and inaccurate in its thinking.

10. (A) NO CHANGE

   (B) thought that is inaccurate and a mind that is confused.

   (C) inaccurate thought and a confused mind.

   (D) bewilderment of the mind and inaccuracy when it comes to thinking.

11. (A) understood

   (B) appropriated

   (C) condemned

   (D) indulged

PRACTICE QUESTION ANSWERS

1. **(D)** Here, you have a dependent clause followed by an independent clause, or complete sentence. You should separate these with a comma.

2. **(A)** This is a word choice question and is correct as is. "Effectively" means "efficiently" or in a way that achieves a desired result. (B) refers to emotions. (D) means without discrepancy or "absolutely," and so is illogical here. (C) is appealing but is too lukewarm for this, suggesting that language use should be just acceptable.

3. **(B)** Since you have two complete sentences here, you can eliminate (A) and (C) right away. (B) is the correct choice here because the semicolon is used just like a period to separate complete sentences, and the comma after "yet" gives a necessary pause.

4. **(C)** This sentence introduces new material—the quality of artists in the United States and Great Britain. At no point in the rest of the passage are artists discussed further. Eliminate (A) and (B). Now, look at the reasoning and choose (C) since the information is not repetitive.

5. **(C)** Be careful. This question has two parts. First, realize we need the semicolon because there are two independent clauses here. Then realize "it's" is correct because it means "it is." "Its" shows possession and so is inappropriate here.

6. **(D)** For questions like this, you want to maintain consistency throughout the sentence and rest of the paragraph. The rest of the verbs in the sentence—"is," "notice," "taste"—are all in present tense, leaving you with (B) and (D). Since the subject is "we," (D) is the correct choice.

7. **(D)** Here, you are looking for the answer choice that is concise and parallel. First, eliminate (B) because it changes the meaning of the sentence and (C) because it is too wordy. (A) is appealing, but doesn't maintain parallelism. (D), however, is parallel and to the point.

8. **(A)** This is correct as is. The transition word is what's in question. You could rephrase this: a great violinist can play good music on a bad violin, but that doesn't mean the person should play on a bad violin. Choose the word most like "but." Another approach is to eliminate (B) and (C) because they do the same thing, and then to get rid of (D) because it means "additionally."

9. **(B)** This is a tough question. You need to consider the sentence in the context of the paragraph. The preceding sentence informs this sentence. The point being made is a great violinist can play well even on the cheapest violin. Thus, (B) is the logical choice here.

10. **(C)** Remember that the PSAT prefers concision. You want the shortest answer with all the information. Eliminate (B) and (D) because they are wordy. (A) is appealing but isn't as concise and parallel as choice (C).

11. **(D)** You are choosing the most logical and precise word for the intended meaning. Try to substitute a word first. If careless language is allowed or ignored, it can have bad effects on the mind. "Indulged" means "allowed" or "yielded to," and is thus the best choice here.

ADVANCED MATH QUESTIONS

1. $25 - 2x = 3y$

   $y - 3x = 1$

   What is $x - y$ equal to?

   (A) −9
   (B) −5
   (C) 6
   (D) 9

Questions 2 and 3 are based on the following information.

A company is giving away gifts to all its employees during the holiday season. Employees are allowed to choose only one out of the following three choices: food processor, vacuum cleaner, and cash card. The ratio of employees who chose food processor to vacuum cleaner to cash card is 1:3:6.

2. Out of everyone who did not choose the cash card, what is the percentage of employees who chose the vacuum cleaner?

   (A) 20%
   (B) 22%
   (C) 40%
   (D) 75%

3. If there are 42 employees who chose the cash card, how many employees are there in the company?

   (A) 48
   (B) 60
   (C) 70
   (D) 82

4. If $6x^2 - 5x = 4$, which is a possible solution for x?

(A) $-\dfrac{1}{2}$

(B) $-1\dfrac{1}{3}$

(C) $\dfrac{4}{3}$

(D) 2

5. There is a ladder leaning against a wall. If the distance between the base of the ladder and the base of the wall is 5 feet and the distance between the top of the ladder and the ground is 10 feet, how tall is the ladder?

(A) 5 feet
(B) $5\sqrt{5}$ feet
(C) 8 feet
(D) 80 feet

6. If a traditional analog clock is showing 6:30, what is the interior angle that is shown between the two hands?

(A) 0°
(B) 15°
(C) 30°
(D) 33°

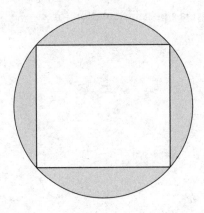

7. In the figure above a square is inscribed inside a circle, If the radius is $2\sqrt{2}$, what is the area of the shaded region?

(A) 8π

(B) $8\pi - 16$

(C) $\dfrac{\sqrt{2}}{2}\pi - 8$

(D) $16\sqrt{2}\pi$

8. Shimi walked from his home to his school in half an hour. The distance between his home and his school is 2.4 km. On the way back from the school to his home, he ran for $\dfrac{3}{4}$ of the distance. His running speed is 1.5 times the speed of his walking. He then walked the rest of the way home. How many minutes did it take for him to get home?

(A) 10 minutes

(B) 22.5 minutes

(C) 23 minutes

(D) 25.5 minutes

9. A store sold two types of sugar, white sugar and brown sugar. The brown sugar cost $6 dollars more. If the store made $391 from selling 43 bags of white sugar and 16 bags of brown sugar, how much money did the store make from selling the brown sugar?

(A) $45

(B) $176

(C) $251

(D) $349

10. If Sammy can finish folding 280 napkins in 2 hours, how many minutes will he take to finish folding 98?

    (A) 0.7
    (B) 1
    (C) 42
    (D) 140

11. $y = 4x - 5$

    $y = 3$

    At which coordinate do the two lines intersect?

    (A) (3, 5)
    (B) (15, 2)
    (C) (5, 5)
    (D) (2, 3)

12. Which point satisfies both $y > 5x - 3$ and $y < \dfrac{5x}{2} + 7$?

    (A) (3, 4)
    (B) (–3, 4)
    (C) (–4, 2)
    (D) (–2, 1)

13. If $3x - 2y = 7$, then what is the value of $\dfrac{y}{3} - \dfrac{x}{2}$?

    (A) $-\dfrac{7}{6}$

    (B) $-\dfrac{5}{7}$

    (C) $\dfrac{1}{7}$

    (D) $-\dfrac{1}{5}$

14. What is y in terms of x, if $9(3^y) = 3^x$? Note: x and y are positive numbers.

    (A) $y - 1$
    (B) $y + 2$
    (C) $x + 1$
    (D) $x - 2$

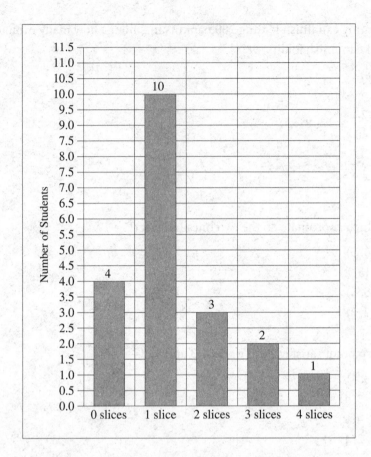

The baking club of a school is having a cake party at the beginning of the year. The secretary of the club is keeping track of how many slices of cake each person has to be able to estimate how many cakes she has to order for the next event. The graph shows how many students have 0 slices, 1 slice, 2 slices, 3 slices, 4 slices, and 5 slices. For example, there are 4 students who did not have any cake.

15. How many slices should she order if there are 30 students attending the next event?

(A) 39
(B) 41
(C) 62
(D) 90

PRACTICE QUESTION ANSWERS

1. **(B)** This is a system of equations problem. First, multiply the second equation by 3 to get $3y - 9x = 3$. Then rearrange this equation to get $3y = 9x + 3$. Then set this equation equal to the first equation to get $25 - 2x = 9x + 3$. Then add $2x$ to both sides to get $25 = 11x + 3$. Then takeaway 3 from both sides to get $22 = 11x$. Then divide both sides by $11x$ to get $x = 2$. Then plug x into the second equation to get y; $y - 3(2) = 1$; $y - 6 = 1$; $y = 7$. Then, find what $x - y$ is equal to; $2 - 7 = -5$.

2. **(D)** This is a ratio to percent question. First find the ratio of the employees who took the vacuum cleaner to the total number of employees who did not take the cash card, which is 3:4 $(1 + 3 = 4)$. Then set up an equation to solve for the percentage, $\dfrac{x}{100\%} = \dfrac{3}{4}$. Then solve the equation to get the percentage $x = \dfrac{3(100\%)}{4}$, $x = 75\%$.

3. **(C)** This is a ratio question. First find the ratio of the employees who took the cash card to the total number of employees, which is 6:10 $(1 + 3 + 6 = 10)$. Then set up an equation to solve for the total number of students, $\dfrac{x}{42} = \dfrac{10}{6}$. Then solve the equation to get the total number of employees in the company, $x = \dfrac{10(42)}{6}$, $x = 70$.

4. **(B)** This is a difficult quadratic equation to solve. First, rearrange the equation by taking away 4 on both sides to get $6x^2 - 5x - 4 = 0$. Then factor this equation to get $(2x - 1)(3x + 4) = 0$. Then solve for the first bracket to get $2x - 1 = 0$; $2x = 1$; $x = \dfrac{1}{2}$. Then solve for the second bracket to get $3x + 4 = 0$; $3x = -4$; $x = -\dfrac{4}{3}$; $x = -1\dfrac{1}{3}$.

5. **(B)** This is a simple trigonometry question. Use the Pythagorean theorem to solve this question, $a^2 + b^2 = c^2$. Solve for how tall the ladder is, $(5 \text{ feet})^2 + (10 \text{ feet})^2 = c^2$; 25 feet square + 100 feet square = c^2; c^2 = 125 feet square; $c = \sqrt{125}$ feet; $c = 5\sqrt{5}$ feet.

6. **(B)** This is a question about the internal angle of a circle. First, the clock is divided by 12 segments corresponding with each hour. Then because the minute hand at 6:30 is at 6 and hour hand is at halfway between 6 and 7, the internal angle between the two hands is 0.5 out of the 12 segments. Next set up an equation to solve for the interior angle that is shown between the two hands and use 360° because that is the internal angle within the circle, $\dfrac{x}{360°} = \dfrac{0.5}{12°}$. Multiply both sides of the equation by 360° to get the answer, $x = \dfrac{0.5(360°)}{12}$; $x = 15°$.

7. **(B)** This is a difficult geometry question. First find the area of the circle, $\left(2\sqrt{2}\right)^2 \pi = 8\pi$. Then because the radius is $2\sqrt{2}$, the diameter is $4\sqrt{2}$. Recognize that the square is made with two special triangles of $1:1:\sqrt{2}$. Then because the sides of the square are 4 and 4, the area of the square is $4 \times 4 = 16$. Then find the area of the shaded region $8\pi - 16$. This question can also be solved by using the angle to find the sides of the square.

8. **(B)** This is a multistep word problem about speed. First, find out his speed of walking, 2.4 km ÷ 30 minutes = 0.08 km/min. Then find out the running speed, 0.08 km/min × 1.5 = 0.12 km/min. Then find out the time it took to walk, 2.4 ÷ 4 ÷ 0.08 km/min = 7.5 minutes. Then find the time it took in the car, 2.4 ÷ 4 × 3 ÷ 0.12 = 15 minutes. Add the number of minutes together to get the answer, 15 min + 7.5 min = 22.5 min.

9. **(B)** This is a difficult multistep word problem. First, set up the equations needed to solve the problem and use y for white sugar and x for brown sugar, $x - y = \$6$, $16x + 43y = \$391$. Manipulate the first equation to get $y = x - \$6$. Then plug the modified equation into the second equation to get $16x + 43(x - \$6) = \$391$. Solve for x, $16x + 43x - \$258 = \$391$; $59x = \$649$; $x = 11$. Then multiply the number of bags of brown sugar by the price of the brown sugar to get $176 (\$11 \times 16 = \$176)$.

10. **(C)** This is a word problem about speed. First, find out the speed of folding napkins, 280 napkins ÷ 2 hours = 140 napkins/hour. Then find how long it will take to finish 98 napkins, 98 napkins ÷ 140 napkins/hour = 0.7 hours. Then convert the number of hours to minutes 0.7 hours = 0.7 × 60 = 42 minutes.

11. **(D)** This is a system of equations problem. First, substitute $y = 3$ into the first equation $(3 = 4x - 5)$. Then add 5 to both sides $(8 = 4x)$. Then solve for x; $x = 2$. The x coordinate will be 2. Because $y = 3$, the y coordinate does not need to be solved and will be 3. The coordinates of the intersection are $(2, 3)$. The correct answer is then (D).

12. **(D)** This is an inequality question. To see which points satisfy both equations, plug each of the points into both equations and find the point that satisfies both equations. For example, plug $(-2, 1)$ into the first equation: $1 > 5(-2) - 3$, and get $1 > -13$. This means that the point satisfies the first equation. Next plug $(-2, 1)$ into the second equation: $1 < \dfrac{5(-2)}{2} + 7$, and get $1 < 2$. This means that the point also satisfies the second equation. Another way of solving this question is to graph out the two equations and see which points satisfies both equations.

13. **(A)** This is a difficult algebra question. Modify $\frac{y}{3} - \frac{x}{4}$ until it looks like $3x - 2y = 7$ to get the answer, $-6\left(\frac{y}{3} - \frac{x}{2}\right) = -2y + 3x = 3x - 2y = 7$. Therefore, $-6\left(\frac{y}{3} - \frac{x}{2}\right) = 7$. The answer is $\frac{y}{3} - \frac{x}{2} = -\frac{7}{6}$.

14. **(D)** This is an exponent question. This question needs the exponents to be manipulated. The power of the same number can be added or subtracted. Therefore, $9(3^y) = 3^x$ is the same as $3^{y+2} = 3^x$. Because the base of the equation is 3 and the two sides equal, $y + 2 = x$. The question asks to express y in terms of x, so $y = x - 2$.

15. **(A)** This is a data analysis question. If she needs to find out how many slices of pizza to order for each student, she needs the average or the mean of the set of data. First find the total number of students $4 + 10 + 3 + 2 + 1 = 20$. Then find the total number of slices $0(4) + 1(10) + 2(3) + 3(2) + 4(1) = 0 + 10 + 6 + 6 + 4 = 26$. Then find the average number of slices of cake each person has $26 \div 20 = 1.3$. Then find how many slices she should order if there are 30 students attending the next event; $30 \times 1.3 = 39$.

PART 7

PSAT Practice Tests

PSAT/NMSQT
Practice Test 1

Answer Sheet

Last Name: _____   **First Name:** _____

Date: _____   **Testing Location:** _____

Administering the Test

- Remove this answer sheet from the book and use it to record your answers to this test.
- This test will require 2 hours and 10 minutes to complete. Take this test in one sitting.
- Use a stopwatch to time yourself on each section. The time limit for each section is written clearly at the beginning of each section. The first four sections are 25 minutes long, and the last section is 30 minutes long.
- Each response must completely fill the oval. Erase all stray marks completely, or they may be interpreted as responses.
- You must stop ALL work on a section when time is called.
- If you finish a section before the time has elapsed, check your work on that section. You may NOT move on to the next section until time is called.
- Do not waste time on questions that seem too difficult for you.
- Use the test book for scratchwork, but you will only receive credit for answers that are marked on the answer sheets.

Scoring the Test

- Your scaled score, which will be determined from a conversion table, is based on your raw score for each section.
- You will receive one point toward your raw score for every correct answer.
- You will receive no points toward your raw score for an omitted question.
- For each wrong answer on a multiple-choice question, your raw score will be reduced by 1/4 point. For each wrong answer on a numerical "grid-in" question (Section 4, questions 29–38), your raw score will receive no deduction.

SECTION 1 **Reading Test** 60 MINUTES

Time: 60 minutes

Start: _____

Stop: _____

1. Ⓐ Ⓑ Ⓒ Ⓓ
2. Ⓐ Ⓑ Ⓒ Ⓓ
3. Ⓐ Ⓑ Ⓒ Ⓓ
4. Ⓐ Ⓑ Ⓒ Ⓓ
5. Ⓐ Ⓑ Ⓒ Ⓓ
6. Ⓐ Ⓑ Ⓒ Ⓓ
7. Ⓐ Ⓑ Ⓒ Ⓓ
8. Ⓐ Ⓑ Ⓒ Ⓓ
9. Ⓐ Ⓑ Ⓒ Ⓓ
10. Ⓐ Ⓑ Ⓒ Ⓓ
11. Ⓐ Ⓑ Ⓒ Ⓓ
12. Ⓐ Ⓑ Ⓒ Ⓓ
13. Ⓐ Ⓑ Ⓒ Ⓓ
14. Ⓐ Ⓑ Ⓒ Ⓓ
15. Ⓐ Ⓑ Ⓒ Ⓓ
16. Ⓐ Ⓑ Ⓒ Ⓓ
17. Ⓐ Ⓑ Ⓒ Ⓓ
18. Ⓐ Ⓑ Ⓒ Ⓓ
19. Ⓐ Ⓑ Ⓒ Ⓓ
20. Ⓐ Ⓑ Ⓒ Ⓓ
21. Ⓐ Ⓑ Ⓒ Ⓓ
22. Ⓐ Ⓑ Ⓒ Ⓓ
23. Ⓐ Ⓑ Ⓒ Ⓓ
24. Ⓐ Ⓑ Ⓒ Ⓓ
25. Ⓐ Ⓑ Ⓒ Ⓓ
26. Ⓐ Ⓑ Ⓒ Ⓓ
27. Ⓐ Ⓑ Ⓒ Ⓓ
28. Ⓐ Ⓑ Ⓒ Ⓓ
29. Ⓐ Ⓑ Ⓒ Ⓓ
30. Ⓐ Ⓑ Ⓒ Ⓓ
31. Ⓐ Ⓑ Ⓒ Ⓓ
32. Ⓐ Ⓑ Ⓒ Ⓓ
33. Ⓐ Ⓑ Ⓒ Ⓓ
34. Ⓐ Ⓑ Ⓒ Ⓓ
35. Ⓐ Ⓑ Ⓒ Ⓓ
36. Ⓐ Ⓑ Ⓒ Ⓓ
37. Ⓐ Ⓑ Ⓒ Ⓓ
38. Ⓐ Ⓑ Ⓒ Ⓓ
39. Ⓐ Ⓑ Ⓒ Ⓓ
40. Ⓐ Ⓑ Ⓒ Ⓓ
41. Ⓐ Ⓑ Ⓒ Ⓓ
42. Ⓐ Ⓑ Ⓒ Ⓓ
43. Ⓐ Ⓑ Ⓒ Ⓓ
44. Ⓐ Ⓑ Ⓒ Ⓓ
45. Ⓐ Ⓑ Ⓒ Ⓓ
46. Ⓐ Ⓑ Ⓒ Ⓓ
47. Ⓐ Ⓑ Ⓒ Ⓓ

SECTION 2 **Writing and Language Test** 35 MINUTES

Time: 35 minutes

Start: _____

Stop: _____

1. Ⓐ Ⓑ Ⓒ Ⓓ
2. Ⓐ Ⓑ Ⓒ Ⓓ
3. Ⓐ Ⓑ Ⓒ Ⓓ
4. Ⓐ Ⓑ Ⓒ Ⓓ
5. Ⓐ Ⓑ Ⓒ Ⓓ
6. Ⓐ Ⓑ Ⓒ Ⓓ
7. Ⓐ Ⓑ Ⓒ Ⓓ
8. Ⓐ Ⓑ Ⓒ Ⓓ
9. Ⓐ Ⓑ Ⓒ Ⓓ
10. Ⓐ Ⓑ Ⓒ Ⓓ
11. Ⓐ Ⓑ Ⓒ Ⓓ
12. Ⓐ Ⓑ Ⓒ Ⓓ
13. Ⓐ Ⓑ Ⓒ Ⓓ
14. Ⓐ Ⓑ Ⓒ Ⓓ
15. Ⓐ Ⓑ Ⓒ Ⓓ
16. Ⓐ Ⓑ Ⓒ Ⓓ
17. Ⓐ Ⓑ Ⓒ Ⓓ
18. Ⓐ Ⓑ Ⓒ Ⓓ
19. Ⓐ Ⓑ Ⓒ Ⓓ
20. Ⓐ Ⓑ Ⓒ Ⓓ
21. Ⓐ Ⓑ Ⓒ Ⓓ
22. Ⓐ Ⓑ Ⓒ Ⓓ
23. Ⓐ Ⓑ Ⓒ Ⓓ
24. Ⓐ Ⓑ Ⓒ Ⓓ
25. Ⓐ Ⓑ Ⓒ Ⓓ
26. Ⓐ Ⓑ Ⓒ Ⓓ
27. Ⓐ Ⓑ Ⓒ Ⓓ
28. Ⓐ Ⓑ Ⓒ Ⓓ
29. Ⓐ Ⓑ Ⓒ Ⓓ
30. Ⓐ Ⓑ Ⓒ Ⓓ
31. Ⓐ Ⓑ Ⓒ Ⓓ
32. Ⓐ Ⓑ Ⓒ Ⓓ
33. Ⓐ Ⓑ Ⓒ Ⓓ
34. Ⓐ Ⓑ Ⓒ Ⓓ
35. Ⓐ Ⓑ Ⓒ Ⓓ
36. Ⓐ Ⓑ Ⓒ Ⓓ
37. Ⓐ Ⓑ Ⓒ Ⓓ
38. Ⓐ Ⓑ Ⓒ Ⓓ
39. Ⓐ Ⓑ Ⓒ Ⓓ
40. Ⓐ Ⓑ Ⓒ Ⓓ
41. Ⓐ Ⓑ Ⓒ Ⓓ
42. Ⓐ Ⓑ Ⓒ Ⓓ
43. Ⓐ Ⓑ Ⓒ Ⓓ
44. Ⓐ Ⓑ Ⓒ Ⓓ

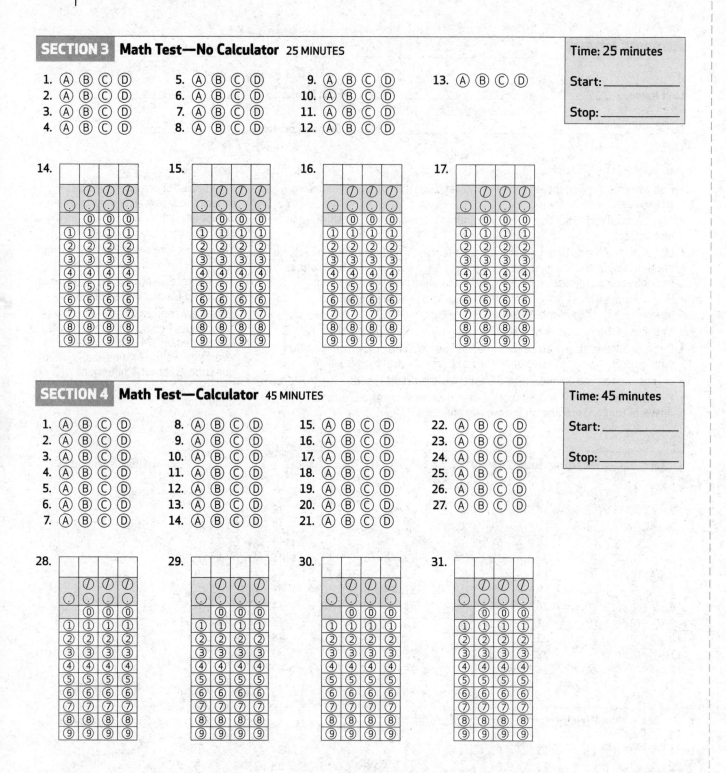

READING TEST

60 MINUTES, 47 QUESTIONS

Turn to Section 1 of your answer sheet to answer the questions in this section.

Directions: Each passage or pair of passages below is followed by a number of questions. After reading each passage or pair, choose the best answer to each question based on what is stated or implied in the passage or passages and in any accompanying graphics (such as a table or graph).

Questions 1–9 are based on the following passage.

This passage is from Charlotte Perkins Gilman's "The Yellow Wallpaper," a short story written in 1892. The setting is a large, aristocratic house where the narrator and her husband have come for the summer. The narrator is describing the house and commenting on her illness and marriage.

It is very seldom that mere ordinary people like John and myself secure ancestral halls for the summer. A colonial mansion, a hereditary estate, I would say a haunted house, and reach the height
5 of romantic felicity—but that would be asking too much of fate! Still I will proudly declare that there is something queer about it. Else, why should it be let so cheaply? And why have stood so long untenanted?

John laughs at me, of course, but one expects
10 that in marriage. John is practical in the extreme. He has no patience with faith, an intense horror of superstition, and he scoffs openly at any talk of things not to be felt and seen and put down in figures. John is a physician, and PERHAPS—(I
15 would not say it to a living soul, of course, but this is dead paper and a great relief to my mind)— PERHAPS that is one reason I do not get well faster.

You see he does not believe I am sick!

And what can one do?
20 If a physician of high standing, and one's own husband, assures friends and relatives that there is really nothing the matter with one but temporary

nervous depression—a slight hysterical tendency— what is one to do? My brother is also a physician,
25 and also of high standing, and he says the same thing. So I take phosphates or phosphites— whichever it is, and tonics, and journeys, and air, and exercise, and am absolutely forbidden to "work" until I am well again.
30 Personally, I disagree with their ideas.

Personally, I believe that congenial work, with excitement and change, would do me good.

But what is one to do?

I did write for a while in spite of them; but it
35 DOES exhaust me a good deal—having to be so sly about it, or else meet with heavy opposition. I sometimes fancy that in my condition if I had less opposition and more society and stimulus—but John says the very worst thing I can do is to think about
40 my condition, and I confess it always makes me feel bad. So I will let it alone and talk about the house.

The most beautiful place! It is quite alone, standing well back from the road, quite three miles from the village. It makes me think of English places
45 that you read about, for there are hedges and walls and gates that lock, and lots of separate little houses for the gardeners and people. There is a DELICIOUS garden! I never saw such a garden—large and shady, full of box-bordered paths, and lined with long
50 grape-covered arbors with seats under them. There were greenhouses, too, but they are all broken now.

GO ON TO THE NEXT PAGE ⟹

There was some legal trouble, I believe, something about the heirs and coheirs; anyhow, the place has been empty for years.

55 That spoils my ghostliness, I am afraid, but I don't care—there is something strange about the house—I can feel it. I even said so to John one moonlight evening, but he said what I felt was a DRAUGHT, and shut the window. I get unreasonably angry
60 with John sometimes. I'm sure I never used to be so sensitive. I think it is due to this nervous condition.

1. Which choice gives the best description of what happens in the passage?

    (A) A wife argues with her husband about which room they will stay in on their summer vacation.
    (B) A husband and brother, both of whom are respected physicians, try to diagnose an ill narrator unsuccessfully.
    (C) The narrator writes about her current surroundings, interrupting her descriptions with personal thoughts.
    (D) One character criticizes her husband's career choice and blames her illness on it.

2. Which choice best describes the passage?

    (A) a stream of consciousness journal entry
    (B) a question and response dialogue
    (C) a detailed analysis of symptoms and possible illnesses
    (D) a cheerful recounting of a memory

3. As used in line 1, "ordinary" most nearly means

    (E) habitual
    (F) prosaic
    (G) standard
    (H) average

4. Why does the narrator believe she is still sick?

    (A) She gets tired very easily.
    (B) Her husband doesn't believe she is sick.
    (C) She ate bad food recently.
    (D) The room her husband chose for them is not well ventilated.

5. Which choice provides the best evidence for the previous question?

    (A) Lines 14–18 ("John is a . . . I am sick!")
    (B) Lines 24–29 ("My brother . . . I am well again.")
    (C) Lines 34–41 ("I did write . . . me feel bad.")
    (D) Lines 55–61 ("That spoils . . . nervous condition.")

6. The narrator's attitude toward her husband is

    (A) utterly indifferent
    (B) wrathful and bitter
    (C) respectful but obligatory
    (D) unquestioningly reverent

7. John's attitude toward his wife is

    (A) passionately affectionate
    (B) condescending disregard
    (C) amusingly engaged and attentive
    (D) respectful equivalence

8. Which choice provides the best evidence for the previous question?

    (A) Lines 1–6 ("It is very . . . much of fate!")
    (B) Lines 6–8 ("Still I will . . . untenanted?")
    (C) Lines 9–14 ("John laughs . . . figures.")
    (D) Lines 30–33 ("Personally . . . one to do?")

9. As used twice in line 43, "quite" most nearly means

    (A) comparatively
    (B) moderate
    (C) slight
    (D) nearly

Questions 10-19 are based on the following passage.

This passage is from James Fergusson's A History of Architecture in All Countries, *published in 1874. This section comes from the chapter on Aryan Races and discusses religion.*

What then was the creed of the primitive Aryans? So far as we can now see, it was the belief in one great ineffable God,—so great that no human intellect could measure His greatness,—so
5 wonderful that no human language could express His qualities,—pervading everything that was made,—ruling all created things,—a spirit, around, beyond the universe, and within every individual particle of it. A creed so ethereal could not long
10 remain the faith of the multitude, and we early find fire,—the most ethereal of the elements,—looked to as an emblem of the Deity. The heavens too received a name, and became an entity:—so did our mother earth. To these succeeded the sun, the stars, the
15 elements,—but never among the pure Aryans as gods, or as influencing the destiny of man, but as manifestations of His power, and reverenced because they were visible manifestations of a Being too abstract for an ordinary mind to grasp. Below this
20 the Aryans never seem to have sunk.

With a faith so elevated of course no temple could be wanted; no human ceremonial could be supposed capable of doing honor to a Deity so conceived; nor any sacrifice acceptable to Him to whom all things
25 belonged. With the Aryans, worship was a purely domestic institution; prayer the solitary act of each individual man, standing alone in the presence of an omniscient Deity. All that was required was that man should acknowledge the greatness of God, and
30 his own comparative insignificance; should express his absolute trust and faith in the beneficence and justice of his God, and a hope that he might be enabled to live so pure, and so free from sin, as to deserve such happiness as this world can afford,
35 and be enabled to do as much good to others as it is vouchsafed to man to perform.

A few insignificant formulae served to mark the modes in which these subjects should recur. The recitation of a time-honored hymn refreshed the
40 attention of the worshipper, and the reading of a few sacred texts recalled the duties it was expected he should perform. With these simple ceremonies, the worship of the Aryans seems to have begun and ended.

45 Even in later times, when their blood has become less pure, and their feelings were influenced by association with those among whom they resided, the religion of the Aryans always retained its intellectual character. No dogma was ever admitted
50 that would not bear the test of reason, and no article of faith was ever assented to which seemed to militate against the supremacy of intellect over all feelings and passions. In all their wanderings, they were always prepared to admit the immeasurable
55 greatness of the one incorporeal Deity, and the impossibility of the human intellect approaching or forming any adequate conception of His majesty.

When they abandoned the domestic form of worship, they adopted the congregational, and then
60 not so much with the idea that it was pleasing to God, as in order to remind each other of their duties, to regulate and govern the spiritual wants of the community, and to inculcate piety towards God and charity towards each other.

65 It need hardly be added that superstition is impossible with minds so constituted, and that science must always be the surest and the best ally of a religion so pure and exalted, which is based on a knowledge of God's works, a consequent
70 appreciation of their greatness, and an ardent aspiration towards that power and goodness which the finite intellect of man can never hope to reach.

10. The passage indicates that the Aryans believed

   (A) fire was God and held ceremonies to honor earthly elements
   (B) God found pleasure in humans gathering often to worship together
   (C) human emotion drove spiritual connection
   (D) in one all-powerful God who was beyond human understanding

11. As used in line 1, the word "creed" most nearly means

   (A) religion
   (B) denomination
   (C) cult
   (D) church

12. The purpose of lines 25–36 ("With the Aryans . . . man to perform.") is to

   (A) explain the family roles in the Aryan culture
   (B) highlight why Aryans eventually changed their beliefs and practices
   (C) describe the daily practice of the Aryans' system of beliefs
   (D) contrast Aryan rituals with other religions

13. The passage indicates that the religious duties of Aryans were straightforward because

   (A) they were outlined clearly in one religious text
   (B) religious gatherings were brief and to the point
   (C) their rituals were simple and could be done at home
   (D) Aryan women were responsible for the family's fate

14. Which choice provides the best evidence for the previous question?

   (A) Lines 14–20 ("To these . . . to have sunk.")
   (B) Lines 37–44 ("A few insignificant . . . begun and ended.")
   (C) Lines 58–64 ("When they . . . towards each other.")
   (D) Lines 65–72 ("It need . . . hope to reach.")

15. The passage indicates that Aryans prioritized

   (A) reason over emotion
   (B) feeling over logic
   (C) ritual over personal faith
   (D) nation over state

16. Which choice provides the best evidence for the previous question?

   (A) Lines 14–20 ("To these . . . to have sunk.")
   (B) Lines 21–25 ("With a faith . . . belonged.")
   (C) Lines 37–44 ("A few insignificant . . . begun and ended.")
   (D) Lines 49–53 ("No dogma . . . passions.")

17. As used in line 54, "admit" most nearly means

   (A) allow entry
   (B) reveal
   (C) receive
   (D) acknowledge

18. The purpose of lines 58–64 is to

   (A) explain a change in religious practice
   (B) offer a counterargument
   (C) contrast Aryan practices with modern religions
   (D) introduce a question

19. According to the last paragraph, it is most important for Aryans to

(A) take careers in the sciences

(B) acknowledge and show gratitude for God's works

(C) remind their friends and family of their religious duties

(D) become God-like in their goodness

Questions 20–28 are based on the following passage.

This excerpt is adapted from Mark Twain's autobiography, 1906.

My experiences as an author began early in 1867. I came to New York from San Francisco in the first month of that year and presently Charles H. Webb, whom I had known in San Francisco as a reporter on
5 *The Bulletin*, and afterward editor of *The Californian*, suggested that I publish a volume of sketches. I had but a slender reputation to publish it on, but I was charmed and excited by the suggestion and quite willing to venture it if some industrious person
10 would save me the trouble of gathering the sketches together. I was loath to do it myself, for from the beginning of my sojourn in this world there was a persistent vacancy in me where the industry ought to be.

15 Webb said I had some reputation in the Atlantic States, but I knew quite well that it must be of a very attenuated sort. What there was of it rested upon the story of "The Jumping Frog." When Artemus Ward passed through California on a lecturing tour, in
20 1865 or '66, I told him the "Jumping Frog" story, in San Francisco, and he asked me to write it out and send it to his publisher, Carleton, in New York, to be used in padding out a small book which Artemus had prepared for the press and which needed some
25 more stuffing to make it big enough for the price which was to be charged for it.

It reached Carleton in time, but he didn't think much of it, and was not willing to go to the typesetting expense of adding it to the book. He
30 did not put it in the waste-basket, but made Henry Clapp a present of it, and Clapp used it to help out the funeral of his dying literary journal, *The Saturday Press*. "The Jumping Frog" appeared in the last number of that paper and was at once copied in
35 the newspapers of America and England. It certainly had a wide celebrity, and it still had it at the time that I am speaking of—but I was aware that it was only the frog that was celebrated. It wasn't I. I was still an obscurity.

40 Webb undertook to collate the sketches. He performed this office, then handed the result to me, and I went to Carleton's establishment with it. I approached a clerk and he bent eagerly over the counter to inquire into my needs; but when he found
45 that I had come to sell a book and not to buy one, his temperature fell sixty degrees. I meekly asked the privilege of a word with Mr. Carleton, and was coldly informed that he was in his private office. Discouragements and difficulties followed, but
50 after a while I got by the frontier and entered the holy of holies. Ah, now I remember how I managed it! Webb had made an appointment for me with Carleton; otherwise, I never should have gotten over that frontier. Carleton rose and said brusquely and
55 aggressively,

"Well, what can I do for you?"

I reminded him that I was there by appointment to offer him my book for publication. He began to swell, and went on swelling and swelling and
60 swelling until he had reached the dimensions of a god of about the second or third degree. Then the fountains of his great deep were broken up, and for two or three minutes I couldn't see him for the rain. It was words, only words, but they fell so densely
65 that they darkened the atmosphere. Finally, he made an imposing sweep with his right hand, which comprehended the whole room and said, "Books— look at those shelves! Every one of them is loaded with books that are waiting for publication. Do I
70 want any more? Excuse me, I don't. Good morning."

Twenty-one years elapsed before I saw Carleton again. I was then sojourning with my family at the Schweitzerhof, in Luzerne. He called on me, shook hands cordially, and said at once, without any
75 preliminaries, "I am substantially an obscure person, but I have at least one distinction to my credit of such colossal dimensions that it entitles me to immortality—to wit: I refused a book of yours, and for this I stand without competitor as the prize ass of
80 the nineteenth century."

20. The main purpose of this passage is to

(A) emphasize the importance of taking risks

(B) stress the difficulty of publishing a book

(C) ridicule a man's biggest mistake

(D) tell an ironic anecdote

21. The lesson of the passage is

(A) don't move to the East Coast to become an author

(B) don't snub someone; you may regret it

(C) don't let one thing determine your reputation

(D) don't show up without an appointment

22. As used in line 7, "slender" most nearly means

(A) limited

(B) slim

(C) willowy

(D) pitiful

23. According to the passage, Webb collected the sketches because

(A) Twain was too lazy to do it himself

(B) Webb had extra time and resources

(C) he wanted to make money off Twain

(D) they were back in California, and Twain couldn't return

24. Which choice provides the best evidence for the previous question?

(A) Lines 11–14 ("I was loath . . . ought to be.")

(B) Lines 17–22 ("What there was . . . in New York,")

(C) Lines 40–42 ("Webb undertook . . . with it.")

(D) Lines 52–54 ("Webb had . . . that frontier.")

25. When Mr. Carleton first meets Twain, he

(A) is sick and cannot stay for the meeting

(B) shakes his hand enthusiastically

(C) treats him disdainfully

(D) recognizes him right away

26. Which choice provides the best evidence for the previous question?

(A) Lines 29–35 ("He did not . . . England.")

(B) Lines 46–51 ("I meekly . . . holy of holies.")

(C) Lines 64–65 ("It was words . . . atmosphere.")

(D) Lines 65–70 ("Finally . . . Good morning.")

27. As used in line 75, "obscure" most nearly means

(A) hidden

(B) unknown

(C) shrouded

(D) invisible

GO ON TO THE NEXT PAGE ⟫

28. What is the purpose of lines 73–80 ("He called . . . nineteenth century.")?

(A) to stress Twain's newly acquired wealth and renown

(B) to illustrate a friendly conversation between old pals

(C) to justify Carleton's earlier decision

(D) to emphasize Carleton's regret for not taking Twain seriously

Questions 29–38 are based on the following passage.

This excerpt is adapted from William Baxter Jr.'s "The Evolution and Present Status of the Automobile," which was included in the Summer 1900 edition of The Popular Science Monthly.

In this closing year of a century which is marked by unparalleled advances in science and its applications to the industrial arts, we are very much inclined to take it for granted that none of the

5 inventions that are regarded by us as indicative of the highest order of progressive tendency, could by any possibility have been thought of by our forefathers; and as the automobile is looked upon as an ultra-progressive idea, no one who has not investigated

10 the subject would believe for a moment that its conception could antedate the present generation, much less the present century. The records, however, show that the subject engrossed the attention of inventive minds many hundreds of years ago.

15 In fact, as far back as the beginning of the thirteenth century a Franciscan monk named Roger Bacon prophesied that, the day would come when boats and carriages would be propelled by machinery. The first authentic record of a self-

20 propelled carriage dates back to the middle of the sixteenth century. The inventor was Johann Haustach, of Nuremburg. The device is described as a chariot propelled by the force of springs, and it is said that it attained a speed of two thousand paces

25 per hour, about one mile and a quarter. Springs have been tried by many inventors since that time, but always without success from the simple fact that the amount of energy that can be stored in a spring is practically insignificant.

30 In 1763 a Frenchman by the name of Cugnot devised a vehicle that was propelled by steam, and a few years after the date of his first experiment, constructed for the French Government a gun carriage. The design was of the tricycle type, and

35 it was intended to mount the gun between the rear wheels. The boiler, which resembles a huge kettle, hung over the front end and was apparently devoid of a smoke stack. Motion was imparted to the front wheel by means of a ratchet. Although this invention

40 is very crude, it must be regarded as meritorious if we consider that it was made before the steam engine had been developed in a successful form for stationary purposes.

The next effort to solve the problem was made by

45 W. Symington in the year 1784. Symington's coach, although pretentious in appearance, was crude mechanically, but it actually ran. Between 1805 and 1830, quite a number of steam vehicles were invented and put into practical operation. Perhaps the most

50 perfect of all the early automobiles was the one devised by Scott Russell, the celebrated designer of the *Great Eastern*. It was operated successfully, and was able to mount the steepest hills and to attain

a high rate of speed, but as coal was used for fuel
and the engines were of large capacity, it is probable
that the smoke, exhaust steam and noise of the
machinery were decidedly objectionable features.
A line of these coaches was put in commission in
Glasgow in 1846, each one having a seating capacity
of twenty-six, six inside and twenty on the top. After
several months of successful operation, the line
was withdrawn on account of the opposition of the
authorities and of the general public.

These few examples of the early attempts to solve
the problem of mechanical propulsion of vehicles
are sufficient to show that the automobile is not

entirely a creation of the progressive mind of the
latter part of the nineteenth century, but that it
engrossed the attention of inventors more than one
hundred and thirty years ago. The success attained
by the workers in this field at different periods was
directly in proportion to the degree to which the
form of power used had been perfected at the time.
The first inventors attained but slight success, owing
to the fact that, in their time, the steam engine was
in a crude form, but as the construction of the latter
improved, so did that of the vehicles operated by it.

*Below is a table outlining the early history of
automobile technology.*

INVENTOR/ENTREPRENEUR	YEAR	DESCRIPTION	LOCATION
Nicolas-Joseph Cugnot	1769	First self-propelled road vehicle	France
Robert Anderson	1869	First electric carriage	Scotland
Karl Benz	1886	First gasoline automobile powered by an internal combustion engine	Germany
Gottlieb Willhelm Daimler	1886	First four-wheeled, four-stroke engine	Germany
George Baldwin Selden	1895	First combined internal combustion engine with a carriage	United States
Charles Edgar Duryea	1893	First successful gas-powered car	United States
Ransom E. Olds	1901	Olds Automobile Factory starts mass production in Detroit	United States
William Durant	1908	Forms General Motors	United States
Henry Ford	1908	Begins production of the Model T	United States

29. As used in line 4, "inclined" most nearly means

(A) biased
(B) favored
(C) leaning
(D) likely

30. An inventor claims that the automobile
originated around 1886. Which statement
contradicts the inventor's claim?

(A) Lines 1–7 ("In this . . . our forefathers;")
(B) Lines 8–14 ("and as the . . . of years ago.")
(C) Lines 22–25 ("The device . . . a quarter.")
(D) Lines 25–29 ("Springs . . . practically
insignificant.")

31. According to the author, the idea of the automobile was first conceived

    (A) as early as the thirteenth century
    (B) in the mid-sixteenth century
    (C) in 1846
    (D) a decade before the writing of this article

32. Which choice provides the best evidence for the previous question?

    (A) Lines 15–19 ("In fact . . . by machinery.")
    (B) Lines 19–22 ("The first . . . sixteenth century.")
    (C) Lines 47–49 ("Between 1805 . . . practical operation.")
    (D) Lines 58–60 ("A line of . . . on the top.")

33. The purpose of the fourth paragraph (lines 44–63 is to

    (A) give an extensive history of the modern automobile
    (B) introduce early inventors
    (C) provide examples of early attempts at the automobile
    (D) point out critical failures in Scott Russell's manufacturing design

34. As used in line 53, "mount" most nearly means

    (A) jump on
    (B) stage
    (C) multiply
    (D) ascend

35. According to the author, the *Great Eastern* ultimately failed because of

    (A) the lack of a smoke stack
    (B) it could not climb hills
    (C) the noise and exhaust smoke
    (D) it wasn't fast enough

36. According to the passage, the author believes

    (A) the automobile is not a new idea, but early inventors didn't have the power technology to be successful
    (B) the automobile is the most significant factor to industrial and economic growth
    (C) the automobile is a new, pioneering invention that came about abruptly
    (D) nineteenth century society happily acknowledges and understands that their forefathers are responsible for current industrial growth

37. Does the table support the author's argument?

    (A) Yes, because it shows that the true automobile originated in 1886.
    (B) Yes, because it illustrates that inventors were working on the automobile before the nineteenth century.
    (C) No, because it doesn't include biographies on each inventor.
    (D) No, because it focuses only on technologies after 1900 in the United States.

38. According to the table, automobile manufacturing in factories began

    (A) many years before this passage was written
    (B) a century after this passage was written
    (C) shortly after this passage was written
    (D) not enough information to determine

Practice Test 1

Questions 39–47 are based on the following passages.

Passage 1 is a student's interpretation of a passage from Friedrich Nietzsche's Beyond Good and Evil. *Passage 2 is adapted from John Stuart Mill's* Utilitarianism.

PASSAGE 1

In the ninth chapter of *Beyond Good and Evil*, titled "What Is Noble?," Nietzsche claims that human excellency is dependent on a caste system. According to Nietzsche, every worthy human
5 advancement can be attributed to the aristocratic class. Not only has this been true in the past; for Nietzsche, it will continue to be true for the duration of humanity. A caste system, of course, relies on difference—there must be a ranking of individuals,
10 a superior class defined as all that is not the inferior class. Ultimately, Nietzsche argues that exploitation is natural and unavoidable. Furthermore, progress necessitates exploitation.

According to this chapter, men, naturally
15 barbaric, seek power and control. Any refusal of this ideology is naive since, for Nietzsche, power is synonymous with life. Civilization, as we know it, is the product of strong men preying on weaker men. Nietzsche does not suggest this itself is morally right
20 but instead that it is merely a fact of life—in fact, he acknowledges that the "weaker" races are usually the more moral and peaceful. Yet, their disinclination to conquer and subordinate other men makes them the inferior; they will never rise to nobility. On the
25 other hand, the noble class firmly believes in its own exceptionality. The members of the upper-class truly understand themselves as greater than the rest, as better than the commoners. As such, the accomplishments and deeds of the ruling class are
30 not what differentiate them, but instead this sense of self-respect—they are destined for greatness.

Since power is a natural instinct, the need for domination and subordination is present in every living organism and structure. Hence, the
35 master-slave dynamic is essential to Nietzsche's

understanding of morality. The upper-class identifies as powerful and healthy, as good, while it sees members of the lower-class as weak and poor, as bad. In contrast, the oppressed see oppressors as bad and
40 define themselves in opposition to wealth and power, representations of evil. As these subjective moralities are passed on through generations, humans develop their character based on their ancestors' status in life. Those who inherit the noble mentality will be
45 above the morality of the common man, setting their own value beyond the "good and evil" which hinders the weak.

PASSAGE 2

The creed which accepts as the foundation of morals, Utility, or the Greatest Happiness Principle,
50 holds that actions are right in proportion as they tend to promote happiness, wrong as they tend to produce the reverse of happiness. By happiness is intended pleasure, and the absence of pain; by unhappiness, pain, and the privation of pleasure.

55 To give a clear view of the moral standard set up by the theory, much more requires to be said; in particular, what things it includes in the ideas of pain and pleasure; and to what extent this is left an open question. But these supplementary
60 explanations do not affect the theory of life on which this theory of morality is grounded—namely, that pleasure, and freedom from pain, are the only things desirable as ends; and that all desirable things (which are as numerous in the utilitarian
65 as in any other scheme) are desirable either for the pleasure inherent in themselves, or as means to the promotion of pleasure and the prevention of pain.

Now, such a theory of life excites in many minds, and among them in some of the most estimable in
70 feeling and purpose, inveterate dislike. To suppose that life has (as they express it) no higher end than pleasure—no better and nobler object of desire and pursuit—they designate as utterly mean and groveling; as a doctrine worthy only of swine, to

GO ON TO THE NEXT PAGE ⟼

75 whom the followers of Epicurus were, at a very
early period, contemptuously likened; and modern
holders of the doctrine are occasionally made the
subject of equally polite comparisons by its German,
French, and English assailants.

80   The comparison of the Epicurean life to that of
beasts is felt as degrading, precisely because a beast's
pleasures do not satisfy a human being's conceptions
of happiness. There is no known Epicurean theory
of life which does not assign to the pleasures of the
85 intellect; of the feelings and imagination, and of the
moral sentiments, a much higher value as pleasures
than to those of mere sensation.

39. As used in line 4, "worthy" most nearly means

(A) blameless
(B) estimable
(C) prime
(D) select

40. What does Nietzsche say about aristocratic rule?

(A) It is pompous and antiquated.
(B) It gives equal rights to all.
(C) It is not only a custom of the past but will
continue indefinitely.
(D) It has hindered human progress throughout
history.

41. According to Passage 1, the need for power is

(A) instinctual and representative of all life
structures
(B) unique to the human species
(C) an adopted mentality that humans acquired
with technological advances
(D) the most significant impediment to human
progress

42. Which choice provides the best evidence for the
previous question?

(A) Lines 4–8 ("According to . . . humanity.")
(B) Lines 14–18 ("According to . . . weaker men.")
(C) Lines 26–31 ("The members . . . for
greatness.")
(D) Lines 32–36 ("Since power . . . morality.")

43. According to the author of Passage 2,
utilitarianism is a theory that

(A) is better suited for farm animals
than humans
(B) doesn't adequately define morality
(C) defines right actions as those that promote
the most happiness
(D) defines wrong actions as those that promote
pleasure

44. The author of Passage 2 indicates that objectors
to utilitarianism fail to

(A) listen to Epicureans
(B) notice that their own beliefs are illogical
(C) understand the theory because they have
never felt pain
(D) recognize that quality, not just quantity, of
pleasure is accounted for

45. As used in line 61, "grounded" most
nearly means

(A) sensible
(B) prevented
(C) instructed
(D) rooted

Practice Test 1 (side tab)

46. The relationship between the two passages can be best described as

(A) Passage 2 refutes the central argument in Passage 1.

(B) Passage 1 more clearly illustrates the phenomenon described in Passage 2.

(C) The passages are two nearly identical philosophical approaches to ethics.

(D) The passages are two very different philosophical approaches to morality.

47. Nietzsche might respond to the idea of utilitarianism discussed in Passage 2 by claiming that

(A) the unhappiness of the common man is a necessary sacrifice for the advancement of humankind

(B) the caste system creates unhappiness and should be abolished

(C) since there are more common men than aristocrats, the commoners should implement utilitarianism and stage a revolt

(D) pleasure is a representation of evil

STOP

If you finish before time is called, you may check your work on this section only.

Do not turn to any other section.

WRITING AND LANGUAGE TEST
35 MINUTES, 44 QUESTIONS

Directions: Answer the following questions on Section 2 of your Answer Sheet. Each passage is accompanied by questions that ask you to revise or edit the passage to improve its flow, organization, clarity, and sentence mechanics. For most questions, you will be directed to an underlined portion of the passage to either choose "NO CHANGE" or to select the appropriate revision. For other questions, you'll be asked to think about the passage as a whole. Some passages may also include a graphic to consider as you edit.

Questions 1–11 are based on the following passage.

A Letter to the Editor

[1] In the *New Yorker's* June 2017 issue, Toni Morrison writes barely a page on the work we do and how it impacts our sense of self. [2] **1** In barely a page, Morrison makes some profound discoveries, which she lists in four **2** snappy bullet points. [3] Her first realization is that regardless of what type of work we do or how well we enjoy it, **3** we should maximize our enthusiasm—not for anybody else, but for ourselves. [4] Her second revelation deals with perception, our ability to "make the job" rather than to be made, molded, and controlled by it. [5] And in her most profound declaration, Morrison suggests that we must always refuse to be defined by the work we do, saying, "You are not the work you do; you are the person you are." [6] Next, **4** she identifies important differences between home and work: insisting that "real life" happens at home rather than at any place of employment. [7] The article is framed by an early experience of hers at a first job during the second world war, but it proves to be increasingly relevant. **5**

1. (A) NO CHANGE
   (B) In barely a page Morrison
   (C) In barely a page Morrison,
   (D) In barely a page—Morrison

2. (A) NO CHANGE
   (B) concise
   (C) abbreviated
   (D) verbose

3. (A) NO CHANGE
   (B) you should take pride in it
   (C) we should do it well
   (D) one should put forth their best effort

4. Which choice flows most logically with the rest of the sentence?

(A) NO CHANGE
(B) she differentiates life at home from life at work;
(C) she distinguishes a job from a career,
(D) she separates home from work,

5. To make this paragraph flow most logically, sentence 6 should be placed:

(A) Where it is now
(B) After sentence 2
(C) After sentence 3
(D) After sentence 4

I recently moved cross country and realized just how constitutive our careers are to our own sense of personhood as well as to other people's understandings of who we are. **6** Every time I disclosed the upcoming move to a family member or friend, the news was met with, "Ohh, what job did you take?" or "What will you be doing out there?" **7** It wasn't until I'd been sharing my decision for three weeks or so that I began to feel unsettled by my loved ones' reactions, and then to ultimately avoid **8** their conversation altogether. I began to wonder if a job was the only socially acceptable reason for a relocation. Couldn't I move for a myriad of reasons? Perhaps, more than the reaction of those closest to me, I was increasingly unnerved by my own hesitation to reveal the uncertainty of my job prospects. **9** I didn't want to admit that I only had temporary employment.

6. (A) NO CHANGE
   (B) Each and every time I vouchsafed
   (C) When I told
   (D) Every single time I explained

7. At this point, the writer is considering adding the following sentence.

   > Not only did I expect this response, but initially I found it sensible.

   Should the reader make this addition?

   (A) Yes, because it adds an important detail and transitions smoothly to the next sentence.
   (B) Yes, because it gives an example of the writer's rebuttal to others' responses.
   (C) No, because it is repetitive.
   (D) No, because it contradicts the main idea of the passage.

8. (A) NO CHANGE
   (B) our
   (C) the
   (D) my

9. The writer wants a concluding sentence that explores how a perception of one's job can impact self-image. Which choice accomplishes this best?

   (A) NO CHANGE
   (B) I felt guilty that my family and friends didn't have similar opportunities.
   (C) If my work was dubious, was I equally suspect?
   (D) Would I learn to love my new career?

Practice Test 1

With my new awareness, I have begun to note how often people name what they do in order to clarify who they are. **10** In a recent NPR podcast, one sociologist claimed that seven out of ten college graduates identify themselves by their job; I couldn't help thinking the estimate sounded low. I wonder what Morrison makes of this: our tendency to quite literally determine a **11** persons value based on the work he or she does. I wonder what she thinks of the larger issue: our tendency to align self-worth with our level of labor.

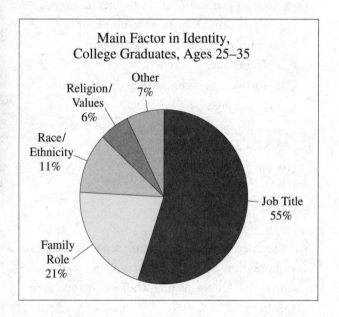

Main Factor in Identity,
College Graduates, Ages 25–35

Other 7%
Religion/Values 6%
Race/Ethnicity 11%
Job Title 55%
Family Role 21%

10. Does the data in the chart support this claim?

(A) Yes, because approximately seven out of ten people surveyed identified by their job title.

(B) Yes, because 7% of people surveyed identified as "Other."

(C) No, because less than 70% identified by their job title.

(D) No, because most people identified by other factors like family role or race.

11. (A) NO CHANGE
    (B) person's
    (C) persons'
    (D) people's

Questions 12–22 are based on the following passage.

The History of Mary Prince serves as an indispensable look into the lives of black women slaves. **12** First published in 1831, it not only tells the story of Prince but incorporates bits and pieces of the experiences of many slaves. **13** Evidently, scholars have used it not only as a record of Prince's personal experience but as **14** a tool for examining the institution of slavery more generally.

Prince herself acknowledges the ways in which her story contributes to a larger abolitionist **15** project. "I have been a slave—I have felt what a slave feels, and I know what a slave knows; and I would have all the good people in England to know it too, that they may break our chains, and set us free." In this declaration, Prince tells the reader two very important things. First, that slaves are human—that they feel and develop relations in the same ways as other humans. **16** Second, Prince aligns her own story with the wider institution of slavery **17** but the eventual goal of emancipation.

12. The writer is considering deleting the underlined portion (beginning the sentence with "It"). Should the writer make this deletion?

(A) Yes, because it distracts the reader from the focus of the passage.
(B) Yes, because it is repetitive.
(C) No, because it defines an important term.
(D) No, because it provides relevant information about the topic of the passage.

13. (A) NO CHANGE
(B) Regardless,
(C) In contrast to,
(D) Consequently,

14. (A) NO CHANGE
(B) an academic tool
(C) a scholarly resource
(D) an instrument of research

15. (A) NO CHANGE
(B) project:
(C) project;
(D) project

16. (A) NO CHANGE
(B) Third,
(C) Also,
(D) And then,

17. (A) NO CHANGE
(B) because
(C) and
(D) so

The letter written by John A. Wood and included in the supplement to this text illuminates the complex cultural and social atmosphere in which Prince tells **18** their story. Interestingly, Thomas Pringle opted to publish the letter **19** as part of Prince's story, which is necessarily problematic, carrying with it its own context as a tool of abolitionist propaganda. Yet, the letter is reportedly copied down word for word and so deserves particular attention.

Wood gives it to Prince as she leaves his house, and it works not only to establish his own credibility and combat any negative assumptions about his character but also to falsify an independence which Mary certainly is not afforded by her white masters. Its contradictions manifest most clearly in Wood's emphasis on the many choices Prince supposedly has; if one were to **20** accept skepticism, the letter suggests that Prince consciously chose her position as slave, her location in London, and her current circumstance as sick and homeless. Wood, while talking to an unknown presumably white audience rather than addressing Prince, **21** write that the letter is for "her [. . .] in order that there may be no misunderstanding on her part". He goes on to express his regret that Prince is leaving his household since "she is a stranger in London" and will obviously be hard-pressed to find lodging and basic necessities.

18. (A) NO CHANGE
    (B) his
    (C) our
    (D) her

19. (A) NO CHANGE
    (B) in addition to
    (C) right before
    (D) as a necessary complement to

20. (A) NO CHANGE
    (B) suspend
    (C) neglect
    (D) fall into

21. (A) NO CHANGE
    (B) writes
    (C) wrote
    (D) has written

GO ON TO THE NEXT PAGE ⟹

Moreover, the circumstance, according to Wood, results from Prince's own actions: her "request," "entreaty," and idleness. While these words in and of themselves may not be surprising, together they form a letter, a historical record, that reveals the utter inconsistency and contradiction of the slavemaster during this time period— 22 this letter was neither written for Prince's benefit nor was she furnished the luxury of choice.

22. The writer is considering deleting the underlined portion (ending the sentence with "period."). Should the writer make this deletion?

(A) Yes, because it is repetitive.

(B) Yes, because it changes the subject of the passage.

(C) No, because it transitions into a new topic.

(D) No, because it clarifies the statement made immediately beforehand.

Questions 23–33 are based on the following passage.

Below is an excerpt adapted from the fourth chapter of Charles Darwin's On the Origin of Species *titled "Natural Selection."*

The preservation of favorable variations and the rejection of injurious variations, I call Natural Selection. Variations 23 neither useful nor injurious would not be effected by natural selection, and would be left a fluctuating element, as perhaps we see in 24 the species called polymorphic.

We shall best understand the probable course of natural selection by taking the case of a country 25 in the midst of a huge change, for instance, of climate. The proportional numbers of its inhabitants would almost immediately undergo a change, and some species might become extinct. We may conclude, from what we have seen of the intimate and complex manner in which the inhabitants of each country are bound together, that any change in the numerical proportions of some of the inhabitants, independently of the change of climate itself, would seriously 26 effect many of the others.

23. (A) NO CHANGE

(B) neither useful nor injurious would not be affected by

(C) neither useful or injurious would not be affected by

(D) either useful nor injurious would not be effected by

24. (A) NO CHANGE

(B) the species we have named polymorphic.

(C) the species given the fitting name of polymorphic.

(D) the polymorphic species, named for their variability.

25. (A) NO CHANGE

(B) which was having some sort of physical change

(C) having a really big change

(D) undergoing some physical change

26. (A) NO CHANGE

(B) have affected

(C) effects

(D) affect

Practice Test 1

If the country were open 27 on its borders new forms would certainly immigrate, and this also would seriously disturb the relations of some of the former inhabitants. But in the case of an island, or of a country partly surrounded by barriers, into which 28 new and better adapted forms could not freely enter, we should then have places in the economy of nature which would assuredly be better filled up, if some of the original inhabitants were in some manner modified; for, had the area been open to immigration, these same places would have been 29 overrun on by intruders. In such case, every slight modification, which in the course of ages chanced to arise, and which in any way favored the individuals of any of the species, by better adapting them to their altered conditions, would tend to be preserved; and natural selection would thus have free scope for the work of improvement. 30

27. (A) NO CHANGE
    (B) on it's borders—
    (C) on it's borders,
    (D) on its borders,

28. (A) NO CHANGE
    (B) newly adapted forms
    (C) the best adaptations
    (D) new, better, and more efficient adapted forms

29. (A) NO CHANGE
    (B) seized
    (C) grabbed
    (D) arrested

30. At this point, the writer is considering making the following addition.

    When an area consists of distinct barriers that don't allow for immigration, natural selection gradually increases variability in order to ensure that the existing species adapt to their current environment.

    Should the writer make the addition here?

    (A) Yes, because it gives a specific example of how natural selection occurs.
    (B) Yes, because it explains how Darwin came to prove his main argument.
    (C) No, because it repeats what the previous sentence says and is unnecessary.
    (D) No, because it abruptly changes the topic of the paragraph.

We have reason to believe that a change in the conditions of life, by specially acting on the reproductive system, causes or increases variability; and in the foregoing case the conditions of life 31 was supposed to have undergone a change, and this would manifestly be favorable to natural selection, 32 by giving a better chance of profitable variations occurring; and unless profitable variations do occur, natural selection can do nothing. Not that any extreme amount of variability is necessary; as man can certainly produce great results by adding up in any given direction mere individual differences, so could Nature, but far more easily, from having incomparably longer time at her disposal. Nor do I believe that 33 one tremendous physical alteration: as of climate, or any unusual degree of isolation to check immigration, is actually necessary to produce new and unoccupied places for natural selection to fill up by modifying and improving some of the varying inhabitants.

31. (A) NO CHANGE
    (B) were
    (C) are
    (D) is

32. Which choice provides the best explanation of natural selection according to the main argument of the passage?

    (A) NO CHANGE
    (B) by giving each species a lesser chance of variability;
    (C) by inhibiting further adaptation;
    (D) by stopping evolution and allowing the weaker species to die off;

33. (A) NO CHANGE
    (B) any great physical change, as of climate,
    (C) any big change; such as climate;
    (D) any huge alteration of climate or other environmental factors,

Questions 34–44 are based on the following passage.

Kevin Yelvington opens his 2006 anthology with his own article, "The Invention of Africa in Latin America and the Caribbean: Political Discourse and Anthropological Praxis, 1920–1940." [34] Yelvington is able through an examination of the work and life of Melville Jean Herskovits to question the conceptual systems and institutional methods in anthropology that govern the shape of knowledge production in diaspora studies. [35] Ultimately, Yelvington suggests that we are able to re-engage "with Afro-American peoples and cultures through an understanding of the historical-contextual and political basis of anthropological endeavors." [36] In other words, a better understanding of the anthropological approaches used to explore African populations in Latin American and the Caribbean yields a better understanding of the peoples and cultures themselves.

Yelvington's anthology takes a dialogic approach to the development of anthropological discourse, emphasizing an inherent interaction between anthropologist, contemporary social positioning, topics (and even objects) of study, and the political context of the moment. For Yelvington, the foundational perspectives of anthropological research need to be reexamined, taking into account [37] their power struggles involved. To do this, Yelvington relies on a certain definition of culture as "a historical process [. . .] that is made and remade," with blacks themselves active in the construction of their own cultural [38] spheres, which they have undoubtedly influenced.

34. (A) NO CHANGE
   (B) Yelvington is able, through an examination of the work and life of Melville Jean Herskovits,
   (C) Yelvington is able; through an examination of the work, and life of Melville Jean Herskovits,
   (D) Yelvington is able, through an examination of the work and life of Melville Jean Herskovits—

35. (A) NO CHANGE
   (B) Moreover,
   (C) Therefore,
   (D) Additionally,

36. The writer is considering deleting the underlined portion. Should the writer make this deletion?

   (A) Yes, because it is repetitive and confusing.
   (B) Yes, because it detracts from the passage's focus.
   (C) No, because it gives relevant detail.
   (D) No, because it simplifies what was said in the previous sentence.

37. (A) NO CHANGE
   (B) his
   (C) the vast number of
   (D) the

38. (A) NO CHANGE
   (B) spheres, which are circular.
   (C) spheres.
   (D) spheres, worlds which they have helped make.

The concept of "Africa," Yelvington argues, has been invented in Western discourse, first as primitive and then as empowered. He is skeptical of both inventions, arguing not for one or the other, but for a scholarship that is aware of the historical processes and problematic social environments that **39** have contributed to what is considered knowledge.

Several of the articles overlap in their attention to a "blending" of African and colonialist cultures characterized by **40** constant fluctuation and reimagining. Yelvington remains cautious of the anthropological approaches that have guided the study of the diaspora, and the subsequent **41** concept's of "Africa" and "Africanness" that have resulted. The collection points at syncretism, adaption, and amalgamation **42** more then at any possibility of discovering or defining an authentic Africa. Through **43** an interpolation of the modes and methodologies used to study and define—or "invent"—Africa and African peoples, a better understanding arises of the inherent fluidity and creolization of diaspora cultures. **44** Anthropology has revealed a lot, but there is still much to learn.

39. (A) NO CHANGE
    (B) contributes
    (C) has contributed
    (D) will contribute

40. Which choice expresses the idea that the cultures are changing and interacting?
    (A) NO CHANGE
    (B) their lengthy relationship with one another.
    (C) conflict and violence.
    (D) continuous conversation.

41. (A) NO CHANGE
    (B) concepts
    (C) concepts'
    (D) concept is

42. (A) NO CHANGE
    (B) more than at
    (C) before
    (D) rather then at

43. (A) NO CHANGE
    (B) an expression
    (C) a division
    (D) a dissection

44. Which choice best concludes this passage?
    (A) NO CHANGE
    (B) Yelvington's anthology stirs conversation among people of different cultures.
    (C) This understanding not only dismantles the Western narrative of Africa, but also challenges any narratives that have evolved therefrom.
    (D) The stories that attempt to answer the questions "What is Africa?" and "What does it mean to be African" are right on, thanks to early anthropologists.

STOP

If you finish before time is called, you may check your work on this section only.

Do not turn to any other section.

MATH TEST—NO CALCULATOR

25 MINUTES, 17 QUESTIONS

To answer questions in this section turn to Section 3 of your answer sheet.

Directions: Choose the best answer choice for questions 1–13 and fill in the answer sheet accordingly. Solve questions 14–17 and fill in the answer sheet accordingly. Before moving on to question 14, refer to the directions on how to fill in the answers on the answer sheet. Use of available space on the test booklet is allowed.

Notes

1. **No calculator use** is permitted.
2. Unless indicated, variables and expressions represent real numbers.
3. Figures are drawn to scale.
4. Figures lie in a plane.
5. The domain of a function f is the set of all real numbers x where $f(x)$ is a real number.

Reference

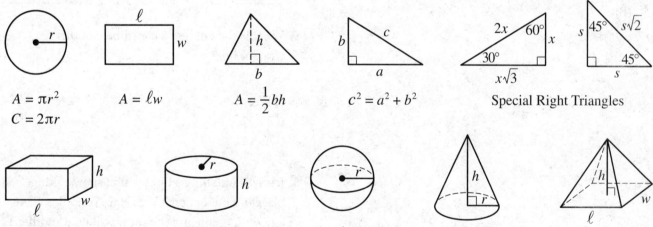

$A = \pi r^2$
$C = 2\pi r$

$A = \ell w$

$A = \frac{1}{2}bh$

$c^2 = a^2 + b^2$

Special Right Triangles

$V = \ell wh$

$V = \pi r^2 h$

$V = \frac{4}{3}\pi r^3$

$V = \frac{1}{3}\pi r^2 h$

$V = \frac{1}{3}\ell wh$

There is a total of 360 degrees in the arc of a circle.

There is a total of 2π radians in the arc of a circle.

There is a total of 180 degrees in the internal angles of a triangle.

GO ON TO THE NEXT PAGE ⟹

1. A teacher buys 5 packs of markers at $12.79 per pack, and a tax of 8.9% is added. How much did the teacher pay in total?

   (A) $51.16
   (B) $56.92
   (C) $63.95
   (D) $69.64

2. If $p = \dfrac{12}{5}$, what is the value of q when $\dfrac{p}{3} = \dfrac{11}{q}$?

   (A) $\dfrac{12}{15}$

   (B) $\dfrac{2}{5}$

   (C) $\dfrac{36}{5}$

   (D) $\dfrac{55}{4}$

3. $n^{2/4} = ?$

   (A) $\sqrt{2n}$

   (B) $\dfrac{n}{2}$

   (C) $\sqrt{n}$

   (D) $\dfrac{2}{n}$

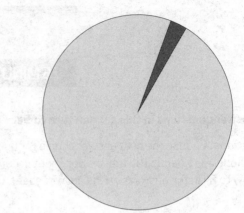

4. A circle with a radius of 18 is cut into slices through the center. One piece has an angle of 10°. What is the area of this piece?

   (A) 9π
   (B) 18π
   (C) 288π
   (D) 324π

x	0	–2	–7	?
y	4	8	18	42

5. What is the missing x coordinate of this straight line?

   (A) –38
   (B) 12
   (C) –19
   (D) –12

6. Jenny is watching a live fashion show, taking place in London, on TV in New York. It is 10:46 a.m. in London and the show will take another 1 hour and 57 minutes to finish. London is 5 hours ahead of New York. What time is it going to be in New York when the show finishes?

   (A) 12:43 p.m.
   (B) 5:46 p.m.
   (C) 7:43 a.m.
   (D) 10:46 a.m.

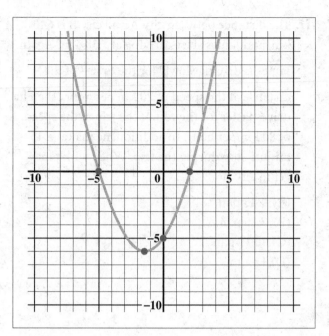

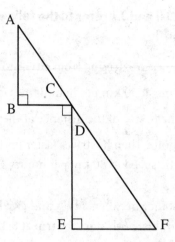

7. Which of the following functions is represented in the graph above?

(A) $y = \dfrac{1}{2}(x + 6)\left(x + \dfrac{3}{2}\right)$

(B) $y = 2(x - 6)\left(x - \dfrac{3}{2}\right)$

(C) $y = \dfrac{1}{2}(x + 5)(x - 2)$

(D) $y = 2(x - 5)(x + 2)$

8. In the figure above, if AF is a straight line and angle A is 33°, what is angle F?

(A) 28°

(B) 33°

(C) 46°

(D) 57°

9. Inertia of a disk rotating around its center is represented by the following equation: $I = \dfrac{1}{2}mr^2$, where I represents inertia, m represents mass, and r represents radius. Which of the following equations represents r in relation to the other variables?

(A) $\dfrac{2I}{m}$

(B) $\sqrt{\dfrac{2I}{m}}$

(C) $\dfrac{1}{2}mI$

(D) $2mI$

GO ON TO THE NEXT PAGE ⇒

Questions 10 and 11 refer to the following information.

Sam and James are driving from city A to city B. Sam is driving at 50 km per hour. James is driving slowly for the first $\frac{1}{4}$ of the distance at the speed of 20 km per hour. Then he drives faster for the rest of the trip at the speed of 80 km per hour.

10. The distance between city A and city B is 400 km, and they both start the trip at 8:35 a.m. What is the difference in their arrival time?

    (A) 0 hour
    (B) 45 minutes
    (C) 1 hour and 35 minutes
    (D) 3 hours

11. The distance between city A and city B is 640 km, and James starts driving at 7:30 a.m. Again, James is driving slowly for the first $\frac{1}{4}$ of the distance at the speed of 20 km per hour. Then he drives faster for the rest of the trip at the speed of 80 km per hour. In addition, he makes a 45 minute stop during the trip. When will James get to city B?

    (A) 4:45 p.m.
    (B) 7:25 p.m.
    (C) 10:15 p.m.
    (D) 12 a.m.

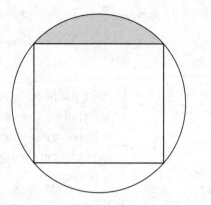

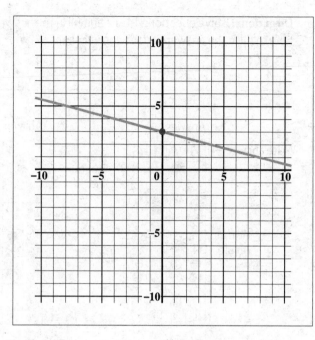

12. In the figure above a square is inscribed inside a circle. If the radius is $6\sqrt{2}$, what is the area of the shaded region?

(A) $16\sqrt{2}\pi$

(B) $36\pi - 9$

(C) $18\pi - 36$

(D) 36π

13. Reflect the line above along the x axis and translate the line 3 units up. What is the new equation of the line?

(A) $y = 4x - 3$

(B) $y = -4x + 3$

(C) $y = \dfrac{1}{4}x - 3$

(D) $y = \dfrac{1}{4}x$

Directions: Solve questions 14–17 and fill in the answer sheet accordingly. Refer to the following directions on how to fill in the answers on the answer sheet.

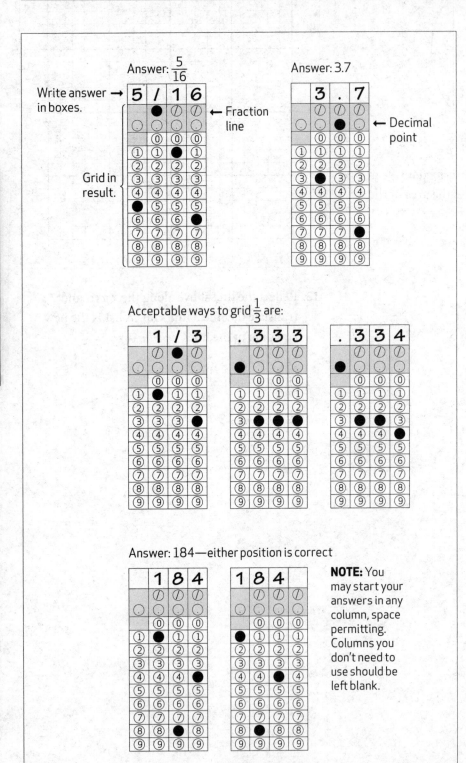

Answer: $\frac{5}{16}$

Write answer in boxes. → Grid in result.

← Fraction line

Answer: 3.7

← Decimal point

Acceptable ways to grid $\frac{1}{3}$ are:

Answer: 184—either position is correct

1. Only the filled-in circles are graded. The directions suggest writing the answer in the box at the top, but it is not scored.

2. Fill in only one circle in any column.

3. There are no negative answers.

4. Only fill in one correct answer, even if there are more than one.

5. **Mixed numbers** like $2\frac{1}{2}$ should be filled in as 2.5 or 5/2.

6. **Decimal answers:** If you obtain a decimal answer with more digits, it should be filled in to fill the entire grid.

NOTE: You may start your answers in any column, space permitting. Columns you don't need to use should be left blank.

14. What is the value of $6x$, when $3x + 6 = 27$?

$y > 5x - 11$

$y < -2x + 12$

15. (x, y) is a solution to the system of equations above. What is the smallest possible integer value of y, if x is 3?

16. The axis of symmetry of the parabola with the equation $y = (x - 6)^2 + 8$ is $x =$?

17. What is the radius of a circle with the equation of $x^2 + 4x + y^2 + 6y - 23 = 0$?

STOP

You can check your work only in this section, if you finished ahead of time.

Do not turn to other sections.

MATH TEST—CALCULATOR
45 MINUTES, 31 QUESTIONS

To answer questions in this section turn to Section 4 of your answer sheet.

Directions: Choose the best answer choice for questions 1–27 and fill in the answer sheet accordingly. Solve questions 28–31 and fill in the answer sheet accordingly. Before moving on to question 28, refer to the directions on how to fill in the answers on the answer sheet. Use of available space on the test booklet is allowed.

Notes

1. **Calculator use** is permitted.
2. Unless indicated, variables and expressions represent real numbers.
3. Figures are drawn to scale.
4. Figures lie in a plane.
5. The domain of a function f is the set of all real numbers x where $f(x)$ is a real number.

Reference

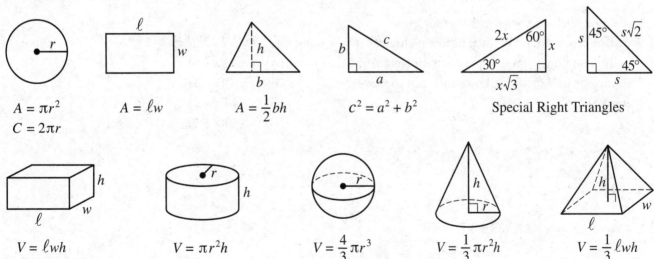

$$A = \pi r^2$$
$$C = 2\pi r$$

$$A = \ell w$$

$$A = \frac{1}{2}bh$$

$$c^2 = a^2 + b^2$$

Special Right Triangles

$$V = \ell wh$$

$$V = \pi r^2 h$$

$$V = \frac{4}{3}\pi r^3$$

$$V = \frac{1}{3}\pi r^2 h$$

$$V = \frac{1}{3}\ell wh$$

There is a total of 360 degrees in the arc of a circle.

There is a total of 2π radians in the arc of a circle.

There is a total of 180 degrees in the internal angles of a triangle.

TYPE OF JAM	NUMBER OF JARS
Mango	45
Grape	37
Fig	46
Berries	97

1. The table above shows the jars of jam on a shelf. If a jar of jam is picked out at random, which type will have the likelihood of $\frac{1}{5}$ being selected?

   (A) Grape
   (B) Fig
   (C) Mango
   (D) Berries

CITY	MONTHLY RENT
New York	$3,500
Austin	$1,500
Vancouver	$1,000

2. The graph shows the average rent for a one-bedroom apartment in three different cities. If Sally is moving from the apartment in New York to the one in Vancouver, how much can she save in a year?

   (A) $1,500
   (B) $2,500
   (C) $5,000
   (D) $30,000

3. 55% of 300 is what % of 200?

   (A) 55%
   (B) 35%
   (C) 82.5%
   (D) 165%

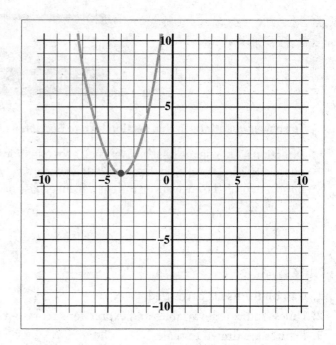

4. The above function is $f(x)$. When $f(x) = 9$, what is x?

   (A) 4
   (B) –4
   (C) –1 and –7
   (D) 0 and –4

5. $x^2 + 6x - 16 = ?$

   (A) $(x + 2)(x - 8)$
   (B) $(x - 4)(x - 4)$
   (C) $(x + 8)(x - 2)$
   (D) $(x + 3)(x + 2)$

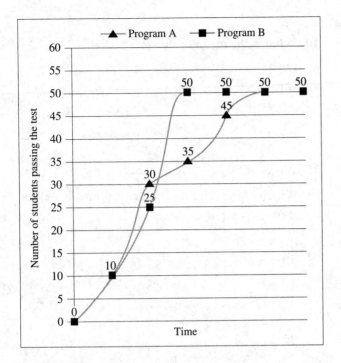

7. The price of a sweater at an outlet store is 30% of the price at the flagship store on Fifth Ave. If the sweater is then subject to another 15% student discount, then the new price of the sweater is $56.53. What was the original price of the sweater at the flagship store?

(A) $52.25

(B) $82

(C) $95

(D) $101.53

8. If $\dfrac{5y}{4x} = -4y^2$, then $xy = ?$

(A) 5

(B) $\dfrac{4}{5}$

(C) $-\dfrac{5}{16}$

(D) $-\dfrac{5}{4}$

6. A school is putting two classes with the same level of computer competency, each of 50 students, into two different programs, Program A and Program B. The programs are designed to help all the students pass the computer competency exam. The school is using this method to decide which program it will be implementing long term. Based on the above graph, which of the following statements below is true?

(A) Program A is faster than Program B at having the students pass the test.

B) Program B is faster than Program A at having the students pass the test.

(C) Program A and Program B are both equally effective at having the students pass the test.

(D) It is impossible to tell which program is more effective at having the students pass the test faster.

Questions 9 and 10 are based on the following information.

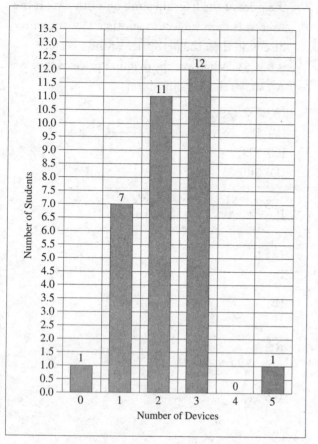

A private school is looking into how many electronic devices its sixth graders have. The electronic devices they are interested in are cellular phones, tablets, laptop computers, and so on. The school is interested because it would like to know if the number of electronic devices children own is related to their academic performance.

9. What is the difference between the mode and range of this set of data?

   (A) 2
   (B) 5
   (C) 11
   (D) 12

10. What is the mean of this set of data?

   (A) 14
   (B) 6.4
   (C) 3
   (D) 2.19

11. $x^2 - x - 42 = 0$

   Which of the solutions of the quadratic equation above is greater?

   (A) $x = -7$
   (B) $x = -6$
   (C) $x = 6$
   (D) $x = 7$

   $x = y + 1$

   $y = 3x + 5$

12. The two lines above meet at point (p, q). Which of the following can be p?

   (A) -4
   (B) 5
   (C) 4
   (D) -3

13. If the percent decrease from 90 to x is the same as the percent increase from 64 to 76.8, what is x?

(A) 77.2

(B) 102.8

(C) 72

(D) 108

14. If $x \times y = y$ for all values of y, what is the value of x?

(A) −1

(B) 0

(C) 1

(D) y

15. $x^2 - 2x + 1 - 100y^4 = ?$

(A) $(100y^2 + x - 1)(-100y^2 + x - 1)$

(B) $(x^2 - 3x)(1 - 100y^4)$

(C) $(3x + 1)(x^2 - 100y^4)$

(D) $x(x - 3) - 1(1 - 100y^4)$

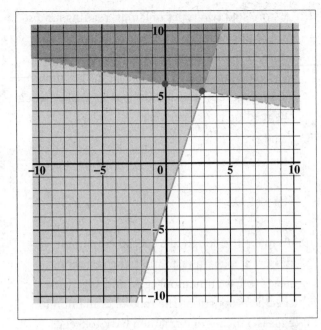

16. $y > -\dfrac{1}{5}x + 6$

$y \geq 3x - 3$

Which of the following is a solution to the two inequalities shown above?

(A) (6, 0)

(B) (5, 5)

(C) (0, 6)

(D) (0, 7)

17. When painting a home, 7.5 cans of red paint was used to paint the bathroom and the office. If the office used 0.87 cans more red paint than the bathroom, what percent of red paint was used on the office?

(A) 44.2%

(B) 55.8%

(C) 75.5%

(D) 87%

18. A store sold two types of lamps, reading lamps and regular lamps. The reading lamps cost $9 more. If the store made $4,671 from selling 71 reading lamps and 55 regular lamps per month, on average, how much did the store make selling the reading lamps per year?

(A) $41
(B) $492
(C) $2,911
(D) $34,932

19. To make the dough of a special cinnamon dessert at a chain restaurant, the restaurant needs to use cinnamon, eggs, and sugar in a specific proportion. The ratio of cinnamon to eggs is 3 inches of cinnamon bark to 5 eggs. The ratio of cinnamon to sugar is 0. 4 feet of cinnamon bark to 9 cups of flour. In a batch of dough the ratio of cinnamon to eggs and cinnamon to flour must be kept the same as described above. The restaurant is making a big batch of dough for a catering event. If 48 eggs are needed for this batch of dough, how many cups of flour are needed?

(A) 648
(B) 54
(C) 324
(D) 27

Questions 20 and 21 are based on the following:

A frame of a picture is 6 inches wide and 8 inches long. The size of the picture is half of the area of the frame. The border of the frame is uniform.

20. What is the length of the picture?

(A) 4
(B) 5
(C) 5.5
(D) 6

21. What is the width of the picture if the frame is 9 inches wide and 12 inches long and the area of the picture is still half of the size of the frame?

(A) 4.5
(B) 5.5
(C) 6
(D) 7

22. Which point satisfies both $y > 4x - 4$ and $y < \frac{3x}{2} + 2$?

(A) (3, 4)
(B) (−3, −4)
(C) (−4, 3)
(D) (3, −4)

23. If $3x - 4y = 5$, then what is the value of $\frac{y}{3} - \frac{x}{4}$?

A) 5

B) $-\frac{5}{12}$

C) $\frac{1}{5}$

D) $-\frac{1}{5}$

GO ON TO THE NEXT PAGE ⟹

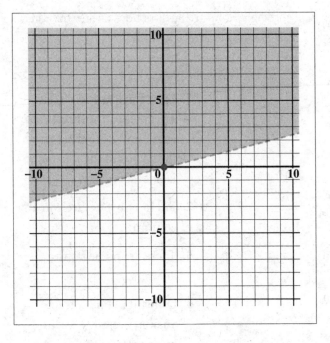

24. The inequality shown in the above graph is which of the following?

(A) $\frac{1}{2}x \le 3y$

(B) $y \le \frac{1}{3}x$

(C) $4y > x$

(D) $y > \frac{1}{3}x$

25. James walked from his home to his friend's home in an hour. The distance between his home and his friend's home is 4.2 km. On the way back from the friend's home to his home, he took the bus for $\frac{2}{3}$ of the distance. The speed of the bus is two times the speed of his walking. He then walked the rest of the way home. How many minutes did it take for him to get home?

(A) 10 minutes
(B) 20 minutes
(C) 30 minutes
(D) 40 minutes

Questions 26 and 27 refer to the following information

A chemistry teacher is making a chemical mixture. She made 1.3 liter of solution by mixing substance A and water. There is 15% of substance A in this 1.3 liters of solution. She also made 2.1 liters of solution by mixing substance B and water. There is 20% substance B in this 2.1 liters. She made a final solution by mixing the two solutions together.

26. What percentage of substance B is in the final solution? Round to the nearest percent.

(A) 5%
(B) 12%
(C) 18%
(D) 20%

27. What percentage of the final solution is water? Round to the nearest percent.

(A) 55%
(B) 60%
(C) 73%
(D) 82%

Directions: Solve questions 28–31 and fill in the answer sheet accordingly. Refer to the directions on how to fill in the answers on the answer sheet.

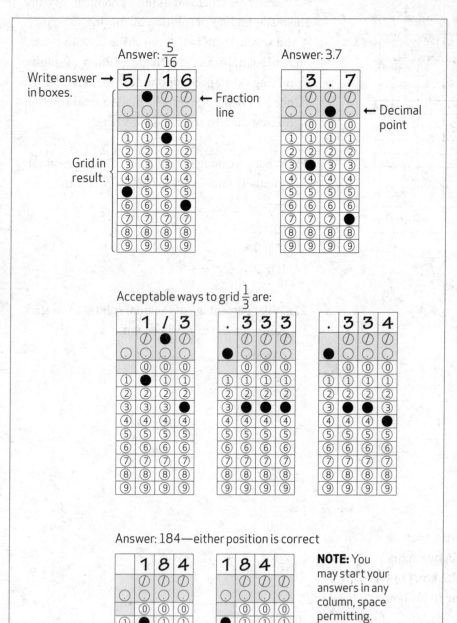

1. Only the filled-in circles are graded. The directions suggest writing the answer in the box at the top, but it is not scored.

2. Fill in only one circle in any column.

3. There are no negative answers.

4. Only fill in one correct answer, even if there are more than one.

5. **Mixed numbers** like $2\frac{1}{2}$ should be filled in as 2.5 or 5/2.

6. **Decimal answers:** If you obtain a decimal answer with more digits, it should be filled in to fill the entire grid.

Answer: $\frac{5}{16}$

Answer: 3.7

Write answer in boxes. → ← Fraction line

Grid in result.

← Decimal point

Acceptable ways to grid $\frac{1}{3}$ are:

Answer: 184—either position is correct

NOTE: You may start your answers in any column, space permitting. Columns you don't need to use should be left blank.

28. If $6n^2 - 24n + 24 = 0$, then what is one of the solutions for n?

29. If Joel can finish 35 paintings in 25 hours, how many minutes will he take to finish 7 paintings?

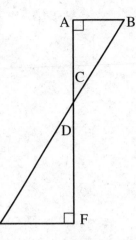

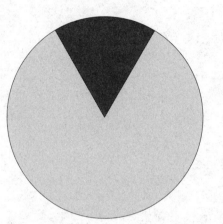

31. In the figure above, if line BC is 13, line BE is 39, angle B is 67.38°, and line AC is 12, what is line EF – line AB?

30. The area of the shaded region is 20π and the area of the shaded region is $\dfrac{1}{5}$ of the area of the circle. What is the diameter of the circle?

You can check your work only in this section, if you finished ahead of time.

Do not turn to other sections.

Practice Test 1 Answer Key

Reading Test

1. **(C)** This question is about the passage as a whole. The narrator is writing about the summer home and commenting on her illness and her relationship with her husband, making (C) the correct choice. (A), (B), and (D) each contain details mentioned in the passage but don't speak to the passage as a whole.

2. **(A)** The narrator is writing whatever she's thinking, so (A) is the correct choice. A dialogue is an exchange between two people. There is no analysis of symptoms happening, although a couple are mentioned. And the narrator is writing about the present, not a memory.

3. **(D)** Here, the writer is referring to herself and her husband as too ordinary for the colonial mansion they are staying at. Hence, she means they are average or common in comparison to the aristocrats who would normally reside there.

4. **(B)** The narrator states that she would be healthy if it weren't for her husband not believing that she's sick.

5. **(A)** In these lines, the narrator specifically states that she is not recovering fast because her husband doesn't believe she's sick.

6. **(C)** The narrator's attitude toward her husband slips out in a few places in the passage. She says she expects her husband to laugh at her rather than take her seriously. She notes that he's a well-respected physician, and every time she tries to talk about her own ideas, he interrupts with his advice. Lastly, she mentions that she gets angry with him, but that it is unwarranted. She is neither indifferent nor reverent. (B) is too extreme since she shows him respect and admiration, not just anger.

7. **(B)** Use the same clues in the passage to discern John's attitude toward the narrator. He doesn't take her opinions or observations seriously. He disregards and even opposes her desire to write and work. He's constantly telling her what to do to the point of being almost parental. John is not very affectionate or attentive. And he definitely doesn't treat her as an equal.

8. **(C)** Look for the best example of John's condescending disregard. In these lines, John laughs at his wife's concern about the house and scoffs at her way of thinking and making sense of the world.

9. **(D)** Here, the house is "nearly" or almost alone. (A) wrongly assumes there is something to compare it to, (B) means average, and (C) means small or delicate.

10. **(D)** You can find this answer in the first few lines of the passage.

11. **(A)** Even if you aren't familiar with the word, read on for context. The author is talking about the Aryan religion. The other answers may be connected with religion or subsections of religion, but they do not encompass a belief system.

12. **(C)** Ask yourself what these lines do. These lines describe how Aryans worshipped and prayed to their God on a daily basis, making (C) correct.

13. **(C)** The religious duties are straightforward because they can be done from home; the relationship between Aryans and their God is a personal one. The passage actually states there are a few religious texts, eliminating (A). There's no evidence for (B) or (D).

14. **(B)** These lines describe the simple daily religious practices of Aryans: reciting hymns and reading sacred texts.

15. **(A)** The passage describes the transformation of the Aryan religion, maintaining that reason and intellect were valued over feelings. Furthermore, it states that science must always be the ally of a religion based on a knowledge of God's works. Eliminate (B) because it's the opposite. Eliminate (C) because Aryan religion was very personal with worship being done mostly from the home. Eliminate (D) because the passage doesn't discuss their national identity.

16. **(D)** It is these lines specifically that state intellect and reason were more valued than feelings and passions.

17. **(D)** Here, Aryans are willing to admit, or acknowledge, the greatness of their God. The other choices are nonsensical. You can always try reading the sentence with each choice if you're unsure.

18. **(A)** This is a tough question. It's asking about the purpose. What do these lines do? They describe how Aryan religion changed its practices while maintaining its character.

19. **(B)** Try to summarize the last paragraph. The goal of Aryans was to understand science as "knowledge of God's works," and strive toward that understanding even though "man can never hope to reach" it. (A) and (C) are not discussed in the final paragraph. And (D) is impossible for Aryans since they believe man can never achieve a God-like understanding.

20. **(D)** For questions like this, think of the big picture. Twain tells a story about his early career that ends up being funny and satirical. It is not persuading the reader to take risks. And while (B) and (C) are details that are brought up, they do not encapsulate the purpose of the passage as a whole.

21. **(B)** The lesson here takes place at the end of the passage: an editor who took no notice of Mark Twain now admits that it was his biggest mistake. That is best described by choice (B).

22. **(A)** Put this sentence in your own words. Twain wasn't well known at this point. His reputation was limited or insufficient when it came to publishing works.

23. **(A)** According to the passage, Twain only agrees to try to publish his work if somebody else compiles the work for him. He states specifically that he doesn't have the "industry" or the energy to do that sort of thing. Hence, he is too lazy.

24. **(A)** In these lines, Twain admits that he was unwilling to gather the work himself because "there was a persistent vacancy" instead of "industry" or productivity.

25. **(C)** When Twain meets Carleton, Carleton is aggressive and disrespectful, failing to even look at Twain's work.

26. **(D)** These lines epitomize Carleton's attitude. He tells Twain he doesn't want his book before even looking at it, and then he excuses himself from the meeting.

27. **(B)** Carleton calls himself obscure or not well known. He compares himself to Twain who is now a popular author, suggesting that he is undistinguished while Twain is very important. (A), (C), and (D) all deal with actually being hard to see, which isn't appropriate here.

28. **(D)** This is another purpose question. What does the quote do? Here, Carleton stresses how big of a mistake it was to treat Twain the way he did. He says his mistake entitles him to immortality, meaning that he will never forget the time he refused Mark Twain's book. His point is not to simply acknowledge that Twain is well known as in (A). The two are not old pals as in (B). And he is not justifying his action as in (C) but instead acknowledging how foolish it was.

29. (D) Try reading the sentence with each choice. We are "likely" to take it for granted is the only choice that makes sense within the context.

30. (B) These lines suggest that the beginning of the automobile is a bit more unclear than many would like to believe, stating instead that people began thinking about and trying to invent such a thing many hundreds of years ago.

31. (A) The author gives credit to Roger Bacon back in the thirteenth century. Even though other dates are mentioned in the passage, they are noted as progressions or turning points in the invention of the automobile, not the first time the idea was conceived.

32. (A) Look within the passage for where the author begins to give the reader a chronological history of the automobile. He begins in these lines at the start of paragraph two, introducing Roger Bacon and his crude idea for the automobile.

33. (C) This is a purpose question, so you are asking what this paragraph does, not what it says. It lists different failed attempts at inventing the automobile, which is most like choice (C).

34. (D) This sentence is discussing the vehicle designed by Scott Russell and noting that it could "mount," or climb, steep hills. "Ascend" is synonymous with "climb." It is not accurate to say the vehicle jumped on, staged, or multiplied hills.

35. (C) The writer discusses the Great Eastern in the fourth paragraph, noting its strengths (speed and the ability to climb hills) before bringing attention to its faults (smoke and noise). According to the author, the public rejected the vehicle because of its exhaust fumes and excessive noise.

36. (A) Eliminate (B) and (D) because there's no evidence in the passage for these choices—the author doesn't directly discuss economic and industrial growth. Then eliminate (C) because it is contrary to the author's main argument.

37. (B) First, remind yourself what the argument is: the automobile is not a new invention, wholly thought up by this generation, but instead has occupied great minds for centuries. The introduction of the passage says it was published in a periodical in 1900; so, to agree with the author, the graph has to show people working on the automobile long before 1900. It does. Eliminate (A) because that's not what the writer is arguing.

38. (C) Look for a mention of manufacturing in factories within the chart. The chart attributes it to 1901, so that's a year after this article was published.

39. (B) Plug the choices into the sentence: every worthy, or notable, advancement. "Estimable" means worthy of great respect.

40. (C) Nietzsche says that the aristocratic class is responsible for all notable advancement and that it will continue to be so "for the duration of humanity."

41. (A) Look for what passage 1 says about power. Basically it says that people naturally want to be powerful and in control—a trait of all life-forms, according to Nietzsche. Eliminate (B) because the passage states this is true for all life. Eliminate (C) because it is natural. Eliminate (D) because it is actually what has propelled progress.

42. (B) These lines are where power is discussed as synonymous with life. It is here that the author defines Nietzsche's belief that a need for power is essential to all life in order to progress.

43. (C) This is a definition question. Utilitarianism is defined in the first lines of the second passage as an understanding of what is right according to whether it promotes happiness.

44. (D) The author addresses this counterargument in the third and fourth paragraphs. Here, the author states that people who do not agree with utilitarianism think that an approach to life based on experiencing the most pleasure is "utterly mean and groveling." The passage then responds to this argument, saying that intellect, imagination, and "moral sentiments" are more pleasurable than mere sensation. So, it isn't just how much happiness or pleasure, but the quality of that pleasure that's accounted for.

45. (D) Here, the author is talking about what the theory is "grounded" on, or rooted in. It is referring to its foundation, or what it's built upon.

46. (D) First try to come up with the main point of each passage. Passage 1 is a philosophical understanding of life as built upon the need for power and control. Passage 2 is a philosophical understanding of life as an attempt to create the most happiness. They are very different, so eliminate (C). They are not addressing one another as in (A). Nor are they expounding upon one another as in (B).

47. (A) These questions are tough. Work backward. Utilitarianism says happiness is what's important. Nietzsche says power and differentiation is what's important. So, what might Nietzsche say if someone told him happiness was the most important? He would probably disagree and say power and advancement relies on exploitation, so unhappiness is inevitable. That sounds like choice (A).

Writing and Language Test

1. (A) This is correct as is. The comma separates the beginning dependent clause (fragment) from the independent clause (complete sentence). (B) has no punctuation and, therefore, creates a run-on; (C) places the comma incorrectly after the subject rather than after the dependent clause; (D) uses the dash, which is used for hard pauses or large breaks in a sentence.

2. (B) Choices (A), (B), and (C) have similar meanings, but are not the same. They are each used for different versions of "brief." (B) matches the tone of the essay and means short but comprehensive, and it is the correct choice. (A) is informal and usually suggests that something is clever or catchy. (C) means shortened or cut. (D) can be eliminated because it is an antonym of brief, meaning wordy.

3. (C) First, eliminate (B) and (D) because they incorrectly change the pronoun and are, therefore, inconsistent with the rest of the sentence. (A) uses awkward elevated language to say what is said more succinctly in (C).

4. (D) Eliminate (C) because it changes the meaning of the sentence. (A) and (B) are wordier than necessary, so go with (D).

5. (D) Look for clues here. Sentence 6 begins with "Next," and so should be part of a list. Sentence 3 and 4 say "first" and "second," while sentence 5 names itself the "most profound" and should probably end the list. So, we want sentence 6 between 4 and 5, making (D) correct.

6. (A) This is correct as is. (B) and (D) are too wordy, and (C) is missing a word.

7. **(A)** This one is tricky. The paragraph seems to work with or without the addition, so read the answers for help. Eliminate (B) since this sentence is not giving an example. Eliminate (C) because it is not repeated information. Eliminate (D) because it doesn't contradict or argue against the main idea. Now, read the paragraph with the addition and see that the next sentence includes "It wasn't until," and now makes more sense when compared to the narrator's initial reaction.

8. **(C)** The author isn't avoiding all conversation, but instead the conversation regarding where he or she will be working after the move. (B) and (D) are illogical. (A) is appealing but suggests that the narrator is avoiding all conversation; to make (A) work, "conversation" would have to be plural.

9. **(C)** Be careful here. You aren't looking for the choice that sounds the best, or that you'd end the paragraph with. Instead, you are looking for a sentence that considers how the work we do influences how we see ourselves. Choice (C) is the only option that suggests how you value yourself can be altered by how you value your job.

10. **(C)** The sociologist claims seven out of ten college graduates identify via their job; 7/10 is equal to 70%. The chart shows 55% of people surveyed identifying by their job, so it does not support the passage's claim. Eliminate (D) because 55% is still a majority.

11. **(B)** Here, "person" is singular so we use apostrophe then "s" to denote possession. The value belongs to the person, so the possessive is needed, making (A) incorrect. (C) puts the apostrophe after the "s," which we only do with plural nouns. (D) changes the meaning of the sentence and refers to a whole population or a section of a demographic.

12. **(D)** First, ask yourself what the underlined portion does. It tells you something important about the main idea, the book *The History of Mary Prince*. Since it hasn't already been said and doesn't distract you from the main idea, eliminate (A) and (B). (C) doesn't work because it isn't a definition.

13. **(D)** This is a transition word, so look what is happening before and after it. What comes previously says that the book includes experiences of many slaves, while what follows says that it can be used to study slavery. So, you are looking for a cause and effect word here, making (D) correct. (A) and (B) are illogical here. (C) would suggest what comes after contradicts what comes before, which is untrue.

14. **(A)** Be concise. Choices (B), (C), and (D) all say about the same thing but are too wordy.

15. **(B)** This one is tricky. If you introduce a quotation, you can use the comma or colon depending on how you introduce it. Here, there is a complete sentence that is clarified by the quote, so the colon is the correct option. Note that the comma is not listed as an option, and that (A) and (C) can be eliminated because they do the same thing. Choice (D) offers no break and therefore creates a confusing run-on.

16. **(A)** This is correct as is. Don't overthink this one. The writer says we will get two things and then introduces one with "First"; therefore, "Second" keeps the passage clear and consistent.

17. **(C)** Here, Prince uses her own story to talk about slavery and emancipation, so (C) is correct. The sentence is not contrasting things as in (A) or showing cause and effect as in (B) and (D).

18. **(D)** Eliminate (B) and (C) right away; Prince is female, and the story is not "ours." (D) can be appealing because you know Prince's story sheds light on the stories of many others, but still she tells only her story.

19. **(A)** You know from the previous sentence the letter was included in the text, so eliminate (B) and (C). (D) is too wordy.

20. **(B)** In order to believe the ridiculous indication that Prince's circumstance is a result of her own choices and actions, the reader would have to temporarily let go of, or suspend, skepticism. (A) and (D) suggest the opposite. (C) means abandoned or not taken care of and is illogical.

21. **(B)** The subject here is "Wood," so read the subject right next to the verb, ignoring what is in between. Since the subject is singular, you can eliminate (A). Now, notice that the sentence and surrounding sentences are in present tense, which helps you to choose (B).

22. **(D)** Ask yourself what this underlined portion is doing. It explains in more detail what the writer means by "reveals the utter inconsistency and contradiction of the slavemaster." Since it is useful and doesn't repeat or change the subject, eliminate (A) and (B). Eliminate (C) because it doesn't introduce a new topic, but effectively concludes this passage.

23. **(B)** Pay attention here; this question tests two different things. First, it tests neither/nor. Second, it tests "affect" vs. "effect." It's easiest to eliminate (C) and (D) because they both get neither/nor wrong. Here, you need the word that means "influenced" or "impacted," so "affected" is the correct choice.

24. **(A)** This is correct as is. Choices (B), (C), and (D) are unnecessarily wordy. Remember to always go with the concise answer, short but with all the necessary information.

25. **(D)** Look for concision and tone. (A) and (C) do the same exact thing and should thus be eliminated. (B) is too wordy.

26. **(D)** "Effect" means result. "Affect" means influence. So, eliminate (A) and (C). Read the sentence without the inessential information surrounded by commas: "We may conclude that any change in the numerical proportions of some of the inhabitants would seriously. . ." This makes it obvious that your choice should be present tense.

27. **(D)** First, eliminate (B) and (C) because "it's" means "it is." Now, notice the sentence begins with "If," which is a good marker of a dependent clause. You need the comma to separate that beginning dependent clause (fragment) from the independent clause (complete sentence).

28. **(A)** This one is tricky. First, decide if you need both "new" and "better." The answer is yes because they don't mean the same thing; hence, (B) and (C) can be eliminated. (D) becomes repetitive since "better" already suggests "more efficient."

29. **(B)** This is another tricky one. Eliminate (C) and (D) because the places won't actually be grabbed or arrested by anything. (A) and (B) both mean "to be taken over," so it's a tough choice. Try reading the sentence with both choices and you'll see that the "on" works with (B) but not with (A).

30. **(C)** What does this sentence really say? It says that in isolated areas natural selection can adapt species to the environment. Read the current last sentence of the passage; it says the same thing, making (C) the correct choice. Another viable approach is process of elimination. It does not give a specific example, discuss how Darwin arrived at his thesis, or change the topic from natural selection.

31. **(C)** The subject here is "conditions," so eliminate (A) and (D) because they do not agree. Now, check the tense and choose (C) because it is in present tense like the rest of the sentence.

32. **(A)** This one asks you for the option that explains natural selection. You don't have to understand every word to know that natural selection as described in the passage is all about species that adapt to survive better. If you didn't get anything else from the passage, that basic understanding is enough to answer this question. Eliminate (B), (C), and (D) because they all talk about stopping evolution.

33. **(B)** Eliminate (A) and (D) because they are wordy and awkward; they overdo it. Now, eliminate (C) because semicolons are used to separate complete sentences or to separate items of a list that already include commas.

34. **(B)** Here, you have inessential information that breaks up the sentence. You know it should be surrounded by commas when you can read the sentence without it and it still makes sense and forms a complete thought. (A) has no pause and creates a run-on. (C) incorrectly uses the semicolon, which separates complete sentences just like the period. (D) uses a comma and a dash, which creates inconsistency; technically this phrase could be surrounded by commas or dashes, but whichever choice the writer makes, he or she must stick with.

35. **(A)** This is correct as is. The sentence puts forward Yelvington's main argument, so "Ultimately" fits well. (B) and (D) can be eliminated because they do the same thing. Since there is no cause and effect relationship, you can likewise get rid of (C).

36. **(D)** Ask yourself what the underlined portion is doing. It restates what was said in simpler terms so that the reader can follow along. It should be kept. But, if you can't decide, find flaws in the other choices. It doesn't change focus or give details, so eliminate (B) and (C). Rather than it being confusing, this sentence clears up any confusion, so (A) doesn't work either.

37. **(D)** You need an article not a pronoun, since the power struggles don't belong to anyone necessarily. That leaves you with (C) and (D), and (C) has extra words you don't need.

38. **(C)** Again, go for short and sweet. (A) and (D) do the same thing and are unnecessarily wordy. (B) is illogical.

39. **(A)** This is correct as is. The subject is "historical processes and problematic social environments," so eliminate (B) and (C) because they do not agree. Here, the writer is talking about something that started in the past and continues into the present, making (A) correct. (D) incorrectly suggests that these things will only influence knowledge in the future.

40. **(A)** This is correct as is. You are looking for the choice that expresses change and interaction, or fluctuation and reimagining. (B) does neither. (C) is too extreme and negative. (D) suggests interaction but not change.

41. **(B)** You do not need this to be possessive, nor do you mean it to be a contraction, so eliminate (A) and (C). (D) is illogical and makes for an awkward sentence.

42. **(B)** This is tricky. First, eliminate (A) and (D). In comparisons like this, you use "than." "Then" is used for time, like something happened, then another thing happened. (C) changes the meaning of the sentence because it suggests the anthology points at syncretism before pointing at authenticity.

43. **(D)** Here is another tough one. This sentence is summarizing the main idea of the passage, which is about a reexamination of anthropological approaches to better understand Africa and its peoples. (D) means taking apart to look at and understand better, so it is the best choice. Choice (A) means an insertion. Choice (B) is too indifferent, merely expressing the methods won't change the knowledge; they must be reexamined. Choice (C) is illogical since a separation of methods won't give rise to a new understanding.

44. **(C)** The passage sums up Yelvington's thesis, reiterating a need to consider power structures influencing anthropologists in order to better understand the African cultures they studied. Yelvington's main point is that the ideas of "Africa" are actually invented rather than just recorded. Thus, (D) is the opposite of his point and can be eliminated. (A) suggests that the passage is about anthropology generally and how it has done a pretty good job, which doesn't align with the argument. (B) is vague and ineffective, failing to conclude the main point. Choice (C) is correct because it explains how a new understanding can influence current discourse.

Math Test—No Calculator

1. **(D)** This is a simple word problem. First find the cost of the 4 pack of gum, $12.79 × 5= $63.95. Then add 8.9% tax on it by multiplying $63.95 by 1.089. The answer is $69.64.

2. **(D)** This is a fraction question. First, plug the value of p into the equation to get $\frac{12}{5} \div 3 = \frac{11}{q}$. Then, simplify to get $\frac{4}{5} = \frac{11}{q}$. Then, cross multiply to get: $4q = 55$. The answer is $q = \frac{55}{4}$.

3. **(C)** This is a question about exponents. $n^{2/4} = \sqrt{n}$. First, simplify $n^{2/4} = n^{1/2}$. Then, $n^{1/2} = \sqrt{n}$.

4. **(A)** This is a simple question about circles. First, find the area of the circle: $A = \pi r^2 = \pi 18^2 = 324\pi$. Then, find out what fraction of the circle is 10°: $\frac{10°}{360°} = \frac{1}{36}$. Then, multiply the area of the circle with the fraction: $\frac{1}{36} \times 324\pi = 9\pi$.

5. **(C)** This is a linear equation question. First, find the slope of the equation by taking two points on the line, $\frac{8-4}{-2-0} = \frac{4}{-2} = -2$. Then plug the slope into the line equation of $y = mx + b$ to get $y = -2x + b$. Then plug in a point to get the constant b, $4 = -2(0) + b$; $b = 4$. The equation of this line is $y = -2x + 4$. Plug in the y value to get the missing y value, $y = -2x + 4$; $42 - 4 = -2x$; $38 = -2x$; $x = -19$.

6. **(C)** This is a word problem. First, find out what time it is in London when the show ends, 10:46 a.m. + 1 hour and 57 minutes = 12:43 p.m. Then because London is 5 hours ahead, take away 5 hours to get to the New York time: 12:43 p.m. – 5 hours = 7:43 a.m.

7. **(C)** This is a parabola question. Plug in the $y = 0$ to the answer choices and find the correct answer. When $y = 0$ is plugged in, only choice C provides the correct answer, $y = \frac{1}{2}(x + 5)(x - 2)$; $x = -5, x = +2$ when $y = 0$.

8. **(D)** This is a medium difficulty geometry question. First find angle C, 180° − 90° − 33° = 57°. Then find angle D, 180° − 90° − 57° = 33°. Then find angle F, 180° − 90° − 33° = 57°.

9. **(B)** This is a simple question where the equation needs to be rearranged. First, rearrange the equation to isolate the r^2, $I \times 2 = \frac{1}{2}mr^2 \times 2$; $2I \div m = mr^2 \div m$; $\frac{2I}{m} = r^2$. Then square root both sides to isolate the r, $r = \sqrt{\frac{2I}{m}}$.

10. **(B)** This is a multistep word problem. Because Sam and James are leaving city A at the same time, the information about both leaving at 8:35 a.m. can be ignored. Sam is driving at 50 km/hr, so it takes 8 hours for him to get to city B (400 km ÷ 50 km per hr = 8 hr). Then find the time it takes for James. First, find the time it takes for the first $\frac{1}{4}$ of the distance. This first $\frac{1}{4}$ of the distance is: 400 km × $\frac{1}{4}$ = 100 km. It took him 5 hours for the first $\frac{1}{4}$ of the distance (100 km ÷ 20 km per hr = 5 hr). Then, find the time it takes for the rest of the distance. This rest of the distance is $\frac{3}{4}$ of the distance, which is: 400 km × $\frac{1}{4}$ = 300 km. It took him 3.75 hours for the rest of the distance (300 km ÷ 80 km per hr = 3.75 hr). It takes James 8.75 hours to get there (5 hr + 3.75 hr = 8.75 hr). The difference between their arrival is 8.75 hr − 8 hr = 0.75 hours, which is 45 minutes (0.75 hours × 60 min per hr = 45 min).

11. **(C)** This is a multistep word problem. To find the time it takes for James, first find the time it takes for the first $\frac{1}{4}$ of the distance. This first $\frac{1}{4}$ of the distance is: 640 km × $\frac{1}{4}$ = 160 km. It took him 8 hours for the first $\frac{1}{4}$ of the distance (160 km ÷ 20 km per hr = 8 hr). Then, find the time it takes for the rest of the distance. This rest of the distance is $\frac{3}{4}$ of the distance, which is 640 km × $\frac{3}{4}$ = 480 km. It took him 6 hours for the rest of the distance (480 km ÷ 80 km per hr = 6 hr). It takes James 14 hours of total driving time (8 hr + 6 hr = 14 hr). Then adding the 45 minute stop in the middle of his trip, it takes him 14 hours and 45 minutes to get to city B. The arrival time will be 10:15 p.m. (7:30 a.m. + 14 hr and 45 min = 10:15 p.m.).

12. **(C)** This is a difficult geometry question. First find the area of the circle, $(6\sqrt{2})^2 \pi = 72\pi$. Then because the radius is $6\sqrt{2}$, the diameter is $12\sqrt{2}$. Recognize that the square is made with two special triangles of 1:1:$\sqrt{2}$. Then because the sides of the square are 12 and 12, the area of the square is 12 × 12 = 144. Then find the area of the shaded region, $\frac{72\pi - 144}{4} = 18\pi - 36$. This question can also be solved by using the angle to find the sides of the square.

13. **(D)** This is a graphing question. Use the equation of the straight line, $y = mx + b$, to find the equation for the line in the graph. First, find the slope by looking at the rise over run. The rise here is −1 and run is 4. The slope is $-\frac{1}{4}$. Then look at the y intercept to find b, which is +3. The equation for the line is $y = -\frac{1}{4}x + 3$. Then reflect the line along the x axis to get $y = \frac{1}{4}x - 3$. Then translate the line 3 units up to get $y = \frac{1}{4}x$.

14. **42** This is a simple algebra question. First, find the value of x, $3x = 21$; $x = 7$. Then find the value of $6x$, $6 \times 7 = 42$.

15. **5** This is a system of equations question. Plug the value of x into both equations to get the y value. Plug into the first equation, $y > 5(3) - 11$; $y > 4$. Plug into the second equation, $y < -2(3) + 12$; $y < 6$. The y value will be between 4 and 6, $4 < y < 6$. The smallest integer value of y would be 5.

16. **6** This is simple parabola question. The equation of a parabola is $y = (x - a)^2 + b$, where (a, b) is the vertex and a is also the axis of symmetry. The axis of symmetry is $x = 6$.

17. **6** First, rearrange the equation, $x^2 + 4x + y^2 + 6y = 23$. Then, change the equation to enable completing the square, $x^2 + 4x + 4 + y^2 + 6y + 9 = 23 + 4 + 9$. Then, change the equation to complete the square, $(x + 2)^2 + (y + 3)^2 = 6^2$. Because the equation of the circle is $(x - a)^2 + (y - b)^2 = r^2$, the radius is 6.

Math Test—Calculator

1. **(C)** This is a simple problem about probability. First, add the number of jars of jam together, $45 + 37 + 46 + 97 = 225$. Then find out what is $\frac{1}{5}$ of 225, $225 \times \frac{1}{5} = 45$. There are 45 jars of Mango jam, so the answer is Mango.

2. **(D)** This is a simple word problem. First find how much she saves per month, $\$3,500 - \$1,000 = \$2,500$. Then multiply by 12 to find how much she saves in a year, $\$2,500 \times 12 = \$30,000$.

3. **(C)** This is a simple question about percents. First find 55% of 300, $55\% \times 300 = 165$. Then find 165 is what percent of 200, $165 \div 200 \times 100\% = 82.5\%$

4. **(C)** This is a simple function question. Find the point on the function where $y = 9$. When $y = 9$, $x = -1$ and -7.

5. **(C)** This is a simple algebra question. Factor the equation. The answer will be $(x + 8)(x - 2)$.

6. **(B)** This is a data analysis question. The graph shows that the students pass the test faster when they are in Program B. Therefore, the answer is (B).

7. **(C)** This is a multistep word problem. It is easiest to set up an equation. Set x as the original price of the sweater. $x(70\%)(85\%) = \$56.53$, because 30% off is 70% and 15% off is 85%; $x(0.7)(0.85) = \$56.53$; therefore $x(0.85) = \$56.53 \div 0.7$; $x(0.85) = \$80.5$; $x = \$80.75 \div 0.85$; $x = \$95$.

8. **(C)** This is a simple algebra question. First divide both sides of the equation by y to get $\frac{5}{4x} = -4y$. Then rearrange the equation to find what xy is equal to: $-4xy = \frac{5}{4}$; $xy = -\frac{5}{16}$.

9. **(A)** This is a simple data analysis question. Find the mode, the number that appears the most often, which is 3. Then find the range, the difference between the biggest and smallest number, which is 5. The difference between 5 and 3 is 2.

10. **(D)** This is a simple data analysis question. First find the total of all the devices, $1(0) + 7(1) + 11(2) + 12(3) + 0(4) + 1(5) = 0 + 7 + 22 + 36 + 0 + 5 = 70$. Then find the total number of students, $1 + 7 + 11 + 12 + 0 + 1 = 32$. Then find the mean of this set of data, $70 \div 32 = 2.19$.

11. **(D)** This is an algebra question. First you have to factor the equation to get $(x + 6)(x - 7) = 0$. To find the two solutions, we have $x + 6 = 0$ and $x - 7 = 0$. The two solutions are $x = -6$ and $x = 7$. The question asks for the greater of the two numbers. Therefore, the correct answer is (D).

12. **(D)** This is a system of equations question. Solve for x and y to get the point (p, q). Plug in y to the first equation to get $y = 3x + 5 + 1$. Then solve for x, $2x = -6$; $x = -3$. Then because p is the x coordinate, $p = -3$.

13. **(C)** This is a medium difficulty percent question. First, find the percent increase from 64 to 76.8, $76.8 \div 64 \times 100\% - 100\% = 20\%$. Then decrease 90 by 20%, $90 - 90 \times 20\% = 90 - 18 = 72$.

14. **(C)** This is a question about the properties of numbers. $x = y \div y$. When a variable is divided by itself it is equal to 1.

15. **(A)** This is a medium algebra question. Factor out the first part of the equation to get $(x - 1)$ $(x - 1) -100y^4$; $(x - 1)^2 - 100y^4$. Then, factor this equation to get $(x - 1 + 100y^2)(x - 1 - 100y^2)$. Then because $(x - 1 + 100y^2)(x - 1 - 100y^2)$ is not one of the solutions, convert it to get $(100y^2 + x - 1)(-100y^2 + x - 1)$.

16. **(D)** This is a system of inequality question. Look though the answer choices to find the set of coordinates that falls in the region where there is shaded area from both inequalities. The answer is (0,7).

17. **(B)** This is a word problem. First find out how much paint is used in the office. If the office used 0.87 cans more than the bathroom, then the office used 4.185 cans of paint. $(7.5 - 0.87) \div 2 = 3.315$; $3.315 + 0.87 = 4.185$. Next find the percent of red paint used on the office: $4.185 \div 7.5 = 0.558$; 0.558 is the same as 55.8%.

18. **(D)** This is a difficult multistep word problem. First, set up the equations needed to solve the problem and use x for reading lamp and y for regular lamp, $x - y = \$9$, $71x + 55y = \$4,671$. Manipulate the first equation to get $y = x - \$9$. Then plug the modified equation into the second equation to get $71x + 55(x - \$9) = \$4,671$. Solve for x, $71x + 55x - \$495 = \$4,671$; $126x = \$5,166$; $x = \$41$. Then find out how much the store makes selling the reading lamps per year, $\$41 \times 71$ per month $\times$ 12 months/year $= \$34,932$.

19. **(B)** This is a difficult word problem about proportions. First start with the proportions given in the question and use c for cinnamon, e for egg, and f for flour; c to e is 3 inches to 5 eggs, and c to f is 0.4 feet to 9 cups. Then convert 0.4 feet to cups by multiplying by 12 to get 4.8 inches to 9 cups. To make sure that the 3 inches and 4.8 inches stay consistent, multiply both sides of c to e by 4.8 and multiply both sides of c to f by 3 to get 14.4 inches to 24 eggs and 14.4 inches to 27 cups. The new ratio of c to e to f is 14.4 to 24 to 27, and the new ratio of e to f is 24 to 27. If 48 eggs are needed the number of cups of flour needed is 54 cups, $48 \div 24 \times 27 = 54$ cups.

20. **(D)** This is a difficult multistep word problem. First, set up an equation setting the difference between the length of the frame and length of the picture as x. Because the border of the frame is uniform, set the difference between the width of the frame and width of the picture also as x. Now find the area of the frame: $6 \times 8 = 48$. Then divide this number by half to find the area of the picture, $48 \div 2 = 24$. Then set an equation. $(6 - x)(8 - x) = 24$. Expand this equation, $48 - 6x - 8x + x^2 = 24$. Simplify, $48 - 14x + x^2 = 24$. Rearrange this equation so that it is equal to 0. $x^2 - 14x + 24 = 0$. Factor the equation to find x. $(x - 12)(x - 2) = 0$. Solve for x. $x = 12$, $x = 2$. Remember the length of the frame is only 8, so in this question the difference between the length of the frame and length of the picture is 2. The length of the picture is then $8 - 2 = 6$.

21. **(C)** This is a difficult multistep word problem. First, set up an equation setting the difference between the width of the frame and width of the picture as x. Because the border of the frame is uniform, set the difference between the length of the frame and length of the picture also as x. Now, find the area of the frame: $9 \times 12 = 108$. Then divide this number by half to find the area of the picture, $108 \div 2 = 54$. Then set an equation: $(9 - x)(12 - x) = 54$. Expand this equation, $108 - 9x - 12x + x^2 = 54$. Simplify, $108 - 21x + x^2 = 54$. Rearrange this equation so that it is equal to 0. $x^2 - 21x + 54 = 0$. Factor the equation to find x. $(x - 18)(x - 3) = 0$. Solve for x. $x = 18$, $x = 3$. Remember the length of the frame is only 12, so in this question the difference between the length of the frame and length of the picture is 3. The length of the picture is then $9 - 3 = 6$.

22. **(B)** This is a simple inequality question. To see which point satisfies both equations, plug each of the points into both equations. For example, plug $(-3, -4)$ into the first equation: $-4 > 4(-3) - 4$ and get $-4 > -16$. This means that the point satisfies the first equation. Next plug $(-3, -4)$ into the second equation: $-4 < 3(-3) \div 2 + 2$ and get $-3 < -2.5$. This means that the point also satisfies the second equation. Another way of solving this question is to graph out the two equations and see which point satisfies both equations.

23. **(B)** This is a difficult algebra question. Modify $\dfrac{y}{3} - \dfrac{x}{4}$ until it looks like $3x - 4y = 5$ to get the answer, $-12\left(\dfrac{y}{3} - \dfrac{x}{4}\right) = -4y + 3x = 3x - 4y = 5$. Therefore, $-12\left(\dfrac{y}{3} - \dfrac{x}{4}\right) = 5$. The answer is $\dfrac{y}{3} - \dfrac{x}{4} = -\dfrac{5}{12}$.

24. **(C)** This is a graphing question. Use the equation of the straight line, $y = mx + b$, to find the equation for the line in the graph. First, find the slope by looking at the rise over run. The rise here is 1 and run is 4. The slope is $\dfrac{1}{4}$. Then look at the y intercept to find b, which is 0. The equation for the line is $y = \dfrac{1}{4}x$. Then because it is a dashed line with a shaded area the inequality shown is $y > \dfrac{1}{4}x$. Because $y > \dfrac{1}{4}x$ is not one of the answer choices, convert the equation to get $4y > x$.

25. **(D)** This is a multistep word problem about speed. First, find out his speed of walking, 4.2 km $\div 60$ minutes $= 0.07$ km/min. Then find out the bus speed, 0.07 km/min $\times 2 = 0.14$ km/min. Then find out the time it took to walk, $4.2 \div 3 \div 0.07$ km/min $= 20$ minutes. Then find the time it took in the car, $4.2 \div 3 \times 2 \div 0.14 = 20$ minutes. Add the number of minutes together to get the answer, 20 min $+ 20$ min $= 40$ min.

26. **(C)** This is a multistep word problem. First find the amount of substance B. To find the amount of substance B, just multiply 2.1 liters by 20% to get 0.42 liter. Then find the total amount of solution by adding 1.3 liter and 2.1 liter to get 3.4 liters. Then find what percentage of solution B is in the final solution, 0.42 liters ÷ 3.4 liters × 100% = 12%

27. **(D)** This is a multistep word problem. First find the amount of water in the first solution. To find the amount of water, just multiply 1.3 liters by 85% to get 1.105 liters. Then, find the amount of water in the second solution. To find the amount of water just multiply 2.1 liters by 80% to get 1.68 liters. Then find the total amount of water by adding 1.105 liters and 1.68 liters to get 2.785 liters. Then find the total amount of solution by adding 1.3 liters and 2.1 liters to get 3.4 liters. Then find what percentage of water is in the final solution, 2.785 liters ÷ 3.4 liters × 100% = 82%.

28. **2** This is a simple algebra question. First, recognize that 6 can be factored out of this equation: $6(n^2 - 4n + 4) = 0$. Next, divide both sides by 6 to get $n^2 - 4n + 4 = 0$. Factor the equation $(n - 2)(n - 2) = 0$. Solve for n, $n = 2$.

29. **300** This is a word problem about speed. First, find out the speed of painting, 35 paintings ÷ 25 hours = 1.4 paintings/hour. Then find how long it will take to finish 7 paintings, 7 paintings ÷ 1.4 paintings/hour = 5 hours. Then convert the number of hours to minutes, 5 hours = 300 minutes (one hour = 60 minutes).

30. **20** This is a medium circle question. First, find the area of the circle, $20\pi \times 5 = 100\pi$. Next find the radius of the circle. Since the area of a circle is πr^2, the radius, r, is the square root of the area divided by π, $\sqrt{100\pi \div \pi} = 10$. The diameter is 10 × 2 = 20.

31. **5** This is a difficult geometry question. First find the ratio between BC and DE, 39 − 13 = 26, 1:2. Then because BC is 12 and AC is 12, triangles ABC and DEF are both special triangles of 5:12:13. Use the ratio to find that AB is 5. Multiply 5 by 2 to get 10 for line EF. Then line EF − line AB is 10 − 5 = 5. This question can also be solved by using angle B to calculate AB then EF.

PSAT/NMSQT
Practice Test 2

Answer Sheet

Last Name: _____ **First Name:** _____

Date: _____ **Testing Location:** _____

Administering the Test

- Remove this answer sheet from the book and use it to record your answers to this test.
- This test will require 2 hours and 10 minutes to complete. Take this test in one sitting.
- Use a stopwatch to time yourself on each section. The time limit for each section is written clearly at the beginning of each section. The first four sections are 25 minutes long, and the last section is 30 minutes long.
- Each response must completely fill the oval. Erase all stray marks completely, or they may be interpreted as responses.
- You must stop ALL work on a section when time is called.
- If you finish a section before the time has elapsed, check your work on that section. You may NOT move on to the next section until time is called.
- Do not waste time on questions that seem too difficult for you.
- Use the test book for scratchwork, but you will only receive credit for answers that are marked on the answer sheets.

Scoring the Test

- Your scaled score, which will be determined from a conversion table, is based on your raw score for each section.
- You will receive one point toward your raw score for every correct answer.
- You will receive no points toward your raw score for an omitted question.
- For each wrong answer on a multiple-choice question, your raw score will be reduced by 1/4 point. For each wrong answer on a numerical "grid-in" question (Section 4, questions 29–38), your raw score will receive no deduction.

SECTION 1	**Reading Test** 60 MINUTES			Time: 60 minutes

Start: _____

Stop: _____

1. Ⓐ Ⓑ Ⓒ Ⓓ   13. Ⓐ Ⓑ Ⓒ Ⓓ   25. Ⓐ Ⓑ Ⓒ Ⓓ   37. Ⓐ Ⓑ Ⓒ Ⓓ
2. Ⓐ Ⓑ Ⓒ Ⓓ   14. Ⓐ Ⓑ Ⓒ Ⓓ   26. Ⓐ Ⓑ Ⓒ Ⓓ   38. Ⓐ Ⓑ Ⓒ Ⓓ
3. Ⓐ Ⓑ Ⓒ Ⓓ   15. Ⓐ Ⓑ Ⓒ Ⓓ   27. Ⓐ Ⓑ Ⓒ Ⓓ   39. Ⓐ Ⓑ Ⓒ Ⓓ
4. Ⓐ Ⓑ Ⓒ Ⓓ   16. Ⓐ Ⓑ Ⓒ Ⓓ   28. Ⓐ Ⓑ Ⓒ Ⓓ   40. Ⓐ Ⓑ Ⓒ Ⓓ
5. Ⓐ Ⓑ Ⓒ Ⓓ   17. Ⓐ Ⓑ Ⓒ Ⓓ   29. Ⓐ Ⓑ Ⓒ Ⓓ   41. Ⓐ Ⓑ Ⓒ Ⓓ
6. Ⓐ Ⓑ Ⓒ Ⓓ   18. Ⓐ Ⓑ Ⓒ Ⓓ   30. Ⓐ Ⓑ Ⓒ Ⓓ   42. Ⓐ Ⓑ Ⓒ Ⓓ
7. Ⓐ Ⓑ Ⓒ Ⓓ   19. Ⓐ Ⓑ Ⓒ Ⓓ   31. Ⓐ Ⓑ Ⓒ Ⓓ   43. Ⓐ Ⓑ Ⓒ Ⓓ
8. Ⓐ Ⓑ Ⓒ Ⓓ   20. Ⓐ Ⓑ Ⓒ Ⓓ   32. Ⓐ Ⓑ Ⓒ Ⓓ   44. Ⓐ Ⓑ Ⓒ Ⓓ
9. Ⓐ Ⓑ Ⓒ Ⓓ   21. Ⓐ Ⓑ Ⓒ Ⓓ   33. Ⓐ Ⓑ Ⓒ Ⓓ   45. Ⓐ Ⓑ Ⓒ Ⓓ
10. Ⓐ Ⓑ Ⓒ Ⓓ   22. Ⓐ Ⓑ Ⓒ Ⓓ   34. Ⓐ Ⓑ Ⓒ Ⓓ   46. Ⓐ Ⓑ Ⓒ Ⓓ
11. Ⓐ Ⓑ Ⓒ Ⓓ   23. Ⓐ Ⓑ Ⓒ Ⓓ   35. Ⓐ Ⓑ Ⓒ Ⓓ   47. Ⓐ Ⓑ Ⓒ Ⓓ
12. Ⓐ Ⓑ Ⓒ Ⓓ   24. Ⓐ Ⓑ Ⓒ Ⓓ   36. Ⓐ Ⓑ Ⓒ Ⓓ

SECTION 2	**Writing and Language Test** 35 MINUTES			Time: 35 minutes

Start: _____

Stop: _____

1. Ⓐ Ⓑ Ⓒ Ⓓ   12. Ⓐ Ⓑ Ⓒ Ⓓ   23. Ⓐ Ⓑ Ⓒ Ⓓ   34. Ⓐ Ⓑ Ⓒ Ⓓ
2. Ⓐ Ⓑ Ⓒ Ⓓ   13. Ⓐ Ⓑ Ⓒ Ⓓ   24. Ⓐ Ⓑ Ⓒ Ⓓ   35. Ⓐ Ⓑ Ⓒ Ⓓ
3. Ⓐ Ⓑ Ⓒ Ⓓ   14. Ⓐ Ⓑ Ⓒ Ⓓ   25. Ⓐ Ⓑ Ⓒ Ⓓ   36. Ⓐ Ⓑ Ⓒ Ⓓ
4. Ⓐ Ⓑ Ⓒ Ⓓ   15. Ⓐ Ⓑ Ⓒ Ⓓ   26. Ⓐ Ⓑ Ⓒ Ⓓ   37. Ⓐ Ⓑ Ⓒ Ⓓ
5. Ⓐ Ⓑ Ⓒ Ⓓ   16. Ⓐ Ⓑ Ⓒ Ⓓ   27. Ⓐ Ⓑ Ⓒ Ⓓ   38. Ⓐ Ⓑ Ⓒ Ⓓ
6. Ⓐ Ⓑ Ⓒ Ⓓ   17. Ⓐ Ⓑ Ⓒ Ⓓ   28. Ⓐ Ⓑ Ⓒ Ⓓ   39. Ⓐ Ⓑ Ⓒ Ⓓ
7. Ⓐ Ⓑ Ⓒ Ⓓ   18. Ⓐ Ⓑ Ⓒ Ⓓ   29. Ⓐ Ⓑ Ⓒ Ⓓ   40. Ⓐ Ⓑ Ⓒ Ⓓ
8. Ⓐ Ⓑ Ⓒ Ⓓ   19. Ⓐ Ⓑ Ⓒ Ⓓ   30. Ⓐ Ⓑ Ⓒ Ⓓ   41. Ⓐ Ⓑ Ⓒ Ⓓ
9. Ⓐ Ⓑ Ⓒ Ⓓ   20. Ⓐ Ⓑ Ⓒ Ⓓ   31. Ⓐ Ⓑ Ⓒ Ⓓ   42. Ⓐ Ⓑ Ⓒ Ⓓ
10. Ⓐ Ⓑ Ⓒ Ⓓ   21. Ⓐ Ⓑ Ⓒ Ⓓ   32. Ⓐ Ⓑ Ⓒ Ⓓ   43. Ⓐ Ⓑ Ⓒ Ⓓ
11. Ⓐ Ⓑ Ⓒ Ⓓ   22. Ⓐ Ⓑ Ⓒ Ⓓ   33. Ⓐ Ⓑ Ⓒ Ⓓ   44. Ⓐ Ⓑ Ⓒ Ⓓ

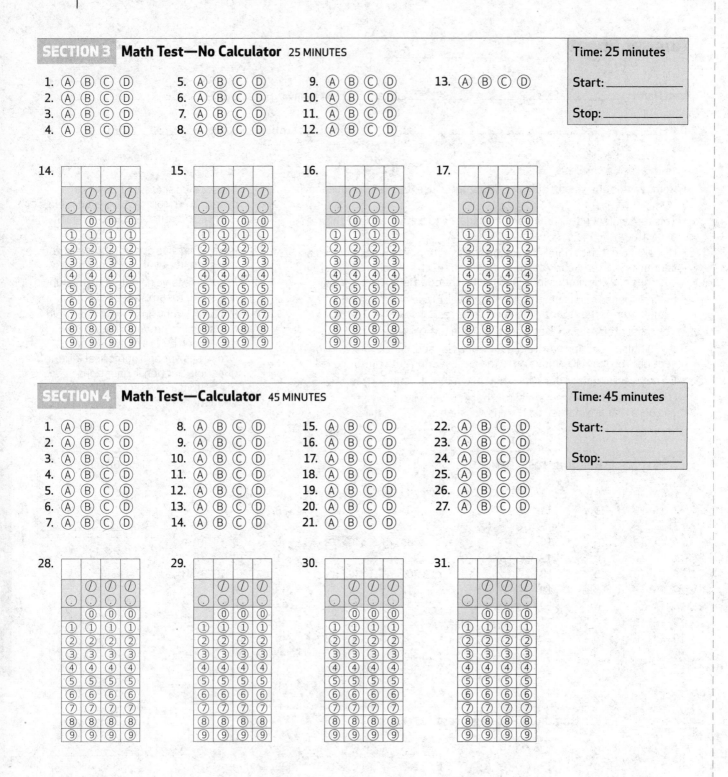

SECTION 3 **Math Test—No Calculator** 25 MINUTES

1. (A) (B) (C) (D) 5. (A) (B) (C) (D) 9. (A) (B) (C) (D) 13. (A) (B) (C) (D)
2. (A) (B) (C) (D) 6. (A) (B) (C) (D) 10. (A) (B) (C) (D)
3. (A) (B) (C) (D) 7. (A) (B) (C) (D) 11. (A) (B) (C) (D)
4. (A) (B) (C) (D) 8. (A) (B) (C) (D) 12. (A) (B) (C) (D)

Time: 25 minutes

Start: _____

Stop: _____

14. 15. 16. 17.

SECTION 4 **Math Test—Calculator** 45 MINUTES

1. (A) (B) (C) (D) 8. (A) (B) (C) (D) 15. (A) (B) (C) (D) 22. (A) (B) (C) (D)
2. (A) (B) (C) (D) 9. (A) (B) (C) (D) 16. (A) (B) (C) (D) 23. (A) (B) (C) (D)
3. (A) (B) (C) (D) 10. (A) (B) (C) (D) 17. (A) (B) (C) (D) 24. (A) (B) (C) (D)
4. (A) (B) (C) (D) 11. (A) (B) (C) (D) 18. (A) (B) (C) (D) 25. (A) (B) (C) (D)
5. (A) (B) (C) (D) 12. (A) (B) (C) (D) 19. (A) (B) (C) (D) 26. (A) (B) (C) (D)
6. (A) (B) (C) (D) 13. (A) (B) (C) (D) 20. (A) (B) (C) (D) 27. (A) (B) (C) (D)
7. (A) (B) (C) (D) 14. (A) (B) (C) (D) 21. (A) (B) (C) (D)

Time: 45 minutes

Start: _____

Stop: _____

28. 29. 30. 31.

READING TEST

60 MINUTES, 47 QUESTIONS

Turn to Section 1 of your answer sheet to answer the questions in this section.

Directions: Each passage or pair of passages below is followed by a number of questions. After reading each passage or pair, choose the best answer to each question based on what is stated or implied in the passage or passages and in any accompanying graphics (such as a table or graph).

Questions 1–10 are based on the following passage.

This passage is adapted from President Woodrow Wilson's speech originally published in 1918, at the closing of WWI.

It will be our wish and purpose that the processes of peace, when they are begun, shall be absolutely open and that they shall involve and permit henceforth no secret understandings of any kind.

5 The day of conquest and aggrandizement is gone by; so is also the day of secret covenants entered into in the interest of particular governments and likely at some unlooked-for moment to upset the peace of the world. It is this happy fact, now clear to the view of

10 every public man whose thoughts do not still linger in an age that is dead and gone, which makes it possible for every nation whose purposes are consistent with justice and the peace of the world to avow now or at any other time the objects it has in view.

15 We entered this war because violations of right had occurred which touched us to the quick and made the life of our own people impossible unless they were corrected and the world secure once for all against their recurrence. What we demand in

20 this war, therefore, is nothing peculiar to ourselves. It is that the world be made fit and safe to live in; and particularly that it be made safe for every peace-loving nation which, like our own, wishes to live its own life, determine its own institutions, be assured

25 of justice and fair dealing by the other peoples of the world as against force and selfish aggression.

All the peoples of the world are in effect partners in this interest, and for our own part we see very clearly that unless justice be done to others it will

30 not be done to us.

The program of the world's peace, therefore, is our program; and that program, the only possible program, as we see it, is this:

I. Open covenants of peace, openly arrived at,

35 after which there shall be no private international understandings of any kind but diplomacy shall proceed always frankly and in the public view.

II. Absolute freedom of navigation upon the seas, outside territorial waters, alike in peace and in

40 war, except as the seas may be closed in whole or in part by international action for the enforcement of international covenants.

III. The removal, so far as possible, of all economic barriers and the establishment of an

45 equality of trade conditions among all the nations consenting to the peace and associating themselves for its maintenance.

IV. Adequate guarantees given and taken that national armaments will be reduced to the lowest

50 point consistent with domestic safety.

V. A free, open-minded, and absolutely impartial adjustment of all colonial claims, based upon a strict observance of the principle that in determining all such questions of sovereignty the interests of the

55 populations concerned must have equal weight with

GO ON TO THE NEXT PAGE ⟶

the equitable claims of the government whose title is to be determined.

VI. The evacuation of all Russian territory and such a settlement of all questions affecting Russia as will secure the best and freest cooperation of the other nations of the world in obtaining for her an unhampered and unembarrassed opportunity for the independent determination of her own political development and national policy and assure her of a sincere welcome into the society of free nations under institutions of her own choosing; and, more than a welcome, assistance also of every kind that she may need and may herself desire. The treatment accorded Russia by her sister nations in the months to come will be the acid test of their good will, of their comprehension of her needs as distinguished from their own interests, and of their intelligent and unselfish sympathy.

VII. Belgium, the whole world will agree, must be evacuated and restored, without any attempt to limit the sovereignty which she enjoys in common with all other free nations. No other single act will serve as this will serve to restore confidence among the nations in the laws which they have themselves set and determined for the government of their relations with one another. Without this healing act the whole structure and validity of international law is forever impaired.

VIII. All French territory should be freed and the invaded portions restored, and the wrong done to France by Prussia in 1871 in the matter of Alsace-Lorraine, which has unsettled the peace of the world for nearly fifty years, should be righted, in order that peace may once more be made secure in the interest of all.

IX. A readjustment of the frontiers of Italy should be effected along clearly recognizable lines of nationality.

X. The peoples of Austria-Hungary, whose place among the nations we wish to see safeguarded and assured, should be accorded the freest opportunity to autonomous development.

XI. Rumania, Serbia, and Montenegro should be evacuated; occupied territories restored; Serbia accorded free and secure access to the sea; and the relations of the several Balkan states to one another determined by friendly counsel along historically established lines of allegiance and nationality; and international guarantees of the political and economic independence and territorial integrity of the several Balkan states should be entered into.

XII. The Turkish portion of the present Ottoman Empire should be assured a secure sovereignty, but the other nationalities which are now under Turkish rule should be assured an undoubted security of life and an absolutely unmolested opportunity of autonomous development, and the Dardanelles should be permanently opened as a free passage to the ships and commerce of all nations under international guarantees.

XIII. An independent Polish state should be erected which should include the territories inhabited by indisputably Polish populations, which should be assured a free and secure access to the sea, and whose political and economic independence and territorial integrity should be guaranteed by international covenant.

XIV. A general association of nations must be formed under specific covenants for the purpose of affording mutual guarantees of political independence and territorial integrity to great and small states alike.

In regard to these essential rectifications of wrong and assertions of right we feel ourselves to be intimate partners of all the governments and peoples associated together against the Imperialists. We cannot be separated in interest or divided in purpose. We stand together until the end.

For such arrangements and covenants we are willing to fight and to continue to fight until they are achieved; but only because we wish the right to prevail and desire a just and stable peace such as can be secured only by removing the chief provocations to war, which this program does remove. We have no jealousy of German greatness, and there is nothing

in this program that impairs it. We grudge her no
achievement or distinction of learning or of pacific
enterprise such as have made her record very bright
145 and very enviable.

   We do not wish to injure her or to block in any
way her legitimate influence or power. We do not
wish to fight her either with arms or with hostile
arrangements of trade if she is willing to associate
150 herself with us and the other peace-loving nations
of the world in covenants of justice and law and fair
dealing.

   We wish her only to accept a place of equality
among the peoples of the world, the new world in
155 which we now live, instead of a place of mastery.

1. It can be implied that the main purpose of this
   passage is

   (A) to outline a peaceful agreement that can
       be used for negotiations toward the end of
       the war
   (B) to suggest an armed enforcement of peace
       and restoration of the borders of the invaded
       countries
   (C) to partner with other nations and form
       a committee to oversee the negotiation
       process
   (D) to outline the negotiation points with other
       nations and to provide resources for all
       nations, including Germany, to restore their
       economy

2. Which choice provides the best evidence for the
   answer to the previous question?

   (A) Lines 1–4, ("It will be . . . any kind.")
   (B) Lines 43–47, ("The removal . . .
       maintenance")
   (C) Lines 130–132, ("we feel . . . Imperialists")
   (D) Lines 135–137, ("For such . . . achieved")

3. As used in line 5, "aggrandizement" most
   nearly means

   (A) defamation
   (B) denigration
   (C) glorification
   (D) aspersion

4. What does point VI of the program suggest
   about Russia?

   (A) Russia will be taking control of its
       neighboring countries and support their
       development post war.
   (B) Russia must evacuate from the neighboring
       countries, which were controlled by Russia
       during the war.
   (C) Russia will be evacuated and allowed to
       operate freely as a sovereign nation.
   (D) Russia's neighboring countries, like Belgium,
       will be evacuated and restored.

5. Which choice provides the best evidence for the
   answer to the previous question?

   (A) Lines 58–64, ("The evacuation . . . national
       policy.")
   (B) Lines 64–66, ("assure her . . . choosing")
   (C) Lines 68–72, ("treatment . . . interests")
   (D) Lines 74–75, ("Belgium . . . restored")

6. As used in line 34, "covenant" most nearly means

   (A) retraction
   (B) adjuration
   (C) agreement
   (D) trust

7. What is the purpose for President Wilson to
   outline the fourteen points?

   (A) to enter into war against violence
   (B) to claim responsibility for the restoration of
       borders of various nations
   (C) to provide a peaceful outline for restoration
       of different nations
   (D) to lead the postwar negotiations

Practice Test 2

8. Which choice provides the best evidence for the answer to the previous question?

(A) Lines 15–17, ("We entered . . . impossible")
(B) Lines 31–33, ("The program . . . program")
(C) Lines 124–128, ("A general . . . alike")
(D) Lines 142–145, ("We . . . enviable")

9. What does the passage mean by impartial adjustment?

(A) to remain unbiased and to restore the borders and powers before the war
(B) to evacuate the colonies of the imperialists and to restore their original power
(C) to consider the interest of the colonies as well as the interest of the colonialists
(D) to bring stability to the region by providing unbiased support

10. Which choice best summarizes the third paragraph of the passage?

(A) The United States defended its interest in the rest of the world.
(B) The United States entered into war to defend its own rights and restore peace.
(C) The United States defended its allies during the war and must be responsible to restore peace.
(D) The United States entered into war to defend justice.

Questions 11–20 are based on the following passage.

This passage is adapted from Ann Howard Shaw's Eulogy to Susan B. Anthony, originally published in 1918.

Your flags at half-mast tell of a nation's loss, but there are no symbols and no words which can tell the love and sorrow which fill our hearts. And yet out of the depths of our grief arise feelings of truest
5 gratitude for the beauty, the tenderness, the nobility of example, of our peerless leader's life.

There is no death for such as she. There are no last words of love. The ages to come will revere her name. Unnumbered generations of the children of men
10 shall rise up to call her blessed. Her words, her work, and her character will go on to brighten the pathway and bless the lives of all peoples. That which seems death to our unseeing eyes is to her translation. Her work will not be finished, nor will her last word be
15 spoken while there remains a wrong to be righted, or a fettered life to be freed in all the earth.

You do well to strew her bier with palms of victory, and crown her with unfading laurel, for never did more victorious hero enter into rest.
20 Her character was well poised; she did not emphasize one characteristic to the exclusion of others; she taught us that the real beauty of a true life is found in the harmonious blending of diverse elements, and her life was the epitome of her
25 teaching. She merged a keen sense of justice with the deepest love; her masterful intellect never for one moment checked the tenderness of her emotions; her splendid self-assertion found its highest realization in perfect self-surrender; she demonstrated the
30 divine principle that the truest self-development must go hand in hand with the greatest and most arduous service for others.

Here was the most harmoniously developed character I have ever known—a living soul whose
35 individuality was blended into oneness with all humanity. She lived, yet not she; humanity lived in her. Fighting the battle for individual freedom,

she was so lost to the consciousness of her own
personality that she was unconscious of existence
40 apart from all mankind.

Her quenchless passion for her cause was that it
was yours and mine, the cause of the whole world.
She knew that where freedom is there is the center
of power. In it she saw potentially all that humanity
45 might attain when possessed by its spirit. Hence
her cause, perfect equality of rights, of opportunity,
of privilege for all, civil and political, was to her
the bed-rock upon which all true progress must
rest. Therefore she was nothing, her cause was
50 everything; she knew no existence apart from it;
in it she lived and moved and had her being. It was
the first and last thought of each day; it was the
last word upon her faultering lips; to it her flitting
soul responded when the silenced voice could no
55 longer obey the will, and she could only answer
our heart-broken questions with the clasp of her
trembling hand.

She was in the truest sense a reformer,
unhindered in her service by the narrowness and
60 negative destructiveness which often so sadly
hampers the work of true reform. Possessed by an
unfaltering conviction of the primary importance
of her own cause, she nevertheless recognized that
every effort by either one or many earnest souls
65 toward what they believed to be a better or saner
life should be met in a spirit of encouragement and
helpfulness.

She recognized that it was immeasurably more
desirable to be honestly and earnestly seeking
70 that which in its attainment might not prove good
than to be hypocritically subservient to the truth
through a spirit of selfish fear or fawning at the
beck of power. She instinctively grasped the truth
underlying all great movements which have helped
75 the progress of the ages, and did not wait for an
individual nor a cause to win popularity before
freely extending to its struggling life a hand of
helpful comradeship. She was never found in the
cheering crowd that follows an already victorious
80 standard. She left that to the time-servers who divide
the spoil after they have crucified their Savior.

She was truly great; great in her humility and
utter lack of pretension.

On her eightieth birthday this noble soul could
85 truthfully say in response to the words of loving
appreciation from those who showered garlands all
about her:

"I am not accustomed to demonstrations of
gratitude or of praise. I have ever been a hewer of
90 wood and a drawer of water to this movement. I
know nothing, I have known nothing of oratory
or rhetoric. Whatever I have done has been done
because I wanted to see better conditions, better
surroundings, better circumstances for women."

11. Which choice best summarizes the first
paragraph of the passage?

(A) to express sadness over her passing and to
remember her honorable attributes

(B) to express indifference over her passing and
the loss of an important figure in history

(C) to remember her achievements and to
educate others about her actions

(D) to educate others about her actions and to
preach for others to follow her lead

12. The main purpose of this passage is

(A) for Susan B. Anthony's students, friends
and loved ones to express love and gratitude
toward her

(B) to remember Susan B. Anthony and to
express her significance in the women's
suffrage movement and in history

(C) to remember Susan B. Anthony's
character and to focus on her role as a wife
and mother

(D) to inform others about Susan B. Anthony's
doings and to introduce her to future
generations as a pioneer in women's suffrage

13. Which choice provides the best evidence for the answer to the previous question?

    (A) Lines 2–3, ("no words . . . hearts")
    (B) Lines 7–10, ("There are . . . blessed")
    (C) Lines 20–22, ("Her character . . . others")
    (D) Lines 41–42, ("Her quenchless . . . mine")

14. As used in line 18, "laurel" most nearly means

    (A) support
    (B) honor
    (C) trivial
    (D) inconsequence

15. According to the passage, what is one of Susan B. Anthony's achievements?

    (A) She was able to stand in front of Congress and deliver an important speech that furthered the women suffrage movement.
    (B) She recognized the importance of freedom and worked to bring freedom to all.
    (C) She taught many students and shared with them her ideology for improved women's rights.
    (D) She was a pioneer who pushed for the passing of laws that allowed women to vote.

16. Which choice provides the best evidence for the answer to the previous question?

    (A) Lines 13–16, ("Her work . . . earth")
    (B) Lines 33–34, ("Here . . . known")
    (C) Lines 43–45, ("She knew . . . spirit")
    (D) Lines 73–75, ("She instinctively . . . ages")

17. As used in line 86, "garlands" most nearly means

    (A) flowers
    (B) praises
    (C) distain
    (D) augmentation

18. What can be inferred from the passage about her characteristics?

    (A) She was fastidious and alluring.
    (B) She was a revolutionary pioneer.
    (C) She was a methodical teacher.
    (D) She was a savior of mankind.

19. Which choice provides the best evidence for the answer to the previous question?

    (A) Lines 22–25, ("she taught . . . teaching")
    (B) Lines 58–61, ("She was . . . reform")
    (C) Lines 68–73, ("She recognized . . . power")
    (D) Lines 80–81, ("She left . . . Savior")

20. What is the purpose of the last paragraph?

    (A) to recognize her for her work on the women suffrage movement
    (B) to praise her excessively for her poise
    (C) to give an example of Susan B. Anthony's characteristics
    (D) to exemplify Susan B. Anthony's doings and to present her as a pillar to her students and followers

Questions 21–29 are based on the following passage.

This passage is adapted from Jane Austen's novel Pride and Prejudice, *originally published in 1813.*

When they were gone, Elizabeth, as if intending to exasperate herself as much as possible against Mr. Darcy, chose for her employment the examination of all the letters which Jane had written to her since her
5 being in Kent. They contained no actual complaint, nor was there any revival of past occurrences, or any communication of present suffering. But in all, and in almost every line of each, there was a want of that cheerfulness which had been used to characterize
10 her style, and which, proceeding from the serenity of a mind at ease with itself and kindly disposed towards everyone, had been scarcely ever clouded. Elizabeth noticed every sentence conveying the idea of uneasiness, with an attention which it had hardly
15 received on the first perusal. Mr. Darcy's shameful boast of what misery he had been able to inflict, gave her a keener sense of her sister's sufferings. It was some consolation to think that his visit to Rosings was to end on the day after the next—and, a still
20 greater, that in less than a fortnight she should herself be with Jane again, and enabled to contribute to the recovery of her spirits, by all that affection could do.

She could not think of Darcy's leaving Kent without remembering that his cousin was to go with
25 him; but Colonel Fitzwilliam had made it clear that he had no intentions at all, and agreeable as he was, she did not mean to be unhappy about him.

While settling this point, she was suddenly roused by the sound of the door-bell, and her
30 spirits were a little fluttered by the idea of its being Colonel Fitzwilliam himself, who had once before called late in the evening, and might now come to inquire particularly after her. But this idea was soon banished, and her spirits were very differently
35 affected, when, to her utter amazement, she saw Mr. Darcy walk into the room. In an hurried manner he immediately began an inquiry after her health, imputing his visit to a wish of hearing that she were better. She answered him with cold civility. He
40 sat down for a few moments, and then getting up, walked about the room. Elizabeth was surprised, but said not a word. After a silence of several minutes, he came towards her in an agitated manner, and thus began:

45 "In vain I have struggled. It will not do. My feelings will not be repressed. You must allow me to tell you how ardently I admire and love you."

Elizabeth's astonishment was beyond expression. She stared, colored, doubted, and was silent. This
50 he considered sufficient encouragement; and the avowal of all that he felt, and had long felt for her, immediately followed. He spoke well; but there were feelings besides those of the heart to be detailed; and he was not more eloquent on the
55 subject of tenderness than of pride. His sense of her inferiority—of its being a degradation—of the family obstacles which had always opposed to inclination, were dwelt on with a warmth which seemed due to the consequence he was wounding, but was very
60 unlikely to recommend his suit.

In spite of her deeply-rooted dislike, she could not be insensible to the compliment of such a man's affection, and though her intentions did not vary for an instant, she was at first sorry for the pain
65 he was to receive; till, roused to resentment by his subsequent language, she lost all compassion in anger. She tried, however, to compose herself to answer him with patience, when he should have done. He concluded with representing to her the
70 strength of that attachment which, in spite of all his endeavors, he had found impossible to conquer; and with expressing his hope that it would now be rewarded by her acceptance of his hand. As he said this, she could easily see that he had no doubt of
75 a favorable answer. He spoke of apprehension and anxiety, but his countenance expressed real security. Such a circumstance could only exasperate farther, and, when he ceased, the color rose into her cheeks, and she said:

80 "In such cases as this, it is, I believe, the
established mode to express a sense of obligation for
the sentiments avowed, however unequally they may
be returned. It is natural that obligation should be
felt, and if I could feel gratitude, I would now thank

85 you. But I cannot—I have never desired your good
opinion, and you have certainly bestowed it most
unwillingly. I am sorry to have occasioned pain
to anyone. It has been most unconsciously done,
however, and I hope will be of short duration. The

90 feelings which, you tell me, have long prevented
the acknowledgment of your regard, can have little
difficulty in overcoming it after this explanation."

Mr. Darcy, who was leaning against the
mantelpiece with his eyes fixed on her face, seemed

95 to catch her words with no less resentment than
surprise. His complexion became pale with anger,
and the disturbance of his mind was visible in
every feature. He was struggling for the appearance
of composure, and would not open his lips till he

100 believed himself to have attained it. The pause was to
Elizabeth's feelings dreadful. At length, with a voice
of forced calmness, he said:

"And this is all the reply which I am to have the
honor of expecting! I might, perhaps, wish to be

105 informed why, with so little endeavor at civility, I am
thus rejected. But it is of small importance."

21. The main purpose of this passage is to

(A) describe why the feelings of one character
toward the other were intensified

(B) describe, in detail the prejudice that one
character feels toward the other

(C) illustrate a marriage proposal and rejection

(D) illustrate a major change in a character's
attitude and the resolution of a conflict

22. Which choice provides the best evidence for the
answer to the previous question?

(A) Lines 1–3, ("When . . . Darcy")

(B) Lines 45–47, ("In vain . . . you")

(C) Lines 52–54, ("But . . . detailed")

(D) Lines 63–65, ("her intentions . . . receive")

23. Which of the following best summarizes the
first paragraph?

(A) Elizabeth understands from her sister Jane's
letters that Jane is upset.

(B) Elizabeth is angry at Mr. Darcy for his
arrogance and impoliteness.

(C) Elizabeth is excited about Mr. Darcy's
pending departure.

(D) Elizabeth is dreading the return of her
unhappy sister.

24. As used in line 3, "employment" most
nearly means

(A) trade

(B) vocation

(C) activity

(D) enrollment

25. According to the passage what does Elizabeth
feel about Colonel Fitzwilliam?

(A) Elizabeth feels coldly indifferent
toward him.

(B) Elizabeth feels positive toward him.

(C) Elizabeth likes to compare him to Darcy.

(D) Elizabeth feels uneasy about Colonel
Fitzwilliam.

26. Which choice provides the best evidence for the
answer to the previous question?

(A) Lines 23–25, ("She could . . . him")

(B) Lines 26–27, ("agreeable . . . him")

(C) Lines 29–31, ("her spirits . . . himself")

(D) Lines 34–36, ("her spirits . . . room")

27. As used in line 39, "civility" most nearly means

(A) politeness

(B) disrespect

(C) bluntness

(D) disdain

GO ON TO THE NEXT PAGE ⟼

28. Which of the following best describes Elizabeth's feelings toward Darcy?

(A) Elizabeth feels extremely angry and ashamed because of the misfortunes of her sister.

(B) Elizabeth is upset with Mr. Darcy and loses her patience.

(C) Elizabeth dreads seeing Mr. Darcy and would prefer a proposal from his cousin

(D) Elizabeth feels indifferent toward him and wishes to ignore him.

29. Which choice provides the best evidence for the answer to the previous question?

(A) Lines 15–17, ("Mr. Darcy's . . . sufferings")

(B) Line 48, ("Elizabeth's . . . expression")

(C) Lines 66–68, ("she lost . . . patience")

(D) Lines 106–107, ("with . . . importance")

Questions 30–38 are based on the following passage.

This passage is adapted from President Teddy Roosevelt's speech originally published in 1918.

I transmit herewith a report of the National Conservation Commission, together with the accompanying papers.

This report, which is the outgrowth of the
5 conference of governors last May, was unanimously approved by the recent joint conference held in this city between the National Conservation Commission and governors of States, state conservation commissions, and conservation
10 committees of great organizations of citizens. It is therefore in a peculiar sense representative of the whole nation and all its parts.

With the statements and conclusions of this report I heartily concur, and I commend it to the
15 thoughtful consideration both of the Congress and of our people generally. It is one of the most fundamentally important documents ever laid before the American people. It contains the first inventory of its natural resources ever made by any
20 nation. In condensed form it presents a statement of our available capital in material resources, which are the means of progress, and calls attention to the essential conditions upon which the perpetuity,

safety and welfare of this nation now rest and must
25 always continue to rest. It deserves, and should have, the widest possible distribution among the people.

The facts set forth in this report constitute an imperative call to action. The situation they disclose demands that we, neglecting for a time, if need be,
30 smaller and less vital questions, shall concentrate an effective part of our attention upon the great material foundations of national existence, progress and prosperity.

This first inventory of natural resources prepared
35 by the National Conservation Commission is undoubtedly but the beginning of a series which will be indispensable for dealing intelligently with what we have. It supplies as close an approximation to the actual facts as it was possible to prepare with
40 the knowledge and time available. The progress of our knowledge of this country will continually lead to more accurate information and better use of the sources of national strength. But we can not defer action until complete accuracy in the estimates can
45 be reached, because before that time many of our resources will be practically gone. It is not necessary that this inventory should be exact in every minute detail. It is essential that it should correctly describe the general situation; and that the present inventory

50 does. As it stands it is an irrefutable proof that the
conservation of our resources is the fundamental
question before this nation, and that our first and
greatest task is to set our house in order and begin to
live within our means.

55   The first of all considerations is the permanent
welfare of our people; and true moral welfare, the
highest form of welfare, can not permanently exist
save on a firm and lasting foundation of material
well-being. In this respect our situation is far from
60 satisfactory. After every possible allowance has been
made, and when every hopeful indication has been
given its full weight, the facts still give reason for grave
concern. It would be unworthy of our history and
our intelligence, and disastrous to our future, to shut
65 our eyes to these facts or attempt to laugh them out
of court. The people should and will rightly demand
that the great fundamental questions shall be given
attention by their representatives. I do not advise
hasty or ill-considered action on disputed points, but
70 I do urge, where the facts are known, where the public
interest is clear, that neither indifference and inertia,
nor adverse private interests, shall be allowed to stand
in the way of the public good.

      The great basic facts are already well known.
75 We know that our population is now adding about
one-fifth to its numbers in ten years, and that by the
middle of the present century perhaps one hundred
and fifty million Americans, and by its end very
many millions more, must be fed and clothed from
80 the products of our soil. With the steady growth
in population and the still more rapid increase
in consumption our people will hereafter make
greater and not less demands per capita upon all
the natural resources for their livelihood, comfort
85 and convenience. It is high time to realize that our
responsibility to the coming millions is like that of
parents to their children, and that in wasting our
resources we are wronging our descendants.

      We know now that our rivers can and should
90 be made to serve our people effectively in
transportation, but that the vast expenditures for our
waterways have not resulted in maintaining, much

less in promoting, inland navigation. Therefore, let
us take immediate steps to ascertain the reasons
95 and to prepare and adopt a comprehensive plan for
inland-waterway navigation that will result in giving
the people the benefits for which they have paid,
but which they have not yet received. We know now
that our forests are fast disappearing, that less than
100 one-fifth of them are being conserved, and that no
good purpose can be met by failing to provide the
relatively small sums needed for the protection, use
and improvement of all forests still owned by the
Government, and to enact laws to check the wasteful
105 destruction of the forests in private hands. There are
differences of opinion as to many public questions;
but the American people stand nearly as a unit for
waterway development and for forest protection.

30. What is the main purpose of this passage?

   (A) a call to action for Americans to conserve
       resources and public lands and areas
   (B) an anxious demand for Americans to reduce
       waste and leave the future generations with
       more natural resources
   (C) a methodical expression spelling out all the
       actions that need to be taken to ensure the
       survival of the nation in the future
   (D) a dialogue with Americans about the plans
       of the nation to conserve land

31. Which choice provides the best evidence for the
answer to the previous question?

   (A) Lines 1–3, ("I transmit . . . papers")
   (B) Lines 55–58, ("The first . . . well-being")
   (C) Lines 63–65, ("It would . . . court")
   (D) Lines 107–109 ("but the . . . forest
       protection")

32. As used in line 14, "concur" most nearly means

   (A) agree
   (B) differ
   (C) obsolete
   (D) collaborate

33. According to the passage, what does President Roosevelt think about the report of the National Conservation Commission?

    (A) The report provides evidence that the actions of Americans are not sustainable and will cause drastic changes immediately.

    (B) The report claims that natural lands and waterways should be conserved because within five years there will be a significant population boost.

    (C) The report provides a wealth of evidence that supports the immediate start of conservation of resources.

    (D) The report undermines environmental factors and provides President Roosevelt with an excuse to seize more public lands.

34. Which choice provides the best evidence for the answer to the previous question?

    (A) Lines 16–17, ("one of . . . people")

    (B) Lines 19–22, ("In condensed . . . conditions")

    (C) Lines 34–38, ("This first . . . have")

    (D) Lines 50–54, ("As it stands . . . means")

35. As used in line 71, "inertia" most nearly means

    (A) apathy

    (B) force

    (C) elation

    (D) vigor

36. What does President Roosevelt believe about the natural resources?

    (A) The waterways are not important, and resources directed toward maintaining the waterways should be redirected.

    (B) The population growth does not pose a problem for the United States but should be used as incentive for Americans to practice more recycling.

    (C) The forests are diminishing, and the country needs to invest in their protection.

    (D) The population growth provides a huge problem for the depletion of resources, and limits should be put on the individual.

37. Which choice provides the best evidence for the answer to the previous question?

    (A) Lines 75–76, ("our population . . . years")

    (B) Lines 77–80, ("present . . . soil")

    (C) Lines 92–93, ("our waterways . . . navigation")

    (D) Lines 98–102, ("We know . . . for the protection")

38. Which of the following is supported by the passage?

    (A) President Roosevelt wanted to start programs that made the conservation of energy easier.

    (B) President Roosevelt believes that Americans have a responsibility to the millions of people that will be part of the growing population.

    (C) President Roosevelt believes that the most important part of conservation is the conservation of public lands and waterways.

    (D) President Roosevelt believes that the first step to starting a conservation program is to conserve the bigger resources.

Questions 39–47 are based on the following passage.

Passage 1 is adapted from "Observations on the Cause of Rickets" by D. Noel Paton, Leonard Findlay, and Alexander Watson from 1918. Passage 2 is adapted from "The Prevention and Cure of Rickets by Sunlight" by Alfred F. Hess, M.D., from 1921.

PASSAGE 1

In the course of an investigation on metabolism in rickets the difficulty of getting satisfactory material from children induced us to produce rickets in a certain number of young dogs, while keeping others

5 free from the disease. The previous experiences in this laboratory had showed that rickets may almost certainly be induced in the great majority of pups of certain breeds of dog by simply keeping them in the animal house of the department, while the

10 experience of every keeper who breeds dogs is that if pups are to be reared without rickets developing they must have abundant exercise in the open air. One of us (L.F.) has already published an experimental investigation on the etiology of rickets in young dogs,

15 in which he records that puppies freely exercised when fed on bread and water, oatmeal and water, etc., did not develop rickets, but became marasmic and died. On the other hand, puppies fed on oatmeal porridge and milk, if allowed to run about, remained

20 free of the disease, but if confined developed it.

Pups kept in the country and freely exercised in the open air, although they had actually a smaller amount of milk fat than those kept in the laboratory, remained free of rickets, while the animals kept in

25 the laboratory all became rickety.

The observations seem to show that some other factor than diet is the prime cause of rickets in dogs, and afford no evidence that milk fat (butter) contains any accessory factor protecting against the

30 development of rickets.

PASSAGE 2

Rickets is the commonest nutritional disorder occurring among infants. In spite of this fact little interest has been manifested in it, either by the clinician or by the laboratory investigator. Its status

35 from an etiological point of view was, until recently, much the same as it had been for the past 250 years, from the time when Glisson and his associates recorded its appearance in England. Broadly speaking, it may be stated that physicians have been

40 divided into two camps regarding its origin, some believing the main cause to be dietetic, and others ascribing its occurrence to faulty hygiene.

During the past few years renewed interest has been aroused in the study of rickets, both in this

45 country and abroad, owing to the fact that some-have ascribed it to the lack of a vitamin, and also because it has become possible to produce the disease with regularity in animals. Studies, however, have not progressed sufficiently far to harmonize

50 opinions as to its causation. The well-known investigations of Mellanby have led him, and others, to the conclusion that the nutritional alterations are due to a deficient diet, the lack of a vitamin identical or closely associated with the fat-soluble vitamin;

55 whereas the work of Findlay and Paton—clinical as well as experimental—have led to the deduction that the disorder is to be ascribed to hygienic factors.

What we wish to emphasize more particularly is rather the prophylaxis against rickets. At the

60 present time it is impossible to state the comparative roles of dietetic and of hygienic factors in its etiology. Probably their influence varies at different times and under different circumstances. During the war, defective diet, no doubt, was a potent

65 factor in increasing the incidence of rickets in the Central Empires. In New York City I believe that lack of sunlight plays a very important role in its development, and I am strengthened in this view by the marked seasonal incidence which it evinces.

70 Now that it has been shown that sunlight is a valuable preventive and curative measure in rickets, those active in infant welfare will have to regulate the care of the baby so that it is not deprived of

GO ON TO THE NEXT PAGE ➠

this simple and beneficent therapeutic agent. At
75 the present time infants are swathed from head to
toe in clothing, so that the sun can fall only upon
their faces; even in the mildest weather their bodies
receive little direct sunlight. Such habits should be
altered. If the baby is in the sun, its arms and legs
80 may be bared without causing discomfort. In cold
weather the body must be particularly well wrapped,
and the hands and feet protected, but the arms and
legs may be exposed.

39. What does the author of Passage 1 suggests
about dietary effect on rickets?

(A) Consumption of milk fat is unable to
prevent rickets in puppies.
(B) Puppies fed a wholesome diet, including
bread water, oatmeal and milk, will not
develop rickets.
(C) Rickets developed in puppies that had been
fed more milk, yet puppies fed little milk did
not develop rickets.
(D) Open air combined with correct diet,
including bread, water, and oatmeal, prevent
the occurrence of rickets, and puppies on
this diet thrived.

40. Which choice provides the best evidence for the
answer to the previous question?

(A) Lines 14–17, ("rickets in young . . . rickets")
(B) Lines 18–20, ("puppies fed . . . developed it")
(C) Lines 21–23, ("Pups kept in . . . laboratory")
(D) Lines 28–30, ("no evidence . . . rickets")

41. As used in line 17, "marasmic" most
nearly means

(A) booming
(B) emaciated
(C) exorbitant
(D) capacious

42. What does the author of Passage 2 suggests
about what scientists thought was the origins of
rickets?

(A) Malnutrition and lack of minerals are
thought to cause rickets.
(B) Hygiene had been thought to cause
rickets, but this theory had recently been
proven false.
(C) The cause of rickets is debated; some think it
is caused by hygiene.
(D) The cause of rickets had been the center of
debates, but the cause has been proven in
recent years.

43. Which choice provides the best evidence for the
answer to the previous question?

(A) Lines 31–32, ("Rickets is . . . infants")
(B) Lines 40–42, ("some believing . . . faulty
hygiene")
(C) Lines 45–48, ("that some . . . in animals")
(D) Lines 48–50, ("Studies . . . its causation")

44. As used in line 71, "curative" most nearly means

(A) remedial
(B) purifying
(C) inimical
(D) consumptive

45. What does the author of Passage 2 suggest about
the role of sunlight?

(A) Seasonality of rickets suggests that sunlight
plays an important role in preventing
rickets.
(B) Sunlight plays a small role in causing rickets
in certain geographical locations.
(C) Direct sunlight on the faces and not the
arms and legs is the correct way to expose
infants to sunlight.
(D) The practical implications of the research
on sunlight and rickets needs to be tested
extensively.

Practice Test 2

46. Which choice provides the best evidence for the answer to the previous question?

(A) Lines 66–68, ("In New York . . . development")

(B) Lines 68–69, ("I am strengthened . . . evinces")

(C) Lines 74–78, ("At the present . . . sunlight")

(D) Lines 79–80, ("If the baby . . . discomfort")

47. Which of the following best describes the relationship between the two passages?

(A) Passage 2 attacks the scientific evidence presented by Passage 1.

(B) Passage 2 details the practical implications for the scientific discoveries made by the author of Passage 1.

(C) Passage 2 presents evidence of more advanced understanding than Passage 1 on the causes of rickets.

(D) Passage 1 and Passage 2 advocate different ideas, and Passage 2 presents more details.

STOP

If you finish before time is called, you may check your work on this section only.

Do not turn to any other section.

WRITING AND LANGUAGE TEST
35 MINUTES, 44 QUESTIONS

Answer the following questions on Section 2 of your answer sheet.

Directions: Each passage is accompanied by questions that ask you to revise or edit the passage to improve its flow, organization, clarity, and sentence mechanics. For most questions, you will be directed to an underlined portion of the passage to either choose "NO CHANGE" or to select the appropriate revision. For other questions, you'll be asked to think about the passage as a whole. Some passages may also include a graphic to consider as you edit.

Questions 1–11 are based on the following passage.

Exclusionary Feminism

Mona Lisa Smile **1** portrays upper-class women and also their education at Wellesley College in 1950s America. The prestigious school contrasts sharply with the film's protagonist, the independent, forward-thinking Katherine Watson, **2** who is hired to teach art history. **3** It embodies Victorian standards, setting a strict feminine ideal that revolves around the women's role in the private sphere; Katherine, on the other hand, represents the modern woman with her determination to be autonomous and career-minded. **4** Thus, Katherine's ideals end up being only slightly more open-minded than those within the conservative finishing school.

1. (A) NO CHANGE
   (B) is a portrayal of the upper-class education of women
   (C) is a film portrayal of upper-class women as they are educated
   (D) portrays the education of upper-class women

2. (A) NO CHANGE
   (B) hired as an instructor to teach art history.
   (C) whom teaches art history.
   (D) a recently hired teacher of art history at the school.

3. (A) NO CHANGE
   (B) The school
   (C) The film
   (D) She

4. (A) NO CHANGE
   (B) Interestingly,
   (C) In contrast,
   (D) Additionally,

In the decade following World War II, America saw the push for women to retreat from the workforce back into their homes. Advertisements and propaganda painted the idyllic woman as one who was wholly fulfilled by **5** they're role within the home. The upper-class women of *Mona Lisa Smile* are a unique group in that they are encouraged to pursue higher education and job training, but still expected to be only wives and mothers. Katherine, a visiting instructor and PhD candidate, **6** has become obsessed with opening the minds of her students to the realization that they are just as capable and ambitious as men, and that they don't have to settle down into monotonous lives confined by the walls of their tidy homes.

Wellesley is home to the best educated and most intelligent women in America at the time. **7** Still, the young women who make up its classrooms are merely being molded into desirable wives for wealthy and similarly educated men. Simply put, the objective is to educate the women just as rigorously as the men are educated at Ivy League schools, **8** but to never let them use that education or experience in any way outside the home. The young women Katherine encounters exhibit extraordinary intelligence, but express no desire to move beyond the role of delicate, agreeable housewives. **9** Katherine is the opposite. She rejects everything which is emblematic of traditional femininity.

5. (A) NO CHANGE
   (B) her
   (C) their
   (D) its

6. (A) NO CHANGE
   (B) became
   (C) becomes
   (D) is becoming

7. (A) NO CHANGE
   (B) Hence,
   (C) Insofar,
   (D) Yet,

8. Which choice is best supported by the sentences that come earlier in the paragraph?

   (A) NO CHANGE
   (B) and to cheer them on as they acquire high-paying careers.
   (C) but to ensure they never make more money than their male colleagues.
   (D) so they can help start new schools and educate their children.

9. Which choice best combines the underlined sentences?

   (A) On the opposite end is Katherine; she rejects traditional femininity.
   (B) Traditional femininity is rejected, however, by Katherine, who is the opposite of an agreeable housewife.
   (C) Katherine, on the other hand, rejects everything which is emblematic of traditional femininity.
   (D) In contrast, Katherine rejects tradition and femininity.

When one student, Joan, decides to marry her boyfriend and assume her wifely duties rather than **10** except an offer to Yale's law school, Katherine insists that Joan can "have her cake and eat it too." In response to Katherine's complete dismissal of the worth of a wife and mother, Joan argues, "You stand in class and tell us to look beyond the image, but you don't. To you a housewife is someone who sold her soul for a center hall colonial. She has no depth, no intellect, no interests. You're the one who said I could do anything I wanted. This is what I want." Herein lies the film's central issue: as early feminist discourse advances, it threatens to be as **11** exclusionary as conventional standards of femininity.

10. (A) NO CHANGE
    (B) accepting
    (C) excepting
    (D) accept

11. (A) NO CHANGE
    (B) exclusionary and separatist
    (C) exclusivity
    (D) exclusively separatist

Questions 12–22 are based on the following passage.

The Original Fireworks Show

On September 1, 1859, British astronomer Richard Carrington made an accidental discovery. While tracking sunspots, Carrington **12** peered at two flashes of white light unlike anything he'd ever seen before. These flashes preceded the largest geomagnetic storm **13** to ever hit Earth, causing red auroras to appear as far south as Hawaii. This phenomenon, **14** which would later be known as the Carrington Event, proved that auroras were caused by solar activity. Yet, it wasn't until 1892 that German astronomer Martin Brendel captured the first **15** picture of an aurora, from northern Norway. And it wasn't until 1909 that **16** Norwegian physicist, Kristian Birkeland, mimicked an aurora in a lab experiment and could finally explain how **17** the suns charged particles create the enchanting light display when they hit Earth's magnetic field.

12. (A) NO CHANGE
    (B) overlooked
    (C) noticing
    (D) observed

13. (A) NO CHANGE
    (B) to ever hit Earth
    (C) to ever, hit Earth,
    (D) to ever hit Earth;

14. (A) NO CHANGE
    (B) later known as the Carrington Event,
    (C) called the Carrington Event by some people,
    (D) named the Carrington Event after Richard Carrington,

15. (A) NO CHANGE
    (B) picture of an aurora from
    (C) picture of an aurora, in
    (D) picture, of an aurora, from

16. (A) NO CHANGE
   (B) Norwegian physicist Kristian Birkeland,
   (C) Norwegian physicist Kristian Birkeland
   (D) Norwegian physicist Kristian Birkeland—

17. (A) NO CHANGE
   (B) the charged particles within the sun
   (C) the sun's charged particles
   (D) the sun is charging particles which then

Auroras 18 —are known as the Northern or Southern Lights depending on which pole they emanate from—are caused by electrons from solar winds. Solar particles race from the Sun at hundreds of miles per second and 19 entice Earth's magnetic poles, colliding with nitrogen and oxygen molecules in a captivating display of glowing greens, blues, reds, and purples. This natural light display usually occurs in areas known as the auroral zone, unfolding over the poles of the Arctic in the north and Antarctic in the south. Most common is the Aurora Borealis, another title for the Northern Lights, which erupts around the north pole in shades of cascading greens and creeps toward the equator during geomagnetic storms. Although forecasters still struggle to predict space weather, geomagnetic storm magnitude is measured using the Planetary K-index on a 1–9 scale. 20 The best places for sightings of the Northern Lights include Alaska, Norway, and parts of Russia, while the Southern Lights can be spotted from Antarctica, New Zealand, and Australia.

18. (A) NO CHANGE
    (B) , known informally as the Northern or Southern Lights—
    (C) —informally known as the Northern or Southern Lights depending on which pole they emanate from—
    (D) , known as the Northern or Southern Lights informally, based on their geographic location,

19. NO CHANGE
    (B) fly to
    (C) are attracted to
    (D) pulls toward

20. At this point, the writer is considering adding the following sentence.

    Once the index hits 4 or higher, auroras are likely and an alert is issued.

    Should the writer make this addition?
    (A) Yes, because it expands on the previous sentence.
    (B) Yes, because the intended audience is aurora chasers.
    (C) No, because it makes an illogical transition.
    (D) No, because it interrupts the main idea with irrelevant details.

Historically, folktales that attempted to explain this grand spectacle of nature told of claps, static, and crackles accompanying **21** the light display. It wasn't until 2016 that scientists discovered evidence to back up these early observations. When pockets of warm air form between layers of cold air without mixing, the accumulated charges discharge and create sparks and sounds, a phenomenon called an inversion. Recently, scientists recorded an inversion during an **22** intense aurora display. A light show accompanied by snaps and crackles? Apparently, Earth has long had its very own fireworks show.

21. The writer is considering revising the underlined portion to the following

    the light display, which may include greens, blues, reds, and purples.

    Should the writer make this revision?

    (A) Yes, because it includes specific information.
    (B) Yes, because it helps orient the reader.
    (C) No, because it gives inaccurate information.
    (D) No, because it is repetitive and unnecessary.

22. (A) NO CHANGE
    (B) intense and extreme
    (C) extremely intense
    (D) extreme, because of the intensity,

Questions 23–33 are based on the following passage.

Drawing Lines on Land

   Mapping, Mishuana Goeman argues in her book, *Mark My Words*, is **23** an implement of conquest. Maps flatten powerful colonial histories that territorialize the physical landscape by creating categories and separating people from their land and communities. As such, Goeman insists that mapping and maps are **24** inseparable; from colonialism, slavery, orientalism, and gendered violence. She shows that erasing Native nations by charting "open" territory meant that colonial settlers could privatize land, reassign it to themselves, and **25** force Native populations onto reservations. Goeman's work therefore attests that there is nothing natural about a border—a line drawn down a piece of paper that separates and frames land and the bodies within. **26** Her text analyzes the consequences of a gendered and racialized mapping on Native populations and offers a counter imagining of colonial spatializing within Native women's literature. **27** Native womens' efforts to document alternative conceptions of border, nation, and place, Goeman argues, are purposefully subversive to empire building.

23. (A) NO CHANGE
   (B) an instrument with
   (C) a tool of
   (D) part of

24. (A) NO CHANGE
   (B) inseparable, from
   (C) inseparable from
   (D) inseparable: from

25. (A) NO CHANGE
   (B) Native populations could be forced
   (C) end up forcing Native populations
   (D) be forced by Native populations

26. At this point the writer is considering adding the following sentence:

   > According to Webster's dictionary, a border is a boundary which separates two political or geographical areas.

   Should the writer make this addition?

   (A) Yes, because it's nice to have multiple definitions of the word.
   (B) Yes, because it gives the reader necessary background information.
   (C) No, because it contradicts the main point of the paragraph.
   (D) No, because it distracts the reader and interrupts the flow of the paragraph.

27. (A) NO CHANGE
   (B) Native women's efforts
   (C) Native women give effort
   (D) Native womens effort

From the reformulation of family and tribe relationships to the recreating of gender norms through the conquest of **28** women's bodies. Goeman presents mapping as a historical categorization of, organization of, and dispossession of bodies that creates a national myth of who does and does not belong. **29** Maps are two-dimensional representations of the surface of the world. Goeman frames her argument on the work of four Native women writers from different Native nations—E. Pauline Johnson (Mohawk), Esther Belin (Diné), Joy Harjo (Muscogee Creek), and Leslie Marmon Silko (Laguna Pueblo)—as they **30** defy and resist the confinement of land and bodies through an understanding of space that is fluid, relational, and layered. **31** Stories become an important part of this project as they unfold, explore, and expand on geography.

28. (A) NO CHANGE
(B) women's bodies, Goeman
(C) women's bodies; Goeman
(D) women's bodies—Goeman

29. The writer wants a sentence that introduces Goeman's unique insight into the implications of Native writers. Which choice accomplishes this?

(A) NO CHANGE
(B) Louise Erdrich, a half German and half Ojibwe woman, is a nationally acclaimed author.
(C) (Re)mapping is the work of Native authors in "simultaneously metaphoric and material capacities of map making, to generate new possibilities."
(D) Authors, like cartographers, use pen and paper to tell a story.

30. (A) NO CHANGE
(B) defy, resist, and reject
(C) defiantly resist
(D) defy

31. The writer wants a concluding sentence that generally sums up the relationship between writers and notions of geography. Which choice accomplishes this?

(A) NO CHANGE
(B) Joy Harjo is a member of the Muscogee Nation and writes poetry that transcends borders.
(C) Leslie Marmon Silko is perhaps the most well-known of the writers; her name is nearly synonymous with the Native American Renaissance.
(D) Native Americans historically have not held the same conceptions of land, borders, and property that Western cultures do, and are thus exploited via capitalism and cultural intolerance.

Mark My Words disappoints only in its reliance on an essentially resistant Native woman while simultaneously insisting that the Native not be romanticized. Native women are allotted a lofty responsibility of deconstructing colonialism and creating the space to imagine and address possible alternatives and creative imaginings that will ensure a better future for the Native and non-Native. **32** Nonetheless, *Mark My Words* accomplishes **33** the author's goal, in successfully developing the work of four Native women writers to argue that colonization is not effective and that Native geographical discourse is available for a national and global (re)mapping. It opens up a wide range of research to be done on geographical alternatives and how those imaginings could play out on a global scale.

32. (A) NO CHANGE
    (B) Likewise
    (C) Therefore
    (D) For instance

33. (A) NO CHANGE
    (B) the authors goal;
    (C) the author's goal
    (D) the author's goal—

GO ON TO THE NEXT PAGE ⟼

Questions 34–44 are based on the following passage.

Cross-Disciplinary for the Win

In recent years, students around the world have flocked to the STEM fields—those beloved programs in science, technology, engineering, **34** and mathematics, coveted for their high job potential and promising salaries. In the U.S., the percentage of high school students planning to pursue a STEM major **35** has remained steady, an increase emboldened by the recent recession. **36** Understandably, coming-of-age college students who witnessed their parents and siblings lose jobs, default on loans, and terminate not only annual vacations but even weekly dining traditions, are hesitant to invest their money and time on a degree that doesn't guarantee a job the day after graduation. And they've been told that when it comes to job security, STEM is the way to go.

The push for STEM undergraduates **37** has propelled a STEM versus liberal arts dichotomy that seems to dominate conversations around higher education, but fails to capture trends and address the complexity of a changing job market. Certainly, there is no denying the surge in engineering students. And if one were to listen to any political exchange on higher education, it wouldn't be long before the familiar dialogue surfaces—a prioritization of STEM fields means we compete better globally. **38** Consequently, innovation is always coupled with science.

34. (A) NO CHANGE
    (B) and math which have
    (C) and areas of mathematics with
    (D) and mathematics, being liked because of

35. Which choice is supported by the rest of the paragraph?
    (A) NO CHANGE
    (B) has jumped to over 30%,
    (C) has quickly fallen,
    (D) has slowly but surely climbed

36. At this point the writer is considering adding the following sentence:

    The recession that began in 2008 and 2009 is now referred to as the Great Recession.

    Should the writer add this?
    (A) Yes, because it supplies necessary details about the early twenty-first century.
    (B) Yes, because it introduces the main topic of the passage.
    (C) No, because it supplies false information.
    (D) No, because it disrupts the flow of the paragraph with unnecessary information.

37. (A) NO CHANGE
    (B) have
    (C) were
    (D) had

38. (A) NO CHANGE
    (B) After all,
    (C) Thus,
    (D) Previously,

Hence, **39** student's everywhere enroll as freshmen with a generalized and vague notion that the world works according to this dichotomy—choose STEM and gain financial success, even if the work is dull, or choose the arts and humanities and find yourself in a financial noose, even if the work is rewarding. Yet, the numbers themselves don't support this thinking.

40 Enrollment in STEM soars. Enrollment in the arts and humanities remains steady. Instead, it appears that the professional fields are taking a hit. Biomedical engineering and computer science go up; **41** business and education go down. Nobody quite knows what this means for the next generation's workforce, but it is promising to hear that the liberal arts haven't been annihilated in the rush to compete with **42** the worlds rocket's and medical scientists.

39. (A) NO CHANGE
    (B) student's enrollments
    (C) students everywhere enroll
    (D) students' enroll everywhere

40. Which choice best combines the underlined sentences?

    (A) Aside from soars in STEM enrollment, there is the steady enrollment in the arts and humanities.
    (B) Arts and humanities, which remain steady, contrast with STEM enrollment, which soars.
    (C) In fact, as enrollment in STEM soars, enrollment in the arts and humanities remains steady.
    (D) Hence, as the interest in STEM soars, it is the arts and humanities which continue to maintain their previous enrollment rates.

41. Which choice makes sense considering the previous statement?

    (A) NO CHANGE
    (B) STEM fields also go up.
    (C) law and business flourish.
    (D) arts and humanities suffer a loss.

42. (A) our world's scientists of rockets and medicine.
    (B) the worlds rocket and medical scientist's.
    (C) the worlds rocket, and medical scientists.
    (D) the world's rocket and medical scientists.

In truth, leading corporations and government agencies have begun voicing the need for more hires from the humanities fields. There reasoning? The need for people who can write and speak about the work being done to non-STEM audiences. They aren't the first to realize this need—U.S. graduate and medical programs have been welcoming more and more students with humanities backgrounds **44** of years now, hoping to produce well-rounded graduates. The hard line between STEM and the liberal arts isn't just blurry, it's artificial.

43. (A) NO CHANGE
    (B) They're
    (C) Its
    (D) Their

44. (A) NO CHANGE
    (B) for
    (C) from
    (D) OMIT the underlined word

STOP

If you finish before time is called, you may check your work on this section only.

Do not turn to any other section.

MATH TEST—NO CALCULATOR
25 MINUTES, 17 QUESTIONS

To answer questions in this section turn to Section 3 of your answer sheet.

Directions: Choose the best answer choice for questions 1–13 and fill in the answer sheet accordingly. Solve questions 14–17 and fill in the answer sheet accordingly. Before moving on to question 14 refer to the directions on how to fill in the answers on the answer sheet. Use of available space on the test booklet is allowed.

Notes

1. **No calculator use** is permitted.
2. Unless indicated, variables and expressions represent real numbers.
3. Figures are drawn to scale.
4. Figures lie in a plane.
5. The domain of a function f is the set of all real numbers x where $f(x)$ is a real number.

Reference

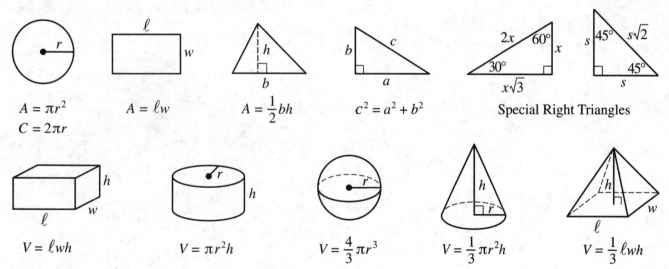

$A = \pi r^2$
$C = 2\pi r$

$A = \ell w$

$A = \frac{1}{2}bh$

$c^2 = a^2 + b^2$

Special Right Triangles

$V = \ell wh$

$V = \pi r^2 h$

$V = \frac{4}{3}\pi r^3$

$V = \frac{1}{3}\pi r^2 h$

$V = \frac{1}{3}\ell wh$

There is a total of 360 degrees in the arc of a circle.

There is a total of 2π radians in the arc of a circle.

There is a total of 180 degrees in the internal angles of a triangle.

Practice Test 2

MEAL PLAN	PRICE PER MONTH
Premium	$500
Regular	$450
Value	$400

1. A school has three different meal plans for students to choose from. The graph shows the three different plans and their prices. Jane started on the regular plan and found that it was not enough. She decided to upgrade her plan to the premium. Half a month of the 4-month semester has already passed. How much more money would she spend on the premium plan versus on the regular plan for the rest of the semester?

(A) $50
(B) $75
(C) $175
(D) $350

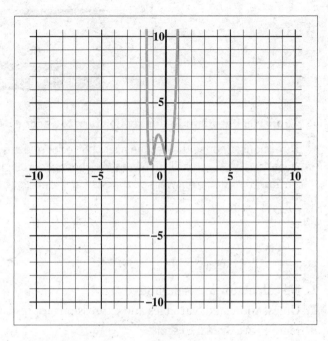

2. The above shows the graph of $f(x)$. Which of the following is $f(0)$ equal to?

(A) 1
(B) 5
(C) –2
(D) Does not exist

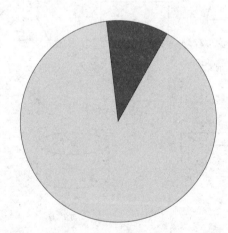

3. A circle with a radius of 10 is cut into slices through the center. One piece has an angle of 36°. What is the area of this piece?

(A) 10p
(B) 36π
(C) 46p
(D) 100π

4. If $\dfrac{4x}{3y} = \dfrac{1}{4}$ then $\dfrac{y}{x} = ?$

(A) $\dfrac{16}{3}$

(B) $\dfrac{4}{3}$

(C) $\dfrac{1}{3}$

(D) 3

5. What is the value of $\dfrac{1}{5}x$, when $\dfrac{2}{x} - 3 = 3$?

(A) $\dfrac{1}{15}$

(B) $-\dfrac{5}{3}$

(C) 3

(D) $\dfrac{3}{5}$

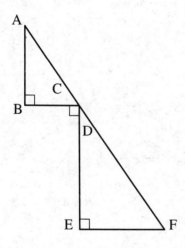

6. In the above if AF is a straight line and angle C is 56°, what is angle F?

(A) 16°

(B) 21°

(C) 34°

(D) 56°

7. Which of the parabola equations has an axis of symmetry of $x = -4$ and a minimal value of 3?

(A) $y = (x + 4)^2 + 3$

(B) $y = (x - 4)^2 + 3$

(C) $y = (x - 3)^2 + 4$

(D) $y = (x + 3)^2 + 4$

8. Inertia of a hollow sphere rotating around its center is represented by the following equation:

$$I = \frac{1}{3}mr^2$$

where I represents inertia, m represents mass and r represents radius. Which of the following equations represents r in relation to the other variables?

(A) $\sqrt{\dfrac{I}{3m}}$

(B) $\dfrac{1}{3}mI$

(C) $\left(\dfrac{3I}{m}\right)^2$

(D) $\sqrt{\dfrac{3I}{m}}$

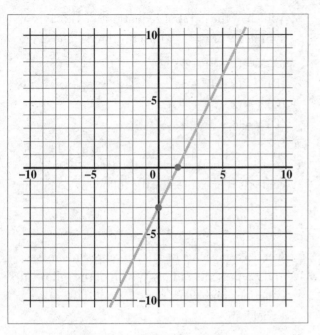

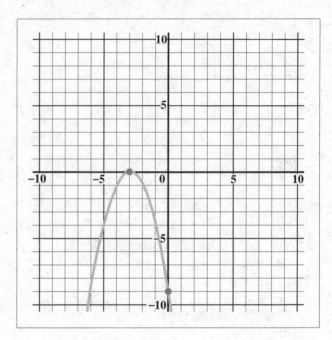

9. Reflect the line above along the *x* axis and translate the line 3 units up. What is the new equation of the line?

(A) $y = -2x + 6$

(B) $y = \frac{1}{2}x - 3$

(C) $y = -\frac{1}{2}x + 6$

(D) $y = 2x$

10. Which of the following functions is represented in the graph above?

(A) $y = -(x + 3)(x - 3)$
(B) $y = (x - 3)(x - 3)^2$
(C) $y = (x + 3)(x - 3)$
(D) $y = -(x + 3)^2$

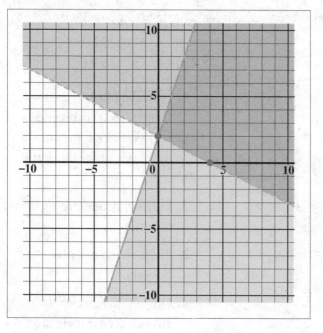

11. $y > -\dfrac{1}{2}x + 2$

$y \le 3x + 2$

Which of the following is a solution to the two inequalities shown above?

(A) (2, 0)
(B) (0, 2)
(C) (1, 2)
(D) (0, 6)

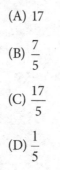

$$\dfrac{3(n-1)-1}{3} = \dfrac{12-(3-n)}{6}$$

12. What is the value of n in the equation above?

(A) 17

(B) $\dfrac{7}{5}$

(C) $\dfrac{17}{5}$

(D) $\dfrac{1}{5}$

13. $y = \dfrac{x}{3} - 4$

$y - 4x = 7$

The two lines above meets at point (p, q). Which of the following can be q?

(A) –3
(B) 3
(C) –5
(D) –8

Directions: Solve questions 14–17 and fill in the answer sheet accordingly. Refer to the following directions on how to fill in the answers on the answer sheet.

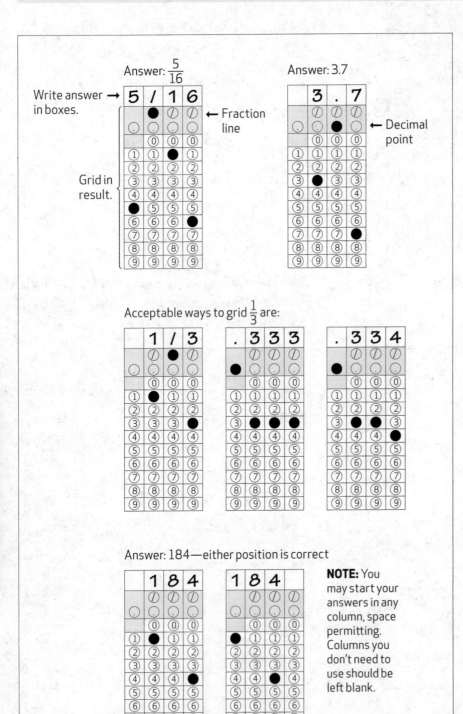

1. Only the filled-in circles are graded. The directions suggest writing the answer in the box at the top, but it is not scored.

2. Fill in only one circle in any column.

3. There are no negative answers.

4. Only fill in one correct answer, even if there are more than one.

5. **Mixed numbers** like $2\frac{1}{2}$ should be filled in as 2.5 or 5/2.

6. **Decimal answers:** If you obtain a decimal answer with more digits, it should be filled in to fill the entire grid.

Answer: $\frac{5}{16}$

Write answer in boxes.

← Fraction line

Grid in result.

Answer: 3.7

← Decimal point

Acceptable ways to grid $\frac{1}{3}$ are:

Answer: 184—either position is correct

NOTE: You may start your answers in any column, space permitting. Columns you don't need to use should be left blank.

14. If $f(x) = -x^2 - x$, $g(x) = x^2 - 187$, and $x = -5$, what is $g(f(x))$?

15. $y < 2x - 6$

$y > x - 12$

(x, y) is a solution to the system of equations above. What is the smallest possible integer value of x, if y is 18?

16. If the circumference of the larger circle is $12p$ and the area of the small circle is 9π, what is the shortest distance between the edge of the small circle and the edge of the big circle?

17. What is the radius of a circle with the equation of $x^2 - 8x + y^2 + 6y - 39 = 0$?

You can check your work only on this section, if you finished ahead of time.

Do not turn to other sections.

MATH TEST—CALCULATOR
45 MINUTES, 31 QUESTIONS

To answer questions in this section turn to Section 4 of your answer sheet.

Directions: Choose the best answer choice for questions 1–27 and fill in the answer sheet accordingly. Solve questions 28–31 and fill in the answer sheet accordingly. Before moving on to question 28 refer to the directions on how to fill in the answers on the answer sheet. Use of available space on the test booklet is allowed.

Notes

1. **Calculator use** is permitted.
2. Unless indicated, variables and expressions represent real numbers.
3. Figures are drawn to scale.
4. Figures lie in a plane.
5. The domain of a function f is the set of all real numbers x where $f(x)$ is a real number.

Reference

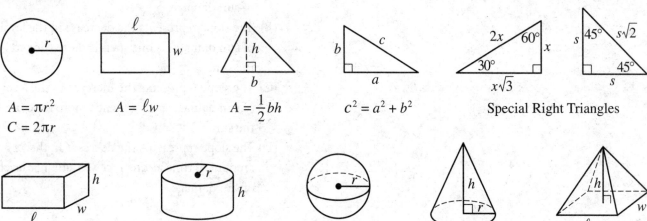

$A = \pi r^2$
$C = 2\pi r$

$A = \ell w$

$A = \frac{1}{2}bh$

$c^2 = a^2 + b^2$

Special Right Triangles

$V = \ell wh$

$V = \pi r^2 h$

$V = \frac{4}{3}\pi r^3$

$V = \frac{1}{3}\pi r^2 h$

$V = \frac{1}{3}\ell wh$

There is a total of 360 degrees in the arc of a circle.

There is a total of 2π radians in the arc of a circle.

There is a total of 180 degrees in the internal angles of a triangle.

GO ON TO THE NEXT PAGE ⟼

1. If $\dfrac{x}{13} = \dfrac{89}{y}$, what is the value of xy?

   (A) 6.85
   (B) 76
   (C) 102
   (D) 1,157

2. What number is halfway between $\dfrac{38}{17}$ and $\dfrac{32}{11}$?

   (A) $2\dfrac{107}{187}$

   (B) $\dfrac{28}{53}$

   (C) $\dfrac{53}{28}$

   (D) 3.572

3. What is the x intercept of $y = 2x$?

   (A) 0
   (B) 2
   (C) x
   (D) $\dfrac{1}{2}$

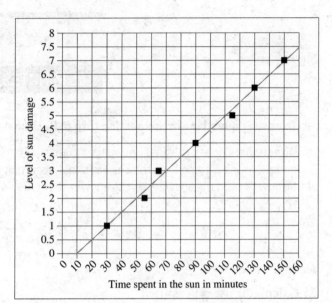

4. A student is conducting a study regarding the amount of time spent in the sun and its relationship with the level of sun damage. Which of the following statements is true regarding the graph above?

   (A) The slope represents the increase in the amount of time as one receives a lower level of sun damage.
   (B) The slope represents the decrease in the level of sun damage as one spends more time in the sun.
   (C) The slope represents the increase in the level of sun damage as one spends more time in the sun.
   (D) The slope represents the decrease in the amount of time as one receives a higher level of sun damage.

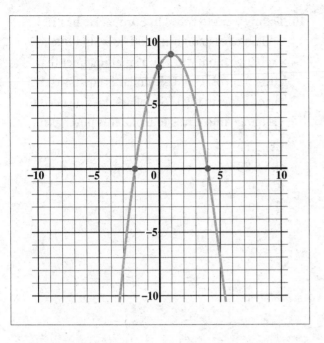

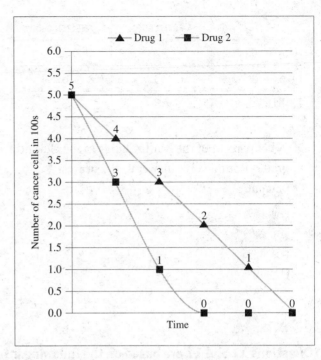

5. The above function is $f(x)$. When $f(x) = 5$, what is x?

   (A) –1 and 3
   (B) –2 and 4
   (C) 8 and 9
   (D) 11 and 9

6. 75% of 180 is what percent of 360?

   (A) 37.5%
   (B) 50%
   (C) 75%
   (D) 135%

7. A cancer researcher is testing two types of drugs on mice. Which of the statements below is true about the two drugs?

   (A) Drug 1 is faster than Drug 2 at killing cancer cells.
   (B) Drug 2 is faster than Drug 1 at killing cancer cells.
   (C) Drug 1 and Drug 2 are both equally effective at killing cancer cells.
   (D) It is impossible to tell which drug is more effective at killing cancer cells.

8. $x^2 + 6x + 9 = ?$

   (A) $(x + 2)(x + 3)$
   (B) $(x + 6)(x + 9)$
   (C) $(x + 3)(x - 3)$
   (D) $(x + 3)^2$

	MATH CLUB	ENGLISH CLUB
10th Grade	37	39
11th Grade	33	67
12th Grade	88	32

9. What percent of the Math Club is in the eleventh grade? Round your answer to the nearest percent.

(A) 15%
(B) 21%
(C) 23%
(D) 40%

10. Danny went to travel in Europe. He has 15 U.S. dollars of cash on him, and he would like to exchange money to buy a small magnet that costs 5 euros. One U.S. dollar is equal to 0.85 euros. How many U.S. dollars does he need to exchange into euros to make this purchase?

(A) 3.11
(B) 5.88
(C) 10
(D) 10.5

Questions 11 and 12 are based on the following information.

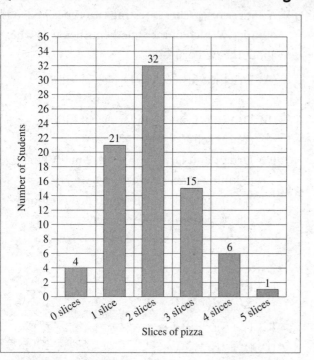

The debate club of a school is having a pizza party at the beginning of the year. The secretary of the club is keeping track of how many slices of pizza each person has to be able to estimate how many pizzas she has to order for the next event. The graph shows how many students have 0 slices, 1 slice, 2 slices, 3 slices, 4 slices, and 5 slices. For example, there are 4 students who did not have any pizza.

11. The secretary is trying to decide how many slices of pizza to order for each student. Which of the following should she base her decision on?

(A) median
(B) mean
(C) mode
(D) range

12. What is the difference between the mode and the median of this set of data?

(A) 1
(B) 11
(C) 17
(D) 0

13. The price of a T-shirt is decreased by 20% during a sale. What is the ratio of the decrease in price to the new price of the T-shirt.

(A) 2 to 5
(B) 10 to 2
(C) 1 to 4
(D) 10 to 80

	AP HISTORY	AP CALCULUS	AP BIOLOGY	AP PHYSICS	AP SPANISH	TOTAL
Grade 9	85	16	32	55	69	460
Grade 10	65	22	67	44	89	511
Grade 11	90	25	54	38	74	420

14. A school is considering starting AP courses. It would like to start two AP courses and conducted a survey to see the most popular courses. Surveys were passed out to students in grade 9, grade 10, and grade 11. Not all surveys were returned. What fraction of grade 9 and grade 10 students out of the total number of grade 9 and grade 10 students selected AP calculus as their choice course?

(A) $\dfrac{16}{511}$

(B) $\dfrac{38}{544}$

(C) $\dfrac{38}{971}$

(D) $\dfrac{16}{38}$

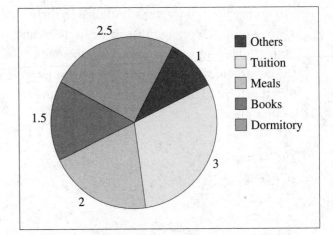

15. A student's school fees are split into 10 portions. 3 portions are used for tuition, 2.5 for dormitory, 2 for meals, 1.5 for books, and 1 for others. If he spent \$6,500 total for his school fees this semester, how many dollars did he spend in total on dormitory and meals?

(A) 650
(B) 2,925
(C) 3,250
(D) 6,500

16. If $4x^2 - 4x = -1$, what is the solution for x?

(A) $-\dfrac{1}{2}$

(B) $\dfrac{1}{2}$

(C) 2

(D) 4

17. If $f(x) = -14$ and $g(x) = x^2 - 58 + x^3$, what is $g\big(f(x)\big)$?

(A) 2,882
(B) 2,744
(C) −2,606
(D) 537,766

Practice Test 2

18. An orange juice concentrate is diluted so that there is only 31% orange juice in 1 cup. This cup is then added into a punch bowl together with 3.5 cups of juice mixture with 23% orange juice. What percent of the new punch bowl mixture is orange juice?

    (A) 23.7%
    (B) 24.8%
    (C) 26.1%
    (D) 53%·

19. If $\dfrac{x}{5} - \dfrac{y}{7} = \dfrac{1}{2}$, then what is the value of $5y - 7x$?

    (A) 35
    (B) 12
    (C) $-\dfrac{35}{2}$
    (D) $\dfrac{1}{2}$

Questions 20 and 21 are based on the following information.

Sally has $556.76 dollars in her bank account, which is only used to pay for her new phone and Internet bills. The phone bill is a total of $30 for the first 3 months and $49.99 for every month after. The Internet bill is a total of $59.99 for the first 2 months then $39.99 for every month after.

20. How much money does she have left after month 3?

    (A) $426.78
    (B) $466.75
    (C) $476.77
    (D) $506.77

21. For how many full months can Sally pay for her new phone and Internet bills with her $556.76 in the bank?

    (A) 4
    (B) 5
    (C) 7
    (D) 10

22. Which point satisfies both $y < 5x + 2$ and $x + 3y < 6$?

    (A) (2, 3)
    (B) (–1, 1)
    (C) (1, 1)
    (D) (–2, –3)

23. To make a special color of paint, the paint factory needs to use red, yellow, and blue in a specific proportion. The ratio of red paint to yellow paint is 3 ml to 5 ml. The ratio of yellow paint to blue paint is 55 ml to 1.2 L. In a batch of paint the ratio of red to yellow and yellow to blue must be kept the same as described above. The paint factory is making a batch of paint for a special client; if 3,864 ml of paint is needed in total, how many ml of yellow paint is needed? (1,000 ml = 1 L)

    (A) 1.2
    (B) 55
    (C) 165
    (D) 3,864

24. Noel has two cylindrical vases. The base of the first vase has a radius of 15 cm, and the base of the second vase has a radius of 12 cm. The first vase is filled with water up to 14.5 cm, and the second is empty. If Noel pours half of the water from the first vase into the empty vase, the second vase now has water filled up to where?

(A) 26.5π

(B) 22.66π

(C) 14.5π

(D) 11.33π

25. James and Ming are working together to pack toys. James can pack 8 bags of toys in one hour. Ming can pack 6 bags of toys in one hour. How long would it take for Ming and James to pack 10 bags of toys if they work together? Round to the nearest minute.

(A) 1 hour 5 minutes

(B) 43 minutes

(C) 1 hour 13 minutes

(D) 2 hours

26. What is the larger of two consecutive negative odd integers whose product is 195?

(A) −11

(B) −13

(C) −15

(D) −17

x	y
−9	−4
−3	0
0	2
9	8

27. If x and y have a linear relationship and above are the x and y values, what is the equation of the line?

(A) $y = \dfrac{2x}{3} + 2$

(B) $y = \dfrac{1x}{2} + 2$

(C) $y = \dfrac{3x}{2} - 3$

(D) $y = \dfrac{2x}{6} - 3$

Directions: Solve questions 28–31 and fill in the answer sheet accordingly. Refer to the following directions on how to fill in the answers on the answer sheet.

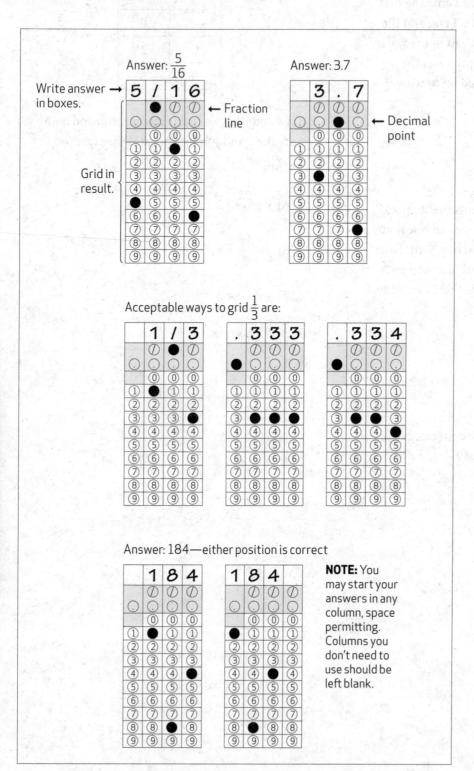

Answer: $\frac{5}{16}$

Write answer → in boxes.

← Fraction line

Grid in result.

Answer: 3.7

← Decimal point

Acceptable ways to grid $\frac{1}{3}$ are:

Answer: 184—either position is correct

NOTE: You may start your answers in any column, space permitting. Columns you don't need to use should be left blank.

1. Only the filled-in circles are graded. The directions suggest writing the answer in the box at the top, but it is not scored.

2. Fill in only one circle in any column.

3. There are no negative answers.

4. Only fill in one correct answer, even if there are more than one.

5. **Mixed numbers** like $2\frac{1}{2}$ should be filled in as 2.5 or 5/2.

6. **Decimal answers:** If you obtain a decimal answer with more digits, it should be filled in to fill the entire grid.

Practice Test 2

Questions 28 and 29 refer to the following information.

A store gets a new shipment of sweaters to sell in January. On the 15th day of each of the months after January, a sweater is marked 15% off until it is 85% off. The original price of the sweater is marked at $89.99.

28. If a sweater is sold on March 17, what is the price that this sweater sold for? Round to the nearest dollar.

29. If Janice bought a sweater on May 30 and there is a 9.7% tax, how much did she pay in total? Round to the nearest dollar.

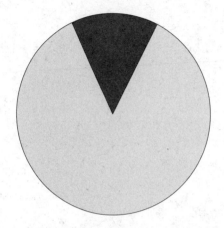

30. The area of the shaded region is 6π and area of the shaded region is $\frac{1}{6}$ of the area of the circle. What is the diameter of the circle?

31. If Janice can finish packing 6 boxes in 3 hours, how many minutes will she take to finish packing $\frac{1}{3}$ of a box?

You can check your work only in this section, if you finished ahead of time.

Do not turn to other sections.

Practice Test 2 Answer Key

Reading Test

1. **(A)** This is a main idea question. It is clear that the passage suggests a peaceful agreement, so (B) is eliminated. Also, choices (C) and (D) are not supported by the passage. Therefore, choice (A) is the correct answer.

2. **(A)** The answer to the previous question is best supported by choice (A) because only (A) supports a peaceful agreement that can be used for negotiations at the end of the war. Choice (B) gives details of the agreement but does not answer the question. Choices (C) and (D) do not provide good support to the answer to the previous question.

3. **(C)** This is a vocabulary question. In the passage "aggrandizement" is used to describe the act of making something look better. Aggrandizement is also used with conquest, so glorification is the best answer. Therefore the correct answer is (C). Choices (A), (B), and (D) express the opposite meaning and are not correct.

4. **(C)** This is a detail question. (D) can be eliminated because the passage does not suggest that Belgium is a neighboring country of Russia. Choices (A) and (B) are also not supported by the passage. The correct answer is (C).

5. **(A)** The answer to the previous question is best supported by choice (A) because only (A) supports the answer from the previous question. Choice (D) is unrelated to the answer to the previous question. Choices (B) and (C) only support part of the answer from the previous question and not the entire answer. Therefore, the answer is (A).

6. **(C)** This is a vocabulary question. In the passage "covenant" most nearly means agreement. Choices (A) and (B) express the opposite idea and are not correct. Between choices (C) and (D), choice (C) is more accurate. Therefore, the correct answer is (C).

7. **(C)** It can be inferred from the points that the purpose of President Wilson was to provide a peaceful outline for restoration of many nations. Choices (A), (B), and (D) are not supported by the passage.

8. **(B)** The answer to the previous question is best supported by choice (B) because only B supports that the purpose of President Wilson was to provide a peaceful outline for restoration of many nations. Choices (A), (C), and (D) do not support the answer to the previous question.

9. **(C)** This is a detail question. The passage expresses that the interests of all parties involved should be considered, therefore (C) is the correct answer.

10. **(B)** This is a summary question. Choice (B) is the most accurate. Choice (D) is too vague. Choices (A) and (C) are not entirely supported by the passage.

11. **(A)** This is a summary question. Choice (A) is the most accurate answer. The first part of the paragraph expresses sadness over her passing, so choices (C) and (D) can be eliminated. The second part is to remember her attribute. Therefore, choice (A) is the correct answer.

12. **(B)** This is a main idea question. It is clear that this passage is a eulogy to remember Susan B. Anthony, so choices (A) and (D) can be eliminated. The focus of the passage is not on Susan B. Anthony's characteristics and tenacity, so choice (C) can be eliminated as well. The correct answer is (B).

13. **(B)** The answer to the previous question is best supported by choice (B) because B supports that the purpose of the passage is to remember Susan B. Anthony and to express her significance in the women suffrage movement and in history. Choices (A) and (C) do not provide good support for the answer to the previous question. Choice (D) is a possible choice, but it only supports part of the answer to the previous question. Therefore, the correct answer is (B).

14. **(B)** This is a vocabulary question. In the passage "laurel" is used with the word "hero" in the same sentence. Therefore, honor is the most close in meaning. Also, choices (A), (C), and (D) do not express this idea and are not correct.

15. **(B)** This is a main idea question. Choices (A), (C), and (D) all provide details that cannot be substantiated by the passage. Therefore, the answer is (B).

16. **(C)** The answer to the previous question is best supported by choice (C) because only (C) supports that Susan B. Anthony recognized the importance of freedom and worked to bring freedom to all. Choices (A), (C), and (D) do not provide good support for the answer to the previous question.

17. **(B)** This is a vocabulary question. In the passage garlands is used in the same sentence as loving affection. Therefore, "praises" is the closest in meaning to garlands in this context, and the correct answer is (B).

18. **(B)** This is a main idea question. It is clear that the passage supports that she was a pioneer and reformer. Therefore, choice (B) is correct. There is no evidence to support choices (A) or (C). Choice (D) is too strong.

19. **(B)** The answer to the previous question is best supported by choice (B) because only (B) supports that Susan B. Anthony was a revolutionary pioneer. The other choices do not support the answer to the previous question.

20. **(C)** This is a main idea question. The last paragraph gives an example of how Susan B. Anthony speaks and gives an example of her characteristics. Therefore, the correct answer is (C).

21. **(C)** This is a main idea question. It is clear that in this passage the most important events are the proposal and the rejection of this proposal. Although choice (B) is also a possible answer, choice (C) is the best answer.

22. **(B)** The answer to the previous question is best supported by choice (B) because only (B) supports that the main purpose of the passage is to illustrate a marriage proposal and rejection.

23. **(A)** This is a summary question. Choice (A) is the correct answer. Choice (C) is not a good summary for the paragraph, and choices (B) and (D) are not supported by the passage.

24. **(C)** This is a vocabulary question. In the passage "employment" is used to describe spending time on an activity. Therefore, the correct answer is (C). Choices (A), (B), and (D) are other definitions of the word *employment* and are not correct.

25. **(B)** This is a main idea question. Choices (A) and (D) are not supported by the passage. Choice (C) is only partially supported by the passage and is too weak. Therefore, the best answer is (B).

26. **(C)** The answer to the previous question is best supported by choice (C). Both choices (B) and (C) support that Elizabeth feels positive toward Colonel Fitzwilliam. However, choice (C) provides stronger support. Therefore, the correct answer is (C).

27. **(A)** This is a vocabulary question. In the passage "civility" most nearly means "politeness." Choices (B), (C), and (D) express the opposite idea and are not correct. Therefore, the correct answer is (A).

28. **(B)** This is a main idea question. Choices (A), (C), and (D) are not supported by the passage. Choice (B) is the only correct answer. There are multiple parts of the passage that express Elizabeth's lack of patience and unhappiness with Mr. Darcy.

29. **(C)** The answer to the previous question is best supported by choice (C) because only (C) supports that Elizabeth is upset with Mr. Darcy and loses her patience. Choices (A), (B), and (D) do not clearly support the answer to the previous question.

30. **(A)** This is a main idea question. It is clear that in this passage the speech is a call to action for Americans to conserve resources. Choice (B) is too strong because President Roosevelt does not seem anxious. Choice (C) and (D) are also not accurate.

31. **(B)** The answer to the previous question is best supported by choice (B) because only (B) supports that this passage is a call to action for Americans to conserve resources and public lands and areas. Choices (A) and (C) are not related. Choice (D) is only partially supportive. Therefore, choice (B) is the best answer.

32. **(A)** This is a vocabulary question. In the passage "concur" most nearly means "agree" because President Roosevelt agrees with the report. Choice (B) expresses the opposite meaning and is not correct. Choices (C) and (D) are not accurate in the context of the passage. Therefore, the correct answer is (A).

33. **(C)** This is a main idea question. It is clear that in this passage President Roosevelt believes the report of the National Conservation Commission provides evidence that supports the conservation of resources. Choices (A), (B), and (D) are not substantiated by the passage. Therefore, choice (C) is the correct answer.

34. **(D)** The answer to the previous question is best supported by choice (D) because only (D) supports that President Roosevelt believes immediate actions must be taken to ensure the future of the next generation. Choice (A) is too vague, and choices (B) and (C) contain details not substantiated by the passage. Therefore, the correct answer is (D).

35. **(A)** This is a vocabulary question. In the passage "inertia" is used to describe apathy because it is used together with indifference. Choices (C) and (D) express the opposite idea and are not correct. Choice (B) is inconsistent with the context. Therefore, the correct answer is choice (A).

36. **(C)** This is a details question. It is important to find support for the answer choice. Answers (A), (B), and (D) all have details that cannot be substantiated by the passage. Therefore the correct answer is (C).

37. **(D)** The answer to the previous question is best supported by choice (D) because only (D) supports that the forests are diminishing, and the country needs to invest in their protection. Choices (A), (B), and (C) do not clearly support the answer to the previous question.

38. **(B)** This is a detail question. Every detail of the answer choices needs to be verified to make eliminations. The correct answer is (B) and evidence for this can be found in lines 85–87.

39. **(A)** This is a detail question. Choice (B) can be eliminated because the passage does not support that diet alone will prevent rickets. Choice (C) is also not supported by the passage, and choice (D) is only partially correct. Only (A) is supported by the passage. Therefore, the correct answer is (A).

40. **(D)** The answer to the previous question is best supported by choice (D). Choice (C) is unrelated to the answer to the previous question. Choices (A) and (B) only provide supplementary evidence and do not directly support the answer from the previous question. Therefore, the answer is (D).

41. **(B)** This is a vocabulary question. In the passage "marasmic" most nearly means emaciated. Here emaciated is most consistent with the context of the sentence. Choices (A), (C), and (D) express the opposite meaning and are not correct. Therefore, the correct answer is (B).

42. **(C)** This is a detail question. Choices (A), (B), and (C) can be eliminated because they are only partially correct. In choice (A), lack of minerals is not mentioned by the passage. Choice (B) is not supported by the passage. In choice (D), the passage does not mention proving the cause in recent years. Only (C) is supported by the passage. Therefore, the correct answer is (C).

43. **(B)** The answer to the previous question is best supported by choice (B). Choice (A) is unrelated to the answer to the previous question. Choices (C) and (D) only provide supplementary evidence and do not directly support the answer from the previous question. Therefore, the answer is (B).

44. **(A)** This is a vocabulary question. In the passage "curative" most nearly means "remedial" because only "remedial" is consistent with the word "preventative," used earlier in the same sentence. Choices (C) and (D) express the opposite meaning and are not correct. Choice (B) is not accurate in the context of the passage. Therefore, the correct answer is (A).

45. **(A)** This is a detail question. Choice (B) and (C) can be eliminated because they are the opposite of what the passage suggests. Choice (D) is also not supported by the passage. Only (A) is supported by the passage. Therefore, the correct answer is (A).

46. **(B)** The answer to the previous question is best supported by choice (B). Choices (C) and (D) are unrelated to the answer to the previous question. Choice (A) only provides supplementary evidence and does not directly support the answer from the previous question. Therefore, the answer is (B).

47. **(C)** The answer choice that best describes the relationship between the two passages is choice (C). Passage 2 presents evidence of more advanced understanding of rickets than Passage 1 by presenting evidence that sunlight exposure, as opposed to outdoor exposure, prevents rickets. Choice (D) is not correct because neither claim is true. Choices (A) and (B) are not supported by the passages.

Writing and Language Test

1. **(D)** Choice (D) is the most concise and clear option. (B) changes the meaning of the sentence, and (A) and (C) are unnecessarily wordy.

2. **(A)** This is correct as is. The sentence is simple, direct, and easy to understand. (B) and (D) are both lengthier and repetitive. (C) improperly uses "whom" rather than the correct "who."

3. **(B)** Without specifying what "embodies Victorian standards," this sentence is confusing. You can read the sentence before and know the paragraph is comparing the school to the instructor, therefore (B) is the correct answer choice.

4. **(B)** Here we need a transition word. The sentence before states that Katherine is emblematic of the modern woman. This sentence suggests that, upon deeper reflection, Katherine is more conservative than she lets on to be. So, this is opposite of what you'd think, making it surprising or interesting. (A) suggests a cause-effect relationship. (D) suggests that we are giving more information, like "also." And (C) can be tricky because the two ideas in these sentences do contrast with one another, but since Katherine is the topic of both, it doesn't make sense to juxtapose Katherine to Katherine.

5. **(B)** This pronoun is referring to "the idyllic woman," which is singular, making (B) the correct choice.

6. **(C)** The passage discusses the action of the film in present tense and there is no need for the present perfect as in (A) or the present participle as in (D). Keep it simple and consistent. If you're still unsure, look at the verb usage later in the sentence: the students "are just as capable." "Are" is present tense, so maintain the same tense.

7. **(D)** Another transition word; it must link the two sentences. The sentence before establishes that these women are the best and brightest. This sentence states that they are only being taught how to be good wives. Therefore, we want to contrast these two ideas with a conjunction like "but" or "yet," making (D) the correct choice.

8. **(A)** Use the context. The smartest women are being trained only to be wives and serve men, so (A) is the correct choice. (B) and (D) mistakenly state that the women are entering the workforce and founding schools. (C) isn't supported by the passage since women aren't even in the workforce to compete for equal salaries.

9. **(C)** Choice (A) is choppy and doesn't combine the ideas. Choice (B) is wordy and hard to read. Choice (D) changes the meaning of the sentence.

10. **(D)** First, eliminate (B) and (C) because the verb needs to be in the same tense as "marry" and "assume" in order for the sentence to be parallel. Then, eliminate (A) because "except" means to not include.

11. **(A)** This is correct as is. (B) and (D) are repetitive. (C) is a noun rather than an adjective.

12. **(D)** Here an astronomer detects or "observes" unexpected lights. (A) means to squint or look closely at. (B) implies that he missed seeing it. And (C) makes the sentence a run-on.

13. **(A)** This is correct as is. (B) fails to include the necessary pause, while (C) has unnecessary pauses that break up the flow of the sentence. Choice (D) is incorrect because the second part is not a complete sentence, and semicolons work just like periods.

14. **(B)** is the most concise answer choice and still includes the necessary information, making it the correct choice.

15. **(B)** This is one thought and, therefore, doesn't need to be broken up by any punctuation. The other choices make the sentence awkward to read.

16. **(C)** Since "Norwegian physicist" is a broad subject, we need the physicist's name to identify the subject. If we need it, no commas, making (C) the correct choice. (D) uses the dash, a hard pause, inappropriately and interrupts the flow of the sentence.

17. **(C)** Eliminate (B) and (D) because they are unnecessarily wordy. (C) is correct because the apostrophe plus *s* denotes possession and the particles belong to the sun.

18. **(C)** Eliminate (B) because it uses a comma and a dash instead of remaining consistent. Eliminate (D) because it's wordy and awkward. (A) is appealing, but the "are" would make it a complete sentence rather than extra information describing auroras, and so it would create a run-on.

19. **(C)** The particles are attracted to the magnetic poles, making (C) correct. The particles do not tempt as in (A) or fly as in (B). (D) doesn't agree with the subject.

20. **(A)** The sentence links the sentence before and after it, connecting the K-index with the alerts for possible sightings; therefore, eliminate (C) and (D). This passage is generally informative for an interested audience; it's not specialized enough for those, like aurora chasers, who know a lot about the topic.

21. **(D)** This addition would repeat information from the last paragraph, making it unnecessary, so eliminate (A) and (B). The information is correct even if it's repetitive, making (C) incorrect.

22. **(A)** Choice (A) is the best and most concise answer choice. Since "extreme" and "intense" are doing the same thing here, (B), (C), and (D) are repetitive and wordy.

23. **(C)** Choice (C) is the appropriate choice here. (B) sounds awkward because of "with." (D) is too vague and doesn't give us as much information. (C) is more direct and precise.

24. **(C)** This is right in the middle of an idea, so no punctuation is needed. (A) doesn't work because there are not two complete sentences. (D) doesn't work because colons go after complete thoughts before lists or clarifications.

25. **(A)** Choose the option that keeps the sentence parallel. In this list, "privatize" and "reassign" are parallel with "force"—they are all verbs in the present tense. Notice that you can eliminate (D) because it is inaccurate.

26. **(D)** Ask yourself what this sentence does. It gives a broad and common definition after the writer has already established the topic of borders. Hence, it is unnecessary and would interrupt the paragraph, making (D) the correct choice. "Border" is a common term, making (A) and (B) incorrect. And since it's still relevant to the topic, eliminate (C).

27. **(B)** Look for the option that shows possession. Since "women" is a plural noun, (A) doesn't exist. Thus, (B) is the only option that shows possession accurately.

28. **(B)** Here we have a dependent clause (fragment) followed by an independent clause (complete sentence). The rule is to separate these with a comma, making (B) correct. (A) and (C) can be eliminated because they do the same thing. (D) is a harder pause than needed, like for voice change or an interruption.

29. **(C)** The question asks for Goeman's insight or contribution to the topic. (C) is the only option that reiterates her argument. (A), (B), and (D) give general information without providing her thesis or claim.

30. **(D)** Look for the concise answer. (A), (B), and (C) all have synonyms or compound words saying the same thing.

31. **(A)** Pay close attention to what the question is asking for: a sentence that links writers to geography. With that in mind, eliminate (B), (C), and (D) because they do not contain both ideas.

32. **(A)** For questions like these, look at the relationship between the previous sentence and the current sentence. Directly before this the author is stating the shortcomings of the book. The current sentence, in contrast, discusses what the book does well. So, we are looking for a word that sets up contrast like "however" or "still," making (A) correct.

33. **(C)** Check both possession and punctuation. The goal belongs to one author, so we need an apostrophe plus *s*; eliminate (B). Since this is one long idea, we don't need to pause or break up ideas, so eliminate (A) and (D). (B) doesn't work because there are not two complete sentences on either side of the semicolon.

34. **(A)** Eliminate (C) and (D) for their wordiness. Then, realize that the dependent clause following describes all the programs, not just mathematics, and so we need a pause there to break up the sentence making (A) correct.

35. **(B)** Consider the context. Students "flocked" to STEM, so there has been an abrupt increase making (A) and (C) obviously incorrect. The increase has been abrupt and "emboldened" by the recession, not slow and steady, making (D) incorrect.

36. **(D)** Ask yourself what the sentence does. It gives broad information about the recession, which is a detail but not the main topic of the paragraph. Hence, it is unnecessary and disruptive, making (D) correct. Since the information is not incorrect, eliminate (C).

37. **(A)** First, recognize that the subject is "The push," so eliminate (B) and (C). Check the tense and eliminate (D) because the passage is not in past tense.

38. **(B)** What is the relationship between these two sentences? The current sentence gives evidence for the previous sentence, making (B) correct. Eliminate (A) and (C) because they are doing the same thing; since they can't both be right, they must both be wrong. Choice (D) is illogical.

39. **(C)** The subject here is plural, but there is no need for possession, so (C) is the only appropriate answer.

40. **(C)** (B) is awkward sounding, and (D) is wordy and unnecessarily formal. "Aside from" makes (A) incorrect because it works like "apart from" or "besides" to convey a contrast. (C) is clear, concise, and shows the intended relationship: despite what you may expect, as one soars, the other remains steady.

41. **(A)** The previous sentence tells us that the professional fields are declining, so (A) is the correct answer. Biomedical engineering and computer science are examples of STEM fields, while business and education are examples of professional fields.

42. **(D)** The scientists belong to the world, so we want "world" to show ownership, making (D) the only appropriate choice.

43. **(D)** Here we want the possessive case of *they* since the sentence refers to "leading corporations and government agencies." (A) refers to location, and (B) means "they are."

44. **(B)** Trust your instinct here. Read it with each option. They have welcomed them "for" years now.

Math Test—No Calculator

1. **(C)** This is a simple word problem. First find how much she spends more per month, $500 – $450 = $50. Then multiply by 3.5 to find how much more she spends for the rest of the semester, $50 × 3.5 = $175.

2. **(A)** This is a simple question about functions. Find the point on the function where $x = 0$. When $x = 0$, $y = 1$.

3. **(A)** This is a simple question about a circle. First, find the area of the circle: $A = \pi r^2 = p10^2 = 100\pi$. Then, find out what fraction of the circle is 36°: $36°/360° = \dfrac{1}{10}$. Then, multiply the area of the circle with the fraction: $\dfrac{1}{10} \times 100\pi = 10\pi$.

4. **(A)** This is a simple algebra question. First, flip both sides of the equation to get $\dfrac{3y}{4x} = \dfrac{4}{1}$. Then multiply both sides of the equation by $\dfrac{4}{3}$ to get the answer. The answer is $\dfrac{16}{3}$.

5. **(A)** This is a simple algebra question. First, find the value of x, $\dfrac{2}{x} = 6$; $x = \dfrac{1}{3}$. Then find the value of $\dfrac{1}{5}x$, $\dfrac{1}{5} \times \dfrac{1}{3} = \dfrac{1}{15}$.

6. **(D)** This is a simple geometry question. First find angle D, 180° – 90° – 56° = 34°. Then find angle F, 180° – 90° – 34° = 56°.

7. **(A)** This is simple parabola question. The equation of a parabola is $y = (x - a)^2 + b$, where (a, b) is the vertex and a is also the axis of symmetry. Therefore, this parabola will be $y = (x - (-4))^2 + 3$; $y = (x + 4)^2 + 3$. The correct answer is (A).

8. **(D)** This is a simple question where the equation needs to be rearranged. First, rearrange the equation to isolate the r^2, $I \times 3 = \dfrac{1}{3}mr^2 \times 3$; $3I \div m = mr^2 \div m$; $\dfrac{3I}{m} = r^2$. Then square root both sides to isolate the r, $r = \sqrt{\dfrac{3I}{m}}$.

9. **(A)** This is a graphing question. Use the equation of the straight line, $y = mx + b$, to find the equation for the line in the graph. First, find the slope by looking at the rise over run. The rise here is 2 and run is 1. The slope is 2. Then look at the y intercept to find b, which is –3. The equation for the line is $y = 2x - 3$. Then reflect the line along the x axis to get $y = -2x + 3$. Then translate the line 3 units up to get $y = -2x + 6$.

10. **(D)** This is a parabola question. Plug in the $y = 0$ to the answer choices and find the correct answer. When $y = 0$ is plugged in, only choice (D) provides the correct answer, $y = -(x + 3)^2$; $x = -3$ when $y = 0$. Also, the graph opens downward, which means that the function is negative.

11. **(C)** This is a system of inequality question. Look though the answer choices to find the set of coordinates that falls in the region where there is shaded area from both inequalities. The answer is (1, 2).

12. **(C)** This is a difficult algebra question. First, simplify $\dfrac{3(n-1)-1}{3} = \dfrac{12-(3-n)}{6}$; $\dfrac{3n-4}{3} = \dfrac{9+n}{6}$. Then, multiply both sides by a common denominator, $6 \times \dfrac{3n-4}{3} = 6 \times \dfrac{9+n}{6}$; $2 \times (3n-4) = 9+n$; $6n - 8 = 9 + n$. Then solve for n, $5n = 17$; $n = \dfrac{17}{5}$.

13. **(C)** This is a system of equations question. Solve for x and y to get the point (p, q). Manipulate the second equation to get $y = 4x + 7$. Then set the two equations as equal to each other, $\dfrac{x}{3} - 4 = 4x + 7$. Then multiply both sides by 3, $3 \times (\dfrac{x}{3} - 4) = (4x + 7) \times 3$; $x - 12 = 12x + 21$. Then solve for x, $11x = -33$, $x = -3$. Then because q is the y coordinate, plug in x to solve for y, $y = 4(-3) + 7$; $y = -5$ and $q = -5$.

14. 713 This is a difficult algebra question. If $f(x)$ $= -x^2 - x$, and $x = -5$, then $f(x) = -(-5)^2 - 5$. Here $f(x) = -25 - 5 = -30$. Then -30 can be plugged into $g(f(x))$. $g(f(x)) = x^2 - 187 = 900 - 187 = 713$.

15. 13 This is a system of equations question. Plug in the value of y into both equations to get the x value. Plug into the first equation, $18 < 2x - 6$; $24 < 2x$; $12 < x$. Plug into the second equation, $18 > x - 12$; $30 > x$. The x value will be between 12 and 30, $12 < x < 30$. The smallest integer value of x would be 13.

16. 3 This is a medium difficulty geometry question. First find the radius of the larger circle $12p \div 2\pi = 6$. Then find the radius of the small circle $9p = r^2\pi$; $r = 3$. Then find the shortest distance between the edge of the small circle and the edge of the big circle, $6 - 3 = 3$.

17. 8 First, rearrange the equation, $x^2 - 8x + y^2$ $+ 6y = 39$. Then, change the equation to enable completing the square, $x^2 - 8x + 16 + y^2 + 6y$ $+ 9 = 39 + 16 + 9$. Then, change the equation to complete the square, $(x - 4)^2 + (y + 3)^2 = 8^2$. Because the equation of the circle is $(x - a)^2 + (y - b)^2 = r^2$, the radius is 8.

Math Test—Calculator

1. (D) This is an algebra question. This question is very simple, just cross multiply. $x(y) = 89(13)$; xy $= 1,157$.

2. (A) This is a simple fraction question. Add the two fractions: $\dfrac{38}{17} + \dfrac{32}{11} = \dfrac{(38)(11)}{(17)(11)} + \dfrac{(32)(17)}{(11)(17)} =$ $\dfrac{418}{187} + \dfrac{544}{187} = \dfrac{962}{187}$. Then divide by 2 to get the answer for this question: $\dfrac{962}{187} \div 2 = \dfrac{481}{187} = 2\dfrac{107}{187}$.

3. (A) This is a simple graphing question. The x intercept is when $y = 0$, so plug 0 in for y. $0 = 2x$. Then divide both sides by 2, $0/2 = 2x/2$. Then the answer is $x = 0$, and the x intercept is 0.

4. (C) This is a data analysis question. The graph shows that as a person spends more time in the sun, he or she will have more sun damage. The x value is the amount of time and y value is the level of sun damage. Therefore the answer is (C).

5. (A) This is a simple function question. Find the point on the function where $y = 5$. When $y = 5$, $y = -1$ and 3.

6. (A) This is a simple question about percents. First find 75% of 180, $75\% \times 180 = 135$. Then find 135 is what percent of 360, $135 \div 360 \times 100\%$ $= 37.5\%$

7. (B) This is a data analysis question. The graph shows that the cancer cells lower in numbers faster when using Drug 2. Therefore, the answer is (B).

8. (D) This is a simple algebra question. This is a perfect square question. Factor the equation $(x + 3)(x + 3)$, which equals $(x + 3)^2$.

9. (B) This is a data analysis question. First, find the total number of students enrolled in the Math Club. This can be found by $37 + 33 + 88$ $= 158$. Then find the percentage by dividing 33 by 158 then multiplying by 100%. The answer is 20.88% and when rounded is 21%. Therefore, the correct answer is (B).

10. (B) This is a multistep word problem. Set up the equation to solve how many U.S. dollars he needs to purchase the magnet, $\dfrac{1 \text{ dollar}}{x \text{ dollars}} = \dfrac{0.85 \text{ euros}}{5 \text{ euros}}$. 5.88 U.S. dollars will be needed to purchase the magnet.

11. **(B)** This is a simple data analysis question. If she needs to find out how many slices of pizza to order for each student, she needs the average or the mean of the set of data.

12. **(D)** This is a simple data analysis question. First find the mode, the number that appears the most often, which is 2. Then find the median, the number in the middle, which is also 2. The difference between 2 and 2 is 0.

13. **(C)** This is a medium difficulty question about percent and ratios. Use an arbitrary number like 100 to start the calculation. If 100 is decreased by 20%, then the new price is 80. Therefore the ratio is 20 to 80, 1 to 4.

14. **(C)** This is a simple statistics question. First, find the total number of grade 9 and grade 10 students, 460 + 511 = 971. Then find the total number of grade 9 and grade 10 students who selected AP calculus, 16 + 22 = 38. Then, find the fraction, $\frac{38}{971}$.

15. **(B)** This is a data analysis question. First, add the two portions together 2.5 + 2 = 4.5 portions. Then find how much is each portion, $6,500 ÷ 10 = $650. Then find the answer $650 × 4.5 = $2,925

16. **(B)** This is a medium algebra question. First set the equation to 0, $4x^2 - 4x + 1 = 0$. Then factor the equation, $(2x - 1)(2x - 1) = 0$. Solve for x, $x = \frac{1}{2}$.

17. **(C)** This is a medium algebra question. If $f(x) = -14$, -14 can be plugged into $g(f(x))$. $g(f(x)) = g(-14) = (-14)^2 - 58 + (-14)^3 = 196 - 58 - 2{,}744 = -2{,}606$.

18. **(B)** This is a word problem. The difficulty of this type of questions is medium, but students tend to struggle on this type of questions. First calculate how many cups of orange juice there are in total. 31% of 1 cup is 0.31 × 1 cup = 0.31 cup; 23% of 3.5 cups is 0.23 × 3.5 cups = 0.805 cups. In total there are 1.185 cups of orange juice (0.31 + 0.805 = 1.115). Now calculate how much fruit punch there is in total (1 + 3.5 = 4.5). Now calculate the percentage of orange juice there is in the fruit punch (0.115 ÷ 4.5 = 0.248 and 0.248 is 24.8%). Therefore the correct answer is (B).

19. **(C)** This is a difficult algebra question. Modify $\frac{x}{5} - \frac{y}{7} = \frac{1}{2}$ until it looks like $5y - 7x$ to get the answer, $-35\left(\frac{x}{5} - \frac{y}{7}\right) = -7x + 5y = 5y - 7x = \frac{1}{2} \times (-35)$. The answer is $\frac{1}{2} \times (-35) = -\frac{35}{2}$.

20. **(A)** This is a multistep word problem. The difficulty is medium. First find out the total amount of the bills for the first 3 months. $30 + $59.99 + $39.99 = $129.98 Then take this total amount from the amount in the bank. $556.76 – $129.98 = $426.78. The answer is $426.78.

21. **(C)** This a multistep high difficulty question. First, find out the total amount of the bills for the first 3 months. $30 + $59.99 + $39.99 = $129.98. Then take this total amount from the amount in the bank. $556.76 – $129.98 = $426.78. This is the amount left after 3 months. Every month after the third month the combined Internet and phone bill is a fixed amount: $39.99 + $49.99 = $89.98. Next, find out the number of months she can pay for after the first 3: $426.78/$89.98 = 4.74. If she can pay for another 4.74 months, it means she can pay for another 4 full months on top of the first 3 months. That is a total of 7 months: 3 + 4 = 7. Choice (A) is a trick answer for those who forget to add the first 3 months.

22. (C) This is a simple inequality question. To see which points satisfies both equations, plug each of the points into both equations and find the point that satisfies both equations. For example, plug (1, 1) into the first equation: $1 < 5(1) + 2$ and get $1 < 7$. This means that the point satisfies the first equation. Next plug (1, 1) into the second equation: $1 + 3(1) < 6$ and get $4 < 6$. This means that the point also satisfies the second equation. Another way of solving this question is to graph out the two equations and see which points satisfy both equations.

23. (C) This is a difficult word problem about proportions. First start with the proportions given in the question and use r for red, y for yellow, and b for blue: r to y is 3 ml to 5 ml, and y to b is 55 ml to 1.2 L. Then convert 1.2 L to ml by multiplying by 1,000 to get y to b = 55 ml to 1,200 ml. To make sure that the 55 ml of yellow and 5 ml of yellow stay consistent, multiply both sides of r to y by 11 to get r to y = 33 ml. The new ratio of r to y to b is 33 to 55 to 1,200. Then find the ratio of the amount of yellow paint to total paint. If there is 55 ml of yellow paint then there is $(33 + 55 + 1,200) = 1,288$ of total paint, and the ratio would be 55:1,288. If 3,864 ml of paint is needed in total, the amount of yellow paint needed is $3,864 \div 1,288 = 3$; $3 \times 55 = 165$ ml.

24. (D) This is a difficult word problem. First, find the volume of the water in the first vase by using the formula for the volume of a cylinder, $\pi(15)^2 \times 14.5 = 3,262.5\pi$. Then find half of the water, $3,262.5\pi \div 2 = 1,631.25\pi$. Then find the height of the water by using the formula for the volume again and dividing by the radius of the second base squared, $1,631.25\pi \div (12)^2 = 11.33\pi$.

25. (B) This is a multistep word problem. Find the number of bags of toys the two can pack in one hour if they work together: $8 + 6 = 14$ bags per one hour. Then find how long it would take if they work together: 10 bags $\div$ 14 bags per hour $= 0.71$ hours, which is the same as 43 min (0.71 hours $\times$ 60 minutes per hour).

26. (B) This is a short word problem. The simple way of solving this problem is to work from the answers back. There are only two numbers, and they are consecutive odd integers. It is simple to use trial and error to find the answer. The other way of solving this question is to set an equation, and this way is a bit more complicated. Set the smaller of the two numbers as x and the larger of the two as $x + 2$. The product of the two numbers is 195. Therefore, $x(x + 2) = 195$. Expand the equation. $x^2 + 2x = 195$. Set the equation equal to 0, $x^2 + 2x - 195 = 0$. Factor the equation, $(x + 15)(x + 13)$. Solve for x, $x = -15x = -13$. The larger of the two numbers is -13.

27. (A) This is a graphing question. In this question we need to find out what the slope is. Slope is equal to rise over run. The rise between the points is 6 and the run is 9. Therefore, the slope of the equation is $\frac{6}{9}$, which is equal to $\frac{2}{3}$. Next find the y intercept or when $x = 0$. When x is 0 y is 2. Using the line equation $y = mx + b$, the equation of the given x and y values is $y = \frac{2}{3}x + 2$.

28. 65 This is a medium level word problem. First find the number of markdowns. There is one markdown on Feb 15 and one markdown on March 15. Then take 15% off two times from $89.99. $89.99 \times 85\% \times 85\% = \$65.02$, which rounds to $65.

29. 52 This is a medium level word problem. First find the number of markdowns. There is one markdown on February 15, one markdown on March 15, one markdown on April 15, and one markdown on May 15. Then take 15% off four times from $89.99. $89.99 × 85% × 85% × 85% × 85% = $45.98. Then add the 9.7% tax by multiplying $45.98 by 1.097 = $51.53, which rounds to $52.

30. 12 This is a medium circle question. First, find the area of the circle, $6\pi \times 6 = 36p$. Then find the radius by working backward from the formula for area, $r = \sqrt{\pi r^2 \div \pi}$, $\sqrt{36p \div p} = 6$. The diameter is $6 \times 2 = 12$.

31. 10 This is a word problem about speed. First, find out the speed of packing, 6 boxes ÷ 3 hours = 2 boxes/hour. Then find how long it will take to finish $\frac{1}{3}$ of a box, $\frac{1}{3}$ box ÷ 2 boxes/hour = $\frac{1}{6}$ hour. Then convert the number of hours to minutes: $\frac{1}{6}$ hour = 10 minutes.

PSAT/NMSQT
Practice Test 3

Answer Sheet

Last Name: _____   First Name: _____

Date: _____   Testing Location: _____

Administering the Test

- Remove this answer sheet from the book and use it to record your answers to this test.
- This test will require 2 hours and 10 minutes to complete. Take this test in one sitting.
- Use a stopwatch to time yourself on each section. The time limit for each section is written clearly at the beginning of each section. The first four sections are 25 minutes long, and the last section is 30 minutes long.
- Each response must completely fill the oval. Erase all stray marks completely, or they may be interpreted as responses.
- You must stop ALL work on a section when time is called.
- If you finish a section before the time has elapsed, check your work on that section. You may NOT move on to the next section until time is called.
- Do not waste time on questions that seem too difficult for you.
- Use the test book for scratchwork, but you will only receive credit for answers that are marked on the answer sheets.

Scoring the Test

- Your scaled score, which will be determined from a conversion table, is based on your raw score for each section.
- You will receive one point toward your raw score for every correct answer.
- You will receive no points toward your raw score for an omitted question.
- For each wrong answer on a multiple-choice question, your raw score will be reduced by 1/4 point. For each wrong answer on a numerical "grid-in" question (Section 4, questions 29–38), your raw score will receive no deduction.

SECTION 1 **Reading Test** 60 MINUTES

Time: 60 minutes

Start: _____

Stop: _____

1. Ⓐ Ⓑ Ⓒ Ⓓ
2. Ⓐ Ⓑ Ⓒ Ⓓ
3. Ⓐ Ⓑ Ⓒ Ⓓ
4. Ⓐ Ⓑ Ⓒ Ⓓ
5. Ⓐ Ⓑ Ⓒ Ⓓ
6. Ⓐ Ⓑ Ⓒ Ⓓ
7. Ⓐ Ⓑ Ⓒ Ⓓ
8. Ⓐ Ⓑ Ⓒ Ⓓ
9. Ⓐ Ⓑ Ⓒ Ⓓ
10. Ⓐ Ⓑ Ⓒ Ⓓ
11. Ⓐ Ⓑ Ⓒ Ⓓ
12. Ⓐ Ⓑ Ⓒ Ⓓ
13. Ⓐ Ⓑ Ⓒ Ⓓ
14. Ⓐ Ⓑ Ⓒ Ⓓ
15. Ⓐ Ⓑ Ⓒ Ⓓ
16. Ⓐ Ⓑ Ⓒ Ⓓ
17. Ⓐ Ⓑ Ⓒ Ⓓ
18. Ⓐ Ⓑ Ⓒ Ⓓ
19. Ⓐ Ⓑ Ⓒ Ⓓ
20. Ⓐ Ⓑ Ⓒ Ⓓ
21. Ⓐ Ⓑ Ⓒ Ⓓ
22. Ⓐ Ⓑ Ⓒ Ⓓ
23. Ⓐ Ⓑ Ⓒ Ⓓ
24. Ⓐ Ⓑ Ⓒ Ⓓ
25. Ⓐ Ⓑ Ⓒ Ⓓ
26. Ⓐ Ⓑ Ⓒ Ⓓ
27. Ⓐ Ⓑ Ⓒ Ⓓ
28. Ⓐ Ⓑ Ⓒ Ⓓ
29. Ⓐ Ⓑ Ⓒ Ⓓ
30. Ⓐ Ⓑ Ⓒ Ⓓ
31. Ⓐ Ⓑ Ⓒ Ⓓ
32. Ⓐ Ⓑ Ⓒ Ⓓ
33. Ⓐ Ⓑ Ⓒ Ⓓ
34. Ⓐ Ⓑ Ⓒ Ⓓ
35. Ⓐ Ⓑ Ⓒ Ⓓ
36. Ⓐ Ⓑ Ⓒ Ⓓ
37. Ⓐ Ⓑ Ⓒ Ⓓ
38. Ⓐ Ⓑ Ⓒ Ⓓ
39. Ⓐ Ⓑ Ⓒ Ⓓ
40. Ⓐ Ⓑ Ⓒ Ⓓ
41. Ⓐ Ⓑ Ⓒ Ⓓ
42. Ⓐ Ⓑ Ⓒ Ⓓ
43. Ⓐ Ⓑ Ⓒ Ⓓ
44. Ⓐ Ⓑ Ⓒ Ⓓ
45. Ⓐ Ⓑ Ⓒ Ⓓ
46. Ⓐ Ⓑ Ⓒ Ⓓ
47. Ⓐ Ⓑ Ⓒ Ⓓ

SECTION 2 **Writing and Language Test** 35 MINUTES

Time: 35 minutes

Start: _____

Stop: _____

1. Ⓐ Ⓑ Ⓒ Ⓓ
2. Ⓐ Ⓑ Ⓒ Ⓓ
3. Ⓐ Ⓑ Ⓒ Ⓓ
4. Ⓐ Ⓑ Ⓒ Ⓓ
5. Ⓐ Ⓑ Ⓒ Ⓓ
6. Ⓐ Ⓑ Ⓒ Ⓓ
7. Ⓐ Ⓑ Ⓒ Ⓓ
8. Ⓐ Ⓑ Ⓒ Ⓓ
9. Ⓐ Ⓑ Ⓒ Ⓓ
10. Ⓐ Ⓑ Ⓒ Ⓓ
11. Ⓐ Ⓑ Ⓒ Ⓓ
12. Ⓐ Ⓑ Ⓒ Ⓓ
13. Ⓐ Ⓑ Ⓒ Ⓓ
14. Ⓐ Ⓑ Ⓒ Ⓓ
15. Ⓐ Ⓑ Ⓒ Ⓓ
16. Ⓐ Ⓑ Ⓒ Ⓓ
17. Ⓐ Ⓑ Ⓒ Ⓓ
18. Ⓐ Ⓑ Ⓒ Ⓓ
19. Ⓐ Ⓑ Ⓒ Ⓓ
20. Ⓐ Ⓑ Ⓒ Ⓓ
21. Ⓐ Ⓑ Ⓒ Ⓓ
22. Ⓐ Ⓑ Ⓒ Ⓓ
23. Ⓐ Ⓑ Ⓒ Ⓓ
24. Ⓐ Ⓑ Ⓒ Ⓓ
25. Ⓐ Ⓑ Ⓒ Ⓓ
26. Ⓐ Ⓑ Ⓒ Ⓓ
27. Ⓐ Ⓑ Ⓒ Ⓓ
28. Ⓐ Ⓑ Ⓒ Ⓓ
29. Ⓐ Ⓑ Ⓒ Ⓓ
30. Ⓐ Ⓑ Ⓒ Ⓓ
31. Ⓐ Ⓑ Ⓒ Ⓓ
32. Ⓐ Ⓑ Ⓒ Ⓓ
33. Ⓐ Ⓑ Ⓒ Ⓓ
34. Ⓐ Ⓑ Ⓒ Ⓓ
35. Ⓐ Ⓑ Ⓒ Ⓓ
36. Ⓐ Ⓑ Ⓒ Ⓓ
37. Ⓐ Ⓑ Ⓒ Ⓓ
38. Ⓐ Ⓑ Ⓒ Ⓓ
39. Ⓐ Ⓑ Ⓒ Ⓓ
40. Ⓐ Ⓑ Ⓒ Ⓓ
41. Ⓐ Ⓑ Ⓒ Ⓓ
42. Ⓐ Ⓑ Ⓒ Ⓓ
43. Ⓐ Ⓑ Ⓒ Ⓓ
44. Ⓐ Ⓑ Ⓒ Ⓓ

SECTION 3 **Math Test—No Calculator** 25 MINUTES

Time: 25 minutes

Start: _____

Stop: _____

1. Ⓐ Ⓑ Ⓒ Ⓓ
2. Ⓐ Ⓑ Ⓒ Ⓓ
3. Ⓐ Ⓑ Ⓒ Ⓓ
4. Ⓐ Ⓑ Ⓒ Ⓓ

5. Ⓐ Ⓑ Ⓒ Ⓓ
6. Ⓐ Ⓑ Ⓒ Ⓓ
7. Ⓐ Ⓑ Ⓒ Ⓓ
8. Ⓐ Ⓑ Ⓒ Ⓓ

9. Ⓐ Ⓑ Ⓒ Ⓓ
10. Ⓐ Ⓑ Ⓒ Ⓓ
11. Ⓐ Ⓑ Ⓒ Ⓓ
12. Ⓐ Ⓑ Ⓒ Ⓓ

13. Ⓐ Ⓑ Ⓒ Ⓓ

14.
15.
16.
17.

SECTION 4 **Math Test—Calculator** 45 MINUTES

Time: 45 minutes

Start: _____

Stop: _____

1. Ⓐ Ⓑ Ⓒ Ⓓ
2. Ⓐ Ⓑ Ⓒ Ⓓ
3. Ⓐ Ⓑ Ⓒ Ⓓ
4. Ⓐ Ⓑ Ⓒ Ⓓ
5. Ⓐ Ⓑ Ⓒ Ⓓ
6. Ⓐ Ⓑ Ⓒ Ⓓ
7. Ⓐ Ⓑ Ⓒ Ⓓ

8. Ⓐ Ⓑ Ⓒ Ⓓ
9. Ⓐ Ⓑ Ⓒ Ⓓ
10. Ⓐ Ⓑ Ⓒ Ⓓ
11. Ⓐ Ⓑ Ⓒ Ⓓ
12. Ⓐ Ⓑ Ⓒ Ⓓ
13. Ⓐ Ⓑ Ⓒ Ⓓ
14. Ⓐ Ⓑ Ⓒ Ⓓ

15. Ⓐ Ⓑ Ⓒ Ⓓ
16. Ⓐ Ⓑ Ⓒ Ⓓ
17. Ⓐ Ⓑ Ⓒ Ⓓ
18. Ⓐ Ⓑ Ⓒ Ⓓ
19. Ⓐ Ⓑ Ⓒ Ⓓ
20. Ⓐ Ⓑ Ⓒ Ⓓ
21. Ⓐ Ⓑ Ⓒ Ⓓ

22. Ⓐ Ⓑ Ⓒ Ⓓ
23. Ⓐ Ⓑ Ⓒ Ⓓ
24. Ⓐ Ⓑ Ⓒ Ⓓ
25. Ⓐ Ⓑ Ⓒ Ⓓ
26. Ⓐ Ⓑ Ⓒ Ⓓ
27. Ⓐ Ⓑ Ⓒ Ⓓ

28.
29.
30.
31.

READING TEST

60 MINUTES, 47 QUESTIONS

Turn to Section 1 of your answer sheet to answer the questions in this section.

Directions: Each passage or pair of passages below is followed by a number of questions. After reading each passage or pair, choose the best answer to each question based on what is stated or implied in the passage or passages and in any accompanying graphics (such as a table or graph).

Questions 1–10 are based on the following passage.

This passage is adapted from Theodore S. Wright's speech originally published in 1837.

Mr. President, with much feeling do I rise to address the society on this resolution, and I should hardly have been induced to have done it had I not been requested. I confess I am personally interested
5 in this resolution. But were it not for the fact that none can feel the lash but those who have it upon them, that none know where the chain galls but those who wear it, I would not address you.

This is a serious business, sir. The prejudice which
10 exists against the colored man, the free man is like the atmosphere, everywhere felt by him. It is true that in these United States and in this State, there are men, like myself, colored with the skin like my own, who are not subjected to the lash, who are not
15 liable to have their wives and their infants torn from them; from whose hand the Bible is not taken. It is true that we may walk abroad; we may enjoy our domestic comforts, our families; retire to the closet; visit the sanctuary, and may be permitted to urge
20 on our children and our neighbors in well doing. But sir, still we are slaves—every where we feel the chain galling us. It is by that prejudice which the resolution condemns, the spirit of slavery, the law which has been enacted here, by a corrupt public
25 sentiment, through the influence of slavery which treats moral agents different from the rule of God,

which treats them irrespective of their morals or intellectual cultivation. This spirit is withering all our hopes, and oftentimes causes the colored parent
30 as he looks upon his child, to wish he had never been born. Often is the heart of the colored mother, as she presses her child to her bosom, filled with sorrow to think that, by reason of this prejudice, it is cut off from all hopes of usefulness in this land. Sir, this
35 prejudice is wicked.

If the nation and church understood this matter, I would not speak a word about that killing influence that destroys the colored man's reputation. This influence cuts us off from everything; it follows us
40 up from childhood to manhood; it excludes us from all stations of profit, usefulness and honor; takes away from us all motive for pressing forward in enterprises, useful and important to the world and to ourselves.

45 In the first place, it cuts us off from the advantages of the mechanic arts almost entirely. A colored man can hardly learn a trade, and if he does it is difficult for him to find any one who will employ him to work at that trade, in any part of the State.
50 In most of our large cities there are associations of mechanics who legislate out of their society colored men. And in many cases where our young men have learned trades, they have had to come to low employments for want of encouragement in those
55 trades.

GO ON TO THE NEXT PAGE →

It must be a matter of rejoicing to know that in this vicinity colored fathers and mothers have the privileges of education. It must be a matter of rejoicing that in this vicinity colored parents can
60 have their children trained up in schools. At present, we find the colleges barred against them.

I will say nothing about the inconvenience which I have experienced myself, and which every man of color experiences, though made in the image of
65 God. I will say nothing about the inconvenience of traveling; how we are frowned upon and despised. No matter how we may demean ourselves, we find embarrassments everywhere.

But sir, this prejudice goes further. It debars men
70 from heaven. While sir, slavery cuts off the colored portion of the community from religious privileges, men are made infidels. What, they demand, is your Christianity? How do you regard your brethren? How do you treat them at the Lord's table? Where
75 is your consistency in talking about the heathen, transversing the ocean to circulate the Bible everywhere, while you frown upon them at the door? These things meet us and weigh down our spirits.

And, sir, the constitution of society, molded
80 by this prejudice, destroys souls. I have known extensively, that in revivals which have been blessed and enjoyed in this part of the country, the colored population were overlooked. I recollect an instance. The Lord God was pouring out His Spirit. He was
85 entering every house, and sinners were converted. I asked, Where is the colored man? who is weeping for them? who is endeavoring to pull them out of the fire? No reply was made. I was asked to go round with one of the elders and visit them. We went and
90 they humbled themselves. The Church commenced efficient efforts, and God blessed them as soon as they began to act for these people as though they had souls.

And sir, the manner in which our churches
95 are regulated destroys souls. Whilst the church is thrown open to everybody, and one says come, come in and share the blessings of the sanctuary, this is the gate of heaven—he says to the colored

man, be careful where you take your stand. I know
100 an efficient church in this State, where a respectable colored man went to the house of God, and was going to take a seat in the gallery, and one of the officers contended with him, and said, "you cannot
105 go there, sir."

In one place the people had come together to the house of the Lord. The sermon was preached—the emblems were about to be administered—and all at once the person who managed the church thought
110 the value of the pews would be diminished if the colored people sat in them. They objected to their sitting there, and the colored people left and went into the gallery, and that, too, when they were thinking of handling the memorials of the broken
115 body and shed blood of the Savior! And, sir, this prejudice follows the colored man everywhere, and depresses his spirits.

1. What is the main purpose of the speaker?

    (A) To convince all African Americans to stand together against racial disparity.
    (B) To lament the prejudice faced by slaves alone.
    (C) To support a resolution that criticizes the prejudice against black people.
    (D) To speak to the U.S. Congress against the African American Exclusion Act.

2. Which choice provides the best evidence for the answer to the previous question?

    (A) Lines 9–11 ("This is . . . by him.")
    (B) Lines 11–14 ("It is true . . . the lash.")
    (C) Lines 21–23 ("But sir . . . of slavery,")
    (D) Lines 31–34 ("Often is the . . . this land.")

3. As used in line 22, "galling" most nearly means

    (A) vexing
    (B) worry
    (C) mollify
    (D) appease

4. What does the passage suggest about the difference between the colored population and the rest of the population in the United States of America?

   (A) There are improvements made in the rights of the rest of the population, but there are no advancements in the rights of the colored population.

   (B) There is not enough human rights advancement because the conditions of colored people are not improved.

   (C) There are some improvements to the rights of the colored population, but there is a trend of reversing these improvements.

   (D) There are small efforts made to improve the conditions of the colored population.

5. Which choice provides the best evidence for the answer to the previous question?

   (A) Lines 62–63, ("the inconvenience . . . myself")

   (B) Lines 79–80, ("constitution . . . souls")

   (C) Lines 81–83, ("revivals . . . overlooked")

   (D) Lines 99–101, ("I know . . . God")

6. As used in line 57, "vicinity" most nearly means

   (A) plot

   (B) faraway

   (C) environment

   (D) range

7. What does the speaker believe about "colored fathers and mothers"?

   (A) They are not optimistic about the future of their children.

   (B) They are hopeful that their children will have good education.

   (C) They should work together for the future of their children.

   (D) They are unable to educate their own children because the parents themselves are uneducated.

8. Which choice provides the best evidence for the answer to the previous question?

   (A) Lines 4–5, ("I confess . . . resolution")

   (B) Lines 31–34, ("the heart . . . land")

   (C) Lines 57–58, ("colored fathers . . . education")

   (D) Lines 59–60, ("colored parents . . . schools")

9. What can be inferred about what the speaker believes about a church?

   (A) A church should be an inclusive environment for all people including people of color.

   (B) All churches do not allow people of color to enter and pray.

   (C) Churches are places where prejudice and exclusion are practiced the most.

   (D) Churches are locations of inclusion, and the few churches that practice prejudice are only the minority.

10. According to the passage, which one is NOT an influence of the prejudice against blacks?

    (A) limits the education opportunities for black people

    (B) isolates black people

    (C) limits the employment of black people

    (D) bans black people from traveling abroad

Questions 11–19 are based on the following passage.

This passage is adapted from Carrie Chapman Catt's speech originally published in 1916.

I am aware that some suffragists do not share this belief. They see no signs nor symptoms today which were not present yesterday; no manifestations in the year 1916 which differ significantly from those in the year 1910. To them, the movement has been a steady, normal growth from the beginning and must so continue until the end. I can only defend my claim with the plea that it is better to imagine a crisis where none exists than to fail to recognize one when it comes; for a crisis is a culmination of events which calls for new considerations and new decisions. A failure to answer the call may mean an opportunity lost, a possible victory postponed.

The object of the life of an organized movement is to secure its aim. Necessarily, it must obey the law of evolution and pass through the stages of agitation and education and finally through the stage of realization. As one has put it:

"A new idea floats in the air over the heads of the people and for a long, indefinite period evades their understanding but, by and by, when through familiarity, human vision grows clearer, it is caught out of the clouds and crystallized into law."

Such a period comes to every movement and is its crisis. In my judgment, that crucial moment, bidding us to renewed consecration and redoubled activity, has come to our cause. I believe our victory hangs within our grasp, inviting us to pluck it out of the clouds and establish it among the good things of the world.

If this be true, the time is past when we should say: "Men and women of America, look upon that wonderful idea up there; see, one day it will come down." Instead, the time has come to shout aloud in every city, village, and hamlet, and in tones so clear and jubilant that they will reverberate from every mountain peak and echo from shore to shore: "The woman's hour has struck."

Suppose suffragists as a whole do not believe a crisis has come and do not extend their hands to grasp the victory, what will happen? Why, we shall all continue to work and our cause will continue to hang, waiting for those who possess a clearer vision and more daring enterprise. On the other hand, suppose we reach out with united earnestness and determination to grasp our victory while it still hangs a bit too high? Has any harm been done? None!

Therefore, fellow suffragists, I invite your attention to the signs which point to a crisis and your consideration of plans for turning the crisis into victory.

First: We are passing through a world crisis. All thinkers of every land tell us so; and that nothing after the Great War will be as it was before. Those who profess to know claim that 100 millions of dollars are being spent on the war every day and that 2 years of war have cost 50 billions of dollars or 10 times more than the total expense of the American Civil War. Our own country has sent 35 millions of dollars abroad for relief expenses.

Were there no other effects to come from the world's war, the transfer of such unthinkably vast sums of money from the usual avenues to those wholly abnormal would give so severe a jolt to organized society that it would vibrate around the world and bring untold changes in its wake.

But three and a half millions of lives have been lost. The number becomes the more impressive when it is remembered that the entire population of the American Colonies was little more than three and a half millions. These losses have been the lives of men within the age of economic production. They have been taken abruptly from the normal business of the world and every human activity from that of the humblest, unskilled labor to art, science, and literature has been weakened by their loss. Millions of other men will go to their homes, blind, crippled, and incapacitated to do the work they once

80 performed. The stability of human institutions has
never before suffered so tremendous a shock. Great
men are trying to think out the consequences but
one and all proclaim that no imagination can find
color or form bold enough to paint the picture of the
85 world after the war. British and Russian, German
and Austrian, French and Italian agree that it will
lead to social and political revolution throughout the
entire world. Whatever comes, they further agree
that the war presages a total change in the status
90 of women.

A simple-minded man in West Virginia, when
addressed upon the subject of woman suffrage in
that state, replied, "We've been so used to keepin'
our women down, 't would seem queer not to." He
95 expressed what greater men feel but do not say.
Had the wife of that man spoken in the same clear-
thinking fashion, she would have said, "We women
have been so used to being kept down that it would
seem strange to get up. Nature intended women for
100 doormats." Had she so expressed herself, these two
would have put the entire anti-suffrage argument in
a nutshell.

In Europe, from the Polar Circle to the Aegean
105 Sea, women have risen as though to answer that
argument. Everywhere they have taken the places
made vacant by men and in so doing, they have
grown in self-respect and in the esteem of their
respective nations. In every land, the people have
110 reverted to the primitive division of labor and while
the men have gone to war, women have cultivated
the fields in order that the army and nation may be
fed. No army can succeed and no nation can endure
without food; those who supply it are a war power
115 and a peace power.

Women by the thousands have knocked at the
doors of munition factories and, in the name of
patriotism, have begged for the right to serve their
country there. Their services were accepted with
120 hesitation but the experiment once made, won
reluctant but universal praise. An official statement
recently issued in Great Britain announced that
660,000 women were engaged in making munitions

in that country alone. In a recent convention of
125 munition workers, composed of men and women, a
resolution was unanimously passed informing the
government that they would forego vacations and
holidays until the authorities announced that their
munition supplies were sufficient for the needs of
130 the war and Great Britain pronounced the act the
highest patriotism. Lord Derby addressed such a
meeting and said,

"When the history of the war is written, I wonder
to whom the greatest credit will be given; to the men
135 who went to fight or to the women who are working
in a way that many people hardly believed that it was
possible for them to work."

Lord Sydenham added his tribute. Said he,

"It might fairly be claimed that women have
140 helped to save thousands of lives and to change the
entire aspect of the war. Wherever intelligence, care,
and close attention have been needed, women have
distinguished themselves."

11. Which statement best describes Carrie
Chapman Catt's purpose for giving this speech?

(A) to promote passing of bills that support
women's equality within the society and in
the work place
(B) to address the important role that women
play within society
(C) to promote further actions to bring human
rights to the women of the rest of the world
(D) to address the importance of women's rights
and the suffragist movement in light of
the war

12. Which choice provides the best evidence for the
answer to the previous question?

(A) Lines 97–99, ("We women . . . get up")
(B) Lines 104–106, ("In Europe . . . argument")
(C) Lines 116–119, ("Women . . . there")
(D) Lines 139–143, ("women . . . themselves")

13. As used in line 79, "incapacitated" most nearly means

   (A) insubstantial
   (B) galvanized
   (C) exhilarated
   (D) debilitated

14. It can be inferred from the passage that Carrie Chapman Catt believes that America's focus after the war should be on

   (A) making changes in light of the end of the war, especially regarding women's suffrage
   (B) advancing toward economic stability and recuperating the losses by having more women join the workforce
   (C) appeasing the citizens of America and remembering the tragedy of the war
   (D) remembering the many men who lost their lives during the war and promoting women's rights as a result

15. Which choice provides the best evidence for the answer to the previous question?

   (A) Lines 56–60, ("that 100 millions . . . War")
   (B) Lines 66–67, ("organized . . . wake")
   (C) Lines 68–69, ("But three . . . lost")
   (D) Lines 72–73, ("These . . . production")

16. As used in line 82, "consequences" most nearly means

   (A) ramifications
   (B) explanation
   (C) inducement
   (D) discomfiture

17. It can be inferred that Carrie Chapman Catt would like to see

   (A) women and men working the same jobs and women taking more positions as educators and professors
   (B) men stop repressing women and to stand up for women suffrage alongside women
   (C) women of America, following the leads of women in the European nations, improve women suffrage in the United States
   (D) women of America granted more rights and equal rights

18. Which choice provides the best evidence for the answer to the previous question?

   (A) Lines 32–34, ("Men . . . down")
   (B) Lines 36–38, ("reverberate . . . struck")
   (C) Lines 93–94, ("We've . . . Not to")
   (D) Lines 106–109, ("Everywhere . . . nations")

19. According to the passage, what does Carrie Chapman Catt believe will happen if suffragists do not believe her causes are critical?

   (A) She believes that the suffragists will believe her causes are critical when she communicates with them and shares with them the losses that the country has suffered as a result.
   (B) Society is changing, and it will be up to women to stand up for themselves and convince the suffragists to further these causes.
   (C) The importance of these causes will be found eventually by others who understand their urgency.
   (D) If these suffragists do not internalize the significance of the causes, great harm will be done to society.

Questions 20-29 are based on the following passage.

This passage is adapted from President Woodrow Wilson's speech originally published in 1917.

Gentlemen of the Congress, I have called the Congress into extraordinary session because there are serious, very serious, choices of policy to be made, and made immediately, which it was neither
5 right nor constitutionally permissible that I should assume the responsibility of making.

On the third of February last I officially laid before you the extraordinary announcement of the Imperial German Government that on and
10 after the first day of February it was its purpose to put aside all restraints of law or of humanity and use its submarines to sink every vessel that sought to approach either the ports of Great Britain and Ireland or the western coasts of Europe or any of the
15 ports controlled by the enemies of Germany within the Mediterranean. That had seemed to be the object of the German submarine warfare earlier in the war, but since April of last year the Imperial Government had somewhat restrained the commanders of its
20 undersea craft in conformity with its promise then given to us that passenger boats should not be sunk and that due warning would be given to all other vessels which its submarines might seek to destroy when no resistance was offered or escape attempted,
25 and care taken that their crews were given at least a fair chance to save their lives in their open boats. The precautions taken were meager and haphazard enough, as was proved in distressing instance after instance in the progress of the cruel and unmanly
30 business, but a certain degree of restraint was observed. The new policy has swept every restriction aside. Vessels of every kind, whatever their flag, their character, their cargo, their destination, their errand, have been ruthlessly sent to the bottom:
35 without warning and without thought of help or mercy for those on board, the vessels of friendly neutrals along with those of belligerents. Even hospital ships and ships carrying relief to the sorely bereaved and stricken people of Belgium, though
40 the latter were provided with safe conduct through the proscribed areas by the German Government itself and were distinguished by unmistakable marks of identity, have been sunk with the same reckless lack of compassion or of principle. I was
45 for a little while unable to believe that such things would in fact be done by any government that had hitherto subscribed to the humane practices of civilized nations. International law had its origin in the attempt to set up some law which would be
50 respected and observed upon the seas, where no nation had right of dominion and where lay the free highways of the world. . . . This minimum of right the German Government has swept aside under the plea of retaliation and necessity and because it had
55 no weapons which it could use at sea except these which it is impossible to employ as it is employing them without throwing to the winds all scruples of humanity or of respect for the understandings that were supposed to underlie the intercourse of the
60 world. I am not now thinking of the loss of property involved, immense and serious as that is, but only of the wanton and wholesale destruction of the lives of noncombatants, men, women, and children, engaged in pursuits which have always, even in the darkest
65 periods of modern history, been deemed innocent and legitimate. Property can be paid for; the lives of peaceful and innocent people cannot be. The present German submarine warfare against commerce is a warfare against mankind.
70 It is a war against all nations. American ships have been sunk, American lives taken, in ways which it has stirred us very deeply to learn of, but the ships and people of other neutral and friendly nations have been sunk and overwhelmed in the waters in
75 the same way. There has been no discrimination. The challenge is to all mankind. Each nation must decide for itself how it will meet it. The choice we make for ourselves must be made with a moderation of counsel and a temperateness of judgment befitting

our character and our motives as a nation. We must
put excited feeling away. Our motive will not be
revenge or the victorious assertion of the physical
might of the nation, but only the vindication of
right, of human right, of which we are only a single
champion.

   When I addressed the Congress on the twenty-
sixth of February last I thought that it would suffice
to assert our neutral rights with arms, our right
to use the seas against unlawful interference, our
right to keep our people safe against unlawful
violence. But armed neutrality, it now appears, is
impracticable. Because submarines are in effect
outlaws when used as the German submarines
have been used against merchant shipping, it is
impossible to defend ships against their attacks as
the law of nations has assumed that merchantmen
would defend themselves against privateers or
cruisers, visible craft giving chase upon the open
sea. It is common prudence in such circumstances,
grim necessity indeed, to endeavor to destroy
them before they have shown their own intention.
They must be dealt with upon sight, if dealt with
at all. The German Government denies the right of
neutrals to use arms at all within the areas of the
sea which it has proscribed, even in the defense of
rights which no modern publicist has ever before
questioned their right to defend. The intimation
is conveyed that the armed guards which we have
placed on our merchant ships will be treated as
beyond the pale of law and subject to be dealt with
as pirates would be. Armed neutrality is ineffectual
enough at best; in such circumstances and in the
face of such pretensions it is worse than ineffectual:
it is likely only to produce what it was meant to
prevent; it is practically certain to draw us into the
war without either the rights or the effectiveness of
belligerents. There is one choice we cannot make, we
are incapable of making: we will not choose the path
of submission and suffer the most sacred rights of
our Nation and our people to be ignored or violated.
The wrongs against which we now array ourselves
are no common wrongs; they cut to the very roots of
human life.

Line numbers: 80, 85, 90, 95, 100, 105, 110, 115, 120

20. What is the main purpose of this passage?

   (A) to request military and economic sanctions
       against Germany, and condemn Germany
       for its violent actions toward multiple
       European countries
   (B) to condemn Germany for its actions against
       the United States and around the world
   (C) to request the United States to declare
       war on Germany and defend itself against
       Germany
   (D) to condemn the German navy and suggest
       a collaboration with Britain and other
       European countries

21. Which choice provides the best evidence for the
    answer to the previous question?

   (A) Lines 8–16, ("the extraordinary . . .
       Mediterranean")
   (B) Lines 70–75, ("American ships . . . way")
   (C) Lines 81–85, ("Our motive . . . champion")
   (D) Lines 118–121, ("There is . . . violated")

22. As used in line 27, "haphazard" most
    nearly means

   (A) scrupulous
   (B) erratic
   (C) careless
   (D) fastidious

23. What does President Wilson mean by
    "minimum of right" in line 52?

   (A) the right to attack submarines from other
       nations that are scouting around the waters
       owned by America
   (B) the right of access to free highways of the sea
       around the world
   (C) the right to dominate the seas in the vicinity
       of one's own sovereign state
   (D) the right to defend one's own sovereign state
       against attacks from submarines while on
       the free highways of the sea

24. What does the passage suggest about the German navy?

   (A) The Germans like other Axis powers have an attack all policy, where they would attack all enemy fleets.
   (B) The Germans passed an internal policy without negotiating with the Allied powers and enforced their own laws in the seas around their vicinity.
   (C) The Germans passed an internal policy that allowed its navy to attack fleets from all nations.
   (D) The Germans are hostile against all other neighboring countries and did not deliberately attack other submarines.

25. Which choice provides the best evidence for the answer to the previous question?

   (A) Lines 31–34, ("The new . . . bottom")
   (B) Lines 37–44, ("Even hospital . . . principle")
   (C) Lines 67–69, ("The present . . . mankind")
   (D) Lines 93–98, ("German . . . cruisers")

26. As used in line 114, "ineffectual" most nearly means

   (A) inadequate
   (B) ample
   (C) sustenance
   (D) galore

27. What does President Wilson mean by "wholesale destruction" in line 62?

   (A) the warfare and slaughtering of military and ordinary men serving other nations
   (B) the destruction of all merchant goods and merchant ships from other countries
   (C) the demolition of economic relationships and destruction of wholesale goods from the enemy countries
   (D) the carnage of civilians

28. Which choice best summarize the last paragraph of the passage?

   (A) President Wilson calls on the U.S. Congress to make a decision to move from armed neutrality to active defense.
   (B) President Wilson expresses his disappointment in the U.S. Congress for failing to take preventative actions earlier on.
   (C) President Wilson suggests immediate action to protect other nations' rights and to assert domination over Germany.
   (D) President Wilson is looking for feedback and suggestions regarding further actions toward Germany.

29. What does President Wilson mean by "armed neutrality" in line 91?

   (A) to use weapons to defend and dominate
   (B) to remain unbiased and protect oneself with weapons
   (C) protect friendly countries with weapons
   (D) to remain unbiased and armed but not to use the weapons

Questions 30–38 are based on the following passage.

This passage is adapted from Jane Austen's novel Pride and Prejudice *originally published in 1813.*

Instead of receiving any such letter of excuse from his friend, as Elizabeth half expected Mr. Bingley to do, he was able to bring Darcy with him to Longbourn before many days had passed after
5 Lady Catherine's visit. The gentlemen arrived early; and, before Mrs. Bennet had time to tell him of their having seen his aunt, of which her daughter sat in momentary dread, Bingley, who wanted to be alone with Jane, proposed their all walking out.
10 It was agreed to. Mrs. Bennet was not in the habit of walking; Mary could never spare time; but the remaining five set off together. Bingley and Jane, however, soon allowed the others to outstrip them. They lagged behind, while Elizabeth, Kitty, and
15 Darcy were to entertain each other. Very little was said by either; Kitty was too much afraid of him to talk; Elizabeth was secretly forming a desperate resolution; and perhaps he might be doing the same.

They walked towards the Lucases, because
20 Kitty wished to call upon Maria; and as Elizabeth saw no occasion for making it a general concern, when Kitty left them she went boldly on with him alone. Now was the moment for her resolution to be executed, and, while her courage was high, she
25 immediately said:

"Mr. Darcy, I am a very selfish creature; and, for the sake of giving relief to my own feelings, care not how much I may be wounding yours. I can no longer help thanking you for your unexampled kindness
30 to my poor sister. Ever since I have known it, I have been most anxious to acknowledge to you how gratefully I feel it. Were it known to the rest of my family, I should not have merely my own gratitude to express."

35 "I am sorry, exceedingly sorry," replied Darcy, in a tone of surprise and emotion, "that you have ever been informed of what may, in a mistaken light, have given you uneasiness. I did not think Mrs. Gardiner was so little to be trusted."

40 "You must not blame my aunt. Lydia's thoughtlessness first betrayed to me that you had been concerned in the matter; and, of course, I could not rest till I knew the particulars. Let me thank you again and again, in the name of all my family, for
45 that generous compassion which induced you to take so much trouble, and bear so many mortifications, for the sake of discovering them."

"If you will thank me," he replied, "let it be for yourself alone. That the wish of giving happiness to
50 you might add force to the other inducements which led me on, I shall not attempt to deny. But your family owe me nothing. Much as I respect them, I believe I thought only of you."

Elizabeth was too much embarrassed to say a
55 word. After a short pause, her companion added, "You are too generous to trifle with me. If your feelings are still what they were last April, tell me so at once. My affections and wishes are unchanged, but one word from you will silence me on this
60 subject for ever."

Elizabeth, feeling all the more than common awkwardness and anxiety of his situation, now forced herself to speak; and immediately, though not very fluently, gave him to understand that her
65 sentiments had undergone so material a change, since the period to which he alluded, as to make her receive with gratitude and pleasure his present assurances. The happiness which this reply produced, was such as he had probably never felt
70 before; and he expressed himself on the occasion as sensibly and as warmly as a man violently in love can be supposed to do. Had Elizabeth been able to encounter his eye, she might have seen how well the expression of heartfelt delight, diffused over his face,
75 became him; but, though she could not look, she could listen, and he told her of feelings, which, in proving of what importance she was to him, made his affection every moment more valuable.

They walked on, without knowing in what
80 direction. There was too much to be thought, and felt, and said, for attention to any other objects. She

soon learnt that they were indebted for their present
good understanding to the efforts of his aunt, who
did call on him in her return through London,
85 and there relate her journey to Longbourn, its
motive, and the substance of her conversation with
Elizabeth; dwelling emphatically on every expression
of the latter which, in her ladyship's apprehension,
peculiarly denoted her perverseness and assurance;
90 in the belief that such a relation must assist her
endeavors to obtain that promise from her nephew
which she had refused to give. But, unluckily for her
ladyship, its effect had been exactly contrariwise.

"It taught me to hope," said he, "as I had scarcely
95 ever allowed myself to hope before. I knew enough
of your disposition to be certain that, had you been
absolutely, irrevocably decided against me, you
would have acknowledged it to Lady Catherine,
frankly and openly."
100 Elizabeth colored and laughed as she replied,
"Yes, you know enough of my frankness to believe
me capable of that. After abusing you so abominably
to your face, I could have no scruple in abusing you
to all your relations."

30. Which of the following best summarizes the
first paragraph?

(A) The characters meet unexpectedly and go on
a stroll.
(B) The characters have a complex history that
results in increasing anxiety.
(C) The Bennets are calm and separated into
groups.
(D) The characters are hostile toward each other.

31. The main purpose of this passage is to

(A) describe a major change in one character's
attitude toward another
(B) describe the personality flaws of both
characters
(C) illustrate a marriage proposal and
acceptance
(D) illustrate the resolution of a conflict

32. Which choice provides the best evidence for the
answer to the previous question?

(A) Lines 26–27, ("Mr. Darcy . . . feelings")
(B) Lines 28–29, ("I can . . . kindness")
(C) Lines 58–60, ("My affections . . . ever")
(D) Lines 64–65, ("her sentiments . . . change")

33. Which of the following best describes
Elizabeth's feelings toward Darcy?

(A) She feels extremely embarrassed and
ashamed.
(B) She feels thankful for his actions.
(C) She feels prejudice against him.
(D) She feels indifferent toward him.

34. Which choice provides the best evidence for the
answer to the previous question?

(A) Lines 30–32, ("I have . . . it")
(B) Lines 54–55, ("Elizabeth . . . word")
(C) Lines 61–62, ("Elizabeth . . . situation")
(D) Lines 73–74, ("she might . . . face")

35. As used in line 24, "executed" most
nearly means

(A) murdered
(B) assassinated
(C) accomplished
(D) dabbled

36. What event does the passage suggests caused
Elizabeth's change in attitude?

(A) Mr. Darcy was enlightened by Elizabeth.
(B) Elizabeth was more open with her emotions
and could finally express her true feelings.
(C) Elizabeth realizes her selfish ways and is able
to change her attitude.
(D) Mr. Darcy helped Elizabeth and her family.

37. Which choice provides the best evidence for the answer to the previous question?

(A) Lines 33–34, ("I should . . . express")

(B) Lines 40–44, ("Lydia's . . . family")

(C) Lines 94–95, ("It taught . . . before")

(D) Lines 101–102, ("Yes . . . that")

38. As used in line 56, "trifle" most nearly means

(A) humor

(B) toy

(C) gloom

(D) sweep

Questions 39–47 are based on the following passage.

Passage 1 is adapted from "The Islets of Langerhans in Relation to Diabetes" by John Rennie, D.Sc., and Thomas Fraser, M.B., M.A from 1906. Passage 2 is adapted from "Insulin and Diabetes" by J. J. R. Macleod, M.B., Ch.B. from 1922.

PASSAGE 1

Now, this relation between pancreas and diabetes is held by many to depend more particularly upon the epithelial cell groups, commonly termed "islets of Langerhans," which are a characteristic of the
5 pancreas in all vertebrates. These islets have a rich blood supply, and have been held by various writers to be elements sui generis. Comparatively recently the view has been advanced (not for the first time by any means) that they are not a distinct tissue,
10 but simply a phase of ordinary pancreatic tissue. The present is not an appropriate opportunity upon which to discuss the merits of these opposing views; that is reserved for another occasion.

Reference is made to them here simply to clear the
15 ground for what follows. One of us has shown that in Teleostei, at all events, these islets are independent of pancreas proper, and that in several species there exists a particular islet which from its definite position and constancy of occurrence may be termed
20 a "principal islet." This islet is in certain fishes of relatively large size, and this, coupled with the fact that in Aberdeen Fish Market we were able to secure exceptional supplies, particularly throughout the winter months, yielded our opportunity. Numbers
25 of *Lophius piscatorius* and other fishes were obtained

almost daily, and from these the larger islets were cut out and supplied for consumption to patients suffering from diabetes. They were generally given in the form of a boiled extract; in one case considerable
30 quantities were consumed in the raw state. In each case will be found indicated the particular form in which the islet substance was taken.

PASSAGE 2

A preliminary paper on the principal clinical effects was published in March by Banting, Best,
35 Collip, Campbell, and Fletcher, and since that date a sufficient number of cases of all degrees of the disease have now been observed—partly in the clinic of Dr. Banting at the Christie Street Hospital of the Soldiers' Civil Re-establishment in
40 Toronto, partly in the clinic of Professor Duncan Graham in the Toronto General Hospital, and partly in certain diabetic clinics in the United States—to justify the statement that when insulin is administered subcutaneously in adequate dosage
45 it is capable, within a remarkably short time, of removing the cardinal symptoms of the disease for a period of several hours. To suppress the symptoms permanently, however, the injections must be repeated, the practice at present being twice daily. So
50 long as the administration is maintained the patient is able to assimilate much more carbohydrate than previously, and he gains weight and with it both physical and mental vigor, so that the despondency and apathy that are prominent in these cases
55 disappear. Whether the diabetic condition is in

any degree cured by the rest which is given to the damaged pancreatic function by insulin cannot as yet be stated. It is perhaps in the adolescent forms of the disease that these results have been
60 most marked, but there can be no doubt that when insulin comes to be more available its exhibition along with intelligent control of diet will have the same beneficial results in all the serious forms of the disease. In cases of threatened coma its value is
65 undoubted, and this is also the case when it is used as a precautionary measure against post-operative risk in surgical practice. Until the clinical effects have been more thoroughly investigated it would be out of place here to discuss in further detail the
70 therapeutic value of insulin.

39. What does the author of passage 1 state about the islets?

(A) Islets from fish were fed to patients.

(B) Islets from fish cause diabetes.

(C) It is important to study the islets from fish because of the important implication that these islets may cause pancreatitis.

(D) Islets from certain fish species will be able to cure diabetes caused by pancreatic disarray.

40. Which choice provides the best evidence for the answer to the previous question?

(A) Lines 1–4, ("diabetes . . . islets of Langerhans")

(B) Lines 17–20, (in several species . . . principal islet.")

(C) Lines 20–23, ("This islet . . . supplies")

(D) Lines 26–28, ("from these . . . diabetes")

41. As used in line 19, "constancy" most nearly means

(A) irresolution

(B) equivocation

(C) allegiance

(D) steadfastness

42. The author of Passage 2 suggests that

(A) when insulin pills are taken, they permanently alleviate symptoms of diabetes

(B) when insulin pills are taken, they temporarily alleviate symptoms of diabetes in women only.

(C) diabetic patients, when they take insulin, are able to consume more carbohydrates

(D) diabetic patients are unaffected by insulin

43. Which choice provides the best evidence for the answer to the previous question?

(A) Lines 36–37, ("a sufficient . . . observed")

(B) Lines 43–47, ("justify the . . . several hours")

(C) Lines 47–49, ("To suppress . . . repeated")

(D) Lines 49–52, ("So long . . . previously")

44. As used in line 46, "cardinal" most nearly means

(A) peripheral

(B) main

(C) vital

(D) auxiliary

45. What does the author of Passage 2 suggest about the practical application of insulin?

(A) Insulin is not suitable for practical application in the form of pills consumed orally.

(B) Insulin only affects the adolescent form of diabetes.

(C) The clinical effects of insulin need to be tested extensively.

(D) Insulin induces coma and poses a threat to cause pancreatic cancer.

46. Which choice provides the best evidence for the answer to the previous question?

(A) Lines 55–58, ("Whether the diabetic . . . stated")

(B) Lines 58–60, ("It is perhaps . . . marked")

(C) Lines 64–67, ("In cases of . . . practice")

(D) Lines 67–70, ("Until the . . . insulin")

47. Which of the following best describes the relationship between the two passages?

(A) Passage 1 and Passage 2 advocate the same idea, but passage 1 gives more experimental details.

(B) Passage 2 provides a practical application for the scientific development on diabetes introduced by Passage 1.

(C) Passage 2 presents evidence of more advanced science in understanding diabetes than Passage 1.

(D) Passage 2 attacks the scientific evidence presented by Passage 1.

You can check your work only in this section, if you finished ahead of time.

Do not turn to other sections.

WRITING AND LANGUAGE TEST

35 MINUTES, 44 QUESTIONS

Answer the following questions on Section 2 of your answer sheet.

Directions: Each passage is accompanied by questions that ask you to revise or edit the passage to improve its flow, organization, clarity, and sentence mechanics. For most questions, you will be directed to an underlined portion of the passage to either choose "NO CHANGE" or to select the appropriate revision. For other questions, you'll be asked to think about the passage as a whole. Some passages may also include a graphic to consider as you edit.

Questions 1–11 are based on the following passage.

The Black River

From 1755 to 1759, James **1** Smith a frontiersman from Franklin County, Pennsylvania, lived among the Native Americans who had captured him at the age of eighteen. In 1799 his narrative outlining his experiences, "Remarkable Adventures in the Life and Travels of Colonel James Smith," was printed. Unlike accounts from other captives, Smith reported being **2** adopted into the tribe and treated agreeably, learning the customs and ways of Indians from an insider perspective. He described his experiences in an encampment on the Canesadooharie River, where he fished and hunted near waterfalls, remarking that the Indians always allowed him to keep a journal. **3** In the 19th Century, historians believed they'd tracked down Smith's mysterious river. They were wrong. What they had found instead was **4** the Black River: a fifteen-mile-long, tributary of Lake Erie in northern Ohio.

1. (A) NO CHANGE
   (B) Smith, who was a frontiersman
   (C) Smith, a frontiersman,
   (D) Smith, a frontiersman

2. (A) NO CHANGE
   (B) adopted into the tribe, and treated agreeably
   (C) adopted by the tribe, and treated agreeably
   (D) adopted, and treated agreeably, into the tribe,

3. Which choice most effectively combines the underlined sentences?

(A) In the 19th Century, historians were wrong: they incorrectly believed they'd tracked Smith's mysterious river down.

(B) They were wrong in the 19th Century when historians believed they'd tracked down Smith's mysterious river.

(C) In the 19th Century, historians believed they'd tracked down Smith's mysterious river, but they were wrong.

(D) 19th Century historians believed they'd down tracked Smith's mysterious river down finally; and they were wrong.

4. (A) NO CHANGE

(B) the Black River. A fifteen-mile-long tributary

(C) the Black River, a fifteen-mile-long tributary

(D) the Black River a fifteen-mile-long tributary –

Later, historians corrected themselves—Smith must have been held captive near the Huron River. The Black River, which forms in the city of Elyria, Ohio **5** where its east branch and west branch come together and meet, doesn't fit Smith's descriptions because of its twin falls. **6** Known as Cascade Falls, the perpendicular waterfalls form in Elyria where the branches converge, featuring steep shale cliffs over forty feet high. Then, the river meanders through what is now the Lorain County Metro Parks before emptying into Lake Erie.

The 300,000 residents who live within the Black River Watershed might not know that for many years **7** they were mistaken for Smith's home away from home. They might even take for granted the charming duo of falls that has been as much a part of their hometown as the courthouse or the library. **8** And so, nearly all those residents will be able to tell you why the river has its current name. They might even offer another name for the river: Tumor Fish River. In 1985, the Black River was federally designated an Area of Concern after years of industrial and wastewater contamination. The main offender, Lorain Steel, is now closed; but, for many years, the steel mill was responsible for heavy metals and polynuclear aromatic hydrocarbons in the lower part of the river. By the 1980s, the near-black, toxic water had degraded habitats and resulted in a loss of biodiversity. **9**

5. (A) NO CHANGE
   (B) where its east and west branches meet,
   (C) where its east branch meets up with its west branch,
   (D) where the two branches, east and west, meet,

6. Which choice transitions best between the preceding and the following sentence?
   (A) NO CHANGE
   (B) Smith's record told about only one waterfall.
   (C) The Huron River, a one-hundred-and-thirty-mile river in southeastern Michigan, also flows into Lake Erie.
   (D) By surface area, Lake Erie is the fourth largest of the five Great Lakes, but it is actually the smallest by volume.

7. (A) NO CHANGE
   (B) it was a mistake
   (C) she was mistook
   (D) it was mistaken

8. (A) NO CHANGE
   (B) Similarly,
   (C) Yet,
   (D) For instance,

9. At this point, the writer wants to add a sentence that clarifies and concludes the main idea of this paragraph. Which choice best accomplishes this goal?
   (A) Those fish that did manage to survive were often deformed with large tumors protruding from different parts of their bodies.
   (B) The residents that only visit the courthouse and the library, but fail to spend time at Cascade falls, are truly missing out.
   (C) Lorain Steel was directly responsible for an economic boost in the 70s and 80s.
   (D) When the steel mill opened and Lorain's population grew, people relied on the Black River for cheap and convenient food sources.

In response to the river's severe condition, the Black River Remedial Action Plan was founded in 1991 to restore the river. **10** In 2002, the fish were redesignated from "Impaired" to "In Recovery." In 2015, the area of concern was reduced and water quality showed significant improvement. And in 2016, the widespread restriction on fish and wildlife consumption was officially removed. Despite the realization that James Smith never set eyes on it, the Black River has quite a history of its own.

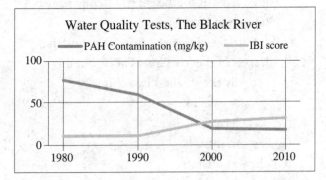

10. The writer is considering adding the following sentence:

> The most dramatic improvements in the biological condition of the Black River occurred during the years between 2000 and 2010.

Should the writer make this change?

(A) Yes, because it adds additional information supported by the graphic.

(B) Yes, because it accurately answers a question the reader might have.

(C) No, because it introduces irrelevant information and distracts the reader.

(D) No, because it is not an accurate interpretation of the graphic.

11. Based on the information given in the passage and the data in the graph, generally, IBI scores:

(A) must stay between 0 and 40

(B) are lower when water quality is higher

(C) are lower when water quality is lower

(D) tell us how deep pollution can be found in a body of water

Questions 12–22 are based on the following passage.

Big Ben

When the iconic clock tower was finished in 12 1859, Big Ben was the biggest, most accurate chiming clock in the world. More formally known as Elizabeth Tower, the clock stands at the north end of the Palace of Westminster and remains the prominent symbol of London and of the United Kingdom as a whole. Films that take place in London often open on one of the four clock faces. For tourists, it is a must see (notwithstanding the fact that the inside is off limits for visitors). For the British, it is a recognizable salute to 13 the nation's renown and resilience. The three-hundred-and-fifteen-foot clock tower, constructed of brick, limestone and cast iron, has a 14 wide interior volume of 164,200 cubic feet, and was originally designed as the focal point of a new palace design after the Westminster fire of 1834.

12. (A) NO CHANGE
    (B) 1859 Big Ben was the biggest most accurate
    (C) 1859, Big Ben was the biggest most, accurate
    (D) 1859 Big Ben was the biggest, most accurate,

13. (A) NO CHANGE
    (B) the nations renown
    (C) the nations' renown
    (D) the nation is renown

14. (A) NO CHANGE
    (B) impressionable
    (C) overwhelming
    (D) staggering

Famous for its reliability, Big Ben has rarely stopped. The steadfast pendulum is an impressive 13 feet long and 660 pounds. **15** Designer, Edmund Beckett Denison, invented a gravity escapement which separates the pendulum from the five-ton clock mechanism. **16** Regardless, the timekeeping is strictly regulated by adding or removing penny coins, which sit atop the pendulum. **17** Because of this stack of coins, the clock's speed can be adjusted by half-seconds. The thirteen-ton bell inside, which first rang out in May 1859, has become the eternal sound of England.

15. (A) NO CHANGE
    (B) Designer Edmund, Beckett Denison
    (C) A designer named Edmund Beckett Denison
    (D) Designer Edmund Beckett Denison

16. (A) NO CHANGE
    (B) Furthermore,
    (C) For example,
    (D) Nevertheless,

17. (A) NO CHANGE
    (B) By adding or subtracting from this stack of coins,
    (C) Using this stack of coins,
    (D) DELETE the underlined portion.

Despite its intricate design and ■18 reputation to accuracy, Big Ben has been interrupted. During WWI and WWII, the clock faces were not illuminated at night so as to avoid guiding enemy bombers. In 1941, a German bombing raid damaged the clock's dials. ■19 In 1949, a flock of birds used Ben's minute hand as a rest stop; consequently, Big Ben ticked four and half minutes behind. On several occasions the clock has slowed or temporarily came to a stop due to heavy snow and ice. Perhaps the most memorable of its freezes occurred on New Year's Eve in 1962 when the clock hands froze over, and the 1963 new year was rung in a full nine minutes late. Until now, Big Ben's only major breakdown occurred in August of 1976 after more than ■20 100 years of use—the clock was down for a total of 26 days that year.

18. (A) NO CHANGE
    (B) reputation for
    (C) having a reputation of
    (D) being reputable when it comes to

19. The writer is considering adding the following sentence:

    Each dial is seven meters in diameter.

    Should the writer make this change?

    (A) Yes, because it restates the main point of the paragraph.
    (B) Yes, because it gives an important detail that is further explained in the following sentence.
    (C) No, because it repeats information.
    (D) No, because it interrupts the flow of the paragraph.

20. (A) NO CHANGE
    (B) 100 year's of use; the clock
    (C) 100 years' of use. The clock
    (D) 100 years of use, the clock

[21] Additionally, 26 days doesn't compare to Ben's impending four years of silence. In early 2017 plans were announced to restore Big Ben. The list of renovations includes cracks in masonry, erosion, rusting, and a lift. The lift will not only comply with health and safety measures in the event of an emergency [22] evacuation, but they will also supply a route to the top of the clock besides the 399 stairs. While the reconstruction is necessary and long overdue, it has been over 150 years since London's been this quiet.

21. (A) NO CHANGE
    (B) Similarly,
    (C) Hitherto,
    (D) However,

22. (A) NO CHANGE
    (B) evacuation—it will,
    (C) evacuation, but it will
    (D) evacuation; but, will

Questions 23–33 are based on the following passage.

Dental Hygienists

You go to the dentist. First, there's an assistant who might take x-rays, update your file, and [23] questions will be asked about any problems you might be having. Lastly, there's the dentist, who examines your mouth and diagnoses, and then treats, any abnormalities, injuries, or diseases. But [24] among the two, there's yet another medical professional, a dental hygienist. Dental hygienists are responsible for cleaning teeth, looking for signs of oral diseases, and educating patients on oral health. And as research continues to link oral health to overall health and the demand for dental services continues to increase, the job outlook for dental hygienists remains [25] promising. [26] Dental hygienists earn an impressive salary in relation to the amount of years they devote to schooling.

23. (A) NO CHANGE
    (B) ask you
    (C) asks you questions
    (D) have questions for you to answer

24. (A) NO CHANGE
    (B) inside
    (C) between
    (D) before

25. (A) NO CHANGE
    (B) bolstering
    (C) arousing
    (D) prominent

26. Which choice best concludes this paragraph?
    (A) NO CHANGE
    (B) In fact, employment of dental hygienists is projected to grow 20 percent in the next decade.
    (C) CODA—the Commission on Dental Accreditation—develops accreditation standards to monitor dental education programs.
    (D) The costs of health care are increasing worldwide.

Unless you are at the dentist for a procedure—like a filling, root canal, extraction, etc.—then most of [27] you're time will be spent with the hygienist. The hygienist not only does the actual cleaning, polishing, and [28] seals the teeth; but also develops the x-rays, assesses oral health, and reports findings to the dentist. It is the hygienist who removes stains and applies fluorides. And in some states, hygienists are permitted to diagnose certain health problems without the direct supervision of a dentist. With so many duties, hygienists need a lot of knowledge and a lot of skills. Understandably, they are well trained—most states require a two-year degree, with four-year degrees becoming more and more common, plus a state licensing test. [29] According to the 2016 Occupational Outlook Handbook, the median annual wage for dental hygienists is [30] over $72,000, with those working in private offices earning more than those in government positions.

27. (A) NO CHANGE
    (B) our
    (C) his or her
    (D) your

28. (A) NO CHANGE
    (B) then the teeth are sealed, but also
    (C) sealing. He or she
    (D) sealing of the teeth, but also

29. The writer is considering adding the following sentence:

    > Moreover, they are well compensated.

    Should the writer make this change?

    (A) Yes, because it transitions into the next idea.
    (B) Yes, because it specifies the requirements of being a hygienist.
    (C) No, because it contradicts information given in the paragraph.
    (D) No, because it is repeats information given in the paragraph.

30. (A) NO CHANGE
    (B) above $72,000; with
    (C) well above $72,000—yet
    (D) over $72,000: with

Considering this, it's good news for those in the field that about 95% of the jobs are in dental offices. Still, it's tough to get a full-time position. Oftentimes dentists hire hygienists only a few days a week, so hygienists usually work **31** under more then one dentist. And the limited number of full-time positions are highly coveted, and thus highly competitive, with the job seekers with previous work experience having a sharp advantage. **32** So this does mean that full-time opportunities aren't guaranteed, and health insurance varies case by case, prospective hygienists shouldn't be deterred. There were more than 200,000 jobs in 2016, and the outlook is expected to grow much faster than average. With more and more people aware of oral health and proactively seeking preventive care, dental hygienists have a bright career outlook **33** for a long time.

31. (A) NO CHANGE
    (B) for more than one
    (C) for more then one
    (D) with one or more

32. (A) NO CHANGE
    (B) Meanwhile
    (C) Likewise
    (D) While

33. (A) NO CHANGE
    (B) into the foreseeable future
    (C) as far as anybody knows
    (D) DELETE the underlined portion.

GO ON TO THE NEXT PAGE ⟼

Questions 34–44 are based on the following passage.

Somewhere, at Some Point

Rarely has ambiguity paid off for someone as well as it paid off for George Lucas, the creator of the *Star Wars* film series who notoriously began his epic space franchise with the words, "a long time ago in a galaxy far, far away." **34** Lucas's first film was released in 1977. It found worldwide acclaim immediately. Lucas leapt at his chance—by 1983, he had **35** a flourishing trilogy. Lucas had given up on a sequel trilogy until the *Dark Empire* comic book series and Timothy Zahn's *Thrawn Trilogy* recommended public interest. With **36** his audience, as large as ever, Lucas told the tragedy of Anakin Skywalker in a three-film prequel, with the final episode, *Revenge of the Sith*, released in 2005. As a result of the criticism surrounding the prequel, Lucas had given up on the idea of a sequel and often denied his original nine-film plan for the series insisting that the story ended with **37** Luke Skywalker, saving the galaxy.

34. Which choice best combines the underlined sentences?

(A) Lucas's acclaimed first film, released in 1977, was immediately worldwide.

(B) Lucas's first film was released in 1977 to immediate worldwide acclaim.

(C) In 1977, Lucas's first film was released and, immediately, it enjoyed worldwide acclaim.

(D) Lucas released his first film in 1977, and then he was immediately acclaimed worldwide.

35. (A) NO CHANGE

(B) a rich

(C) an advantageous

(D) a futile

36. (A) NO CHANGE

(B) his audience—as large as ever—

(C) his audience (as large as ever)

(D) his audience as large as ever,

37. (A) NO CHANGE

(B) Luke Skywalker

(C) Luke Skywalker saving the galaxy

(D) Luke Skywalker: who saves the galaxy

38 Luke Skywalker also redeems his father, making the sixth movie an appropriate place to end the series. In 2008, he produced the animated *Star Wars: The Clone Wars* film. And in 2011, he began working on the final three *Star Wars* films. When Walt Disney acquired Lucasfilm in 2012, the studio **39** officially announced a sequel trilogy. The trilogy begins 30 years after the events of **40** *Return of the Jedi*; for the first installment was released in December 2015. Two more films are expected by December 2019. Fans **41** flock to see *Rogue One* in 2016, wondering where it fit in the series, but it has since been established as a standalone anthology film. As of 2015, the *Star Wars* franchise was valued somewhere around $42 billion. We may not know exactly when or where these space adventures take place, but we know there is an astronomical appetite for them.

38. Which sentence best transitions from the preceding paragraph to the current paragraph?

   (A) NO CHANGE
   (B) George Lucas lost much of his fortune in a divorce.
   (C) The first film was later subtitled *Episode IV: (A)New Hope.*
   (D) But Luke, or rather Lucas, wasn't done yet.

39. Which choice best sets up the remainder of the paragraph?

   (A) NO CHANGE
   (B) spent $4 billion.
   (C) celebrated after a one-and-a-half-year pursuit of George Lucas's empire.
   (D) brought on Lucas as a creative consultant.

40. (A) NO CHANGE
   (B) *Return of the Jedi*, and the
   (C) *Return of the Jedi* yet, the
   (D) *Return of the Jedi*, and—the

41. (A) NO CHANGE
   (B) did flock
   (C) flocked
   (D) have flocked

The film series has spawned the most successful merchandising franchise ever, according to Guinness World Records. From books and television series to video games and theme parks, the universe of *Star Wars* has **42** moved into a cultural phenomenon. And **43** Lucas original vision will manifest in 2019 when the nine-part series is complete. The first of the sequel, the seventh film chronologically, picks up with the demise of the new Jedi Order and a missing Luke Skywalker. *The Force Awakens*, then, is the First Order versus the New Republic, with princess/general Leia leading the Resistance. Kylo Ren, son of Leia and Han Solo turned evil, aspires to be like his grandfather, Darth Vader, and find Luke before the Resistance can. What's to come in episodes VIII and IX is, at this point, speculation at best. What we can be sure of is **44** those happened a long time ago, somewhere far, far away.

42. (A) NO CHANGE
    (B) emerged
    (C) evolved
    (D) retracted

43. (A) NO CHANGE
    (B) Lucas's original visions'
    (C) Lucas' vision is original
    (D) Lucas's original vision

44. (A) NO CHANGE
    (B) that it
    (C) this did
    (D) DELETE the underlined portion.

You can check your work only in this section, if you finished ahead of time.

Do not turn to other sections.

MATH TEST—NO CALCULATOR

25 MINUTES, 17 QUESTIONS

To answer questions in this section turn to Section 3 of your answer sheet.

Directions: Choose the best answer choice for questions 1–13 and fill in the answer sheet accordingly. Solve questions 14–17 and fill in the answer sheet accordingly. Before moving on to question 14 refer to the directions on how to fill in the answers on the answer sheet. Use of available space on the test booklet is allowed.

Notes

1. **No calculator use** is permitted.
2. Unless indicated, variables and expressions represent real numbers.
3. Figures are drawn to scale.
4. Figures lie in a plane.
5. The domain of a function f is the set of all real numbers x where $f(x)$ is a real number.

Reference

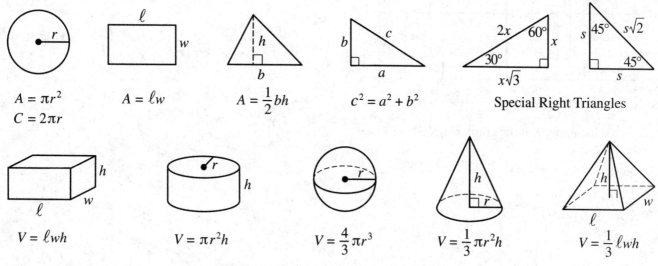

$A = \pi r^2$
$C = 2\pi r$

$A = \ell w$

$A = \frac{1}{2}bh$

$c^2 = a^2 + b^2$

Special Right Triangles

$V = \ell wh$

$V = \pi r^2 h$

$V = \frac{4}{3}\pi r^3$

$V = \frac{1}{3}\pi r^2 h$

$V = \frac{1}{3}\ell wh$

There is a total of 360 degrees in the arc of a circle.

There is a total of 2π radians in the arc of a circle.

There is a total of 180 degrees in the internal angles of a triangle.

GO ON TO THE NEXT PAGE ⟹

1. If $a = \dfrac{33}{16}$, what is the value of b when $\dfrac{a}{8} = \dfrac{9}{b}$?

(A) $\dfrac{6}{11}$

(B) $\dfrac{384}{11}$

(C) $\dfrac{33}{18}$

(D) 297

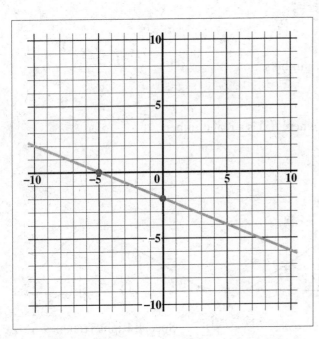

2. What is the slope of the graph above?

(A) $\dfrac{2}{5}$

(B) $-\dfrac{2}{5}$

(C) $\dfrac{5}{2}$

(D) $-\dfrac{5}{2}$

3. A student has a $50 allowance, which she uses to pay for her lunch every day. If her lunch is $4.50 every day, how much does she have left after 5 days of paying for lunch?

(A) $5.00

(B) $22.50

(C) $27.50

(D) $45.50

4. An airplane flew for 8 hours and 32 minutes from France to New York. It left France at 7:33 p.m., and the time in France is 6 hours ahead of New York. What was the time in New York when this plane landed?

(A) 4:05 a.m.

(B) 9:35 a.m.

(C) 10:05 p.m.

(D) 12:35 p.m.

5. What number is halfway between $\dfrac{7}{3}$ and $-\dfrac{12}{5}$?

(A) $-\dfrac{1}{15}$

(B) $-\dfrac{1}{30}$

(C) $-\dfrac{5}{2}$

(D) $\dfrac{19}{8}$

Questions 6 and 7 refer to the following information.

Sally is starting a baking business, and she needs to buy a professional oven for $1,500 and to buy other products to start the business costing another $3,000.

6. If she sells her baked goods for $5 each, how many items must she sell to make money from the business?

   (A) 900
   (B) 324
   (C) 3,000
   (D) 4,500

7. If she sells her baked goods for $6 and is also renting her store for $6,000 per month, how many items must she sell in the first year to cover all the costs of the business and make money from the business?

   (A) 875
   (B) 6,000
   (C) 8,900
   (D) 12,750

8. If $x^{\frac{3}{2}} = 27$, what is x?

   (A) 43.5
   (B) 3
   (C) 19.33
   (D) 9

9. $y = \frac{1}{2}x + 6$

   What is the value of y, when $2x = \frac{1}{2}$?

   (A) $\frac{27}{4}$

   (B) $\frac{1}{6}$

   (C) $\frac{49}{8}$

   (D) 6

10. What is the x intercept of $y = -\dfrac{3x}{4} + 1$?

    (A) $\dfrac{4}{3}$

    (B) $-\dfrac{3}{4}$

    (C) $+1$

    (D) $\dfrac{3}{4}$

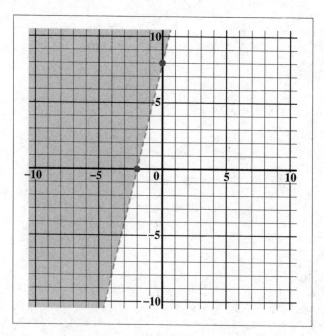

11. The inequality shown in the above graph is which of the following?

    (A) $y \geq 4x + 8$
    (B) $y \leq 4x + 8$

    (C) $y > -\dfrac{1}{4}x + 4$

    (D) $\dfrac{y}{4} > x + 2$

12. $y^{\frac{3}{2}} = ?$

(A) $\dfrac{3y}{2}$

(B) $\sqrt{y^3}$

(C) $\sqrt[3]{y}$

(D) $\dfrac{2y}{3}$

13. May is using a grid to draw a map. She drew a line represented by the equation $y = \dfrac{1}{3}x + 5$. Each unit on the grid is 1 cm long. If she drew two points on the graph $(3, p)$ and $(q, 7)$, how far are these points from each other in cm?

(A) 5

(B) $\dfrac{1}{3}$

(C) $\sqrt{10}$

(D) 11

Directions: Solve questions 14–17 and fill in the answer sheet accordingly. Refer to the following directions on how to fill in the answers on the answer sheet.

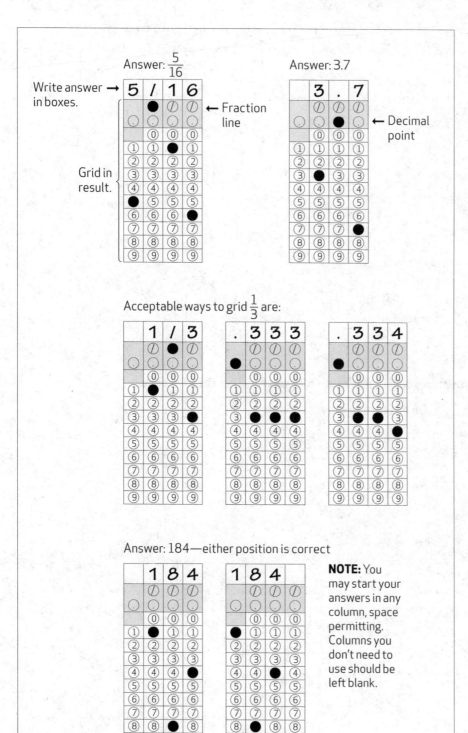

1. Only the filled-in circles are graded. The directions suggest writing the answer in the box at the top, but it is not scored.

2. Fill in only one circle in any column.

3. There are no negative answers.

4. Only fill in one correct answer, even if there are more than one.

5. **Mixed numbers** like $2\frac{1}{2}$ should be filled in as 2.5 or 5/2.

6. **Decimal answers:** If you obtain a decimal answer with more digits, it should be filled in to fill the entire grid.

Answer: 184—either position is correct

NOTE: You may start your answers in any column, space permitting. Columns you don't need to use should be left blank.

14. If $y^2 - 7y + 12 = 0$, what is the bigger of the two solutions of y?

16. If $f(x) = 18$ and $g(x) = x^2 + x - 189$, what is $g(f(x))$?

17. What is the diameter of a circle with the equation of $x^2 - 4x + y^2 + 8y - 29 = 0$?

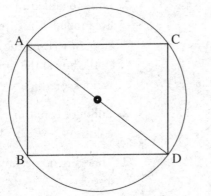

15. In the figure above, if line AB is 6 and the radius is 5, what is the area of rectangle ABCD?

 STOP

You can check your work only in this section, if you finished ahead of time.

Do not turn to other sections.

MATH TEST—CALCULATOR

45 MINUTES, 31 QUESTIONS

To answer questions in this section turn to Section 4 of your answer sheet.

Directions: Choose the best answer choice for questions 1–27 and fill in the answer sheet accordingly. Solve questions 28–31 and fill in the answer sheet accordingly. Before moving on to question 28, refer to the directions on how to fill in the answers on the answer sheet. Use of available space on the test booklet is allowed.

Notes

1. **Calculator use** is permitted.
2. Unless indicated, variables and expressions represent real numbers.
3. Figures are drawn to scale.
4. Figures lie in a plane.
5. The domain of a function f is the set of all real numbers x where $f(x)$ is a real number.

Reference

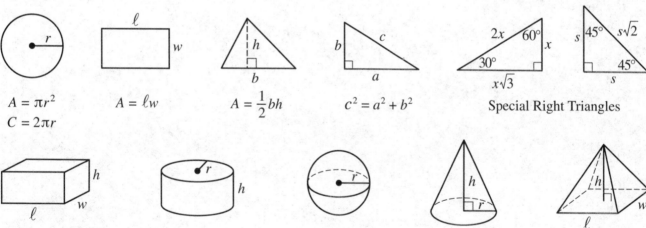

$A = \pi r^2$
$C = 2\pi r$

$A = \ell w$

$A = \dfrac{1}{2}bh$

$c^2 = a^2 + b^2$

Special Right Triangles

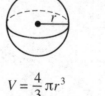

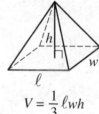

$V = \ell w h$

$V = \pi r^2 h$

$V = \dfrac{4}{3}\pi r^3$

$V = \dfrac{1}{3}\pi r^2 h$

$V = \dfrac{1}{3}\ell w h$

There is a total of 360 degrees in the arc of a circle.

There is a total of 2π radians in the arc of a circle.

There is a total of 180 degrees in the internal angles of a triangle.

GO ON TO THE NEXT PAGE ⟶

1. If $p = \dfrac{11}{24}$, what is the value of q when $\dfrac{q}{22} = \dfrac{3}{p}$?

(A) $\dfrac{1}{4}$

(B) 4

(C) $\dfrac{1,584}{11}$

(D) 144

COLOR OF JELLY BEANS	NUMBER OF JELLY BEANS
Blue	8
Red	11
Green	12
Yellow	13

2. The table above shows the jelly beans in a bag. If a jelly bean is picked out at random, which color will have the likelihood of $\dfrac{1}{4}$ being selected?

(A) yellow

(B) blue

(C) green

(D) red

3. If $\dfrac{7x}{4y} = \dfrac{1}{3}$, then $\dfrac{y}{x} = ?$

(A) $\dfrac{21}{7}$

(B) $\dfrac{21}{4}$

(C) 12

(D) 21

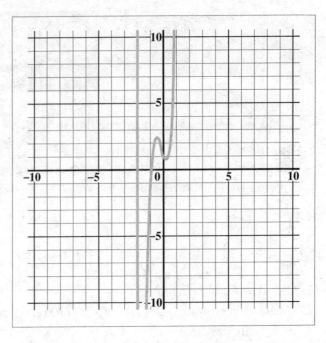

4. The above shows the graph of $f(x)$. What is x when $f(x) = 0$?

(A) 1

(B) –1 and –2

(C) 0

(D) 1 and 3

	CRACKERS	COFFEE	APPLES	SPINACH	CORN	TOTAL
Group A	3	5	5	9	8	30
Group B	7	9	9	18	12	55
Group C	6	3	8	4	4	25

5. A pharmaceutical company is conducting a survey with its 3 study groups to see what foods participants selected after taking a new taste-altering pill that the pharmaceutical company developed. Out of the total number of people in all three groups, what is the fraction of people selecting apples?

   (A) $\dfrac{5}{110}$

   (B) $\dfrac{14}{110}$

   (C) $\dfrac{21}{110}$

   (D) $\dfrac{1}{5}$

6. Sammy is paying off her bills at the end of the month. She starts with $4,600 and uses 25% of the money to pay rent. Then she uses 50% of what is left to pay credit card bills. With the rest of the money, she will put one-fifth into her savings. How much will she have for her savings?

   (A) $345
   (B) $450
   (C) $1,725
   (D) $3,450

7. What is y in terms of x, if $4(4^y) = 4^x$? Note: x and y are positive numbers.

   (A) $y - 1$
   (B) $y + 1$
   (C) $x + 1$
   (D) $x - 1$

8. Which point satisfies both $y > \dfrac{1x}{4} - 3$ and $y < -\dfrac{3x}{4} + 4$?

   (A) $(5, 2)$
   (B) $(2, 2)$
   (C) $(2, -5)$
   (D) $(5, -2)$

9. The price of a house is increased by 30% during a sale. What is the ratio of the increase in price to the new price of the house.

   (A) 1 to 3
   (B) 3 to 13
   (C) 3 to 10
   (D) 1 to 10

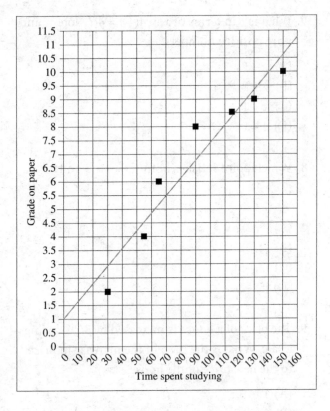

10. A school is conducting a study regarding the amount of time spent studying history and its relationship with the grade on the students' history paper. Which of the following statements is true regarding the graph above?

(A) The slope represents the increase in the amount of time studying as one receives a lower score on the history paper.

(B) The slope represents the decrease in the grade on the students' history paper as students spend more time studying.

(C) The slope represents the increase in the grade on the students' history paper as students spend more time studying.

(D) The slope represents the decrease in the amount of time studying as one receives a higher score on the history paper.

11. If the percentage increase from 9 to x is the same as the percent increase from 4 to 10, what is x?

(A) 14.4

(B) 15

(C) 23

(D) 22.5

12. What is the minimum value of a parabola with the equation $y = (x - 11)^{-2} + 12$?

(A) -12

(B) -11

(C) 11

(D) 12

13. If $7y^2 - 18y = -11$, what is one of the solutions of y?

(A) $-\dfrac{7}{11}$

(B) -1

(C) $\dfrac{1}{7}$

(D) $\dfrac{11}{7}$

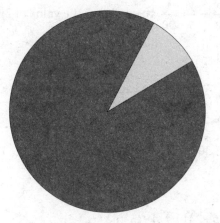

13. A circle has a diameter of 12 and the angle of the shaded region is 330°. What is the perimeter of the shaded region?

(A) 12 + 11π

(B) 30

(C) 12p+ 6

(D) 33π

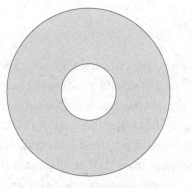

15. If the circumference of the larger circle is 14p and the circumference of the small circle is 8π, what is the area of the shaded region?

(A) 14p

(B) 33π

(C) 64p

(D) 72π

16. Mike and Zach are working together to fill a pool. Mike can fill the pool in 5 hours. Zach can fill the pool in 8 hours. How long would it take for Mike and Zach to fill the pool if they work together? Round to the nearest minute.

(A) 3 hours and 5 minutes

(B) 2 hours and 15 minutes

(C) 4 hours and 55 minutes

(D) 6 hours

17. A yo-yo is swung at the end of a 5.5-inch string. How far does the yo-yo travel in one full circle?

(A) 5.5π inches

(B) 10.5π inches

(C) 11π inches

(D) 25π inches

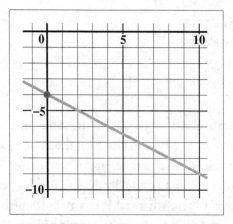

18. In the graph above, where does the line intersect the x axis?

(A) –4

(B) $5\frac{1}{4}$

(C) –8

(D) $-6\frac{1}{2}$

19. If $f(x) = -15$ and $g(x) = |-x^3 + 2x| - x^3$, what is $g(f(x))$?

(A) $-3,120$

(B) $-2,865$

(C) $2,865$

(D) $3,120$

20. How many solutions would the following system of equations have?

$2x + 3y = 2$

$6x + 9y = 6$

(A) 0

(B) 1

(C) 2

(D) more than 2

21. If $f(x) = |-x - x^2| + x^2$, $g(x) = x - x^3$, and $x = -3$, what is $g(f(x))$?

(A) $-3,360$

(B) $-3,375$

(C) 15

(D) 989

22. Sam and Ally both start at the same time to drive from city A to city B on the same route. The cities are 200 miles apart. Sam drives 50 miles per hour, and Ally drives 76 miles per hour. When Ally reaches city B, how much longer will it take Sam to get there? Round your answer to the nearest minute.

(A) 77 min

(B) 82 min

(C) 88 min

(D) 90 min

23. If $\dfrac{x}{2} + \dfrac{y}{5} = \dfrac{1}{30}$, then what is the value of $2y + 5x$?

(A) $\dfrac{1}{3}$

(B) 7

(C) $-\dfrac{1}{30}$

(D) 30

$$\frac{4(p+2)+1}{5} = \frac{4-(5-p)}{2}$$

24. What is the value of p in the equation above?

(A) $\dfrac{13}{3}$

(B) $\dfrac{2}{5}$

(C) $-\dfrac{23}{3}$

(D) 10

25. James has two cylindrical glasses. The first glass has a base with a radius of 11 cm, and the second glass has a base with a radius 6 cm. The first glass has water filled up to 12.5 cm, and the second glass is empty. If James pours one-third of the water from the first glass into the empty glass, the second glass now has water filled up to where?

(A) 14π

(B) 12.5π

(C) 11π

(D) 5π

Questions 26 and 27 refer to the following information.

Andy and Garry are driving from city A to city B. Andy is driving at 80 km per hour. Garry is driving fast for the first $\frac{1}{4}$ of the distance at the speed of 100 km per hour. Then he drives slower for the rest of the trip at the speed of 70 km per hour.

26. Andy starts driving at 10:55 a.m. and needs to be at city B for a meeting. The distance between city A and city B is 300 km, and Andy needs to arrive at 2:15 p.m. How early or late will Andy be?

    (A) 2 hours 45 minutes early
    (B) 1 hour 15 minutes early
    (C) 25 minutes late
    (D) 1 hour 15 minutes late

27. If the distance between city A and city B is 280 km and Garry starts driving at 7:45 p.m., when will Garry get to city B?

    (A) 10:42 p.m.
    (B) 11:27 p.m.
    (C) 12:28 p.m.
    (D) 2:15 p.m.

Directions: Solve questions 28–31 and fill in the answer sheet accordingly. Refer to the following directions on how to fill in the answers on the answer sheet.

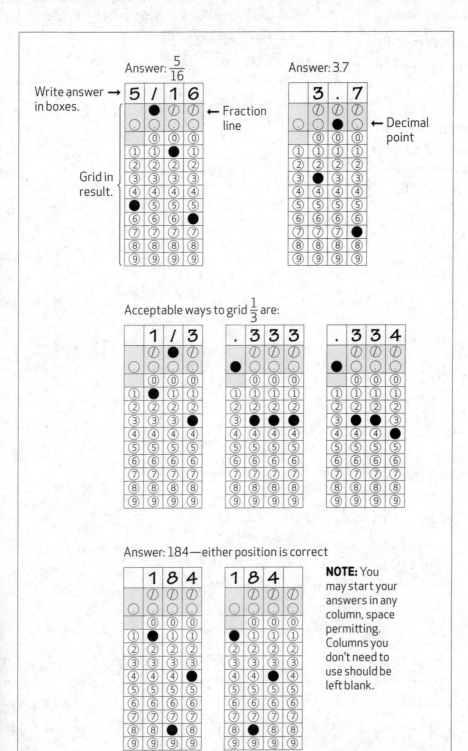

1. Only the filled-in circles are graded. The directions suggest writing the answer in the box at the top, but it is not scored.

2. Fill in only one circle in any column.

3. There are no negative answers.

4. Only fill in one correct answer, even if there are more than one.

5. **Mixed numbers** like $2\frac{1}{2}$ should be filled in as 2.5 or 5/2.

6. **Decimal answers:** If you obtain a decimal answer with more digits, it should be filled in to fill the entire grid.

NOTE: You may start your answers in any column, space permitting. Columns you don't need to use should be left blank.

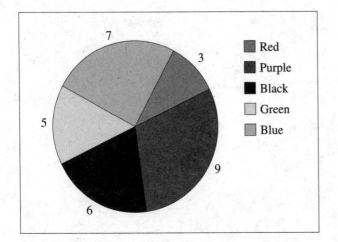

28. Jim bought a box of 30 collectable figurines. There are 3 red ones, 5 green ones, 6 black ones, 7 blue ones, and 9 purple ones. If he sold all of his purple ones to his friend, what percent of the box of figurines does he have left?

29. 30 buckets of paint will finish 45 fences. How many buckets of paint will be needed to finish 15 fences?

Questions 30 and 31 refer to the following information.

A store gets a new shipment of bags to sell in March. On the 10th day of each of the months after March, a bag is marked 15% off until it is 75% off. The original price marked for the bag is $200. The cost of purchasing each bag from the supplier is $35.

30. If a bag is sold on May 8, what is the price that this bag is sold for? Round to the nearest dollar.

31. If a bag is sold on June 12, how much profit is the store making from this bag sold? Round to the nearest dollar.

STOP

You can check your work only in this section, if you finished ahead of time.

Do not turn to other sections.

Practice Test 3 Answer Key

Reading Test

1. **(C)** This is a main idea question. It is clear that in this passage the speech criticizes the prejudice against black people. Therefore, the correct answer is (C). Answer (B) is not detailed enough. Choices (A) and (D) are not supported by the passage.

2. **(C)** The answer to the previous question is best supported by choice (C) because only (C) mentions a resolution that criticizes the prejudice against black people. Choices (A) and (B) express the opposite idea. Choice (D) is incorrect because it is not about supporting the resolution.

3. **(A)** This is a vocabulary question. In the passage "galling" is used to describe inflicting distress and pain. This is supported in lines 29–31, "causes the colored parent as he looks upon his child, to wish he had never been born." Choices (C) and (D) express the opposite and are not correct. Choice (B) is also a negative word but does not fit with the context. Therefore the correct answer is (A).

4. **(A)** This is a detail question. It is clear this passage states that there are advancements in the rights of only the citizens who are not colored citizens. Therefore choice (A) is the correct answer. Choices (B) and (C) are not supported by the passage. Choice (D) is incorrect.

5. **(C)** The answer to the previous question is best supported by choice (C) because only (C) supports that there are advancements in the rights of only the citizens who are not colored. Choices (A), (B), and (D) do not clearly support the answer to the previous question.

6. **(C)** This is a vocabulary question. In the passage "vicinity" is used to describe environment. Choice (B) expresses the opposite idea. Choices (A) and (D) do not fit into the context correctly, even though they express similar meanings. Therefore, the correct answer is (C).

7. **(A)** This is a main idea question. It is clear that in this passage the speech supports that parents of color are worried about the future of their children. Choices (B), (C), and (D) are not supported by the passage.

8. **(B)** Choice (A) is unrelated to colored parents and is not correct. Choice (B) clearly supports that parents of color are worried about the future of their children. Therefore, choice (B) is the correct answer. Choices (C) and (D) do not support the answer to the previous question.

9. **(A)** Choice (A) is the correct answer because it is clearly supported in the passage. Choice (B) is too strong. Choices (C) and (D) are not supported by the passage. Therefore, choice (A) is the correct answer.

10. **(D)** is the correct answer because all the other choices are supported by the passage. The passage mentions that black people are allowed to "walk abroad," but this use of "abroad" means "away from one's home" rather than travel to other nations.

11. **(D)** This is a main idea question. It is clear that in this passage the speech addresses the importance of the women's movement. It is also clear that this is during war times. Therefore, the correct answer is (D). Choice (A) is not directly supported by the passage. Choice (B) is not specific. Choice (C) is incorrect.

12. **(D)** The answer to the previous question is best supported by choice (D) because only (D) addresses the importance of the women's movement in the context of the war. Choices (A), (B), and (C) do not clearly support the answer to the previous question.

13. **(D)** This is a vocabulary question. In the passage "incapacitated" most nearly means debilitated. Choices (B) and (C) express the opposite idea. Choice (A) is less accurate than choice (D). Therefore, choice (D) is the correct answer.

14. **(A)** This is a main idea question. It is clear that in this passage Carrie Chapman Catt thinks America should focus on making changes in light of the end of the war. The passage also discusses women's rights extensively. Therefore, the correct answer is (A). Choices (C) and (D) are not the main focus of the passage. Choice (B) is not supported by the passage.

15. **(B)** The answer to the previous question is best supported by choice (B) because only (B) supports the idea that America should focus on making changes in light of the end of the war. Choices (A), (C), and (D) do not clearly support the answer to the previous question.

16. **(A)** This is a vocabulary question. In the passage "consequences" most nearly means ramifications. Choices (B), (C), and (D) express the opposite idea and are not correct.

17. **(D)** This is a main idea question. It is clear that in this passage the speech focuses on women rights and promotes more human rights. Therefore, the correct answer is (D). Choice (A) and (B)'s details cannot be verified by the passage. Choice (C) is not supported by the passage.

18. **(B)** The answer to the previous question is best supported by choice (B) because only (B) supports that the speech focuses on women's rights and promotes more human rights. Choices (A), (C), and (D) do not clearly support the answer to the previous question.

19. **(C)** This is a main idea question. Choice (C) is the correct answer. Choice (A) and (B) are both too vague, and choice (D) is incorrect.

20. **(C)** This is a main idea question. It is clear that in this passage President Wilson was asking the United States Congress to make a decision. Therefore, answer choice (B) can be eliminated. Also, there is no suggestion to collaborate with European countries, so choice (D) is incorrect. Between choices (A) and (C), choice (C) is the answer because there is no suggestion of economic sanctions.

21. **(D)** The answer to the previous question is best supported by choice (D) because only (D) supports this answer. In choice (D) President Wilson urges Congress not to choose the path of submission. This supports that he is requesting the nation to declare war. Choices (A), (B), and (C) do not clearly support the answer to the previous question.

22. **(C)** This is a vocabulary question. In the passage "haphazard" is used in combination with "meager." This suggests that the precautions were not enough. Choice (C) is the best choice. Choices (A) and (D) express the opposite meaning and are not correct. Between choice (B) and (C), choice (C) is the better choice and is the correct answer.

23. **(B)** This is a detail question. It is clear from the previous sentence that the minimum of right refers to the free highways of the sea. Therefore, answers (A) and (C) can be eliminated. Also, choice (D) can be eliminated because the passage does not support that the minimum right gives nations the right to attack others. Therefore, choice (B) is the correct answer.

24. **(C)** This is a main idea question. This passage clearly supports that Germany passed a new policy that is hostile against other nations. There are no mentions of the Axis powers or the Allied powers, so choices (A) and (B) can be eliminated. The passage also suggests that the Germans deliberately attacked ships. Therefore, choice (D) is also eliminated. The correct answer is (C).

25. **(A)** The answer to the previous question is best supported by choice (A) because only choice (A) supports that the Germans passed an internal policy which allowed attacks on all fleets. Choices (B) and (D) only give details about the policy but do not mention the actual policy and are not correct. Choice (C) is unrelated.

26. **(A)** This is a vocabulary question. In the passage "ineffectual" most nearly means inadequate. Choices (B), (C), and (D) express the opposite idea and are not correct. The correct answer is (A).

27. **(D)** This is a detail question. It is clear that "wholesale" does not refer to wholesale goods, so choices (B) and (C) can be eliminated. Also, the passage suggests that the destruction included all. Therefore, the correct answer is (D).

28. **(A)** This is a summary question. Choices (B) and (D) are not supported by the passage. Choice (C) is too strong. The correct answer is choice (A).

29. **(B)** This is a detail question. It is clear that in this passage that armed neutrality refers to the right to defend oneself while armed. Therefore the correct answer is choice (B).

30. **(A)** This is a summary question. Choice (A) is the correct answer. Choice (C) is not a good summary for the paragraph, and choices (B) and (D) are not supported by the passage.

31. **(C)** This is a main idea question. It is clear that in this passage the most important events are the proposal and the acceptance of this proposal. Although, choice (A) is also a possible answer, choice (C) is the best answer.

32. **(C)** The answer to the previous question is best supported by choice (C) because only (C) supports that the main purpose of the passage is to illustrate a marriage proposal and acceptance.

33. **(B)** This is a main idea question. Choices (C) and (D) are not supported by the passage. Choice (A) is only partially correct and is too strong. Therefore, the best answer is (B).

34. **(A)** The answer to the previous question is best supported by choice (A) because only (A) supports the idea that Elizabeth feels thankful for Darcy's actions. Choices (B), (C), and (D) do not clearly support the answer to the previous question.

35. **(C)** This is a vocabulary question. In the passage "executed" most nearly means accomplished. Choices (A) and (B) are different meanings of the word *executed* and do not fit in the context. Choice (D) expresses the opposite idea and is not correct.

36. **(D)** This is a main idea question. It is clear in the passage that Elizabeth is thankful toward Darcy. The details in the passage further indicate that Elizabeth is thankful because of Mr. Darcy's help toward her family. Therefore, the correct answer is (D).

37. **(B)** The answer to the previous question is best supported by choice (B) because only (B) supports that Elizabeth is thankful because of Mr. Darcy's help toward her family. Choices (A), (C), and (D) do not clearly support the answer to the previous question.

38. (B) This is a vocabulary question. In the passage "trifle" most nearly means toy. Choices (C) and (D) do not express this idea and are not correct. Choice (A) is also a possible choice, but choice (B) is more accurate.

39. (A) This is a detail question. Choices (C) and (D) can be eliminated because the passage does not mention either pancreatic disarray or pancreatitis. Choice (B) is also not supported by the passage. Only (A) is supported by the passage. Therefore, the correct answer is (A).

40. (D) The answer to the previous question is best supported by choice (D). Choice (A) is unrelated to the answer to the previous question. Choices (B) and (C) only provide supplementary evidence and do not directly support the answer from the previous question. Therefore, the answer is (D).

41. (D) This is a vocabulary question. In the passage "constancy" most nearly means steadfastness. Here steadfastness agrees with the word "definite," which is used earlier in the same sentence as the word "constancy." Choices (A) and (B) express the opposite meaning and are not correct. Choice (C) is not accurate in the context of the passage. Therefore, the correct answer is (D).

42. (C) This is a detail question. Choices (A) and (B) can be eliminated because the passage does not mention insulin pills. Choice (B) is also not supported by the passage. Only (C) is supported by the passage. Therefore, the correct answer is (C).

43. (D) The answer to the previous question is best supported by choice (D). Choice (A) is unrelated to the answer to the previous question. Choices (B) and (C) only provide supplementary evidence and do not directly support the answer from the previous question. Therefore, the answer is (D).

44. (B) This is a vocabulary question. In the passage "cardinal" most nearly means main because only "removing the main symptoms" would work in this sentence. Choices (A) and (D) express the opposite meaning and are not correct. Choice (C) is not accurate in the context of the passage. Therefore, the correct answer is (B).

45. (C) This is a detail question. Choice (A) can be eliminated because the passage does not mention insulin pills. Choice (B) is also not supported by the passage. Choice (D) can also be eliminated because the passage does not mention pancreatic cancer. Only (C) is supported by the passage. Therefore, the correct answer is (C).

46. (D) The answer to the previous question is best supported by choice (D). Choice (A) is unrelated to the answer to the previous question. Choices (B) and (C) only provide supplementary evidence and do not directly support the answer from the previous question. Therefore, the answer is (D).

47. (C) The answer choice that best describes the relationship between the two passages is choice (C). Passage 2 presents evidence of more advanced science in understanding diabetes than passage 1 by presenting evidence of understanding what suppresses the disease. Choice (A) is not correct because neither claim is true. Choice (B) is not supported by the passages, and choice (D) is too strong.

Writing and Language Test

1. **(D)** Since the passage gives a specific name, any other information becomes extra and is, therefore, surrounded by commas, making (D) correct. (A) doesn't include punctuation at all. (B) adds unnecessary words. (C) breaks up "a frontiersman from Franklin County" with an extra comma.

2. **(A)** This is correct as is. Smith reported both these things, so they do not need to be split up with a comma as in (B), (C), and (D). The comma after "agreeably," however, is needed because it separates the independent clause from the dependent clause and provides a necessary pause.

3. **(C)** Don't overthink this. These two sentences are related and can be combined with a comma conjunction. Since there is a contrasting relationship, "but" is effective, making (C) correct. (A) illogically makes it sound as if historians were all wrong for the entire nineteenth century. (B) sounds awkward, and who "they" are is unclear. (D) uses a semicolon where a comma should be and uses "and" where "but" or "yet" is more accurate.

4. **(C)** Eliminate (A) because there shouldn't be a comma between "long" and "tributary." Eliminate (B) because it forms a fragment. Eliminate (D) because it doesn't use any punctuation between "Black River" and its description, and then uses a dash, or hard pause, right in the middle of an idea. (C) is what's left, and it's correct.

5. **(B)** Remember to be concise. (A) and (C) are wordy. (D) is difficult to read because of all the excess punctuation.

6. **(A)** This is a difficult question. The preceding sentence introduces the idea that the Black River begins at a set of two waterfalls. The following sentence tells the reader where the Black River ends. To transition between these ideas, there must be a sentence discussing the falls or describing the features of the river before it empties into Lake Erie, making (A) correct. (C) and (D) present new topics or go off topic to give irrelevant information. (B) may be appealing since the previous sentence talks about Smith, but it fails to connect it to the following sentence.

7. **(D)** First, decide what the subject is. What was mistaken? The river. So, the proper pronoun is "it." Eliminate (B) because it's inaccurate and doesn't flow well with the sentence.

8. **(C)** For transition words, establish the relationship between the sentences. The writer is talking about things the residents might not know and then something they definitely know—so the writer is making a contrast. (A) is cause and effect. (B) is for something alike or similar. (D) is for giving examples.

9. **(A)** First, notice that the paragraph's main point is about the local name for the Black River and the circumstances that earned it its name. (B), (C), and (D) expound upon details from the passage but fail to reference the pollution problem and the effect on wildlife.

10. **(D)** According to the graph, the contamination decreased most dramatically between 1990 and 2000, so the information given in the sentence is inaccurate, making (D) the correct choice.

11. **(C)** Even without knowing what IBI stands for, its relationship to contamination is clear in the graph. As contamination decreases, IBI increases. It must have something to do with quality of the water. Hence, when contamination is high and water quality is low, IBI is low. When contamination is low and water quality is high, IBI increases.

12. **(A)** This is correct as is. First, notice that you need the comma after 1859 to separate the dependent clause (fragment) from the independent clause (complete thought). Since these adjectives can be switched around, they do need to be separated by a comma, but there is no need for a comma after "most accurate" as well. And you definitely don't want to pause between "most" and "accurate" since that's one idea.

13. **(A)** This is correct as is. The "renown" and "resilience" refer back to the nation; they belong to the nation, so speak. (B) doesn't show ownership because there is no apostrophe. (C) refers to many nations, but the clock is only in one nation. And (D) changes the meaning of the sentence.

14. **(D)** "Staggering" is the best word choice here since it means it is an astonishing size. Volume is the amount of space the clock occupies, and is three dimensions, so width alone, as in (A), isn't appropriate. (B) means trusting or easily influenced. (C) means large to the point of being overpowering.

15. **(D)** No commas here. If we add commas around the name it signifies that we could read the sentence without the name, but "designer" is too vague for that. And it is inaccurate to break up the name as in (B). (C) has unnecessary words.

16. **(B)** Look at the context. The paragraph is giving evidence for Big Ben's reliability. An additional reason is its regulation via penny coins, so "furthermore" is appropriate. (A) and (D) are like "despite" and can be eliminated because they do the same thing. (C) can be eliminated because we are not giving an example but instead introducing further support.

17. **(C)** Be concise when possible. (A) is vague, and (B) is wordy because the sentence before gives this information. (D) removes necessary information from the sentence.

18. **(B)** Big Ben has a reputation "for" accuracy, making (B) the correct choice. It doesn't have a reputation "to" accuracy; (C) isn't parallel; (D) is wordy.

19. **(D)** For these, ask what the sentence does. Here, it gives a detail about the size of the clock's dials. While the information is relevant to the topic, it breaks up a list of breakdowns or mishaps and so interrupts the flow. If this information was included in the passage, it should be in the beginning when the writer is describing the clock in detail.

20. **(A)** This is correct as is. Here, there are two complete sentences. They can be separated by a dash, a semicolon, or a period. However, "years" is just plural; it does not need an apostrophe because it doesn't show ownership.

21. **(D)** For transition words, check the sentence before and the current sentence. Right before this, the writer was discussing 26 days that the clock wasn't working properly. In this sentence, the writer is comparing that downtime to four years. Since this is a contrast, "however" is the appropriate choice.

22. **(C)** Eliminate (A) because the subject is "the lift," so "they" is not an appropriate pronoun. Eliminate (B) because no comma is needed after "it will." Eliminate (D) because the semicolon is used to separate two complete sentences, and since the subject, "it," is removed from the second part, it is no longer a complete sentence. (C) separates two complete sentences with a comma and conjunction and so is correct.

23. **(B)** Be consistent and parallel. "Take x-rays," "update your file," and "ask you about any problems" is the only choice that makes this sentence parallel.

24. **(C)** Here, the writer literally means you see the hygienist after the assistant and before the dentist, so "between" them. "Among" is used for more than two things (split the cookies between the two children, or among three children). (B) and (C) are awkward and inaccurate.

25. **(A)** This is correct as is. Here, the writer means that the job outlook is favorable, so "promising" is the correct choice. (B) is a verb meaning to reinforce. (C) is a verb meaning awakening or triggering. (D) means important or famous.

26. **(B)** Ask yourself what this paragraph is about. It introduces the profession of a dental hygienist and then establishes it as a field with good prospects. Therefore, look for the answer choice that supports this idea and it will lead you to (B), evidence for the previous sentence. While (A), (C), and (D) might all be true, they introduce seemingly new ideas instead of wrapping up the ideas in this paragraph.

27. **(D)** "Your" shows possession. "You're" means "you are." Eliminate (B) and (C) because the beginning of the sentence is in second person and you want to maintain consistency.

28. **(D)** This question tests parallelism and punctuation. First, notice that to be consistent with "cleaning" and "polishing," the writer should use "sealing." Then, eliminate (C) because there are not two complete sentences here.

29. **(A)** Here, the writer transitions from education and training to wages, so this sentence is needed to orient the reader. It does not go into any requirements of being a hygienist, so eliminate (B).

30. **(A)** This is correct as is. Here, the comma separates an independent clause and a dependent clause, adding a needed pause. Eliminate (B) because there are not two complete sentences. Eliminate (C) because "yet" makes the sentence sound awkward. Eliminate (D) because the colon is used before a clarification or list.

31. **(B)** When comparing things of a greater number or degree, use "more than." This rule alone allows us to eliminate (A) and (C). (D) doesn't work because "dentist" would have to be plural.

32. **(D)** This indicates a contrast like "although," so "while" is the correct answer. (A) incorrectly indicates a cause and effect. (B) means at the same time and is used like "simultaneously." (C) is used like "also" to transition into a point similar to the one just made.

33. **(D)** Be concise when you can. (A), (B), and (C) are all vague and doing the same thing—eliminate them. The sentence is fine without the underlined portion.

34. **(B)** Eliminate (A) because it breaks up "worldwide" and "acclaim" to the point that the sentence doesn't make sense. Eliminate (C) because it is wordy with unnecessary punctuation. Eliminate (D) because it changes the meaning of the sentence. (B) is clear and concise.

35. **(A)** Here, the writer means that the trilogy was successful and thriving, so "flourishing" is appropriate. The trilogy itself was not wealthy as in (B). (C) means favorable or beneficial, which is too mild here. (D) means pointless and doesn't make sense here.

36. **(D)** This is one idea that doesn't need to be broken up. There does, however, need to be a comma after "ever" to separate the dependent clause (fragment) from the independent clause (complete sentence).

37. **(C)** Eliminate (A) because we don't need to pause here. (B) loses information. And (D) doesn't work because colons are used after complete ideas before a clarification or list.

38. **(D)** Ask yourself what the last paragraph ended with and what this paragraph discusses. The last paragraph ends with the idea that Lucas insisted the series was done after six films. This paragraph is about Lucas continuing to write and produce other films. So, we are looking for a sentence that links the two ideas. The only option that transitions to Lucas continuing his work is (D).

39. **(A)** The sentences following this one give details on the sequel trilogy, so this is correct as is. (B), (C), and (D) don't mention the trilogy.

40. **(B)** Here, we have two complete sentences that are connected. The sentences do not show cause and effect, so "for" isn't appropriate. The sentences do not show contrast, so "yet" isn't appropriate. That leaves us with (B) and (D). The dash in (D) is unnecessary.

41. **(C)** The subject is "fans," and the sentence is past tense, making (C) the correct choice.

42. **(C)** Here, the writer uses other *Star Wars* merchandise to show how the franchise has grown or expanded, so "evolved" is the correct choice. It didn't relocate as in (A). (B) is appealing but means to appear or materialize. (D) means to take back or be drawn in.

43. **(D)** Here, the original vision belongs to Lucas, so there needs to be an apostrophe. (B) has an unnecessary apostrophe on "vision." (C) makes Lucas plural and has more words than needed.

44. **(B)** Trust your instinct here. The writer is talking about "what's to come," so we can be sure "that it happened."

Math Test—No Calculator

1. **(B)** This is a fraction question. First, plug the value of a into the equation to get $\frac{33}{16} \div 8 = \frac{9}{b}$. Then, simplify to get $\frac{33}{128} = \frac{9}{b}$. Then, cross multiply to get: $33b = 1,152$. The answer will be $b = \frac{384}{11}$.

2. **(B)** This is a simple graphing question. To find the slope find the rise and run, rise is -2, and run is 5. Therefore the slope is $-\frac{2}{5}$.

3. **(C)** This is a simple word problem. Find out how much money the student needs to pay for the 5 days of lunch: $4.50 \times 5 = $22.50. Then take $22.50 away from the $50 allowance that the student has: $50 − $22.50 = $27.50. Choice (B) is a trick answer; it is only the cost of lunch for the 5 days.

4. **(C)** This is a word problem. First, find out what time it is when the plane landed in France: 7:33 p.m. + 8 hours and 32 minutes= 4:05 a.m. of the next day. Then because France is 6 hours ahead, take away 6 hours to get to the New York time when the plane landed: 4:05 a.m. – 6 hours = 10:05 p.m.

5. **(B)** This is a simple fraction question. Add the two fractions: $\frac{7}{3} + (-\frac{12}{5}) = \frac{(7)(5)}{(3)(5)} - \frac{(12)(3)}{(5)(3)} = \frac{35}{15} - \frac{36}{15} = -\frac{1}{15}$. Then divide by 2 to get the answer for this question: $-\frac{1}{15} \div 2 = -\frac{1}{30}$.

6. **(A)** This is a multistep word problem. First, find the total cost of the running the business, $1,500 + $3,000 = $4,500. Then divide $4,500 by $5 to get the number of baked goods she must sell to make money from the business, $4,500 ÷ $5 = 900.

7. **(D)** This is a multistep word problem. First, find the total cost of the running the business without the rent, $1,500 + $3,000 = $4,500. Then, find the cost of the rent for the year, $6,000 × 12 = $72,000. Add the cost without the rent and the cost of the rent to get the total cost for the first year. $4,500 + $72,000 = $76,500. Then divide $76,500 by $6 to get the number of baked goods she must sell to make money from the business, $76,500 ÷ $6 = 12,750.

8. **(D)** This is a question about exponents. $x^{\frac{3}{2}} = 27$. First cube root both sides of the equation. $\sqrt[3]{x^{\frac{3}{2}}} = \sqrt[3]{27}$. Then the equation becomes $x^{\frac{1}{2}} = 3$. Then square both sides of the equation and get: $\left(x^{\frac{1}{2}}\right)^2 = (3)^2$. Then the answer will be 9 because $x = 9$.

9. **(C)** This is an algebra question. First, find the value of x, $x = \frac{1}{4}$. Then plug x into the equation to solve for y, $y = \frac{1}{2}(\frac{1}{4}) + 6$; $y = \frac{1}{8} + 6$; $y = \frac{49}{8}$.

10. **(A)** This is a simple graphing question. The x intercept is when $y = 0$, so plug 0 in for y. $0 = -\frac{3x}{4} + 1$. Take away 1 on both sides, $-1 = -\frac{3x}{4}$. Then multiply both sides by -4, $4 = 3x$. Then divide both sides by 3, $\frac{4}{3} = x$. The x intercept is $\frac{4}{3}$.

11. **(D)** This is a graphing question. Use the equation of the straight line, $y = mx + b$, to find the equation for the line in the graph. First, find the slope by looking at the rise over run. The rise here is 4 and run is 1. The slope is 4. Then look at the y intercept to find b, which is 8. The equation for the line is $y = 4x + 8$. Then because it is a dashed line with a shaded area, the inequality shown is $y > 4x + 8$. Because is $y > 4x + 8$ is not one of the answer choices, convert the equation by dividing both sides by 4 to get $\frac{y}{4} > x + 2$.

12. **(B)** This is a question about exponents. $y^{\frac{3}{2}} = \sqrt{y^3}$.

13. **(C)** This is a linear equation and Pythagorean question. First, plug the number into the equation to solve for p, $p = \frac{1}{3}(3) + 5$; $p = 6$. Second, plug the number into the equation to solve for q, $7 = \frac{1}{3}q + 5$; $2 = \frac{1}{3}q$; $q = 6$. Find the distance between the y coordinates, $7 - 6 = 1$. Find the distance between the x coordinates, $6 - 3 = 3$. Then use $a^2 + b^2 = c^2$ to solve for the distance between the two points, $3^2 + 1^2 = 10$, $c = \sqrt{10}$. Then find the answer, $\sqrt{10} \times 1$ cm = $\sqrt{10}$ cm.

14. **4** This is a simple algebra question. The first step is to factor this question. $(y - 3)(y - 4) = 0$. Then, solve for y, $y = 3$, $y = 4$. The answer is 4.

15. **48** This is a medium difficulty geometry question. To find the area of ABCD, first find the length of AD, 5 × 2 = 10. Then find the length of BD. Recognize that triangle ABD is a special triangle of 3 to 4 to 5. Use this ratio to find that BD is 8. Then find the area of rectangle ABCD is 8 × 6 = 48.

16. 153 This is a medium algebra question. If $f(x) = 18$, 18 can be plugged into $g(f(x))$. $g(f(x)) = g(18) = (18)^2 + (18) - 189 = 324 + 18 - 189 = 153$

17. 14 First, rearrange the equation, $x^2 - 4x + y^2 + 8y = 29$. Then, change the equation to enable completing the square, $x^2 - 4x + 4 + y^2 - 8y + 16 = 29 + 4 + 16$. Then, change the equation to complete the square, $(x - 2)^2 + (y - 4)^2 = 7^2$. Because the equation of the circle is $(x - a)^2 + (y - b)^2 = r^2$, the radius is 7. The diameter is 14.

Math Test—Calculator

1. (C) This is a fraction question. First, plug the value of p into the equation to get $\dfrac{q}{22} = 3 \div \dfrac{11}{24}$. Then, get $\dfrac{q}{22} = 3 \times \dfrac{24}{11}$. Simplify to get $\dfrac{q}{22} = \dfrac{72}{11}$. Multiply both sides by 22 to get:
$$q = \frac{1,584}{11}$$

2. (D) This is a simple problem about probability. First, add the number of jelly beans together, $8 + 11 + 12 + 13 = 44$. Then find out what is $\dfrac{1}{4}$ of 44, $44 \times \dfrac{1}{4} = 11$. The answer is red.

3. (B) This is a simple algebra question. First, flip both sides of the equation to get $\dfrac{4y}{7x} = \dfrac{3}{1}$. Then multiply both sides of the equation by $\dfrac{7}{4}$ to get the answer. The answer is $\dfrac{21}{4}$.

4. (B) This is a simple question about functions. Find the point on the function where $y = 0$. When $y = 0$, $x = -1$ and -2.

5. (D) This is a simple statistics question. First, find the total number of people, $30 + 55 + 25 = 110$. Then find the total number of people who selected apples, $5 + 9 + 8 = 22$. Then, find the fraction, $\dfrac{1}{5}$.

6. (A) This is a word problem about percentages. First, find out how much she has left after rent, $\$4,600 \times 75\% = \$3,450$. Then find out how much is left after she pays her bills, $\$3,450 \times 50\% = \$1,725$. Then divide by 5 to get the answer, $\$1,725 \div 5 = \$345$.

7. (D) This is an exponent question. This question needs the exponents to be manipulated. The power of the same number can be added or subtracted. Therefore, $4(4^y) = 4^x$ is the same as $4^{y+1} = 4^x$. Because the base of the equation is 4 and the two sides equal, $y + 1 = x$. The question asks to express y in terms of x, so $y = x - 1$.

8. (B) This is a simple inequality question. To see which points satisfies both equations, plug each of the points into both equations and find the point that satisfies both equations. For example, plug (2, 2) into the first equation: $2 > \dfrac{1(2)}{4} - 3$ and get $2 > -2.5$. This means that the point satisfies the first equation. Next plug (2, 2) into the second equation: $2 < -\dfrac{3(2)}{4} + 4$ and get $2 < 5.5$. This means that the point also satisfies the second equation. Another way of solving this question is to graph out the two equations and see which points satisfy both equations.

9. (B) This is a medium difficulty question about percent and ratios. Use an arbitrary number like 100 to start the calculation. If 100 is increased by 30%, then the new price is 130. Therefore the ratio is 30 to 130, 3 to 13.

10. (C) This is a data analysis question. The graph shows that as a person spends more time studying, he or she will have a higher score on his or her history paper. The x value is the amount of time and y value is the score on the paper. Therefore the answer is (C).

11. **(D)** This is a medium difficulty percent question. First, find the percent increase from 4 to 10, $10 \div 4 \times 100\% = 250\%$. Then multiply 9 by 250%, $9 \times 250\% \div 100\% = 22.5$.

12. **(D)** This is simple parabola question. The equation of a parabola is $y = (x - a)^2 + b$, where (a, b) is the vertex and a is also the axis of symmetry. Here the minimal value of the equation is 12.

13. **(D)** This is a medium algebra question. First set the equation to 0, $7y^2 - 18y + 11 = 0$. Then factor the equation, $(7y - 11)(y - 1) = 0$. Solve for y, $y = \frac{11}{7}, y = 1$.

14. **(A)** This is a medium circle question. First, find the radius, $12 \div 2 = 6$. Then find the circumference of the circle, $2p6 = 12\pi$. Find the ratio of the shaded region to the circle $330° \div 360° = \frac{11}{12}$. Then find the arch of the shaded area, $12p \times \frac{11}{12} = 11\pi$. Then add the sides to find the circumference, $11\pi + 6 + 6 = 12 + 11\pi$.

15. **(B)** This is a medium difficulty geometry question. Solve for the area of the larger circle. First find the radius, $14p \div 2\pi = 7$. Then find the area of the large circle $7^2\pi = 49\pi$. Solve for the area of the smaller circle. First find the radius $8p \div 2\pi = 4$. Then find the area of the smaller circle, $4^2\pi = 16\pi$. Then find the area of the shaded region, $49p - 16\pi = 33p$.

16. **(A)** This is a speed problem. First find the amount of pool that Mike can fill in one hour, 1 pool $\div$ 5 hours = 1 pool/5 hours. Then find the amount of pool that Zach can fill in one hour, 1 pool $\div$ 8 hours = 1 pool/8 hours. Then add the amounts together: $\frac{1}{5} + \frac{1}{8} = 0.2 + 0.125 = 0.325$ pool/hour. Then find how long it takes for Mike and Zach to fill the pool if they work together, 1 pool $\div$ 0.325 pool/hour = 3.07 hours = 3 hours + .07 hours $\times \frac{60 \text{ min}}{1 \text{ hour}}$ = 3 hours and 5 minutes.

17. **(C)** This is a geometry question. If the length of the string is 5.5 inches, then the radius of the circle will be 5.5 inches. Next just calculate the circumference, which is $2\pi \text{ (radius)} = 2 \times 5.5\pi = 11\pi$ inches.

18. **(C)** This is a graphing question. Use the equation of the straight line, $y = mx + b$, to find the equation for the line in the graph. First, find the slope by looking at the rise over run. The rise here is –1 and run is 2. The slope is $-\frac{1}{2}$. Then look at the y intercept to find b, which is –4. The equation for the line is $y = -\frac{1}{2}x - 4$. Then to find where the line intersects the x axis plug in $y = 0$, $0 = -\frac{1}{2}x - 4$. Solve to find the x value, $0 = -x - 8$; $8 = -x$; $x = -8$. The answer is –8.

19. **(A)** This is an algebra question. Since $f(x) = -15$, we can put –15 into $g(f(x))$. $g(f(x)) = g(-15) = |-(-15)^2 + 2(-15)| - (-15)^3 = |-225 - 30| - 3,375 = 255 - 3,375 = -3,120$.

20. **(D)** This is a system of equations question. This question tests the student's knowledge about the system of equations. When the two equations can be derived from each other there will be more than two solutions to the equation. (If we multiply $2x + 3 = 2$ by 3 we will get $6x + 9 = 6$.)

21. **(A)** This is a difficult algebra question. If $f(x) = |-x - x^2| + x^2$, and $x = -3$, then $f(x) = |-(-3) - (-3)^2| + (-3)^2$. Here $f(x) = |3 - 9| + 9 = |-6| + 9 = 15$. Then 15 can be plugged into $g(f(x))$. $g(f(x)) = x - x^3 = 15 - (15)^3 = 15 - 3,375 = -3,360$.

22. **(B)** This is a word problem. This question is difficult and requires multiple steps. If Ally and Sam start at the same time, by the time Ally reaches city B it would have already taken 2.63 hours (200 miles ÷ 76 miles per hour = 2.63 hours). We can use this 2.63 hours to find how much of the 200 miles Sam has already driven (2.36 hours × 50 miles per hour = 131.57 miles). Using this we can then find out how much more Sam has to drive (200 miles – 131.57 miles = 68.43 miles). Then we can find out how much longer it is going to take Sam to drive to city B (68.43 miles ÷ 50 miles per hour = 1.36 hours). Now as a final step we can convert this into minutes because we see that all of the answer choices are in minutes and round the answer (1.36 hours × 60 minutes = 82 min). The correct answer is thus (B).

23. **(A)** This is a difficult algebra question. Modify $\frac{x}{2} + \frac{y}{5} = \frac{1}{30}$ until it looks like $2y + 5x$ to get the answer, $10\left(\frac{x}{2} + \frac{y}{5}\right) = 5x + 2y = 2y + 5x = \frac{1}{30} \times 10$. The answer is $\frac{1}{30} \times 10 = \frac{1}{3}$.

24. **(C)** This is a difficult algebra question. First, simplify $\frac{4(p+2)+1}{5} = \frac{4-(5-p)}{2}$; $\frac{4p+9}{5} = \frac{-1+p}{2}$. Then, multiply both sides by a common denominator, $10 \times \frac{4p+9}{5} = 10 \times \frac{-1+p}{2}$; $2 \times (4p+9) = 5(p-1)$; $8p + 18 = 5p - 5$. Then solve for p, $3p = -23$; $p = -\frac{23}{3}$.

25. **(A)** This is a difficult word problem. First, find the volume of the water in the first glass by using the formula for the volume of a cylinder, $\pi(11)^2 \times 12.5 = 1{,}512.5\pi$. Then, find one-third of the volume by dividing $1{,}512.5\pi$ by 3 to get 504.17π. Then find the height of the water by using the formula for the volume again, $504.17\pi \div \pi(6)^2 = 14\pi$.

26. **(C)** This is a multistep word problem. First find out how long it will take for Andy to drive. Andy is driving at 80 km/hr, so it takes 3.75 hours for him to get to city B (300 km ÷ 80 km per hr = 3.75 hr; 3 hours and 45 minutes). Then find out when Andy will arrive: 10:55 a.m. + 3 hours 45 minutes = 2:40 p.m. Andy will arrive 25 minutes late for the 2:15 p.m. meeting (2:40 p.m. – 2:15 p.m. = 25 minutes).

27. **(B)** This is a multistep word problem. To find the time it takes for Garry, first find the time it takes for the first $\frac{1}{4}$ of the distance. This first $\frac{1}{4}$ of the distance is: 280 km $\times \frac{1}{4} = 70$ km. It took him 42 minutes for the first $\frac{1}{4}$ of the distance (70 km ÷ 100 km per hr = 0.7 hr; 0.7 hr × 60 minutes per hour = 42 minutes). Then, find the time it takes for the rest of the distance. This rest of the distance is $\frac{3}{4}$ of the distance, which is: 280 km $\times \frac{3}{4} = 210$ km. It took him 3 hours for the rest of the distance (210 km ÷ 70 km per hr = 3hr). It takes Garry 3 hours 42 minutes of total driving time. The arrival time will be 11:27 p.m. (7:45 p.m. + 3 hours 42 minutes = 11:27 p.m.).

28. **70** This is a data analysis question. First, find the number of figurines he sold to his friend, which is 9. Then find what percent of the box 9 is, 9 ÷ 30 × 100% = 30%. If he sold 30% of the box, then he has 70% of the box left.

29. **10** This is a word problem about proportions. Set up the equation to solve for the number of buckets of paint that will be needed to finish 15 fences, $\frac{30 \text{ buckets}}{45 \text{ fences}} = \frac{x \text{ buckets}}{15 \text{ fences}}$. Solve the equation by simplifying the fractions and cross multiplying to find that 10 buckets will be needed to finish 15 fences.

30. **170** This is a medium level word problem. First find the number of markdowns. There is one markdown on April 10. Take 15% off the price of the bag, $200 × 85% = $170.

31. 88 This is a medium level word problem. First find the number of markdowns. There is one markdown on April 10, one markdown on May 10, and one markdown on June 10. So take 15% off three times from $200. $200 × 85% × 85%× 85% = $122.82. Then take away the cost to get the profit the store made from this bag, $122.82 – $35 = 87.82, which rounds to $88.

Acknowledgments

I would like to thank those who have supported me personally and professionally throughout this project. Thank you to my parents Jing Zou and Long Ming Wang, who are my biggest supporters. I would also like to thank my grandparents, Professor Weiqian Zou, Professor Changlan Qiu, Guoli Wang, and Cuiying Qian, for sparking my interest in education and in life. Thank you to Shimi Shmooely who has been a great partner in life. Thank you to Dr. Avraham Kadar and Ambassador Ido Aharoni, my two mentors. Thank you to the many of you who had helped in anyway though out this project. Thank you to Mercedez, Garret, Daina, and the rest of the McGraw-Hill team for all of your support and guidance throughout the entire project.

Felicia Wang